F.P. GROVE IN EUROPE AND CANADA
Translated Lives

The University of Alberta Press

F.P. GROVE

in Europe and Canada

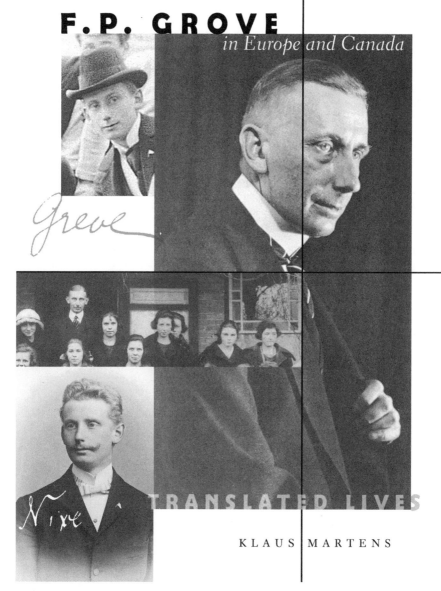

Greve

Nixe

TRANSLATED LIVES

KLAUS MARTENS

Translated by
PAUL MORRIS
in collaboration with the author

Published by
The University of Alberta Press
Ring House 2
Edmonton, Alberta T6G 2E1

Printed in Canada 5 4 3 2 1
Copyright © The University of Alberta Press 2001

National Library of Canada Cataloguing in Publication Data

Martens, Klaus, 1944–
    F.P. Grove in Europe and Canada

    Translation of: Felix Paul Greves Karriere.
    Includes bibliographical references and index.
    ISBN 0–88864–364–0

    1. Grove, Frederick Philip, 1879–1948. 2. Grove, Frederick Philip, 1879–1948—
Correspondence. 3. Grove, Frederick Philip, 1879–1948—Homes and haunts—Germany.
4. Authors, Canadian—20th century—Biography. I. Morris, Paul Duncan, 1961– II. Title.
PS8513.R83Z69813 2001   C813'.52   C2001–910115–5
PR9199.3.G77Z69813 2001

Printed and bound in Canada by Hignell Book Printing Ltd., Winnipeg, Manitoba.
∞ Printed on acid-free paper.
Copyedited by Chris Wangler.
Index prepared by Carol Berger.

Main cover image: Frederick Philip Grove, ca. 1935 (Collection A. Leonard Grove /
Elizabeth Dafoe Library, University of Manitoba); used by permission. Back cover: Frederick
Philip Grove drawn by Charles F. Comfort (Association of Canadian Clubs program, 1928);
used by permission.

The University of Alberta Press acknowledges the financial support of the Government of Canada
through the Book Publishing Industry Development Program for its publishing activities. The
Press also gratefully acknowledges the support received for its program from the Canada Council
for the Arts. A grant toward the cost of translation was provided by Inter Nationes.

The Canada Council | Le Conseil des Arts
FOR THE ARTS | DU CANADA
SINCE 1957 | DEPUIS 1957

Canadä

For Eva, Johanne and Klaus-Konstantin Martens with love

CONTENTS

FOREWORD

MANY YEARS AGO, while beginning to read Grove's *In Search of Myself*, I remember being struck by the opening phrase — "It was a dismal November day" — and reading further to find the author stuck in a mud hole. As he began sinking into a "profound feeling of misery," I followed him there, particularly moved by the distinction he drew between a Frenchman he knew many decades before and himself, both at the time "aflame with a great enthusiasm for life and art." As he remarked of the Frenchman, "he must have achieved things which had focused on him the eyes of a world," while he, the author, was nowhere "but on the lonely prairies of western Canada."

Despite the self-pity that arises in Grove's musings, the incident drove him to write what he wanted to be known as the story of his life. It was a story, he tells us, that began in Russia, where he was born prematurely while his parents were trying to return to their luxurious house in Sweden. Thanks to the groundbreaking work of Douglas Spettigue, we now know that the story should be understood as a grand confidence trick that friends and readers were willing to play into for several decades. Grove's story of himself as Greve was successfully undone, and to such an extent that the gap between early promise in Europe and remembrance in Canada is greater and therefore more poignant. By the time Greve turned thirty in Germany, he had accomplished enough to say *vixi*, that he had lived thoroughly and fully. He had overcome the humble circumstances of his childhood and was enviably proficient in several languages both ancient and modern, which he later used to astounding advantage. A glance at his German bibliography indicates that in less than a decade his accomplishments as a translator would have been sufficient for a professional career. The magnitude and difficulty of the styles employed by the authors he translated is well known, and most translators would be satisfied with the reputation acquired by successfully rendering any one of Balzac, Swift, Flaubert or Cervantes. Some of these translations, furthermore, have become definitive in German culture. Driven partly by ambition and partly by financial need, Greve at times appears doomed for success, but, like an inattentive skier whose skis occasionally overlap, ambition exceeded financial need and he fell.

Although falling was a pattern in Greve's life and reputation, it is worth noting that he believed it possible to gain recognition by being a translator. It is equally worth noting that with his knowledge of languages he might have had a correspondingly brilliant career in Canada, were it not for the entirely different culture he found there. (His languages, however, were not so many and various as those listed in a 1914 letter to Warkentin, in which he mentions that he speaks "English, French, German, Italian, and Arabian" and has "a fair knowledge of Latin, Greek, Sanskrit, Spanish and Swedish [his supposed mother tongue].") It is difficult to imagine what the market might have been for, say, the French novel in the 1920s and early 1930s, when Grove was widely known among Canadian readers. One is tempted to ask what it is now, some eighty years later. In Greve's time, however, all the efforts of the English-Canadian literary establishment were bent upon acquiring self-recognition, endeavouring in such literary histories as those of Archibald MacMechan and J.D. Logan to find a national literature and determine what made it "distinctive." Few translations—and these only from the literature of Québec—have found their way into the canon. For Greve, there would have been no financial reward and certainly no prestige in being a translator in Canada.

Grove found himself in Canada after faking his suicide in Germany. Given the scope of his education, he had little choice but to teach, and, given his inclinations, to write. His decision to leave Germany meant abandoning a particular profession. It is particular inasmuch as it requires more than a knowledge of another language. It requires a certain kind of sympathy for something Other—another idiom, culture, ideology, which, for the sake of understanding, one adopts as one's own. This, in Professor Martens's telling, is Greve's greatest gift. Witness the enjoyment with which he "does" Oscar Wilde, not simply translating him, but by insinuating himself into Wilde so as to imitate the merest gesture, his way of using his eyes, perhaps his turn of phrase. It is evident that Greve had such skills and that his abilities to translate worked in two directions. He could translate himself as well as his authors. A notable example is the skill with which he could mimic the "neurasthenia" of Else's husband, August Endell. Indeed, to play the role of the contemporary decadent was so easy for him that he was taken for one, and he did so readily, despite his extremely robust physical constitution. But Decadence was *de rigueur* in the circles into which Greve desired access, and so decadent he appeared. Greve became, then, the translator's translator by seamlessly moving over borders, so that the movement became more significant than whatever the border surrounded. Reification became anathema; substance was dissolved in style; "acting" was more desirable than being. As he remarks in the same letter to Warkentin: "I…am for knowledge for knowledge's sake," which is hardly different from such slogans of his youth as "art for art's sake." The invention of a text that serves as a foundation—a *texte de départ* as they say in French—is a given; it has already occurred for the translator. The translator's task is to elicit the nearest, most hermeneutically accurate uncovering of sense, and so he or she dwells not so much on language but rather on connotations, nuances, gestures. The text that is produced is unlike those that he or she might produce by writing fiction, for it is at once dependent on and independent of a text in another language. To be between languages, to move through someone else's fiction, means to abandon the firmness of the shaping perception of one's life, in which cherished ideologies and beliefs are hidden, and to set forth into a range of signifiers with which one does not always have an immediate acquaintance. It means, finally, to feel at home where no home rises on the horizon. One is always on the way, in search of oneself as other. Needless to say, such a search would not have been appealing in Grove's Canada. Curiously enough, it could very well have today, which is why Martens's book strikes me as so timely.

Significantly, Greve's first book was entitled *Wanderungen* (rambles or walking tours). Leaving aside the totally derivative character of the book, the title points to Greve's restless nature which returns in Grove and is especially, but not exclusively, evident in *Over Prairie Trails*, in which the journey of the narrator is of far greater importance than his scattered moments with his family. *Wanderungen* is also emblematic of the position of the translator, particularly the kind Greve was—not so much in language but rather between languages. Moreover, it could be remarked that he moves there and everywhere like Goethe's Faust, as a man for whom simply to err is its own reward, not to speak of pleasure and pain. Of course, his literary life in Germany was in many ways a period of juvenilia in which movement between styles and authors can be understood as a period of self-discovery. Although one is at first inclined to view Greve's arrogance as simply another manifestation of the Faustian ideal, one is struck by his inability to feel remorse. Hence, when one asks who Greve/Grove might be, it may not be possible to arrive at an answer that will satisfy all readers. There seems to be no core to the man or, if there is one, it is Faustian, always in flux. If this is true, it would suggest that his naturalism was only another guise of his aestheticism. For naturalism is not merely a style; it is the inscription of the inevitable and would find contemporary notions of the will such as Nietzsche's—then widely accepted by Greve and his contemporaries in Europe—as sadly ridiculous. As a consequence, one cannot help to be moved by a man who, as Martens argues, was doomed in many ways from birth to be always on the outside, despite abilities that might have made him welcome among the young, cosseted artists and intellectuals whom he so desperately courted. Will and talent were simply insufficient. And such a world it was! Not only André Gide and Stefan George belonged to it, but Rilke and d'Annunzio were also somewhere in the background, not to speak of Hugo von Hofmannsthal. Greve made an impression on both Hermann Hesse and Thomas Mann, and he may even have partially served as a model for the latter's Felix Krull. To arrive and not to appear a parvenu would have required more than simply skill and desire; it would have required just the luck that Greve never seemed to have.

The compensation for Greve's lack of luck was to find a way of inventing himself, that is, to become a fiction in which he was the author. In that way he could assume the illusions of authorship as an act of will. If a character or role was not well received, it could be re-conceptualized and presented in another way. Becoming Wilde, one might say, was simply an apprenticeship in a larger, more existentially risky game in which the self as a character could be translated as necessary. Such a game can only be entered upon if one accepts that the self is a fiction, rather than the plaything of the forces of determinism represented, for example, by naturalism. Thus the function of will is to a certain extent redeemed only insofar as it remains attentive to the response of the audience. It means, however, that characters are not only always in flight, but also must be ready to take cover, as Greve frequently did. Nevertheless, the playfulness of it makes it persuasive as a lived style and understanding of the world, and one is reminded of such novels as Hubert Aquin's *Trou de Mémoire* in which the authority of authors and editors is challenged. Which story can be believed? Instead of asking, however, who is to be believed, we are invited to understand that all claims to truth are equally valid and, therefore, so problematic as to defy unravelling. One is also reminded of a question Grove posed to Watson Kirkconnell on March 7, 1927. "What is *truth*?" an unperturbed Grove asks. His answer is that "Plato has a value apart from truth," inasmuch as "the value of a philosophic system is largely aesthetic." The narrator is unreliable, but that is the source of his charm. Even more so, the author is also unreliable and, to a certain extent, an obstacle to full understanding of a text.

In another of his letters to Gide, an edition of which we owe with gratitude to Martens, dated February 7, 1905, Greve writes that while he loves Gide's *L'Immoraliste*, "*je méprise l'auteur.*" I think it is evident that it was not his friend Gide he scorned, but rather the attachment of an author to the book he admired so much. In a letter written later in the same year, dated August 17, 1905, he complains of his name having for a long time been associated with that of Oscar Wilde. Immediately one wonders what has happened. Greve is here not so much abandoning another role, and one which suited him so well, but rather making an effort to separate author from text. As he says, there is no one he would rather have lived with less than Flaubert, but "*Madame Bovary et Bouvard et Pécuchet*—voilà ce qui est *quelque chose…*" Such a comment comes tantalizingly close to saying that he would rather live with fictional representations than their authors. In fact, the very "*odeur de l'auteur*" (a pun which neatly displays Greve's facility with French) which cannot be separated from a text has made it impossible for him to read Goethe, George and Hofmannsthal.

It is not difficult, therefore, to understand the attraction translation in every sense would have had for Greve. It provided access to a world, if only a secondary world, without fear of rejection. In such a world, the text could claim autonomy without fear of human interference, in which Emma Bovary was Flaubert, but, presumably, Flaubert was not, as he famously declared, Emma. Furthermore, as a translator, content, indeed substance, was not his concern, as he remarks in his letter to Gide about *L'Immoraliste*. All that concerned him was the text's temperature, its tone and "*le sens,*" as if to say, "You provide the story; I will give it its meaning." Such a position allowed Greve to move unscathed into the world of literature as a multi-lingual world of textual experience, and to be Fanny Essler was, in a word, to be.

In the "Author's Note" to the fourth edition of *A Search for America* truth comes up again, this time in a special context. "Imaginative literature," we are told, "is not primarily concerned with facts; it is concerned with truth." So Plato and the aesthetic character of truth return once more. Facts, however, belong ineluctably to truth. As a result, "in imaginative literature, no fact enters as mere fact; a fact as such can be perceived; but to form subject-matter for art, it must contain its own interpretation, and therefore made capable of being understood becomes fiction." Imaginative writing, as a consequence, is translation to the degree that it inscribes interpretation; it is truth inasmuch as it transforms "the real." To make his text even more persuasive, the author has chosen to reveal himself pseudonymously because "while pseudonym ostensibly dissociates the author from his creation, it gives him at the same time an opportunity to be even more personal than, in the conditions of our present-day civilization, it would be either safe or comfortable to be were he speaking in the first-person, unmasked." Only the persona reveals because transformation, of which it is the sign, is the only viable way of reaching truth without any fear of the odour of the author.

The truth of me is only apparent in what is not I. Of course such an assertion draws upon the truth of lying, but what it implies, after all the role-playing Greve/Grove indulged in for the sixty years of his life until this revelation, is that the narrator, whoever he may be, appears to want to be "unmasked." Writing deliberately obscures, but ideally "it must contain its own interpretation." But while Grove may think it is truth disguised that he is offering, the truth of the author, it is in fact the truth of the text that is proposed. Fiction is truth; truth is fiction.

The Greve/Grove, however, that Martens has so carefully revealed constitutes the most detailed notion of his life we have and probably will have, drawing on the recollections of Else Baroness von Freytag-Loringhoven, many hitherto unknown documents—particularly regarding his stays in Bonn and Rome—and much new information about Greve's German publishers. It also enlarges upon, and corrects aspects of, the German biography Martens published in 1997. Greve/Grove may now be said to be definitive to the degree that such is possible. No one, after all, can be true to Greve/Grove and make truly authoritative statements. We may have the facts, but they remain profoundly subject to interpretation, as Greve/Grove would say, and no one is more sensitive to this issue than Martens, who currently holds the chair in North American Literature and Culture in Saarbrücken and has himself earned an international reputation as a poet, translator and translation critic. He has spent some fourteen years in search of Greve/Grove, tracking him down in a number of publications, including a volume of Greve/Gide correspondence and work on Greve's relationship to the publishing house of J.C.C. Bruns. His efforts, particularly the German version of this book, have given Greve a rightful place in German letters and made him the object of lengthy discussions in such prestigious forums as *Der Spiegel* and the *Frankfurter Allgemeine Zeitung*. While Martens's biography will unquestionably claim an equally deserving place as the definitive biography of Greve/Grove, it should also open the way for more in-depth scholarship on an author still insufficiently recognized on both sides of the Atlantic.

I began by commenting on *In Search of Myself*, a text that appears driven by a desire for the recognition Grove felt he had missed in his life, written under the sign of the Danish astronomer Tycho Brahe's last words, *ne frustra vixisse videar* ("lest I seem to have lived in vain"). The awards that followed upon the book's publication suggest that his life was not lived entirely in vain. Indeed, as this biography implies, his life and what he could do with it was his best piece of fiction in Grove's sense, with all of his novels revealing and concealing, indeed reinventing the life as it was variously understood by its author. So well contrived was it, and so well "played," that one might infer that he was not only a great confidence man, but also Canada's first post-modernist, who perhaps unknowingly created the literary conditions for such writers as Hubert Aquin and Robert Kroetsch, whose own postmodernity paid homage to Greve/Grove in "FPG:" "inventing (beyond/ America) a new world."

E.D. BLODGETT

ACKNOWLEDGEMENTS

UNAVOIDABLY, in the course of long years of research one incurs more debts to persons and institutions than one dares remember. In alphabetical order, I gratefully acknowledge advice, documents, information and permissions received from: Angus Stewart Q.C. and Catherine A. Smith (Advocates Library, Parliament House, Edinburgh); Dr. Schirn, Hannelore Erlekamm (Akademie der Künste, Berlin); Amtsgericht Bonn; Amtsgericht Hamburg; Amtsgericht Saarbrücken; Amtsgericht Schöneberg; Dr. Wilfred Geominy and Dr. Andreas Scholl (Archäologisches Institut der Rheinischen Friedrich-Wilhelms-Universität, Bonn); Dr. Thomas Becker, Renate Schindler, Dr. Paul Schmidt and Christoph Waldecker (Archiv der Rheinischen Friedrich-Wilhelms-Universität, Bonn); Dr. W. Schultze (Archiv der Humboldt-Universität, Berlin); R. Haasenbruch and Ms. Weikert (Archiv der Martin-Luther-Universität, Halle); Claude Martin (Association des Amis d'André Gide); Axel Juncker Verlag; Dr. Gerhard Stamm (Badische Landesbibliothek, Karlsruhe); Penelope Bullock (Balliol College, Oxford); Dr. Otto-Karl Tröger (Bayerisches Hauptstaatsarchiv, Munich); Dr. Franz Pointner (Bayerische Staatsbibliothek, Munich); Dr. K. Klauss (Berlin-Brandenburgische Akademie der Wissenschaften, Berlin); Dr. Ida Buttitta and Dr. Francesca Migneco (Biblioteca di Giovanni Verga, Catania); Dr. Dario D'Alessandro (Biblioteca Provinciale G. D'Annunzio, Pescara); Yves Peyré, Jean-Luc Berthommier, Béatrice Calendrier (Bibliothèque littéraire Jacques Doucet, Paris); Valérie Neveu (Bibliothèque Municipale, Rouen); Dr. Judith Priestman (Bodleian Library, University of Oxford); Beatrice del Bondio-Reventlow; Jürgen Hespe and Hermann Staub (Börsenverein des Deutschen Buchhandels e.V.,

Frankfurt a.M.); Mick Scott (Bromley Central Library); Gregor Pickro and Mr. Bauer (Bundesarchiv, Koblenz); Ms. Zundeck (Bundesarchiv, Freiburg); Ms. Hufeland and Dr. Ritter (Bundesarchiv, Potsdam); Ms. Kipper (Bürger- and Standesamt, Bonn); Prof. Pierre Coustillas; Dr. Richard Bennett and staff (Department of Archives and Special Collections, Elizabeth Dafoe Library, University of Manitoba, Winnipeg); S. Grittner (Deutsche Bank, Munich); Marie-Luise Hahn (Deutsche Bibliothek, Frankfurt); Vera Deininger (Deutsches Bucharchiv, Munich); Ms. Bertram (Deutsche Bibliothek/ Deutsche Bücherei, Leipzig); Dr. Heide Frielinghaus (Deutsches Archäologisches Institut, Athens); Dr. Antje Krug and Dr. Klaus Junker (Deutsches Archäologisches Institut, Berlin); Ms. Lehnert (Deutsche Dienststelle, Berlin); Silke Becker, Thomas Kemme, Dr. Jochen Meyer and Dr. Reinhard Tgahrt (Deutsches Literaturarchiv, Marbach); Andrea Hauer and Gabriele Jäckl (Deutsches Theatermuseum, Munich); Marita Wetzel (Deutsche Verlags- Anstalt, Stuttgart); M. Wermes (Deutsche Zentralstelle für Genealogie, Leipzig); Michel Drouin; Dr. Joachim Endell; Fondazione 'Il Vittoriale degli Italiani'; Dr. Renate Moering (Freies Deutsches Hochstift/Frankfurter Goethe Museum, Frankfurt); Brenda Hawkins, Alice Johnson (Gallatin County Public Library, KY); Gisi Baronin Freytag von Loringhoven; Prof. Dr. Claus Victor Bock (Friedrich Gundolf-Archiv, London); Ms. Nossol (Geheimes Staatsarchiv Preussischer Kulturbesitz, Berlin); Mr. Deprosse (Gemeinde Pullach); Dr. Freifrau v. Andrian-Werburg (Germanisches Nationalmuseum, Nürnberg); Hilde Glapa; Barbara Glauert-Hesse; Nikola Greif; Gertraude Benöhr (Gutenberg-Gesellschaft, Mainz); Irmgard Bröning (Hessische Landes- und Hochschulbibliothek, Darmstadt); John R. Hammond (The H.G. Wells Society, Nottingham); Dr. Groten (Historisches Archiv der Stadt Köln); Dr. Dietmar Schenk (Hochschule der Künste, Berlin); Jennie Rathbun (The Houghton Library, Harvard University, Cambridge, MA); Carolyn Powell, Gayle M. Barkley (The Huntington Library, San Marino, CA); Jürgen Hertel (Industrie- und Handelskammer Rhein-Neckar); Dr. R. Jansen (Institut für Sportwissenschaft und Sport der Rheinischen Friedrich-Wilhelms-Universität, Bonn); Dr. Horst Blanck (Istituto Archeologico Germanico, Rome); Dr. Uwe Petersen (Gymnasium Johanneum, Hamburg); Justizvollzugsanstalt Bonn; John Pritchard (Kentucky Department of Libraries and Archives, Frankfort); Rebecca Campbell Cape (Lilly Library, Indiana University, Bloomington); Charles T. King (Kenton County Public Library, Covington, KY); Adelheid Ganzoni and Dr. Willy Ryffel (Klages-Stiftung, Zürich); Bruno Klein; Christian Scheffler (Klingspor-Museum der Stadt Offenbach); Palle Ringsted (Det Kongelige Bibliotek, Copenhagen); Theo Kümin (Korporation Wollerau); Sabine Preuss and Jürgen Sprau (Landesarchiv Berlin); Ms. Scheiff (Landgericht Bonn); Prof. Dr. H.-E. Joachim

(Landschaftsverband Rheinland; Rheinisches Landesmuseum, Bonn); Hermann V. Lassaulx; Ulrich Lempp; Carlpeter Lepsius; Prof. Dr. M. Rainer Lepsius; Fred Bauman (The Library of Congress, Washington, DC); A.T. Morgan (Owenton); Prof. Dr. Laetitia Boehm and Dr. Wolfgang J. Smolka (Universitätsarchiv, Ludwig-Maximilians-Universität Munich); R. Haasenbruch and Ms. Weikert (Archiv der Martin-Luther-Universität, Halle); Horst Meyer (Medienbüro, Berlin); M. Müller and H. Birka (Militärgeschichtliches Forschungsamt, Potsdam); Dr. Ursula Hummel (Monacensia, Munich); P.-J. Foulon (Musée Royal de Mariemont, Morlanwelz); Nicole Dony (Musée de la Vie Wallonne, Liège); Dr. Iain G. Brown (National Library of Scotland, Edinburgh); Stephen Crook and Stephen Wagner (The New York Public Library, New York); Karen Noel (New Liberty, KY); Dr. Reinicke and Dr. Stahlschmidt (Nordrhein-Westfälisches Hauptstaatsarchiv, Düsseldorf); Ms. Weber-Hermey (Nordrhein-Westfälisches Personenstandsarchiv, Rheinland, Brühl); Dr. Ernst Gamillscheg (Österreichische Nationalbibliothek, Wien); Bettina Somerville, David Washborn, Kathy Mathews, Susan Hampton (Owen County Library, KY); Doris Riley (Owen County Historical Society, KY); Dr. Peter-Hubertus Pieler; Robert E. Parks (The Pierpont Morgan Library, New York); Klaus Piper; Erwin Hippe (Reclam Verlag, Leipzig); Mechthild Purrmann; Louise Craven (The Royal Commission on Historical Manuscripts, London); Edward Skipworth (Rutgers University Libraries, New Brunswick, NJ); Gertraude Gebauer (Sächsisches Staatsarchiv, Leipzig); Dagmar Schreiber and Cristina Klostermann (S. Fischer Verlag, Frankfurt); Werner J. Schweiger; Dr. Hofmeister (Staatsarchiv, Bremen); Mr Bollmann, Iris Groschek and Ms. Koschlig (Staatsarchiv, Hamburg); Prof. Dr. Tilo Brandis, Dr. Gabriele Spitzer, Inge Wojtke, Helga Döhn and Eva Ziesche (Staatsbibliothek zu Berlin); Dr. Harald Weigel and Sabine Schröder (Staats- und Universitätsbibliothek, Hamburg); Hans-Georg Riemann and Mr Schmidt (Stadt Wyk auf Föhr); Ms. Alef, Hans Kleinpass and Dorothea Zeipel (Stadtarchiv und Stadthistorische Bibliothek, Bonn); Mr Nickel and Dr. M. Garzmann (Stadtarchiv, Braunschweig); Steffen Kober (Stadtarchiv, Cottbus); Dr. F.W. Kniess (Stadtarchiv, Darmstadt); Mr. Bönicke and Mr. Hoppe (Stadtarchiv, Dresden); Mr. Heppner and Dr. Mlynek (Stadtarchiv, Hannover); Dr. Heimers (Stadtarchiv, Munich); Dr. Ute Oelmann (Stefan George-Archiv, Stuttgart); Christa Rudnik and Wolfgang Ritschel (Stiftung Weimarer Klassik/Goethe- und Schillerarchiv, Weimar); Rose and Dr. Martin String; Cornelia Bernini (Thomas Mann-Archiv, ETH Zürich); Wolfgang Störmer (Universitäts- und Landesbibliothek, Bonn); Anne Caiger (The University Library, University of California, Los Angeles); Paula Lee (The University of Chicago Library, Illinois); Susan Stead (University College, London); Bruce W. Swann and Madeline J. Gibson (Rare Book and

Special Collections Library, University of Illinois at Urbana-Champaign); William Abbey (Institute of Germanic Studies, University of London); Beth Alvarez (Special Collections, University of Maryland, College Park); the staff of the Cincinnati Historical Society; Prof. Dr. Raimund Theis; Dr. Don Henry Tolzmann, Curator of the German-Americana Collection, Archives and Rare Book Department, Blegen Library, University of Cincinnati; Fabienne (Le Musée de le Touquet); Heidi Vollmoeller; Rainer-Hans Vollmöller; Vincent Giroud (Yale University Library, New Haven, Connecticut); Dr. Walter Obermaier (Stadt- und Landesbibliothek, Vienna); Dr. J.P. Bodmer (Zentralbibliothek, Zürich); Christel Benner (Zentrum für Theaterforschung, Hamburg); Alma Zsolnay and Olga Kaindl (Paul Zsolnay Verlag, Vienna).

I owe a special debt of gratitude to Ulrich Reipert and Dr. Fritz Kasten for their support in locating documents and securing permissions to reproduce. I thank Rainer Thomas, owner of J.C.C. Bruns, for permissions to quote and reprint materials as well as for access to the firm's archives. I also thank Horst Schweichardt for sensible advice and help at every stage of my research on the Bruns premises. I wish to acknowledge a special debt of gratitude to the late Dr. Hans Gressel, a pioneering Bruns scholar.

This book would not have been possible without the enthusiastic support of Catherine Gide and A. Leonard Grove, who graciously gave permission to print copyrighted material and allowed unlimited access to other published and unpublished sources. In addition, Mary and A. Leonard Grove very generously gave of their time and resources, smoothing the way whenever possible. They shared their memories of Frederick Philip Grove with me and patiently answered my many queries. Knowing them has been a privilege and a pleasure. In the same spirit of friendship I would like to thank James and Katherine Gibson of Sparta, Kentucky, for their help and hospitality.

Thanks are due to the following archives and copyright holders for the use of their resources and their permissions to reproduce: Stadtarchiv Braunschweig (Huch family), Staats- and Universitätsbibliothek Hamburg (Alfred Janssen), The Getty Research Institute, Special Collections and Visual Resources, Los Angeles (Melchior Lechter), Schulbibliothek des Gymnasiums Johanneum, Kongelige Bibliothek in Copenhagen (Axel Juncker), Deutsches Literaturarchiv in Marbach (Franz Blei, Helene and Ludwig Klages, Karl Wolfskehl, Oscar A.H. Schmitz, Karl Gustav Vollmoeller), Stadtbibliothek München, Sammlung Monacensia (Herbert Koch, Franziska Gräfin zu Reventlow), Rare Book and Special Collections Library of the University of Illinois at Urbana-Champaign (F.P. Greve and H.G. Wells;

W.H. Heinemann Publishers), Department of Archives and Special Collections, University of Manitoba (F.P. Grove documents and photographs), Württembergische Landesbibliothek Stuttgart (Stefan George), National Archives of Canada, Ottawa (passenger arrival records), the Carroll, Gallatin, Kenton, and Owen County Libraries, Kentucky (land titles, mortgage and tax records).

In Saarbrücken, I owe a debt of gratitude to my competent and loyal long-time research assistants Dr. Jutta Ernst and Dr. Margit Peterfy (now of the University of Mainz). Andreas Hau, Susanne Korte (M.A.), Mick Lee Kuzia and Arlette Warken (M.A.) helped with the corrections, index, bibliography and the time-consuming tasks of requesting materials and proofreading. Susanne Balzert, my able secretary, helped to coordinate our many activities. Without the inventiveness and perseverance of this excellent team, more than one stone might have been left unturned.

I want to give special thanks to those who, in various capacities, have patiently read and commented upon versions of the manuscript or parts of it, in particular my Canadian colleagues Professors E.D. Blodgett, Milan Dimic, Irene Gammel and Paul I. Hjartarson.

The English translation of the parts of the 1997 German edition not since rewritten was a joint effort. Chapters 1–5 were translated by Dr. Paul Morris. My previously published English-language versions of parts of chapters were used when necessary. I completely rewrote the Introduction, Chapters 6–7 and the Afterword in English, with much new material added. Chapter Five I significantly reworked. Some of the material contained here was taken from my published articles, written since the 1997 edition, and from the 1999 edition of the Greve-Gide correspondence by Dr. Jutta Ernst and myself. It goes without saying that the final responsibility for any shortcomings in the present book is mine.

Finally, I wish to thank the Press Committee, editors and staff of the University of Alberta Press, particularly Christopher Wangler and Leslie Vermeer, for their support in the realization of this project.

Without the trust, patience and generosity of colleagues, students and other patient audiences in Bonn, Charlottetown, Edmonton, Hamburg, Ottawa, Saarbrücken, Toronto, Winnipeg and elsewhere, and without the support of my friends, enthusiastic family and help from many chance acquaintances made in the course of my research and lecturing on two continents, this would have been a lesser book.

A·NOTE·ON·THE·TEXT

ALL QUOTATIONS IN LANGUAGES OTHER THAN ENGLISH
were transcribed from their original sources according to conventions observed
by their respective authors. Seeming or apparent mistakes have only been
pointed out [sic] when a possible misreading might be avoided. Crossed-out
words or phrases in manuscripts or typescripts have only been transcribed
where they might be regarded as significant variants or additions to the final
version of a text. For translations of extended foreign-language quotations, or
of English paraphrases of such texts, the source texts will be provided in the
endnotes to facilitate verification. References to primary and secondary
sources have been included throughout. All translations of German-language
citations into English were done by Paul Morris or myself.

Portions of this book have previously appeared elsewhere. Chapter Two was
published in an earlier version as "Nixe on the River: Felix Paul Greve in
Bonn (1898–1901)" in *Canadian Literature* 151 (Winter 1996): 10–43. Different
versions of parts of the Gide sections in Chapter Six were published as
"Fieberhaftes Schreiben: Leidenschaftliches Zuhören" and "'Blei et Grève
se canardent:' On the Making and Unmaking of Reputations" in *"Je vous
écris, en hâte et fiévreusement:" Felix Paul Greve—André Gide. Korrespondenz
und Dokumentation.* Ed. Jutta Ernst and Klaus Martens. St. Ingbert: Röhrig
Verlag, 1999. An additional version appeared as "Battles for Recognition:
Greve, Gide, also Blei" in *Canadian Review of Comparative Literature/Revue
Canadienne de Littérature Comparée* 25: 3–4 (September-December 1998):
328–47. An earlier version of parts of Chapter Seven was published as

"Frederick Philip Grove in Kentucky: Spartanic Preparations—An Exploration" in my *Pioneering North America: Mediators of European Literature and Culture.* Würzburg: Königshausen & Neumann, 2000.

<u>ABBREVIATIONS</u>

W	*Wanderungen*
HD	*Helena und Damon*
FE	*Fanny Essler*
OPT	*Over Prairie Trails*
SOM	*Settlers of the Marsh*
SFA	*A Search for America*
FOE	*Fruits of the Earth*
NS	*It Needs To Be Said*
ISM	*In Search of Myself*
Letters	*The Letters of Frederick Philip Grove*
BE	*Baroness Elsa*
GG	*Correspondence Greve-Gide*
FPG	D.O. Spettigue, *Frederick Philip Grove: The Early Years*

INTRODUCTION

ISSUES OF GERMAN AND CANADIAN LIFE, literature and culture combine in the person of one internationally significant author to form the subject of this book. Frederick Philip Grove's role as a long-canonized novelist, poet, essayist and short-story writer stands in inverse relation to the almost complete neglect of his early life as Felix Paul Greve, a poet, translator, essayist and novelist in Germany. Apart from his two national identities, there are good reasons for approaching him in both his professional roles as a writer and a formidably productive and influential translator. Unfortunately, Grove's role as a translator has often been considered inferior to his work as an author. Such an assessment is only possible when literature and literary translation are construed as different fields and their respective meanings and functions held separately from one another. There are additional reasons for researching Grove's German period again. The empirical foundation of his German biography has not yet been firmly enough established to serve as a point of departure in the study of the intellectual relevance of his fiction or in an analysis of his translations. Finally, although there is a wealth of published material about Grove's life as an author in Canada, works that aim to integrate the German and Canadian parts of his life are few and far between.

Since Douglas O. Spettigue's discovery that Frederick Philip Grove was none other than the German writer and translator Felix Paul Greve, it has become possible to speak with relative clarity of three incomplete biographies of the double figure, FPG for short. The first consists of two highly fragmentary narratives by the author himself, namely, A Search for America

(1927) and *In Search of Myself* (1946). A second, crucially amended biography was the result of primarily Canadian biographical research conducted by D.O. Spettigue (aided by Anthony Riley), Desmond Pacey (aided by J.C. Mahanti) and Margaret Stobie. The third adds an unexpected dimension to FPG's intricate story and derives from the recollections of his erstwhile "most important companion" Else Ploetz, known as Else Endell until her divorce, then perhaps as Else Greve and later as the New York Dada artist Else Baroness von Freytag-Loringhoven. Here, Paul Hjartarson discovered and first published (with D.O. Spettigue) most of the relevant material found among the papers of the American writer Djuna Barnes, inaugurating an entirely new line of research vigorously pursued since by Irene Gammel and others. Any attempt to fashion an altered and partially new fourth description of the life and work of Greve/Grove as an *interculturally* important author, as I do, cannot but build on the first two and must closely observe the third as it touches upon the story told here.

What I have briefly observed here has made it apparent, I believe, why it has not thus far been possible to construct a complete narrative of Greve's (and by extension Grove's) life, despite several important finds and editions. Part of the reason for this is that the primary work on Grove's biography and oeuvre was conducted by scholars for whom unmediated access to the sources was not always possible.

For their research, they were often forced to rely on papers in German archives (sometimes written in the archaic Sütterlin script) or on correspondents who were not always able to provide the information required. Accordingly, occasionally erroneous conclusions could not always be avoided. My narrative no less suffers from its own difficulties with uncertain data.

With regard to Grove's biography, German literary scholars on FPG (with the exception of Michael's early contribution) have, on the whole, followed the example set by Canadian scholars before turning their attention to issues primarily of intellectual history. The late Walter Pache was the first to form a German-Canadian link in conjunction with the early Canadian researchers. In Canada, a new approach to FPG was undertaken in an essay by Richard Cavell (1997), which deals with the role of homosexuality in turn-of-the-century Berlin.

More than a quarter of a century after the discovery of FPG's German descent, it appeared to me that the available German- and French-language sources were in need of a new reading, and that some of the ground in Canada and the U.S.A. had to be gone over again. These (re-)examinations led, in turn, to new insights regarding Greve's presence in Grove's Canadian oeuvre. While not a few readers harboured doubts that the dual identity of Greve and Grove could be substantiated on the basis of textual evidence alone, I have been able, with the help of many of the earliest pictures and letters of Greve that I have found, to verify this identity with certainty. This research has taken me beyond consultation of the letters deposited in Marbach, Munich, Stuttgart, Urbana-Champaign, Weimar, Winnipeg or in private hands; beyond the two previously known snapshots of Greve in Gardone (August 1902); and beyond assorted published documents, mostly letters, or Else von Freytag-Loringhoven's papers (those published in 1992 as well as those remaining in manuscript at the University of Maryland). Thanks to this new material, it will be possible to provide more detailed documentation of the earlier phases of FPG's German period than was formerly the case. This applies equally well to several important, previously overlooked details from his time in Hamburg, and for almost all aspects of Greve's six semesters as a student in Bonn. I have also found new documentary material regarding his two semesters in Munich, conclusive evidence of a previously unverifiable stay in Rome and his immensely important activities as an author and translator for the publisher J.C.C. Bruns in Minden, as well as others such as Alfred Janssen in Hamburg, Insel in Leipzig and Axel Juncker/Karl Schnabel in Berlin and Stuttgart. Furthermore, the whole extant correspondence between FPG and André Gide—previously available only in excerpts and English paraphrase (Spettigue 1992)—provides much additional insight into FPG's life as a literary translator and mediator between 1903 and 1909. On the basis of this and additional contextual material, it is now possible to read one or two more layers from the palimpsest of autobiography and fiction in Grove's Canadian writing.

I wish to emphasize that the narrative in the following chapters unavoidably extends out of the background of, and is in part a result of, previous research and attempts to contextualize new facts. I gratefully acknowledge the work conducted by the authors of these studies. In the most important instances, my work identifies divergences from other published accounts. Further information is provided in the notes.

The vast majority of the photographic reproductions in the text and documentation consists of previously unknown and unpublished documents from or by Greve, or of the circles in which he moved and the milieu in which he lived. These should be read in conjunction with the text. One of the functions of the present book is to flesh out the private life and literary figure of Felix Paul Greve in the context of his time and the society to which he belonged. In Germany, Greve has been, until recently, wholly missing from established accounts of the first decade of the twentieth century. In Canada, furthermore, Grove's reputation has suffered something of an eclipse in recent years. Future depictions of literary developments in both countries— to which this study seeks to contribute—will not be able to leave him out.[1]

Finally, the recent renaissance of literary translation as an important research topic has inescapably led to the greater visibility of translators such as Felix Paul Greve. In Germany, the late nineteenth and early twentieth centuries combined their original avant-garde literary art with the art of translation to form a perfected translation culture. Not only such poets as Stefan George, Rudolf Borchardt, Hugo von Hofmannsthal, Rainer Maria Rilke and Rudolf Alexander Schröder serve as evidence of this (carried on by Arno Schmidt and Hans Magnus Enzensberger in more recent decades). To this group belongs Felix Paul Greve—often overlooked but, for a time, clearly in a leading, if not dominating, position—who, as an author and unbelievably productive translator, almost ideally combined two inseparable functions during a crucial time of transition.

While Felix Paul Greve's own novels, plays and poems garnered little praise, there is no reason to give short shrift to his work as a translator or to neglect him as a German-language author. His influential role as a pioneering translator, seen in the context of the translation culture in which he moved, has not yet been adequately recognized. All in all, and in spite of the constant pressure upon him to make money, his translations were more than merely preludes to his own writings—more, too, than the hack work his critics then and now (and occasionally Greve himself) have made it out to be.

For Felix Greve, as for many others, translation was more than just a means of "testing your own style," as has been said of Stefan George and Rainer Maria Rilke. Translation was also used to scout out and appropriate what was new. It was an instrument for detecting the Other in various literatures and incorporating it. Whatever censure accorded Greve's often hurried translations—and linguistic accuracy is, heretical as this may sound, the most pedestrian aspect of a translation—they are much more than fodder for the cursory reader. In many cases, Greve's work achieved exactly what may be regarded as the highest measure of a literary translation: to bring authors and literatures of different countries into creative contact. There is probably no better way to judge the enduring effect of a translated author than the testimony of the authors themselves. In Greve's case, no less a figure than the Nobel Prize-winning German novelist Hermann Hesse testified to his lasting effect as a mediator. For those authors not conversant in a source language, the boldness of a new translation strikes them as a work of art in its own right, exerting its own traceable influence.[2]

The present work is divided into an introduction, seven chapters and an afterword. Chapter One revises, expands and reinterprets known facts about Greve's childhood in a number of significant ways. Supported by new material from many sources, I add to other accounts an analysis of the crucial final period of Greve's education before going to Bonn.

Chapter Two concentrates on a phase of Greve's early manhood almost entirely undocumented to date, namely, his formative years as a student of philology and archaeology in Bonn from 1898 to 1901. This new information, especially as it relates to details of the fascinating social milieu in which he moved, may help to untangle the knot of autobiographical narrative strands in parts of *A Search for America* and *In Search of Myself.*

In Chapter Three, I discuss new evidence that helps document Greve's archaeological efforts and preoccupations, as well as a period he spent in Rome and elsewhere—a sojourn that was first suspected on the grounds of Bonn university records and Greve's own claims in *In Search of Myself*, but had never before been documented.

In Chapter Four, I expand and contextualize what is known about FPG's Munich and Berlin experiences in 1901–02 with extensive new material. I again make use of Greve's published "recollections." I have also introduced some new findings about a platonic relationship Greve had with the sister of a member of the George circle as it relates to Greve's much-discussed love affair with Else Endell, later the Baroness von Freytag-Loringhoven.

Dealing in part with the same period in Berlin, Chapter Five provides many details regarding FPG's professional relations to his most important German publisher, J.C.C. Bruns. Discussions of Greve's work as a translator of Wilde's plays and newly recovered correspondence with several other publishers round out the chapter.[3]

Using new evidence and a number of letters to and from hitherto little-known correspondents, I discuss various aspects of FPG's most profitable period as a German translator and author in Chapter Six. The papers consulted include the correspondence with H.G. Wells and with the publishers and agents involved in translating six of the Englishman's novels; the papers surrounding Greve's translations of three of George Meredith's novels; and the materials documenting the grand failure of Bruns and Greve's Flaubert edition. These are discussed in relation to Greve's own novels and the evidence of his close relationship with André Gide, including his rivalry with the author and literary promoter Franz Blei for the Frenchman's texts. The Blei-Greve materials recently became available through the work of Raimund Theis, editor of a notable recent Gide edition in Germany.

Chapter Seven contains a short account of FPG's arrival in the New World and an exploration of his likely sojourn in Kentucky (first mentioned by Freytag-Loringhoven). I speculate on the obscure period between his disappearance from Germany and his re-surfacing in Winnipeg in late 1912. I close with a number of observations regarding Grove's Canadian career in an attempt to round out the picture of FPG's early and later life. These observations are based on a reading of Grove's book for boys, *The Adventures of Leonard Broadus*, and some new material, including recollections that A. Leonard and Mary Grove shared with me.

The Afterword contains a short assessment of Felix Greve as a turn-of-the-century artistic type and a possible model for Thomas Mann's Felix Krull. It also sketches F.P. Grove's major role in Canadian literature. A later book, however, will have to take up these issues in more detail.

The facts I have found myself or gathered from sources will help, I believe, to close the formerly wide gap in our knowledge of Greve's early years. By reconstructing FPG's German career as a whole, I hope to place my own research and hypotheses in context, forming, for the first time, the most comprehensive biographical narrative of that most elusive life.

1

A·PRIZE·STUDENT
IN·HAMBURG
Capable and Competent

AS D.O. SPETTIGUE FIRST DISCOVERED, Frederick Philip
Grove was born on February 14, 1879 in Radomno, in the vicinity of Prussian
Eylau (West Prussia), and christened Felix Paul Berthold Friedrich Greve.
His father, Carl Eduard Greve (1847–1918), came from Niendorf (in
Schleswig-Holstein). His mother, Johanna Julia Anna Bertha (1855–98), was
born into the Reichentrog family of Carlshöhe. They were married on
November 14, 1876 in Cramon and moved to Turow in Pomerania, where
their daughter Henny Frieda Anna Martha Greve was born on August 25,
1877. From May 1881 on, the four-member family lived in Hamburg, where,
as of December 1884, the father worked on the streetcar lines, first as a
Conducteur or "driver," and then as a "cashier" or, as it is called today,
conductor.[1] As an employee on the drafty streetcars of the day, he was designated—according to linguistic usage still occasionally encountered in various
parts of Germany—as a *Beamter* or "official." He was not, however, provided
with the security and relative comfort of a government post. He was certainly
not a "civil servant" (Spettigue, *FPG* 36). In 1904, before Grove had transformed his father into a landholder, he had recast him as an "industrialist
from Mecklenburg" in conversation with André Gide (GG 222). (In reality,
the elder Greve had merely been active in an administrative capacity on
Turow Estate in Pomerania—not unlike his son's alter ego many years later

on a company farm in North Dakota [SFA 339f.]). Carl Eduard Greve left his family in 1892, henceforth leaving his son absolute freedom in forming his elective affinities.

Between May 12, 1881 and the death of Bertha Greve on May 1, 1898, the family had twelve different addresses in Hamburg. From the presumed date of the father's departure on March 12, 1892, the family lived at 40 Besenbinderhof, where Mrs. Greve operated her boarding house. For the last four years, they lived on the fourth floor at 16 Neuburg, an address in the old city close to the Alster basin. While the apartments in St. Pauli were located close to primary and secondary schools, the addresses in the inner city provided convenient access to the *Gymnasium* and *Gelehrtenschule* ("academic school") of the renowned *Gymnasium Johanneum*, established in 1529 by Luther's friend Johann Bugenhagen, who had assisted in the translation of the Bible. It appears as if Bertha, a single mother, saw to it that Felix never had too far to go to school. Perhaps more than anyone else, it was she who cared for the environment and education of her son, who in turn far exceeded that which had previously been achieved in education in the family. It seems fair to assume that Carl Eduard Greve troubled himself little with either education or its costs.

◆ SCHOOLS

While the family's surroundings in St. Pauli were certainly lower-middle class, they were in no way as poor and dubious as has been suggested elsewhere. The professions of the fathers of Felix Greve's fellow pupils at the secondary school of the Protestant Reformed Congregation at 42 Seilerstrasse reveal not only that the majority of pupils lived in the vicinity, but that their parents were presumably financially stable (*Jahresbericht der Realschule* 1895, 25). Of the twenty-five professions mentioned, there were two customs officials, three merchants, one medical doctor, one professor, a captain and even a telegraph director.

Felix began his secondary school education at the *Realschule* at Easter 1889. He seems to have been a little sickly and had typhus, although his results in German, English and French were from good to excellent. He was permitted to take his final examinations with the following recommendation:

> A well-disposed pupil of a serious, mature nature who, despite being hindered by sickness on several occasions, followed his studies with interest and good results and who also strove to attain a level of well-rounded knowledge through private study. The conference proposes his admittance.

From February 19 to 22, 1895, "the written examinations of the twenty-five pupils of the first Easter class were completed." After the oral examinations of March 18 and 19, the entire class received graduation diplomas from the rector, Reinmüller. With respect to curriculum, Felix had to read the following in German: Friedrich Schiller's *Wilhelm Tell* and *Die Jungfrau von Orleans*; G.E. Lessing's *Minna von Barnhelm*; and J.W. von Goethe's *Hermann und Dorothea*. In addition, he read "lyrical-didactic poems by Schiller" and "occasionally one or more odes by Klopstock." The students were also expected to read "biographical material concerning the main representatives of modern literature" and to prepare "individual presentations on the basis of independent readings" and "studies of poems from the canon." In French, the fifteen- to sixteen-year-old pupils were required to read "Jules Verne, *Le Tour du Monde*; Pierre Souvestre, five stories from *Au coin du feu*; Henri Michaud, *Histoire des Croisades*." At this school, in the markedly anglophile city of Hamburg, students read in English an anonymous "*Collection of Tales and Sketches*; Charles Lamb, *Six Tales from Shakespeare*; Walter Scott, *History of Scotland*" (*Jahresbericht* 1895, 4). Felix was excused from drawing, gymnastics and singing.

An overview of the graduates suggests that Felix Greve, the "cashier's son," would have intended to continue his studies, like the sons of the professor, the doctor and the watchmaker. However, in comparison with his schoolmates, the children of more prosperous parents, the financial outlay for the Greves must have been high. It is possible that Felix did in fact contribute to his mother's finances with an unbelievably excessive eighty hours of tutoring per week, as Greve later claimed in his highly (and purposefully) contradictory confessions to André Gide: "j'ai donné jusqu'a 80 leçons par semaine" ("I gave about 80 lessons per week," GG 222). He carefully reported the same in his Canadian autobiographical writings.[2] Given the amount of work waiting for him at the next secondary school, this may have been a terribly difficult, although extremely useful exercise, since it encompassed the entire curriculum, as he also indicated to Gide: "j'ai du l'apprendre tout en donnant mes leçons" ("I had to learn it all in giving my lessons," GG 222).

Three years earlier, on April 21, 1892, Felix's sister Henny Greve had moved into her own apartment at "27 Reitbrook at the W. Lübbe household." Apparently, secondary school was not an option for her. Was she required, like so many daughters of less-than-prosperous parents, to enter into service as a maid at a young age? We know nothing of her later whereabouts. It remains certain, however, that Felix's older sister was not provided the opportunity to continue her schooling, as he was. The financial costs would have been prohibitive, since school monies had to be paid as well as study materials, to say nothing of the cost of living. Four months before her fifteenth birthday Henny moved out of her mother's house. It appears she had received her Easter Graduation Certificate and had to leave home to earn a living. There may have been a connection between her leaving and the departure of her father, since the municipal registry states merely that she had previously lived with her mother. According to evidence from the office of the city registrar, Carl Eduard Greve moved to 56 Kirchenallee after the death of his wife. Did they share the costs of raising the children? Apparently Mrs. Bertha Greve was able to support at best only one child. The formidable expense of continuing Felix's schooling may have been the result of a revolt against her husband.

Here it is worth recalling that in at least three of Frederick Philip Grove's novels a mother takes up the cause of her children against her husband—in *Our Daily Bread* (1928), *Fruits of the Earth* (1933) and *Two Generations* (1939). There is also the semi-fictional autobiography *In Search of Myself* (1946), in which young "Phil" leaves "Castle Thurow" with his mother in order to continue his education in Hamburg and elsewhere, accompanied and financed by her.

What became of Henny? Spettigue assumed that by 1898 she was no longer alive, although it seems that she did not die in Hamburg. If she had, her death would have been recorded, which is not the case. Perhaps there is something of her in Greve's novel *Fanny Essler* (1905), in which a young woman leaves her home to become an actress but dies young (*FPG* 39). The accepted theory that Else von Freytag-Loringhoven was the model for Fanny does not preclude the inclusion of other lives. Elsewhere Grove indicated a sister—"a widow of forty, with two children" (ISM 175)—who had lived in Cincinnati, though she had died young. The latter point is referred to in another context as well. In his first conversation with Gide (1904), Greve claimed that Henny had been married in the United States and that he had not informed his mother of her death, which was not registered after 1898: "je lui ai caché la mort de la dernière [fille], qui était mariée en Amérique" ("I hid from her the death of the latter [daughter], who was married in America," GG 222). If Henny did indeed emigrate to America—like so many others, first in domestic service and perhaps even as Henny Lübbe (Lübbe was the last name mentioned alongside hers in the official registry)—and were she still alive, then Felix could have counted on a temporary *pied-à-terre* in the New World when he made up his mind to go.

This hypothesis also acquires substance from information in the Hamburg Municipal Registry. The page which includes the last addresses of the remaining Greves and notice of Bertha's death also contains data concerning

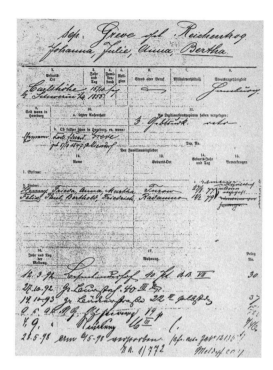

✺ *Excerpt from the Hamburg Municipal Registry for Bertha, Felix and Henny Greve after separation from Carl Eduard Greve*

(Staatsarchiv Hamburg)

the children, Henny and Felix. Under the rubric "Remarks," three short entries appear after a clear arrow-point, which may indicate a later entry and classification. The upper entry reads "residing in America," the middle one "living in Bonn" and the bottom entry has been struck out and could have read "[moved?] t[o]. America." Vertical to these entries is an almost illegible word that could be read as "presumably." Do these entries concern Felix, as the arrow seems to indicate? If so, when were they made? At the death of Greve's father in 1918, who was perhaps informed of his place of residence? And by whom? The entries appear to have been made by at least two, if not three different scribes at various times. On the other hand, at the time of Greve's feigned suicide in 1909, he would have been entered into the official registries as dead. Perhaps the upper entry was intended for Henny after all. The middle one with the reference to Bonn undoubtedly refers to Felix and appears to be dateable. The hand which registered the death of his mother may also have entered his new place of residence, Bonn. Did Felix provide the information regarding Henny's emigration when her estate was settled? Or was it the mysterious "Uncle Jacobsen," who was in attendance during the settlement of the estate (FPG 46–47)?

✳ *Gymnasium Johanneum, 1900 (Gymnasium Johanneum, Hamburg)*

◆ JOHANNEUM

At the beginning of the new school year, Greve transferred to the Johanneum *Realgymnasium*, useful for a business career, which he attended until Easter 1897. He prepared himself with great intensity for the classical language branch of the Johanneum, the academically oriented *Gelehrtenschule*. Frederick Philip Grove later described the situation:

> I was leading my classes at school. Since I had for years not had to take moderns, mathematics had always been my strong point; I was intensely interested in the sort of science which was taught, physics and chemistry. In my type of school, therefore, progress was a walkover. I did my written assignments, of course; and that took a modicum of my time—time, not exertion. I never really worked at my school tasks; my memory was phenomenal. So I had much leisure outside of school hours; but I concealed the fact: I worked at my Greek instead. By this time I had firmly made up my mind, if we remained in Germany, to transfer, for my final year at school, to a gymnasium where classics stood in the centre of the curriculum. If I did that, I should be five or six years behind in Greek: not in reading but in grammar and so-called composition which was really translation into Greek. Now, I was not in the least interested in these aspects of the language: I wanted to be

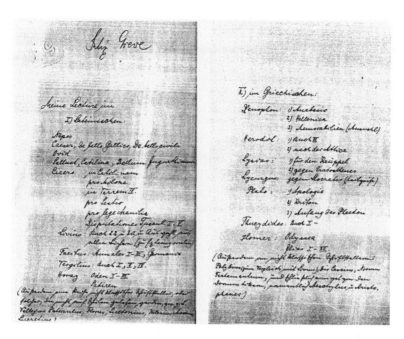

✵ *Felix Greve's list of readings in Latin and Greek, autumn 1897*
(Gymnasium Johanneum, Hamburg)

able to read Greek; and I was able to do so; I had taught myself by
reading. But there were teachers in my Realschule who knew better;
and one or two of them gave me a little time, when a spare period of
mine coincided with one of theirs, to drill me in declensions and
conjugations. Just how much my mother knew or divined of this, I
cannot tell at this distance of time (ISM 103–04).

To this day, the meticulously kept archives of the Johanneum contain two
sheets of paper with the handwritten name "Felix Greve" and the embossed
initials "F.G."—an indication of Greve's lifelong preference for "appropriateness," indeed luxurious appearances.[3] These sheets also provide concrete
evidence of the classical philology curriculum that the students covered with
tremendous speed. There are two detailed lists of Felix's readings:

[Page 1]
My readings in
I) Latin:
    Nepos

Caesar:	De bello Gallico, De Bello civili
Ovid	
Sallust:	Catilina, Bellum Jugurthinum
Cicero:	in Catilinam
	pro Milone
	in Terrem IV
	pro Sestio
	pro lege Manilia
	Disputationes Tuscul. I.V
Livius:	Book 22 a[nd] 30 a[nd] Selections from
	all the books (for Extemporalen)
Tacitus:	Annales I–II, Germania
Vergilius:	Book I, II, IV
Horace:	Odes I–II
	Satires

(As well a selection of non-canonical writers, or those who are not read at schools, such as Vellejus Paterculus, Florus, Suetonius, Valerius Maximus, Lucretius)

[Page 2]
II) In Greek:

Xenophon:	1) Anabasis
	2) Hellenica
	3) Memorabilia (Selections)
Herodotus:	1) Book III
	2) after Attica
Lysias:	1) for the cripple
	2) against Erathosthenes
Lycurgus:	against Socrates (in part)
Plato:	1) Apology
	2) Crito
	3) Beginning of the Phaedra
Thucydides:	Book I
Homer:	Odyssey
	Iliad I–XII

(As well, from the non-canonical writers: Polybius [for comparison with Livius], Dio Cassius, Novum Testamentum, and lastly something from the dramatists, namely Aeschylus a[nd] Aristophanes)

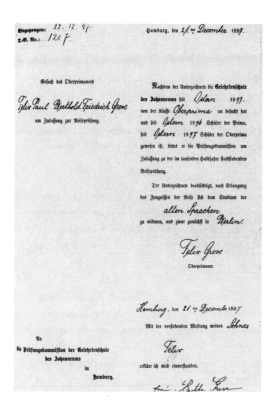

✻ *Permission to write final exams. Signatures of Bertha and Felix Greve, December 1897*

(Gymnasium Johanneum, Hamburg)

This list, impressive as it may seem to contemporary readers, shows little more than the incredible breadth of the then-unexceptional canon in classical languages. As he proudly reported, Greve read further in this canon, predominantly through his readings of historians. Even more impressive, and that which justifies his pride, was the diligence which enabled him to complete this list of his readings in only one year—1897–98—after acquiring the basic linguistic ability in the two preceding years.[4] As late as 1919, in his new identity as Frederick Philip Grove, he would recall this exceptional achievement, the remarkable ability and the promise which it seemed to presage in a manuscript which he never published: "A strange, nearly uncanny facility at mastering languages seemed to point the way for me" (Grove, "Rebels" 67). The list would have been added to Greve's application of December 21, 1897 for permission to write his final exams, which was signed by Felix and his mother and which reveals the striking similarity of their handwriting, assuming that Felix did not sign for both of them.

The records of the Johanneum contain a report on the "Scholarly Progress of the Prospective Secondary School Graduate Greve." In religion he is deemed "good." His oral command of German is only "good," while in written form he is "satisfactory." In Latin, the grades "very good" and "good" are indicated for his oral and written ability. In Greek, the grade of "good" was awarded for his oral proficiency. In French he is consistently "good," and in English "very good." In physical education he received yet another "satisfactory." The "Description of the Prospective Graduate," a summary handwritten by the school director, is positive:

> G. is well gifted, not without acumen and knows how to work success-fully on his own. Through pronounced diligence, supported by a very good memory, he has been able to make up for the gaps originally present at the beginning of his studies which resulted from the manner in which he was prepared and his knowledge and ability.

Greve's statement, also handwritten, that he wished to devote himself "to the study of classical languages…initially in Berlin" is also informative. Had he already had an opportunity to see Berlin? Greve probably discovered that a former Johanneum teacher, Hermann Diels (1848–1922), had made an impressive career for himself as a classical philologist there, first at the Berlin Academy (from 1881) and later at Berlin University (from 1882). Diels had been a teacher at the Johanneum from 1873 to 1878. If Felix had taken an interest in Diels, whom he would have heard about in Hamburg, and made the effort to seek him out in Berlin, he would have had the opportunity to make the acquaintance of Botho Graef, a reputable professor of archaeology, and his circle of gifted pupils, including Marcus Behmer, the famous book artist, and the young Ernst Hardt, the poet and dramatist—both subsequent lovers of Greve's future companion Else. Graef was related to the painter Reinhold Lepsius through his sister, and all three stood in good contact to Stefan George, who had organized one of his first private readings in Lepsius's apartment at 162 Kantstrasse on November 17, 1897 (Zeller, *George* 138).

On December 23, 1897, two days after applying for permission to write his final exams, the school director signed the "character reference" Felix required for acceptance as a one-year volunteer recruit in the military. Without the threat of mandatory military service, the possibilities were endless. Felix Greve, however, did not go to Berlin to Diels and Graef. He travelled instead to Bonn, home of the highly regarded classical philologists

Franz Bücheler, Hermann Usener and Georg Loeschke, professors who were also interested in the new discipline of archaeology. What could have caused these changes to his original intentions?

It was surely not an objective comparison of the two equally renowned departments in Berlin and Bonn which led him to choose Bonn. Apart from Berlin, Bonn was known "as the original Prussian State University, where members of the [Hohenzollern] dynasty were accustomed to studying" (Grupp, *Bonn* 30). The exercise of personal influence would have tipped the balance just as much; Felix Greve's incredible diligence and shining exam results had aroused the interest of his school director. The director was not, however, the former school principal Dr. Hoche (*FPG* 44)—who had long since become the senior school administrator of the district—but rather Professor Dr. Friedrich Schultess. Schultess, who was well regarded outside Hamburg as an experienced teacher and classical philology scholar, was a man who loved to flavour his speech with citations, especially from Seneca and Horace, and who himself wrote verse in Greek and Latin.[5] He had even translated poetry by Schiller into Latin. He is considered one of the period's most well-educated school masters, individuals who as authors and translators acted as mediators between cultures and literatures, contributing to the good reputation of the school system and some of its scholarly philologists (Martens, *Longfellow* 159–64). That this reputation was not maintained everywhere in Germany—that the system had its "Oberlehrer Neubauers" (from Wilhelm Raabe's novella *Horacker*) and "Wulickes" (from Thomas Mann's *Buddenbrooks*)—is attested to in Harry Count Kessler's memories of the Johanneum, as well as in Henry Adams's of his time at a school in Berlin (Adams, *Education* 70–81; Kessler, *Tagebuch* 29). But the First World War experiences of these democratically raised aristocrats may have negatively coloured their respective reminiscences.

In his commencement address for the graduation ceremonies on March 9, 1898, the director quoted his favourite author, Friedrich Schiller, with words from the prologue to the drama *Wallensteins Lager*: "Humans develop in relation to their noblest goals" (Schultess, *Johanneum* 144–48). Schiller had artistic matters in mind, Schultess continued, whereas he wanted to remind the graduates that they were to direct themselves toward the attainment of knowledge and not amusement. Greve was probably thinking more of art and pleasure, although he must have impressed the director as a model of tenacious single-mindedness who managed to advance despite all obstacles.

As it turned out, Schultess did not confine himself to poetic words alone, but took active interest in supporting his pupil. It was probably Schultess Grove was thinking of when he later wrote of "a revered teacher" who had told him that it was unimportant whether he chose to devote himself to classical or modern languages, for "you are sure to leave your mark on whatever you choose. Genius is bound to win."[6] His mentor would not only have directed him to Bonn, where he himself had studied under Usener and Bücheler, and to whom he could in turn recommend Greve, but he also arranged for lasting financial support. Thus on February 28, 1898, one week after the conclusion of final exams, Schultess presented his pupil with a second prize for outstanding achievement. This was the "Schrader'sche Award," a sum derived from the interest accrued by a scholarship fund. In Greve's case, it would amount to 370 gold marks. It was not a fortune, but rather a monetary form of recognition that would be paid once. Had it remained at that, Greve would not have been able to undertake greater challenges or continue his studies. Schultess, however, submitted three further applications, all of which were successful.

The first application solicited a request from a Dr. Amsinck—apparently the estate trustee—for a small stipend of 30 gold marks from the estate of Berend and Catharina Münden, to be paid bi-annually for the duration of the candidate's course of studies. Here, as in the next two instances, the director's reply is on the overleaf of the request:

> The senior Felix Paul Berthold Friedrich Greve, 16 Neuburg Street is above [stroked out: all the] others suited for recommendation for your very kind request for the next Münden Stipend.
>
> He is gifted and diligent and capable, which has already led to his having successfully completed the unusual route from occupational secondary school [Realschule] to secondary school [Realgymnasium] to academic secondary school [Gelehrtenschule] without loss of time while acquiring all the Latin [stroked out: which he lacked] and afterwards the Greek...
>
> He lacks financial support [stroked out: unfortunately also sick...?] and has an ailing mother whom he cares and provides for.[7]

Schultess was obviously impressed not only by Greve's accomplishments as a student, but was also aware of the poor physical health of his student,

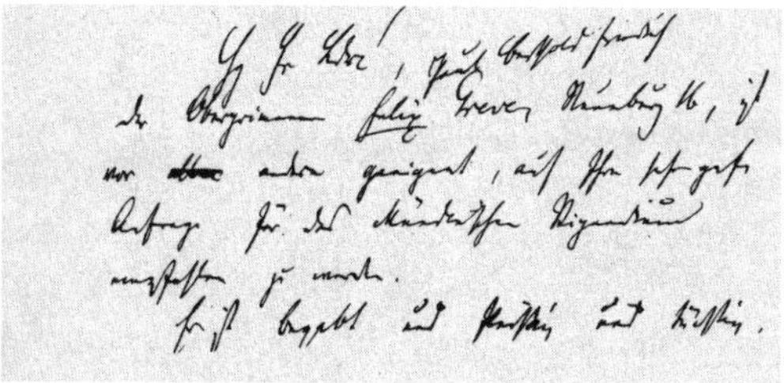

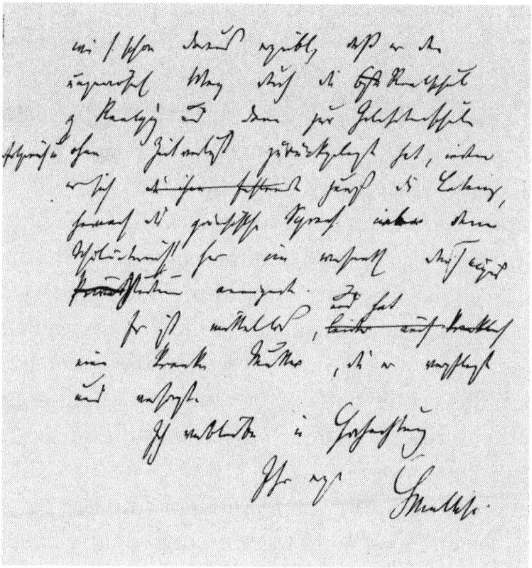

⌘ *Schultess's handwritten evaluation of Greve for the Münden stipend, 1898*

(Gymnasium Johanneum, Hamburg)

who selflessly devoted himself to his sick mother. Greve's seemingly precarious health may also have been the factor which spared him from performing military service. Felix was not—for health reasons?—a member of the highly active Rowing Club of the Johanneum (U.F., *Bootsmannschaft* 1930). He seems not to have accompanied the club on either the Alster or Elbe or on any of its other numerous excursions on Germany's rivers and along the Baltic coast. Given the financial situation of his mother, his enormous quota of work as a student and possibly a very busy tutor, where would he have found the time for costly excursions? For perhaps the same reasons, Felix Greve was also not a member of any of the bustling literary groups organized by the Johanneum students.[8]

Although honourable, the monies from the estates of the Schrader and Münden families were not sufficient to allow Greve to live in Bonn, let alone command the services of expensive tailors. Only a third stipend furnished Felix Greve with more or less sufficient means. Here one thing becomes perfectly clear. It was not an "Uncle Jacobsen" who provided for an income that would be higher than that of his father, but his teacher Schultess. In the minutes to the staff meeting of March 23, 1898, "at noon, 11:55," it was decided that money from the "Professor Fischer Scholarship Foundation" would be awarded to "stud. Greve for 4 years at most" or for the "duration of his actual studies." Fischer, a former teacher at the Johanneum, had bequeathed his library and considerable estate to the school. As with the other benefactors, the interest raised was given out in scholarships. As preconditions, the recipient was to be "needy and capable," Protestant and was to study at a university, "but not theology." Felix Greve would receive 1000 gold marks per annum for a maximum of four years.

The Fischer Scholarship was thus the one Grove refers to as the "scholarship payable in eight half-yearly instalments during the next four years, provided only I was enrolled in some recognized university" (ISM 141). Grove the Canadian failed to mention that such scholarships were only awarded to those "talented" students who were also in need of financial support. Shortly after receiving the handsome scholarship, Greve would begin to emphasize his talents in the presence of others while playing down the impression that he was needy. On the other hand, it was this impression of a poor but deserving student which Schultess contributed to creating and which most certainly helped Greve at other times. Were there other, less selfless reasons for Schultess to support the young Greve?

Grove's discussion of scholarships in *In Search of Myself* contains statements regarding his (hetero-)sexual initiation in the arms of a young woman named "Broegler," whose first name he claims to have forgotten (ISM 167). She was supposedly the wife of his impotent chemistry teacher, a man who had taken him into his trust and supported him. "Dr. Broegler's" sexual inadequacies and his friendly support of the young man who would abuse this trust may be read as a mixture of several sources: August Endell's impotence and Greve's affair with Endell's wife Else (see Chapter Five), as well as the care and charity of his Hamburg school director. Had Grove been thinking not only of Endell but also of Schultess, then it would constitute an example of extreme ingratitude, since Schultess's concern for Greve did not end with the departure of his student.

Even as Greve was preparing for lectures with Schultess's former instructors in Bonn, the director learned on April 1, 1898 that his pupil was being considered for the "Campe'sche Scholarship," supported by the Campe family, a well-known publishing dynasty in Hamburg. Surprisingly, in his comments regarding the nomination, Schultess advised against granting the scholarship: "Felix Greve, son of an impoverished widow, stud. phil. (philology student) is very capable and competent although adequately supported through the Academic School by the generous Fischer Scholarship." It does not appear as if Greve ever learned of the missed scholarship. Had Felix Greve—as may be concluded from Schultess's words—misinformed his mentor of his mother's situation, perhaps because he was ashamed of his parents' separation? Was his father "dead for him" in a moral sense? Or had Schultess simply wanted to give the boy's family situation a socially acceptable appearance?

Schultess did not lose sight of Greve. Two years later in the summer of 1900, when the administrator of the Münden Scholarship complained to Schultess that Greve had not maintained contact with him, Schultess wrote him conciliatory lines:

> Stud[ent]. Greve is, as I hear, in It[aly]; I will be able to report of his whereabouts before the beginning of Easter, when he is to meet with me regarding his schol[arship]. I do not believe that he will be forced to suffer difficulty if you award the schol[arship]. to someone else; he seems to have received a lot from my recommendation.[9]

The question remains whether Schultess was referring by "recommendation" only to the larger Schrader and Fischer scholarships, or whether there were additional sources which he had secured for Greve. This possibility cannot be excluded; the report covering Greve's 1903 trial in Bonn would mention sums additional to his scholarships which totalled from two to three thousand gold marks. During the trial such sums were attributed to his father, whom Greve had falsely called a businessman. Spettigue suggested that "Uncle Jacobsen" could have been the benefactor. Schultess probably recommended that another person or institution support Greve. Schultess himself—and not an "Uncle Jacobsen"—was without doubt the successful mediator of increasingly large sums, some of which may have remained undocumented. In any case, the Johanneum could boast of a significant number of famous and unusually wealthy graduates, among them the banker Aby Warburg and Harry Count Kessler (Kessler, *Tagebuch* 29), who, at least in theory, might have contributed to Greve's upkeep.

Schultess's note reveals more than Greve's financial indebtedness alone. Greve stayed in Italy while he was registered as a student in Bonn, although not before the summer of 1900. He would not have travelled alone "before the beginning of Easter" of that year to see Schultess in Hamburg. He made that trip throughout the course of his studies in Bonn and Munich twice a year—in spring and autumn—in order to report on his progress and to take possession of his scholarship monies, perhaps including any new sources made available by Schultess. Another longer meeting between Schultess and

Greve is also possible. In 1900, at the very time Greve was demonstrably in Italy with the knowledge of his professor, Schultess took, for the first time in his career, a four-and-a-half-month vacation—"a trip to the south…from February 10 until June 25."[10]

It is known that Greve prepared himself for his first stay abroad soon after the death of his mother and the dissolution of her estate in Hamburg. On June 25, 1898, he applied for a passport in Hamburg registered under the number 1232, which was initially valid until January 31, 1899.[11] It remains unclear whether the widowed Bertha Greve ever received anything from Felix Greve's sudden windfall of scholarship monies. Equally unclear is whether she or "Uncle" August Jacobsen, who was also present along with Eduard Greve at the settling of Mrs. Greve's estate, were ever informed of Felix's financial blessings. At any rate, Felix Greve was still identified as a minor, as the protocol in the settlement of Mrs. Greve's estate indicates. His surviving father was his guardian. Given the limited value of Bertha Greve's estate, her son may have said nothing concerning his own financial situation (Carl Eduard Greve swore an oath that she had had no "liquid assets" and that "the debts, costs and rent would not quite be covered by the proceeds from the liquidation of her furniture and estate"). The transformation of the soon-to-be orphan from a gifted though needy high school graduate from a broken home into a member of an ambitious, class-conscious Bonn elite must have seemed like a veritable about-face of character. During Count Kessler's time at the Johanneum—a time when the sentiment was that "we are not gentlemen here, rather Germans who are forced to work because we are poor" (Kessler, *Tagebuch* 30)—it appears that at least one industrious former student was preparing himself for the life of a gentleman. Not only would he regularly move among wealthy and often highly educated people, but he would also become a member of this society and play a new, self-defined role. Luckily, his entrance would not be delayed by military service. Although the character reference necessary for one-year voluntary service remains in the archives of the Johanneum, there are no further records of medical examinations, dispensations or even a subsequent summoning. Nothing other than his Hamburg diplomas and the fruits of his perseverance accompanied him out of his old life and into the new. Before fleeing to the New World, he would practise making himself anew in Bonn. He would seek out a circle of acquaintances in his new place of studies—a circle which would replace his missing family.

2

A·STUDENT·IN·BONN

"Nixe" on the Rhine

WITH MORE MONEY THAN HE HAD EVER POSSESSED in his life, Felix Paul Greve arrived in Bonn during the first days of April 1898. He was registered as a student of philology in the Faculty of Humanities at the Rheinische Friedrich-Wilhelm's University on April 20, paying an enrolment fee of 24.80 marks.[1] He presented himself to his Bonn classmates not only in a new suit and tie but also as a new man: proficient in the modern and ancient languages, young, successful, well-heeled. No one would have suspected his lowly origins.

Greve initially took lodgings in the centre of Bonn's old city at 18 Dreieckstrasse, as Spettigue first established. For the 1899–1900 winter semester, he moved to 32 Koblenzerstrasse (today's Adenauerallee), a prime location close to the Rhine. Apart from these changes of address, it is also known that in November of the following winter semester Greve was granted a leave of absence. He was allowed another retroactive leave of absence for the summer semester of 1901, shortly before his enrolment for the 1901–02 winter semester in Munich. These formalities and most of the courses Greve took with Usener and Loeschke have already been discussed (FPG 49–50). The rest has remained speculation. How did Greve settle upon the desire to become a writer? Who or what influenced him in making such a decision? What was his life as a student like? Did he have close personal friends? Was he on good terms with his fellow students? Who were they? Did he have acquaintances interested in literature? Who or what was responsible for Greve's "desertion in the autumn of 1900?"

To answer these and other questions, it seemed obvious to some scholars that conclusions about Greve's life in Bonn could be drawn from his later literary work and his sporadic proximity to the circle surrounding Stefan George's precious magazine *Blätter für die Kunst*. Accordingly, Spettigue wrote of a hedonistic milieu in which Greve must have moved: "some group of avant-garde students in Bonn" (*FPG* 87). However, many references and episodes in Frederick Philip Grove's works refer not only to elite literary circles but also to the author's preference for water sports. Despite these numerous references and the obvious importance they would seem to imply, an explicit connection between art and athletics in Greve research has yet to be drawn. Artistic depictions from the period, especially in the Anglo-Saxon countries, show how water sports were practised by well-situated students in America at Princeton and at England's Oxford and elsewhere. And although the more modest regattas in Bonn did not compare with those in Henley, Bonn's tradition in water sports earned it the distinction as the "Prussian Oxford" at the turn of the twentieth century (Kessler, *Tagebuch* 32). In many ways, this reputation was centrally important for the academic standing and social position of former and future graduates. Entries in the Hamburg students' academic record (*Belegbuch*) provide decisive early evidence concerning the relationship between studies and sport in Bonn. Apart from his studies in philology, archaeology and art history, Felix Greve had taken a course in sports, although it was not recognized as such by previous critics. It is now evident that he participated in a "Fencing Course" for several semesters.

Felix Paul Greve presented himself as a dapper, self-confident young man who had no cause to be ashamed of his background. Perhaps he bore in mind the German words which, as he would later report to André Gide, his mother had passed on to him "from her deathbed:" "*Kind, dass du stolz bleibe[st]*" ("that you may remain proud," *GG* 223). He would be welcomed as a desirable addition to the higher strata of town and gown. Indeed, at that very time of year, certain groups of academics were recruiting suitable new members for their circles. Greve was looking for such companionship and thus he was found.

◆ RHENUS

The cover of a now-tattered booklet, privately printed in Cologne in 1898, bears the Greek motto "ARISTON MEN YΔΩP" in capital letters above the entwined initials T and R, followed by an exclamation mark. It is the coat of arms of an "arms-bearing fraternity," a *Waffentragende Verbindung*, which by

Greve's time had shifted its crest from duelling to (water)sports.[2] The booklet, entitled *Semester Bericht des ARC Rhenus*, contains the semi-annual report of a Bonn academic fraternity, the rowing-club ARC Rhenus, for the summer semester of 1898 (April to July). Entries were made at irregular intervals by club members who were elected to various offices on a rotational basis each semester. Among these offices were those of the treasurer, the head of the boats committee and the four positions filled by members elected to take charge of the club for the semester. The entries in the log consist of summary accounts of social and sporting events, the minutes of various meetings, reports on rowing events, festive occasions, outings, accounts of the club's income, records of gifts and trophies given and received, reports on admissions and expulsions, competitions, comments and questions, mentions of thanks, praise and censure, reports of new and departing members, reference to births, deaths and marriages, changes in the professional occupations and addresses of all the members, as well as reports on visits from former members and teams of associated local and foreign clubs.

In the spring of 1898, ARC Rhenus proudly announced to its "inactive" members (senior members in good standing of usually more than four or five semesters and close to their exams) and its alumni (or *Alte Herren*) that the club had entered the new semester with eleven new *Füxe* ("foxes," or new members on probation), a record number. We do not know whether the new foxes were met promptly upon their arrival at the Bonn Train Station by "well-instructed representatives" or whether it was apparent from Greve's opulent luggage—as it was from that of Otto Julius Bierbaum's protagonist Henry Felix Hauart (in the novel *Prince Kuckuck*)–that "his monthly allowance left nothing to be desired" (Bierbaum, *Prinz* 305–07). Among the new arrivals, entered as no. 119 in the "List of Members," is "Felix Greve, stud. phil. [philology student], 1 semester, from Hamburg." Greve had quickly found a new home within the type of hierarchical structure he was accustomed to from home and school.

Other freshmen listed—two of whom would withdraw from the club for health reasons in the course of the semester—include the students Arnold Cappenberg and Hans Lomberg, about whom more later. Another, a straggler already entering his third semester, was registered as no. 124 on May 13, 1898, having transferred from the Polytechnic Institute in Dresden. He was "Hermann Kilian, stud. rer. nat." who was later to be identified as Greve's "nemesis."[3] Herman (he preferred the English single "n" spelling) came from a very wealthy and highly regarded family.

Herman Kilian's father, Dr. E. Paul Kilian, was from Leipzig and had been medical chief of staff before retiring from his duties. He seems to have been less respected than Herman's grandfather, Dr. Herman Friedrich Kilian

❧ *Felix Greve (2nd row, 2nd from the left) with friends Cappenberg (in the middle, 3rd from below, with glasses) and Kilian (on the right, with mustache and pipe). Excursion to Hönningen, summer 1898* (Collection Klaus Martens)

(1800–63). Raised in St. Petersburg and proficient in several languages, Dr. Kilian had been a renowned gynecologist and professor at Bonn University. During the course of his many travels, he had befriended Lord Rutherfurd-Clark, a peer and member of the Scottish High Court of Justice in Edinburgh. Rutherfurd-Clark's daughter, Jane Grace, married Professor Kilian's son and became the mother of Greve's friend in Bonn (who also named his daughter Jane).

Such details help to establish the full meaning of Greve's friendship with Kilian and to decipher some of the exotic details from Grove's autobiographical writings. Kilian's accounts of his grandfather, for instance, could well have played a role in Greve's budding interest in translation; for Dr. Herman Friedrich Kilian had shown literary inclinations and had translated English and Russian medical works into German. His grandson, the son of a Scottish woman, would have spoken fluent English, which would have attracted a young man from the anglophile harbour city of Hamburg. Furthermore, thanks to his family's general cultural knowledge, including legal matters, Kilian would have known about the sensational Wilde affair and subsequent trial, making Wilde's *Intentions* a possibility for joint translation in 1902. Even in appearance, Greve's new friend seemed fully, even parodistically Anglo-

Saxon. In the photographs of the new Rhenus members, in which Greve is repeatedly shown together with his friends Cappenberg, Lomberg and Kilian, Kilian is easily recognizable as the somewhat older, more serious and reserved man with the long drooping moustache, smoking a pipe with a curved stem, dressed in a tweed suit with a tweed cap. By contrast, Greve appears not only slim and blond, but fair, light, almost delicate and dainty with an enigmatic smile. Fortunately, pencilled notes on the remaining group photographs definitively identify Kilian such that supposition is unnecessary. In his relationship with Kilian, Greve found a new family which he could superimpose on to his own as he saw fit. Kilian seemed enveloped in an imposing aura, the aura of the foreign and the exotic, the inspired air of literature which Greve would make his own. Translation would be made to serve Greve as it had served Kilian's grandfather.

Before exploiting the transformative power of literary translation, however, Grove "translated" himself into Kilian's family by making his mother Bertha into a born "Rutherford" (in this spelling). The account in *In Search of Myself* reveals additional layers of Greve's autobiographical palimpsest in relation to Kilian. The novel includes a probable source of the apparently extensive travels with "Uncle Rutherford" to St. Petersburg and other parts of Russia (ISM 147, 151). Here, the connections to the real grandfather Kilian are more than obvious. The origins of other "world tours" by Grove may also be deduced from his life in Bonn, as will later be shown. That Grove had appropriated part of the extensive renown of Lord Rutherfurd-Clark in *In Search of Myself* must have seemed like poetic justice to the memoirist Frederick Philip Grove, who would later be condemned for fraud thanks to Kilian.

Although he had a much heavier build than Felix Greve, Kilian was anything but an athlete. Thus it must have been difficult to attract the son of the wealthy Kilian family to Rhenus. Is it possible that Greve had earlier formed an acquaintance with Kilian? No one could have known in the spring of 1898 that one of the new club members would win great honour and publicity for Rhenus and soon thereafter succumb to a scandal of personal indebtedness and public disgrace.

For the time being, however, the newly arrived Felix Greve had found a haven among a new "family" of mostly dedicated sportsmen. Each was eager to test his intellectual and physical prowess and to distinguish himself among young men of equal ambition. What could have been more welcome to a nineteen-year-old from the lower classes, just recently graduated from the renowned Johanneum? Of course there were other fraternities, but it would have been impossible for Greve to join Bonn's most prominent fraternity, the Borussia, which counted the Emperor among its illustrious alumni, and would soon accept the Crown Prince into its membership. Borussia was exclusively for the sons of royalty, noblemen, lesser gentry, diplomats and other rich and influential people. One of these was the turn-of-the-century collector and connoisseur of art Harry Count Kessler, familiar to Greve from the Johanneum.

The example of Count Kessler, along with those of Schultess and Kilian, may also have figured in Grove's semi-fictional account of his youth. The first volume of Kessler's memoirs, *Gesichter und Zeiten* (*Faces and Times*), appeared in 1935, early enough for Grove to have made use of it. A substantial analogy between *In Search of Myself* and Count Kessler's account of his life is evident in Grove's portrayal of his European journeys—journeys which Kessler actually took in the company of his mother and which Greve claimed to have taken with "Bertha Grove, née Rutherford." The Kesslers indeed knew "tout le monde" and "l'élite du high-life étranger à Paris" ("the élite of Paris' expatriate high society") from the world of art, politics and nobility, including Chancellor Count Bismarck and Emperor Wilhelm I, who appeared at the soirées organized by the "charmante comtesse de Kessler" (Kessler, *Tagebuch* 21). The following account by Grove may have its origins in Kessler's travels with *his* mother:

> No matter where we were, even in Egypt and Turkey, the people who called on my mother or on whom she called; who crowded her drawing room or sat down at her table when she gave one of her rare dinner parties, were the men and women—fewer then—who were more or less internationally known as "good Europeans," and whose names are quoted today, in the world of letters, of music, of art, of science…No matter where my mother went, she dropped automatically into milieus where it established a higher claim to attention and even distinction to have written a notable book, to have painted an enduring picture, to have carved a fascinating statue than to have amassed wealth or even to have ruled nations (ISM 82–83).

Among Bonn fraternities, only Borussia would have facilitated entrance into social circles of this kind. Acceptance into Borussia, however, would depend upon financial independence of the highest order and probably certifiable social status (Kessler, *Gesichter und Zeiten* 89–201).

Membership in Rhenus was less expensive, although only attainable with a surety of 400 gold marks. This sum represented more than the Schrader'sche Prize and the Münden Scholarship combined, and although the money was refundable it was nevertheless inaccessible. Rhenus's dedication to sports apparently made it possible for a former social outsider like Greve to join, making up in performance for what he lacked in real wealth and social standing. That Felix Greve had been a student at the *Realschule* and the *Realgymnasium* in Hamburg before entering the *Gelehrtenschule des Johanneums* prepared him for Rhenus. Almost all its members were either active in practical pursuits or preparing for them. They were doctors, engineers, teachers, pharmacists and lawyers. Three tobacco planters and overseas traders were also among them. Thus Felix Greve's intended path in life was already suggested in his choice of fraternity, a choice which in the ordinary course of things would have determined his career. In point of fact, however, he could only have become a school teacher like Schultess or perhaps a university professor in philology or archaeology like Loeschke. Grove later referred specifically to this institutionally prescribed arrangement: "Since university 'standing' has become the prerequisite for position in the hierarchy of the state, the institute has become too large and unwieldy; within the student body social distinctions define themselves as rigidly as they do elsewhere" (ISM 160).

It is here that a fundamental dichotomy—never to be resolved—between his scholarly preparation and his academic and social ambitions begins to reveal itself in Greve's character and development. His pragmatic, school-boyish formation refused to harmonize with his academic and social ambitions. This discrepancy between education and ambition points to a potential source for his extravagant lifestyle and his yearning for the life of a gentleman. Indeed, one reason for Felix Greve's reckless spending even then is his fortuitous acquisition of more money than he (or anybody else in his family) had ever had, as well as his aspiration to an elevated status in society. (The imaginary boyhood among the minor landed gentry in *In Search of Myself* would have prepared him for exactly such a position.) His exemplary performance at school encouraged him to reach for the stars. He did not, however, use his academic preparation for the prodigious work he was to accomplish later as an author and translator. Instead, he used the financial windfall to project the image of an independently wealthy man of letters in Bonn. Felix Greve had fallen victim to the widespread "romantic" image of the writer, rising by sheer effort from lowly beginnings to a glamorous place in society. If this were the case, then Greve did not realize that almost all the great careers in letters and science—including Stefan George's—were securely founded on comfortable family incomes, especially among those members of the Berlin and Munich circles which he would soon join. Greve's naïveté in the world of literature and the triple bounty of his scholarship money combined to ruin his clean-cut youth.

But Felix Greve still looked the model of the innocent, upstanding and promising freshman. The once-poor Hamburg student now sported an

✳ *Felix Paul Greve, 1898*
(*Collection Klaus Martens*)

elegant silk tie and a dark suit, proudly displaying the Rhenus insignia on the left lapel: a blue and white flag with a red eight-pointed star—the outward sign of new status in society. He was a young man of substance and promise.

◆ ATHLETE

The young Hamburg student would need his scholarship money. Rhenus members were required to spend not inconsiderable sums, in addition to the sizeable security deposit upon their entrance into the club. Although the monthly dues amounted to only five marks, rowing and sailing were not to be had for nothing. It was necessary not only to compete in social and athletic arenas, but also to maintain outward appearances. Sporting jerseys, sweaters and hats in the club colours—at first marine blue and then white—had to be purchased, along with respectable everyday clothing. Tailored evening dress was also required and, for executive members, the costly golden-white uniforms. Everything was approached with a heightened sense of formality: rituals were a major part of fraternity life.

Active and inactive members lunched at noon in the Hotel Kronprinz ("Crown Prince"). For the evening meal it was customary to meet at the Restaurant Hähnchen ("Cockerel"). Throughout the year, there were excursions and picnics, sometimes—as at dances in the the oft-visited Hotel Kley—in the company of young women. Weather permitting, members took a motorboat or the train, assuming they preferred not to hike along the towpath to the gardens of the Hotel Mundorf in Plittersdorf or even as far as the towns of Hönningen, Sinzig or Koblenz. There were more than enough opportunities for festivities, invitations and return invitations. It was customary to show generosity; autographed photographs were presented to club members and more than a few rounds of beer or champagne were bought at the larger festivities, such as at the "Founders Day Celebration," which took place annually in July and which in 1898 was celebrated in high style in the ballroom of the Hotel Kley.

As to the rowing activities proper, here, too, things were done in style. Trophies and other prizes were presented to successful members of one's own or competing clubs. Prizes were custom-made by local craftsmen and were paid for by the donor. Members had to keep up appearances and sustain their real or assumed social standing inside and outside of club circles. Delegations of other clubs stopped by in their boats and had to be accommodated, fed and entertained. During the fall break of 1898, for instance, the club established contact with a foreign rowing team: "During the fall vacations we were visited by a crew from London on an excursion down the Neckar and Rhine in their *kanadischen Kanoe" (Festschrift* 1906, 51). The names of the visitors were not recorded. Perhaps Greve used the occasion to practice his English and establish contacts that would be useful later.

Felix Greve must have been quick to grasp the social advantages provided by his new circle. If a member sought popularity, distinguishing oneself as a sportsman went far in compensating for other deficiencies. In this, Rhenus was not unlike its equivalents in the English-speaking world. Presenting oneself on occasions of high social visibility was also effective. One such occasion was the wake for former *Reichskanzler* Count Otto von Bismarck in Bonn's Beethoven Hall on November 28, 1898. It was attended by all Rhenus members in their club finery, the three students in charge standing at attention with lowered silver-plated ceremonial rapiers, their basket hilts padded with cloth in the Rhenus colours red, blue and white. Felix Greve, "third-in-charge" although only in his second semester, was among the three who were certainly admired by the crowd watching the spectacle.

And yet it was not occasions such as these which provided the club with its *raison d'être*. Daily life for Rhenus members was less a matter of the iron countenance at public festivities than that of the so-called "iron butt," a typical rowing formation. Rowing was done singly or in crews of two, three, four or even five men. Boats were taken off their racks in the large lower hall of the boathouse and carried through the open wooden portals to the slip and down an incline into the river. For the inexperienced, there was a danger of being carried away by the swift waters or turned over and drowned. In order to compensate for the lack of a safe training environment, beginners took part in regular exercises and "dry" training in a stationary trainer. Although Rhenus crews participated in numerous races in Bonn, Frankfurt, Berlin and elsewhere, they had yet to score a success comparable to the one in 1904, when a Rhenus boat with a crew of four won the Emperor's Trophy at the Grünau race near Berlin.

Apart from regular rowing activities during the semester, members were expected to engage in two hours of gymnastics on the Rhenus premises, particularly during the winter. Greve may have done "exercises on horizontal bars"—which he claims his "father" performed at "Castle Thurow" (ISM 28)—in the boathouse yard, a kind of "open-air gymnasium," and in the training facilities on the first floor of the boathouse. If the young and agile Felix was not able to complete a "giant's turn," others would have been able to show him. One very likely tutor, besides Fritz Schröder, the university's professional gymnastics trainer, was the muscular and heavily whiskered Theo Thiel, a widely travelled, adventurous medical doctor and an older mentor much beloved by Rhenus members.

The noble art of fencing, then requisite for anyone in a *Schlagende Verbindung*, was also a mandatory Rhenus activity. Greve took a twelve-hour course in fencing (a *Schlägercurs*) from the university's professional fencing master, Mr. Wilhelm Ehrich. Greve's first course lasted until July 1898, and was followed by another during the summer vacation. During the winter term of 1898–99, he took two more courses, the last one devoted to the techniques of handling the rapier. Felix Greve realized that regular training in fencing enabled him to hold his own at the often bloody fencing rituals requisite for acceptance as a regular member in good standing. University fencing courses were supplemented by regular practice at the clubhouse, also under the supervision of coach Ehrich (Anon., *65 Jahre* 12). After performing these rites of passage, Greve and his *confrères* Arnold Cappenberg and Hans Lomberg were admitted together as *Burschen* ("full active members") on October 22, 1898; Kilian followed one week later. To commemorate the occasion, Greve presented Cappenberg with a studio portrait of himself (ca. 16 x 11 cm, cardboard), the first that we have of him. Similar photographs of all the members encircled clubhouse rooms like a frieze above the wainscoting. Such decorations were more the rule than the exception. Bierbaum portrayed the initiation of his hero Henry Felix Hauart in precisely such surroundings:

✳ *Assembly room with library, Rhenus boathouse. Frieze of studio portraits of Rhenus members above the wainscoting. To the right, the collection of Malaysian kris presented by Robert von Kraft, December 1899* (Collection Klaus Martens)

He was almost dazed by all of these colours, to which were added still more caps worn by accompanying members from associated fraternities celebrating with them and the bright standards and coats of arms on the walls; everything was in the golden light of numerous candles standing in old, brass candle-holders already duskily cloaked by the clouds of tobacco smoke from long and short pipes. In addition, there was much flashing metal from the swords, sabres and spears grouped together radially and the paler dazzle of the photographs and silhouettes of former fraternity members hung closely together and appearing as if contained in one single glass surface (Bierbaum, *Prinz* 314–15).[4]

The Rhenus boathouse contained many additional decorative items. Greve was unsparing not only with purchases for himself. Shortly after his arrival, the Rhenus *Journal* lists various gifts presented by the new member. With his own funds he purchased a gas heater which was installed in the change room located on the lower level of the boathouse. He also donated special prizes for exceptional rowing achievements. In May 1898, shortly after his first boat-tour in a Rhenus jersey, he offered a prize to the "four-man team which, in the course of the summer semester, would make the longest journey up river

❅ *Rhenus boathouse, 1904 (Collection Klaus Martens)*

in one day." He gave "a splendid glass goblet engraved with the club coat of arms in gothic style" to a team that rowed from Bonn to Niederlahnstein and back in one day on June 9. The trophy, engraved with the names of the winners, was displayed on the mantelpiece as a decorative adornment until it was destroyed, with the building, in a 1945 bombing raid. In August 1898 Greve donated a stopwatch to the club. And as if that weren't enough, in October of the same year he again displayed his generosity: "For the adornment of the club bar, our d[ear] active member Greve, on the occasion of his reception, dedicated two etchings by Mack representing [the castles] Rheinstein and Lichtenstein."[5] Numerous photographs from Greve's time with Rhenus and later show the crystal goblet on the mantelpiece and the two engravings above the fireplace in the assembly room. Felix Greve presented himself as a gifted and talented individual, one accustomed to success himself and who showed generosity to acknowledge the success of others. He no longer appeared impoverished or dependent upon the charity of others. He had become a patron who presented awards with an open hand.

Although Felix Greve always occupied rooms in Bonn, many activities took place in the club's residence or *Bootshaus*, the hub of the club's activities. Compared with Grove's subsequent descriptions, the building has more in common with the fictive manor house "Castle Thurow" of *In Search of Myself* than with the house in Turow where Greve's parents stayed during the birth of their daughter Henny. The boathouse had been erected in 1897 to replace an earlier, more modest structure, a simple boatshed. The first floor now housed the racks that held the club's assorted boats. A number of surviving photographs of its interior, exterior and surroundings provide us with a good impression of its appearance at the time.

The building was situated on a spacious lot about a hundred feet from the bank of the Rhine; it was surrounded by shrubs and bushes. The front of the large, white two-storey house faced the river. On its right, set back from the front yard, was an attached three-storey square tower with a peaked turret, topped by an iron weathervane. A footpath and boatslip led from the river bank to the house. The second floor resembled a verandah, featuring decorative woodwork and glass. Behind the verandah was a large assembly and dining hall, as well as the study and the library. Pennants, medals, trophies and other memorabilia were displayed on the mantelpiece and along the walls. On the tower's second floor were guest rooms, with living quarters for the caretaker and his family above (Grove speaks, in German, of servants' quarters, or a "Leutehaus," at "Castle Thurow," ISM 24). Photographs show that the dining hall and library were large enough to accommodate fifty or more people. All the rooms were finished with dark panelling.

The following analogies and clues suggest that Grove borrowed significant elements from the boathouse on the Rhine for his "Castle Thurow" on the Baltic Sea. When Grove's reminiscences turn to "Thurow's" premises and hospitality at the breakfast table, he must have imagined the following scene, reminiscent of the gatherings in the boathouse:

> It was always a noisy gathering; for, in contrast to the later meals, everybody helped himself, and people ate and drank sitting or standing in groups. Huge sideboards were loaded with cold viands. Where carving was needed a girl or a lackey stood ready to do it (ISM 25).

The exterior also invites analogies with the boathouse:

> To my memory, the house looks enormous; and it was pretentiously called "Castle Thurow"…Its front faced the sea; and a wide flight of

steps, built of some basaltic rock, led up to an open sort of terrace, used as a driveway and a veranda, and paved with slabs of the same sort of stone, unhewn; in the middle there was the main entrance. To the right, the cliff-like structure was flanked by a tower which reached to twice the height of the main building. The lower three stories of this tower were an integral part of the house; its upper three stories, above the main roof, had contained the children's quarters...It is half a century ago that I saw it last; but my impression of it is, today, one of quiet dignity and straight-lined power, most impressive when approached from the sea. The lawns in front must have comprised twenty-five or thirty acres; and they were dotted with fine old elms and oaks. What a place for a novelist to live in! (ISM 21–22).

"Castle Thurow" was not a castle for a budding novelist, but rather the house which Grove constructed himself in his mind. As regards the other house, the beach fronted by its turreted and gabled structure was not that of the Kattegatt or any other rocky strip of coast on the Skagerrak (familiar to the young "Phil" of *In Search in Myself*), but that of the Rhine. Whatever Grove meant by the "cliff-like structure" of "Castle Thurow," the large tower "flanking" the building was there, and so were the terrace and driveway. "The hall" that "was the scene of the everyday life of the household which never consisted of less than twenty people, exclusive of servants" corresponds to the large assembly hall on the second floor of the boathouse.

The building was certainly not "within about twenty miles from the ancient city of Lund" or "within about a hundred yards of the sea" (ISM 18), but within a few miles of the university city of Bonn and about fifty yards from the Rhine (although in my view it can be considered the basis of young "Phil's" lost home as Grove presented it to his Canadian readers). By the time Felix Greve got to the *Bootshaus*, he was already "an expert oarsman, a bold swimmer, and very self-reliant" (ISM 35) — and determined to improve his talents.

On the up-river side, the house and its grounds were bordered by a commercial brick-kiln with a towering chimney. Both the chimney and the tower of the boathouse served the rowers as useful landmarks for their navigation, and perhaps anticipated the "lighthouse" and "tower near the beach" close to the "Thurow" estate where young "Phil" set out on a trip in a small rowboat, risking the danger of "being swept out, through the Sound, into the Kattegatt" (ISM 36ff.). In any event, the impressive new boathouse and the many trips taken from there to various places may have inspired dreams of drifting from here "into the North Sea, or the Atlantic, whence the Gulf Stream might take me into the Arctic Ocean" (ISM 39).[6]

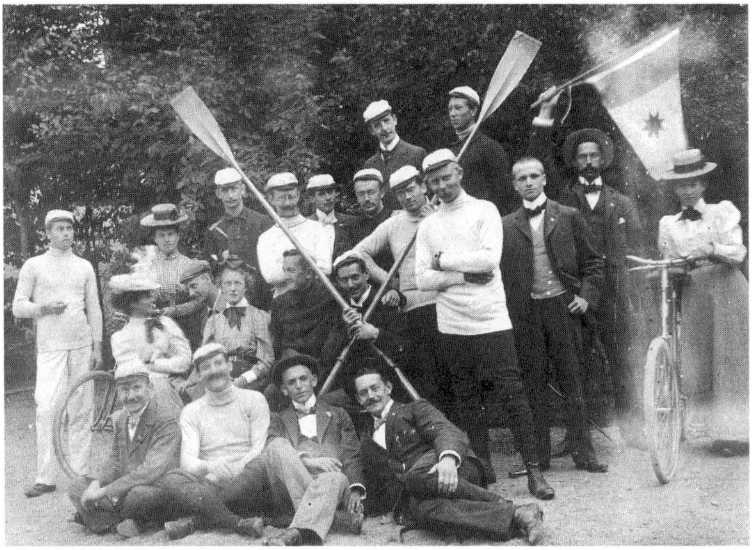

⁂ *Excursion to Hönningen, summer 1899. Felix Greve (3rd row, 3rd from the left, next to the oar blade), Dr. Georg Thiel (2nd row, first from the right), Kilian (in the back with the Rhenus pennant)* (Collection Klaus Martens)

The *Bootshaus* must have struck Felix Greve as a singular and imposing structure. In terms of social ambition, it was indeed the proving ground for the young man. If the university exposed him to the world of learning, then the elite society at the boathouse, with its competitiveness, virile fencing rituals and festive celebrations, provided a sheltered entry into high society by means of a new kind of "family." Indeed, it was not at all unusual in such clubs to designate a circle as a "family." Greve belonged to Dr. Theo Thiel's "family" and, as described above, he adopted some of his fictional "father's" athletic skills from Thiel. A photograph from a trip to Bad Hönningen in 1899 shows this "family" assembled around a pair of crossed oars: a moustached Thiel is standing with crossed arms in the foreground; to the right and back is Kilian, also with a moustache, waving the Rhenus flag; to the left and in the rear, beside the left oar, is Greve (also with a short moustache); above, beside the right oar, is Lomberg. Cappenberg had by this time transferred to Berlin for further studies. Greve was now part of a network of wealthy and influential men all over the world who considered the *Bootshaus* a shared home after they had left university. Conversely, for those expelled from the club or the few removed for other reasons, leaving not only meant social disgrace, but jeopardizing a promising future within the bounds of established society.

✷ *Picnic excursion Bonn-Linz-Bonn, November 1, 1898. Lomberg (1st row, 1st from the right), Greve (1st row, 3rd from the right), Kilian (2nd row, 2nd from the right, with pipe), Cappenberg (standing, 4th from the left)* (Collection Klaus Martens)

✷ *Picnic excursion Bonn-Linz-Bonn, November 1, 1898. Greve (1st row, in the middle), Lomberg (2nd row, first from the right), Cappenberg (2nd row, standing, 1st from the left), Kilian (3rd row, 2nd from the right, with pipe)*
(Collection Klaus Martens)

But there was not the least mention of expulsion in the autumn of 1898. As the third-in-charge, Greve remained in Bonn throughout the winter semester of 1898–99. The Rhenus *Journal* contains numerous entries in his handwriting signed by him, along with references to financial matters and plans for a beer-soaked Christmas party. Greve had already been elected member of the "boat commission" at a meeting of club members. He also figured as one of the two auditors and as one who remained in the boathouse throughout the spring break of 1899 (February 28 to April 17). Prior to this, one of the festive highpoints of the year, Shrovetide Carnival, was celebrated at the Hotel Kley on February 8. The Rhenus finances must have been in a poor state following the event, since Greve sent letters of reminder to fellow members requesting that outstanding dues be paid. During his first years in Bonn, Felix Greve had become a club member to whom responsibility and respect had been given. Nothing stood in the way of his continued success. Thus it was natural for him to exchange his city centre apartment for one on Koblenzerstrasse, a street close to the boathouse and in which the young poet and philologist Rudolf Borchardt lived.

Greve had achieved more than official recognition. In the autumn of 1898, he also participated in hikes to Linz and, via Remagen, to the ancient abbey of Maria Laach on the eponymous lake. On other occasions he rowed with friends to and from the town of Bendorf, close to Koblenz. At the beginning of May 1898, the novices rowed a few kilometres upstream to Linz. Two photographs show a relaxed and merry group of young men with a happy Felix Greve among them. Greve, Lomberg and Kilian are close to one another.

◆ DRAMA AND THE STAGE

Early in the summer of 1899, the regular June training schedule had to be occasionally interrupted to rehearse for a major event in which numerous Rhenus members took part. A committee of Bonn professors and citizens had decided to honour the famous literary historian, poet-professor and translator Karl Simrock by erecting a monument to his memory. To help defray the expenses, Bonn students decided to stage two performances, on July 7 and 9, 1899, at the Bonn Stadttheater, then under the direction of Julius Hoffman. The production was further supported by Berthold Litzmann, a conservative but influential professor of German (Höroldt 400–03). No fewer than three plays were selected to be staged on each of the two evenings, beginning at 7 p.m. and ending at 9:45 p.m.: *Philotas*, a tragedy by Gotthold Ephraim Lessing; Johann Wolfgang Goethe's one-act play *Die Laune des Verliebten*; and the first of the three parts of Friedrich Schiller's drama *Wallenstein*.

⁑ Newspaper advertisement for a student theatre performance in Bonn, July 1899

6. Juli 1899

Stadt=Theater in Bonn.

Freitag ben 7. und Sonntag den 9. Juli 1899:

Aufführungen der Bonner Studentenschaft
zum Besten des

Simrock=Denkmals.

Regie: Herr Ludwig Zimmermann.

Philotas.
Trauerspiel von Lessing.

Die Laune des Verliebten.
Schäferspiel von Goethe.

Wallenstein's Lager.
von Schiller.

Preise der Plätze:
I. Rang u. I. Parquet M. 3.00, Fremdenloge M. 2.00, II. Rang
Proscenium M. 2.00, II. Parquet M. 2.00, II. Rang M. 1.50,
Parterre M. 1.00, Gallerie 50 Pfg.
Billets werden bis 4 Uhr Nachmittags des betreffenden Tages in
der Musikalienhandlung W. Sulzbach, Münsterplatz 19, neben der
Post, ausgegeben.
Die Karten sind nur für den Tag gültig, für welchen sie gelöst
werden.
Der Billetverkauf für beide Vorstellungen beginnt Montag den
3. Juli, Morgens 8 Uhr.
Kasseneröffnung 6¹/₄ Uhr. Anfang 7 Uhr. Ende 9³/₄ Uhr.

According to the newspapers, both performances were considered great successes. A net income of 1,121.50 marks was raised with which a monument was installed and dedicated in 1904. Despite the success of the project and Greve's prominence as a Rhenus member, we have no concrete proof that Greve participated in the performances or even played a part. No cast of characters has been found. However, the Rhenus log contains the following entry: "Of the Rhenus officials, three were cast in major roles, three others played minor speaking parts." At the time, Greve was "a Rhenus official." It would have been strange, given Greve's ambition, if he had not been one of the participants. One would like to know whether Greve played the part of "Lamon" to a young lady playing "Egle" in Goethe's short play, with its classical presentation of two couples in love (Goethe, *Werke* 1968). Pictures from the period also show him in the company of young women. Was Egle among them? Greve's own *Helena und Damon* (1902), although reduced in format to a pair of actors, may have profited from dramatic experience in Bonn. Or did Greve, like Max Piccolomini in *Wallensteins Lager*, wield the weapon he had so assiduously learned to handle? In any event, the classical background of *Philotas* would have suited his scholarly preparation.

Felix Greve's immersion in classical and modern authors during his school years and his involvement in financing the Simrock memorial were hardly his sole literary experiences before his Munich period. It has been suggested that he must have had contact with a small group of avant-garde young people and perhaps had been present at a reading by George: "George did make public appearances when they served the cause, and one of them was a poetry reading at Friedrich-Wilhelms University, where Greve was a student" (*FPG* 58). With these hypotheses, two separate spheres are conflated. The group of students from the rowing club was—apart from Kilian and the people involved in the Stadttheater—little interested in literature. No traces of engagement with trends in contemporary literature remain, which is not to say that no such engagement took place. Even those associated with the Department of German were little interested in contemporary avant-garde authors. Nevertheless, the classical philologists who were enthusiastic about literature, above all Hermann Usener, maintained contacts in Berlin to the circle surrounding Botho Graef, to the painter Reinhardt Lepsius and his wife Sabine and to the gifted poet and dramatist Ernst Hardt—all of whom were closely associated with Stefan George. In fact, at the beginning of May 1898, shortly after the settling of Mrs. Greve's estate in Hamburg, a literary event took place at which Greve may well have been present.

It was arranged by the young poet, philologist and later translator Rudolf Borchardt, who, after a period of time with Graef in Berlin, had transferred to Bonn in 1896. In Berlin, Borchardt had made the acquaintance of the literary historian Richard M. Meyer, who in 1897 had published a pioneering article on Stefan George and the Viennese poet and dramatist Hugo von Hofmannsthal entitled "A New Circle of Poets." In Bonn, Borchardt was on the board of directors of a *Dramatische Verein* ("dramatic club"), a group which included artists, university teachers and citizens devoted to art and culture. (Such clubs were common in other cities such as Munich.) These circles were also of interest to publishers. J.C.C. Bruns, Greve's later publisher, inserted advertisements in the announcements and programs of the Bonn *Dramatische Verein*. Borchardt intended to direct the interest of the Bonn circle towards contemporary literature.

On April 13, 1898, Borchardt wrote to R.M. Meyer in Berlin requesting support for his plan to stage a reading of new poetry:

❆ *Ernst Hardt* ·
(Schiller Nationalmuseum/
Deutsches Literaturarchiv,
Marbach)

The *Dramatische Verein* in Bonn, of which I am a member of the
board of directors, intends in the course of the coming months to trans-
form itself into a free literary society; publication is to follow a reading
before an invited audience in which young Viennese poets are to
express themselves (Tgahrt, *Borchardt* 41).[7]

He requested issues of the privately distributed *Blätter für die Kunst*, of which
he wished to make copies. After consultation with Usener and others,
Borchardt succeeded in having Ernst Hardt invited to read poetry by
Hofmannsthal and George. Hardt's reading was announced in the *Bonner
Zeitung* of May 24, 1898 under the heading "Viennese Poets in Bonn." The
salon of the Hotel Kley, which was used for some of the Rhenus festivities
and in which the meetings of the *Dramatische Verein* took place, was chosen
for the reading. Here is Borchardt's tongue-in-cheek report on the event:

> The apparatus that the minstrel had ordered—a darkened, candle-lit
> room, upset and irritated—the human appearance and youthful

charm of the man were not raised but rather made suspicious by the affected attempt to appear distinguished while the pretentious pseudo-elegance of Berlin's "exceptional" literati, the celebrated reading style—so effective in a light voice before a single listener, so false-sounding in front of hundreds in a sober room—this and more, which I am not going to mention, angered and incensed/disappointed. Usener, with his resplendent silver-stranded head thrown back waited with inscrutable countenance…the audience laughed/mumbled and threatened to grow loud, and as [professor] Justis's huge body slowly emerged out of the darkened seats to stand and go, he lay his heavy hand soothingly on my shoulder—his words "allow me to go, I cannot stand the opium any longer" were overheard by those sitting in the vicinity, spread from mouth to mouth, and half the room left, chairs scraping, exploding the artificial night (Tgahrt, *Borchardt* 43).[8]

We may assume that not only Professor Usener was in attendance but also his son, the student Walther Usener, who, like Hardt, Vollmoeller and Delbrueck, was interested in literature and a good friend of theirs. Walther Usener was also a friend and correspondent of Botho Graef in Berlin and had produced an unpublished volume of poetry (Usener, "Erste Verse" 1906).[9] This may well be the basis of the "circle of talented young men" which had been assumed to exist but whose early connections to Greve could not be established. Usener was as successful in his studies as the rest of Greve's friends and acquaintances, and was also present as a disputant during Herman Kilian's doctoral defence on July 29, 1908. The athletic and cultural circles in Bonn clearly overlapped.

On the day after Ernst Hardt's reading, Borchardt patiently allowed the general censure to pass over him. In brief, a scandal had taken place. A young man with philological interests and literary ambitions could not have been unaware of it, even if he were not present himself at the reading. Greve was well acquainted with the location of the reading and would have been intrigued that the Viennese poetry had caused a sensation. Ernst Hardt himself characterized the evening as a success in a letter to Karl Wolfskehl. It is hardly surprising that his perspective differed from that of Borchardt:

The George evening in Bonn was impressive—approximately 100 invited guests—who left with an impression stronger than all expectations—I had the light dimmed as I read such that two candles at the sides of my head were the only sources of light in the rather large hall. The holiness of the verses accumulated in the darkness, causing the audience to feel itself before an altar—the [breath?]less quiet which

✻ *Karl Gustav Vollmoeller*
(Collection Heidi Vollmoeller)

extended some time beyond the conclusion counts among the most beautiful that I have ever experienced in my life.[10]

Did Greve use the evening to make Hardt's acquaintance and through him make contact with Else Ploetz, August Endell and Richard Schmitz or even with the "priest" of the new art himself, Stefan George? Was he already aware that Professor Usener had more cultural contacts than Hardt alone? Or that both had met Karl Gustav Vollmoeller in Berlin? Or that Vollmoeller, himself a student of archaeology in Bonn since June 1900, knew another young Bonn archaeologist and former student of Loeschke, the promising Richard Delbrueck, who had matriculated in Bonn on May 4, 1898? The world of modern art, like that of archaeology, was small and intimately connected to the world of literature. Endell, for example, had, like Borchardt, already published a volume of poetry. However the channels of influence may have flown (see Chapter Three), Greve discovered a situation in Bonn which was not only beneficial for his athletic and philological/ archaeological inclinations, but also one which offered examples of poetic composition (and as Hardt demonstrated and Borchardt observed, the appropriate mixture of priest-like attitude and gentlemanly allure). Felix Greve's *Wanderungen* and *Helena und Damon* undoubtedly owe something to this demonstrative preciousness.

◆ TRAINING IN A SINGLE SCULL

Readers of Frederick Philip Grove's books, especially *Over Prairie Trails*, *The Turn of the Year*, *A Search for America* and *In Search of Myself*, are time and again confronted with knowledgeable, even professional comment concerning the sea, rivers, water sports and, above all, sailing. As no research has been able to establish any sailing activity in Sweden or Hamburg, and since the existence of Grove's "Uncle Jacobsen," whom the author depicted as an experienced and able sailor, is unlikely in the financial capacity presented, the only remaining source for Grove's early experience with water sports is his time as member of Rhenus.

In the Rhenus *Journal*, Felix Greve is registered as the owner of two boats. Neither was brought from Hamburg; rather, they were both built in Rotterdam according to his specifications. The following was recorded in the *Journal* for October-November 1899 in Greve's handwriting: "O[ur]. d[ear]. active member Greve acquired for himself a smart-looking training scull which was built by Deichmann & Richie and which has turned out to be very nice indeed." The new boat was immediately tested on a "solo run by Greve of approximately 50 km to Leubsdorf (above Linz)." Clearly, Greve's lung ailment had subsided, if it ever existed. Greve presented this boat, the *Nixe*, to the club at the following year's Christmas party on December 16, 1899, which he presided over as the first-in-charge. Recorded in the *Journal*, again in Greve's handwriting: "o[ur]. d[ear]. active member Greve, in consideration of the poor condition of our racing single *Bierjunge* (*Beer Boy*) presented as club boat his training scull built by Deichmann and Ritchie one year ago."[11] His second boat, likewise a single scull with a gliding seat, was called *Faultier* (*Sloth*). Greve later sold the boat to the club. No details concerning the transaction are available. It can be said with assurance, however, that neither of Greve's boats were sold before his departure to America, as Grove would later write (he speaks of "a small yacht," ISM 175), nor did he take one of his boats with him after leaving Bonn. The fact that both boats were built for him in Rotterdam provides indication of Greve's early familiarity with the Dutch harbour city from which Else would depart Europe on June 10, 1910 (BE 24).

"I trained for a boat-race in a single scull" (ISM 145), wrote Frederick Philip Grove. This training was certainly undertaken by Felix Paul Greve,

✷ *Greve with mustache, winter semester, 1899–1900. Verso: "Nixe" Greve's dedication to "Bebe"* (Collection Klaus Martens)

although not in Hamburg but in Bonn. The club's *Journal* of June 1899, for instance, reports: "Besides our dear active member H. Ottendorf II, our dear active member Greve has been training since the middle of June for Mainz in his personal single scull which was built by Deichmann in Rotterdam and which has turned out absolutely perfect." More than Greve's first single scull was baptized with the name "Nixe," however. "Nixe" was also Greve's drinking or club name. The first incidence of this nickname is on the back of the second surviving studio portrait of Greve. It shows Greve in the autumn of 1899. He is sporting a blond moustache with up-turned tips in precisely the style of Kaiser Wilhelm II, from whom Grove's mother Bertha had predicted "nothing but evil" would come.[12] On the back of the photograph is a dedication in Greve's handwriting: "Nixe/ to h[is] d[ear] Bebe/ W.S. 1899/ Bonn. For h[a]pp[y] memories." "Bebe" could not be identified; perhaps Kilian was intended.

"Nixe" was a fitting name, for, as an excellent rower and swimmer, the slender and waif-like Greve was a veritable water creature. In *A Search for America* he describes himself as such when he saves a man from drowning by jumping into the deep and cold waters of the Ohio River without hesitation, claiming "I am—or was—by nature nearly amphibious, swimming and diving being my favourite pastimes" (SFA 252).[13] A *Nixe* is a nixie or mermaid,

✸ *Greve as "Nixe" (on the pushcart); Cappenberg (with enamel urn). Probably in the garden of Hotel Mundorf in Plittersdorf, early summer 1898*
(Collection Klaus Martens)

while a "nix," *nöck* or sprite in Germanic mythology, is its male counterpart, the *Wassermann* — the astrological figure appropriate to the Aquarius Felix Greve, born on February 14. That he named his boat *Nixe* is not surprising, given that boats are frequently given feminine names. That the feminine designation was also extended to the owner, however, may be an indication of Greve's androgynous aura. This aura is powerfully expressed in an early group photograph, probably from the summer of 1898. Greve and his friends are posed on a terrace (probably the terrace of the Hotel Mundorf in Plittersdorf), creating an allegorically suggestive tableau. Felix Greve forms the centre. He is resting on a pushcart with a garland crown in the foreground, his arms crossed over his chest. The long handles of the cart seem to extend his legs and give his "fish tail" an upward twist. Behind his head another club member, possibly Lomberg, is holding a footstool as if he were plucking the strings of a harp, while their common friend Cappenberg seems to sprinkle him with water from an enamel urn. Behind Cappenberg another is standing, in front of a grapevine, blowing into the spout of another watering can as if it were a pan-flute. Five others are standing and sitting around a table set for coffee. Are we looking at the *Nixe Loreley* by Heinrich Heine? At least four of the nine are more than aware that they are making erotic gestures with their tableau. They know, and are showing, what it is supposed to mean. A joke? Certainly, although homoerotically suggestive nevertheless.

That Felix should not object to "Nixe" as his club name and give the same name to his single scull (or vice versa) may, however, be explained not only by the erotic implications of the nickname or its phonetic similarities to his first name. Felix followed a Rhenus tradition by choosing *Nixe* as a name for his boat. Indeed, a 1906 anniversary publication tells us "*Nixe* was the only sailboat ever owned by the club" (*Geschichte* 84). In addition, in the club's lists of boats, the first *Nixe* is specifically identified as a "Norwegian sailboat." If, by analogy, Felix's *Nixe* and the club's earlier sailboat of the same name are perceived in relation to his nickname, then the recurrent tales in Grove's autobiographical narratives about sailboats cease to appear wholly fictitious. In fact, they seem to have a factual basis here—including the Norwegian origin of the sailboat which may indeed have once sailed in the Scandinavian waters so often mentioned by Grove. As it happens, Grove turned "Uncle Jacobsen" into the instrument for the "purchase of the yacht" in which they sailed from "Lübeck to Haparanda and Helsingfors and even down the Baltic, past Thurow into the Skagerrak, along Jutland, and down the North Sea to Hamburg" (ISM 91). The old Rhenus sailboat *Nixe* was known more for capsizing and giving its crews unexpected baths than for traversing the Baltic or making the notoriously rough trip from the Baltic into the North Sea. Grove may have enjoyed another inside joke here.

Indeed, most of the episodes concerning "Jacobsen," boating and sports in Grove's recollections seem to have verifiable roots in Greve's Bonn period. Consider, for instance, Grove's other account of "Jacobsen's" days of sailing with him:

> Whenever we were near water, he had one of his fleet of boats shipped out from Hamburg: a double skiff, or a half-outrigger boat; and finally two single-seaters with full outrigger row-locks and sliding seats. In these boats, some of them no more than sixteen inches wide, we travelled thousands of miles, on the Rhine, the Elbe, the Oder penetrating thence into the Mosel, the Main, the Neckar, the Havel. We went to England to attend the great regattas and thus saw much of the countryside. And finally he taught me to sail (ISM 90).

Was there someone in Hamburg who owned several boats and who allowed the pupil Greve to use them? Perhaps it had been possible for him to sail on the Alster. Some opportunity to practice, perhaps with the rowing team at the Johanneum, can be assumed since Greve began to participate in long rowing trips almost immediately upon arrival in Bonn. According to the

Rhenus *Journal*, in the summer semester of 1898 (from May 1–5), he had travelled no less than 270 km on the Bonn-Trier-Bonn stretch with a companion in the two-seater *Vega*. Shortly afterwards, he rowed only 7 km less as member of a six-man team in the *Fiducit*. This was only fourteen days after his acceptance in the club. Between July 7 and 9, 1898, he again rowed with a six-man team in the *Salamander* from Bonn to Frankfurt and back, a journey of no less than 200 km. In the same month he was again in the *Vega*, rowing 135 km to Bad Ems and back. In the summer semester of 1899, training for a regatta in Mainz took place, although Greve pulled a tendon and was thus unable to participate. Nevertheless, there was a relaxing picnic tour to the confluence of the Rhine and Sieg on June 18. In the middle of these activities, in the pouring rain of June 21 in Bonn, the club participated *in corpore* in a torch-lit procession in honour of Bismarck. At the end of the procession, all the torches were thrown into a pile and the traditional student song "Gaudeamus igitur" was sung. On the same day, in a four-man boat, Greve took part without success in a race in Frankfurt. Rather than take the train, he and a fellow member rowed back to Bonn in the *Vega*. On June 29, the club took one of many boat trips to the "wilderness" of Hammerstein, an island in the Rhine. Felix Greve was, without doubt, one of the most active rowers in the club. When did he learn the sport? Where had he trained? Whatever may have taken place with the legendary "Jacobsen" in Hamburg, it is beyond doubt that in 1899 there were twelve boats of various sizes in the Rhenus clubhouse, including the *Vega* which, along with his own boats, Greve often used.

It goes without saying that custom-built boats like the *Nixe* or the *Faultier* did not come cheaply. In fact, they cost approximately 150 gold marks each. In contrast to Greve, the wealthy Kilian had not bought a boat or participated in any long, taxing journeys on the water. He played a more marginal role and occupied only one position, *Fuxmajor*, the one responsible for new members. Of Kilian it could not be said what Grove would later write of himself, namely, that "I had already found that I had a talent for forming the centre of certain groups" (ISM 161). After an ambitious rise through the hierarchy, Felix Paul Greve was elected as the first-in-charge of the club in October 1899. Prior to the election, he had definitively shown the necessary athletic qualifications for the position.

◆ "NIXE" ON THE RIVER

The longest and most arduous boat trip in the annals of the ARC Rhenus was undertaken from August 3 to 15, 1899. The record distance of 758 km still holds today.[14] Five men — Dr. Georg Thiel, Matthias Schmitz, Carl Hartmann,

Hans "Hanne" Lomberg and Felix "Nixe" Greve—comprised the crew that rowed *Prosit* from Bonn up the Rhine to Wiesbaden, from there into the Main as far as Frankfurt, and from Frankfurt to Würzburg and Heilbronn and back again to Bonn. The two-week journey was not only taxing and memorable, but also well documented. Thiel, who apparently accompanied his "family" in the role of old friend and advising member, made notes of the trip. Of the participants, only "Nixe" and "Hanne" (both later firsts-in-charge) are precisely identified in his notes. Thiel's description provides us with the only extended account of a private venture in which Grove played a role in the social milieu of the period, precisely as several of his fictional characters would later do in Canada.

After departing from Bonn in the early morning, the rowers took their first break on an island near Neuwied. Their attempts at cooking were miserable. The group was grateful when a member living in the vicinity, accompanied by his two daughters in a bark, brought them something appetizing to eat. At Douqué's Inn in Niederlahnstein that evening, they tied into the alcohol more modestly than usual:

> During the day we drank only coffee and water. The wonderful mineral water that everywhere springs from the ground, we were able to find water everywhere we landed…The coffee we transported in earthenware jugs which were freshly replenished every morning.

The August temperatures pressed upon the rowers. "The sun burned from the sky to such an extent," writes Thiel,

> that I very soon realized that…my skin was not up to the sun's rays. I attached a handkerchief under my hat as neck protection and bound a pair of white washcloths around my legs; soon the rest of the team followed my example, apart from "Hanne" and "Nixe," who had avidly rowed that summer and already brought some colour to the trip; yet on the next day, they had to make themselves comfortable with our attire. In this tropical guise we continued on.

As will be seen, Thiel was not the only one with knowledge of the tropics. Greve acquired here something for Grove's memories. A few days later they left Bacharach. They faced their first adventure:

On another morning, the sound of the rushing current seemed to come through the still of the morning dawn as if from far away as we walked through the Bacharach city gates down to the Rhine. First the dew was wiped from the boat and oars, then the packs and supplies stored away and already we were continuing our journey upriver. We had hardly warmed ourselves up when we were forced into the water again; just above the town, as "Nixe" was steering us around the head of a mole which projected far out into the Rhine and against which the water rushed powerfully into the valley, we found ourselves suddenly sitting on a boulder laying just under the surface of the water. In a flash the current took the stem and threw it around against the current, the boat made a polite bow back to the port and an audible crack was heard. We all quickly leaped overboard and the boat was saved; we were washed a good ways downriver before we found ourselves, dripping wet, in the boat again.

"Nixe" was responsible for more than incidents of this sort; he also showed his talents as a scout, especially in the evenings when everyone was tired. It becomes abundantly clear that Felix "Nixe" Greve played the central role in the memories of the chronicler, as, for example, on the following evening at Kostheim:

> Our quarter-master "Nixe," whom mother nature had outfitted with such unusual length that he couldn't go lost for long, was sent out on reconnaissance. He didn't return until we had already safely put the boat away and were just about to instruct some of the village lads, who had helped in transporting the boat, in the essentials of the proper conduct with beer at a local garden bar. Only after some searching had he been able to find quarters for us as a celebration was to take place in the village on the following day. Thus we spent the evening with wine and pork sausages—wine from the barrel in huge 5/10 glasses; a new era had begun.

After a stay in Frankfurt with an associated club, where they sat under old trees resting and watched a boat race, "Nixe" was able once again to demonstrate his talents in Rumpenheim:

> As we walked through the empty streets of the village, we were somewhat concerned about our quarters; "Nixe," however, who had been

sent out ahead, again revealed what an astonishingly fine nose he had developed, for the robust female inn-keeper with whom we were to stay inspired an unusually strong impression of competence.

The next day they rowed further, through the dark woods of the Spessart as far as Aschaffenburg. This was a region which once formed the border of the Roman empire. Thus they were sure not to forget that the "Pompeianum" lay in the vicinity close by. They passed the evening in a tiny inn lit by a single oil lamp and slept on straw bedding which the innkeeper had spread out on the dance floor. After they had passed the woods of the Odenwald on a rainy afternoon, they reached the ancient city of Miltenberg where they dried their wet possessions in a baker's oven. There was certainly something important to see in the area. Miltenberg, in fact, was a must for a student of Georg Loeschke, who with his colleagues (in the Reich Limes Commission) studied Roman cities in Germany and the extent of the limes (the fortified boundary of the Roman Empire). They climbed up the castle hill and found something that must have struck a chord with Greve, the philologist and prospective archaeologist, who may have initiated the trip in the first place. Thiel writes:

> [F]or a long time we fellows of the *alma mater Bonnensis* stood devoutly in the castle courtyard in front of a unimposing weathered sandstone column; it was found in the forest close by. In almost illegible Latin letters it proclaimed to the epigones: 'Here is the boundary between the Teutons and the Romans.'[15]

After leaving, they passed the mouth of the Tauber at Wertheim and Castle Tiefenstein and drank beer from mugs that were brought to them by boat. The days went by with few stops for visits. Although they felt great, the rowers soon looked "like a real band of robbers." Sometimes they went hungry, while at other times they feasted on "roasts and baked fish accompanied by fine-tasting wine." Finally they reached Würzburg where they paused while having their boat transported by train to Heilbronn. They found it there two days later in the evening. As ragged and tattered as they were, little remained for them other than to stay in the strangely named and rather dubious *Gasthaus zur Kettenschiffahrt* ("Chain Shipping Inn"). From Heilbronn they reached Bonn after three days of rowing by way of Worms, Mainz and Geisenheim.

Felix Greve would later complain to Karl Wolfskehl of health problems, which were as fashionable as occasionally timely but which had also been a reality in Hamburg. According to *In Search of Myself*, in fact, Grove later developed a back problem (ISM 232; 340; 342–44). However, at the time of the journey to Heilbronn and back and throughout many other rowing trips, there was no talk of health impairments. On the contrary, the sentence which Grove wrote in his first Canadian book, *Over Prairie Trails*, applied to both the Rhineland and Manitoba: "I am naturally an outdoor creature." He had indeed presented himself as a willing outdoorsman, at home far from the everyday comforts of civilized life and unintimidated by deprivation. In this respect, the life of the aesthete, which he would cultivate in Munich in the *Blätter für die Kunst* circles, is more the exception than the rule, given the simple life he actually lived in Bonn and Manitoba. Frederick Philip Grove's almost superhuman efforts on weekly trips with horse and wagon through the deep snow in freezing winds (1917–19) were—as was his record-breaking swim across the Gardasee in August 1902—not the result of Wildean libertinage but rather his training in the company of his Rhenus friends. His training is also evident in the first-person narrators and protagonists in Grove's novels such as Niels Lindstedt. These lonely, taciturn, isolated and self-isolating characters had little in common with Felix Greve, who in Bonn developed into an increasingly admired figure who occupied the centre of a large group of peers.

This was clearly demonstrated on the boat trip with Thiel, Lomberg and the others. In times of hunger and fatigue, "Nixe" is the member everyone depended upon. He was resourceful and could be counted upon to achieve results as expected. Despite the presence of the older Dr. Thiel, he was undoubtedly *primus inter pares*. This respect was confirmed with his election as leader of the club.

Greve's experiences on his long boat trip through a famous romantic region of Germany may very well have found more concrete expression in his Canadian autobiographical books. One such example is Grove's report on a trip on the Ohio River in *A Search for America* (SFA 239f.). Here, the narrator is in a foreign environment—alone, bedraggled, often despondent and entirely without possessions. While Thiel could happily apostrophize Greve and his friends from Bonn as a "band of robbers," the 1920s narrator no longer found himself on the Rhine, the Lahn, the Main or the Neckar but rather on the "Beautiful River," the Ohio, "as a nomad who lived from what he could find" (SFA 253). His clothes are in tatters and his appearance is highly conspicuous. Instead of a meal being brought to him in a boat, he receives a kick in the ribs as he shivers from the wet and cold: "Move on, there! Or I'll have you run in. No vagrants wanted" (SFA 242). Instead of a picnic tour to the "wilderness" on Hammerstein or to Hönningen, Grove finds himself in a wilderness in which he must remind himself that he is on "no pleasure outing" (SFA 244), and where river water is the only available drink.

Grove's early Canadian books are indeed full of allusions, metaphors and concrete descriptions which betray intimate knowledge of things to do with water. The shape of river banks, changing currents, islands in rivers, fish, boatmen, raftsmen—all this is found not only in reference to a dangerous raft trip on the Ohio, but also in the deepest interior of Manitoba as the drifting snow causes the narrator to think of sailing on another river, the St. Lawrence:

> This was indeed like nothing so much as like being out on rough waters and in a troubled sea, with nothing to brace the storm with but a wind-tossed nutshell of a one-man sailing craft. I knew that experience from having outridden many a gale in the mouth of the mighty St. Lawrence River (OPT 129).

Although the allusion here is to the sea, Grove's adventures are usually played out on rivers. In *A Search for America*, for example, the strongest impressions are created by the narrator's experiences with his raft on the Ohio River—an episode strongly reminiscent of *Huckleberry Finn*. Greve could well have read the book as a St. Pauli *Realschule* student, since Twain's novel was available in the school library. Grove himself writes:

> The story of my trip on the raft stands out with great clearness in my memory. There were fun and disaster, comedy and quasi-tragedy enough in those two weeks to fill a book by themselves. But all that has little bearing upon the present story; I must skip. I shall, after a few brief hints, explain only how my raft came to harm (SFA 247).[16]

It is not surprising that *both* the Bonn Rhine-Main-Neckar trip aboard the *Prosit* and the Ohio River raft journey lasted approximately two weeks, especially since Grove claimed to have arrived in the New World in 1892. Thus, according to Grove's vague time estimations, they could well have merged together. The American trip seems to be the fictional variant of the German one. Yet it was only the German trip which contained all of the elements, including the pleasant ones. And there were certainly enough adventures on the *previous* trip which could easily "fill a book by themselves" but which had "little bearing upon the present story." They belong to the many details that Grove repeatedly refers to and yet never develops. Frederick Philip Grove could never have imagined that one of his former friends would one day produce a travel account in which he would play so prominent a role as a tall young man who "couldn't go lost for long." When one considers the clues which remain in Grove's Canadian writings, along with the elements which are left out, it becomes increasingly difficult to believe, as is often repeated, that Grove really wished to conceal his former German incarnation. Perhaps he was thinking of his time in Bonn as an water-sports enthusiast when composing the following passage in A *Search for America*:

All my life I have been a lover of water—rivers, lakes, the sea. I had made many an inland and outland voyage. Water is nothing inanimate: It responds to the moods of sky and clouds as we do. The mere fact that water is rarely silent has something to do with it. Water is company. Instinctively I clung for a large part of my tramps to the courses of rivers (SFA 237).

◆ JAVA, NOT FAR FROM BATAVIA

As the newly elected first-in-charge in the winter semester of 1899–1900, Felix Greve took part in several important official events in and outside the boathouse. The lavish ball held on November 27, 1899 in the Hotel Kley, for instance, was one such event. In his new position, Felix was responsible not only for keeping track of various club events but also for planning and supervising their organization. For this reason alone he would have maintained contact with all active members as well as the various alumni. Greve undoubtedly awaited the guests for the Christmas party with particular impatience, for among them was an unusual visitor from a great distance. This individual plays an important role in Grove's autobiographical writings, for he served, as did Thiel, as one of the models used for the fictional depiction of Grove's father. Robert von Kraft, a Rhenus member since 1890, served as the chief administrator of a Dutch tobacco plantation close to the city of Medan on the island of Sumatra. He was in Germany for a few weeks of vacation in his homeland. Von Kraft was without doubt an imposing presence. As a young man he measured 196 cm in height and weighed in at a full 90 kilograms. Grove wrote of his "father," the "competent athlete," that he had weighed "225 pounds" (ISM 29). At the time of their meeting, the guest from Sumatra would certainly have had "fatherly" weight for Greve. Von Kraft's colourful, exotic life must have impressed Greve and his friends as they listened to his stories of life on a plantation, of his Chinese "boy" and of his promising prospects for the future. A (remaining) photograph was probably passed around which showed von Kraft and Thiel posing before palm trees while a Chinese servant squats holding a sign emblazoned with the Rhenus coat-of-arms.

Felix Greve recorded the visit with an entry in the *Journal*, writing that von Kraft had presented the club with a gift: "unusually valuable decorations, his collection of antique Malaysian weapons." These weapons, primarily *kris*, were mounted along with the etchings Greve presented to the club. The *kris* are easily recognizable in a photograph of the club's assembly room. There can be no doubt that von Kraft's visit, stories and gifts provide the actual background for another reference to "Uncle Jacobsen" by Frederick Philip Grove:

> Of his other hobbies, I remember distinctly only one, that of collecting 'kris' and other native weapons from the East Indies where he had relatives in the Dutch settlements. This was to be of some slight importance to me a year or so later when I spent three months with a cousin of his on the island of Java (ISM 130).

Von Kraft's importance for Greve lay much less in material things than in the example his colourful personality, international career and physical appearance provided. Along with Thiel, von Kraft may have contributed important elements to the personalities who populated Grove's past. Apart from the composite image Grove drew of his "father," there is also his "Uncle Jacobsen" and Jacobsen's equally obscure "cousin Van der Elst, a settler on the island of Java, not far from Batavia" (ISM 154). He elsewhere refers to a "von Els" as one of the "parasitic young men of Europe" he had met earlier (SFA 29; cf. Chapter Seven). In short, Grove gave "Van der Elst" the Dutch-Indonesian background and von Kraft's collection of Malaysian daggers to "Jacobsen." Just as the ARC Rhenus boathouse provided Grove with the essential architectural elements of his "Castle Thurow," so at least three Rhenus members—Thiel, Kilian and von Kraft—helped the Canadian author to create "family connections" and travel accounts which included journeys to Russia and southeast Asia. Von Kraft's description of his journey to the East (along with Thiel's accounts) presumably form part of Grove's travel itinerary. This included Omsk and Semipalatinsk, arrival in "Nikolaievsk, which at the time was a half-arctic harbour," "followed by a long journey home" from south-east Asia "via Java, the Malysian peninsula, two or three Indian cities, the Red Sea and the familiar Mediterranean" (ISM 149-55). The following could also be added: past Gibraltar and into the Channel until safe arrival in Rotterdam, the city from which von Kraft's plantation "Rotterdam Estate" derived its name.

In conclusion, it should also be noted that another poet, Maximilian Dauthendey, an early contributor to Stefan George's *Blätter für die Kunst* and then highly regarded, travelled to China, Java and Sumatra in 1906 and 1914. He died in 1918 as an internee in Medan near the Deli railway line where, on August 8, 1900, shortly after his return from Bonn, Robert von Kraft also died. Like von Kraft, Dauthendey eventually attempted to support himself through tobacco cultivation in a distant land—a land which must have so entranced Greve that Grove still remembered it in 1946 in the course of his continuing search for a self which he could consider his own.[17]

There is no evidence to suggest that Felix Greve accompanied von Kraft to Rotterdam. It is equally unlikely that he could have visited him on Sumatra in 1900, although a Rhenus obituary does mention the visit of an unnamed Rhenus member to Medan (perhaps Thiel) who laid a wreath at von Kraft's grave. The obituary concludes: "Still lying on his lonely palm-shaded grave are perhaps the faded blue-white-red Rhenus ribbons which a friend of the deceased took over in the name of Rhenus and [the author of the obituary]" (*Festschrift* 1906, 275).

◆ THE KAISER'S BIRTHDAY

Unlike the Corps Borussia, the Rhenus Rowing Club could not claim to count among its members any German royalty, the Hohenzollerns. Nevertheless, it still sought to attain a "place in the sun" through the figure of its newly elected first-in-charge Felix Greve. In October 1899, Greve impelled Rhenus to enter the ultra-patriotic and very influential *flottenverein* ("Naval Association"), a lobby group which promoted a strong Imperial German Navy meant to rival England's (which possessed its own "Naval League").

Immediately after he was elected, Greve took the club on a course which was to bring both him and the club recognition from high places. This was certainly not the time to be travelling with von Kraft or undertaking a pilgrimage to Rome for the turn of the millennium, as Grove later indicated (ISM 198). Greve was interested not in seeing the Pope but in honouring the Kaiser. Indeed, like so many others, he was already sporting a moustache in the style of the Kaiser—with the ends made to rise straight upward, popularly thought to mean *"Es ist erreicht!"* ("It has been achieved!").

An opportunity soon presented itself which would allow Greve to reach his goal and to propel himself into the light of public recognition. Every year the various student organizations in Bonn recognized the Kaiser's birthday (January 27) a day early with a public celebration, the *Kaiserkommers*. Rhenus had never played a particularly prominent role, as the Hohenzollern princes were engaged with Borussia. With considerable pride the Rhenus *Journal* provides the following information concerning the upcoming celebration: "While in previous years we were elected to the executive committee, this time the presidency has been entrusted to us." As Greve had been an executive member throughout the previous year and a half, he must certainly have worked hard to achieve this result—indeed, he would have sought it for himself. Unfortunately, due to a conflict the entire Bonn student body was not represented at the celebration which Greve organized. Instead, two events were organized on two successive days. Nevertheless, the majority of the students were present, as a Bonn newspaper, the *General-Anzeiger*, reported:

> Yesterday's Imperial Celebration in the Beethoven Hall developed... into a wonderful demonstration of the patriotic mood among our student body. The Hall presented a lively, splendidly colourful picture. Its exterior outlines almost disappeared beneath wreaths of leaves, flags and coats-of-arms. The back of the hall with its organ was veiled with a strikingly large painting that depicted the Kaiser mounted on horse-back with his entourage. On both sides of the hall the imposing banners of the student bodies were resplendent in proud unity. While the hall was tightly surrounded with tables, the tables of honour on the podium showed some gaps. The number of professors to attend the festivities was relatively slight. Among the guests of honour present, apart from the Rector and the university judge, generals Bartholomäus and Krummacher, the retired *Oberberghauptmann* His Excellency von Huyssen and the First Public Prosecutor Müller. They were later joined by Colonel Frhr. V. Gayl. The presidency was occupied by the student Greve from the Academic Rowing Club Rhenus.[18]

This was undoubtedly the apex of Felix Greve's career in Bonn. He must have seemed an unusual figure on the podium—tall, blond and slim, a cap on his head with golden cord, on his body a white suit with the red, blue and white sash of his office, before him on the table a sword of honour, perhaps the president's bell. And, as the *Journal* laconically reported, he made a good showing:

> Our first-in-charge Greve conducted himself with complete competence in his simultaneously demanding and honourable task as the leader of the entire celebration and thus did not fail to receive recognition from various sources.[19]

It was not recorded whether Greve himself delivered a speech, although it was his task to present speakers and to preside over the proceedings of the ceremony. This would not have been easy. At the beginning of the ceremony, news was spread of the dowager Empress' death, necessitating the improvisation of a commemoration. Apparently Felix handled this well. This was all the more important—and perhaps all the more delicate—as Prince Friedrich

Wilhelm of Prussia was also present among the Borussia members.[20] The formal high point of the celebration was a speech by the rector of the university. In words which are not unfamiliar today, he complained of a loss of values among German youth since unification.

The importance of this event for Greve's potential career as a government official should not be underestimated. The young man from a modest background had come a long way. His work for Rhenus had helped him achieve broad recognition and, following the birthday celebration, would help him form even better contacts with people who could promote him further. He might well have applied to himself the thrice-repeated "hurrah" for the Kaiser which marked the closing of the celebrations. With Rhenus Felix Paul Greve had reached the zenith of his career with remarkable speed, a high point soon matched by an equally precipitous descent. Regardless of what was to come, however, the editor of the *Bonner Zeitung* was not mistaken when he told Greve's Minden publisher, J.C.C. Bruns, on June 23, 1903 that "For a time, Greve played a prominent role in this town."

That the club was once again entrusted with the organization of the Imperial Celebration the following year may well have been due to his exemplary performance. But by February 1901 he no longer played a role with Rhenus, nor did he appear in Bonn on behalf of the Kaiser, having left for Rome.

◆ **A DEATH BY WATER**

Felix Paul Greve's career with Rhenus reached its nadir almost a year after his glorious appearance at the Imperial Celebration. What happened? We gather from university records that Greve left Bonn for Italy at the beginning of December 1900. It has been argued that "Felix's flight from Bonn in the late autumn of 1900 had a specific reason, namely, news of the final collapse and, in the night of November 30, the death of Wilde in Paris" (*FPG* 58). It seems doubtful, however, that news of Wilde's death prompted Greve's departure. The immediate cause was different—no less tragic, but much closer to home.

In late autumn of 1900, Greve's friend and fellow club member Hans "Hanne" Lomberg died a tragic death. The Rhenus *Journal* for December 1, 1900 contains the following laconic entry: "As has become known through our circular of October 31, we lost our dear inactive member Lomberg through an unfortunate accident." What was this accident and why did it take the whole month of November until it was recorded?

Lomberg had gone missing after a dance at the Hotel Mundorf in Plittersdorf which many club members had attended. Greve and Kilian must

Vermisst!

Der cand. jur. Hans Lomberg aus Bonn wird seit Dinstag den 30. October, Abends, vermißt. Es liegt die Vermuthung vor, daß derselbe im Rhein verunglückt ist. L. war von kleiner, hagerer Statur, hatte blondes Haar, wenig Schnurrbart. Bekleidet war er mit grünlichem Joppen-Anzug, schwarzem Ueberzieher mit Sammtkragen, steifem, schwarzen Hute und Schnürstiefeln. Im linken Rockaufschlage trug er ein Vereinsabzeichen in Form eines blau-weißen Emaille-Fähnchens mit rothem Stern. Jeder, der irgend etwas über den Verbleib des Vermißten angeben kann, wird gebeten, sofort der nächsten Polizeibehörde Mittheilung zu machen.

have also been in attendance, for the dance took place in the middle of the winter semester, when their tuition fees had been paid and Greve had not yet requested a leave of absence. After his friend had been reported missing, the Bonn newspapers carried the story of "Lomberg's mysterious disappearance" and provided almost daily updates on the search. A reward of 3000 marks was offered.

The body was found three weeks later, at Hersel, downriver from Bonn. It was a sensational affair. The handwritten Rhenus log states that after the dance at the Hotel Mundorf some of the students took the train back to Bonn, while others (no names were mentioned) waited for the regular motor boat to ferry them home. Unfortunately, those who chose to wait were forced to spend the night when fog prevented the boat from leaving. Lomberg, however, had "apparently" decided to walk back to Bonn. During the memorial service, the Protestant university pastor used his homily to ask, somewhat melodramatically, the questions that must have occurred to all:

> How did he come to be in the water? As his friends agreed to remain overnight due to the thick fog, did he decide to walk home alone in order to spare his waiting mother unnecessary worry? Did he lose his way in the thick fog? Did he accidentally stumble on the steep edge

of the riverbank and fall into the river? Was he knocked unconscious by the fall? Did the cold water cause a sudden heart attack which ended his life? Or, as a strong swimmer, did he struggle with the current until his strength gave out? Did he cry out for help, with none to hear him in the still night? No one here is able to answer these questions and thus we remain standing before a mystery (*General-Anzeiger*, November 23, 1900, 6).[21]

The mystery was never solved, at least not publicly. Lomberg, Greve and Kilian entered the club at almost the same time. When Greve was first-in-charge, Lomberg became second; as Greve became inactive, Lomberg followed him in the position of first-in-charge. The only rowing trip Kilian ever took was with Lomberg in the summer of 1898. The three appear close together in numerous photographs. "Nixe" Greve and "Hanne" Lomberg (both were given androgynous nicknames) also participated in the 758-kilometre rowing trip together. The three knew each other very well and were close friends. Thus it is all the more astounding to read the following handwritten note in the club *Journal*:

We were forced to expel our inactive member Kilian due to his total lack of interest and his dishonourable behaviour — he was present neither when Lomberg's body was moved nor at the burial, wrote not a single word to excuse himself and in general took very little notice of the entire unfortunate event.[22]

Was Herman Kilian more than impolite and cold-hearted in his behaviour? Were there other motives for his obviously pointed detachment regarding the accident? Had accusations been made or had internal conflicts arisen? Did something come between Lomberg and Kilian, perhaps involving Greve, on the fatal evening which could not be referred to or publicly mentioned? If Kilian had been the "young man, very slightly my senior in years…(who) incredibly subordinated himself to me" (ISM 161), had he then been jealous of Lomberg, who after all shared the closest contact to Greve in the club executive and on rowing trips?[23] Beyond educated speculation, little more can be safely ventured. This much remains clear, however: Kilian was the first member in the history of ARC Rhenus to be expelled. Given the highly unusual nature of this action, something unusual must have happened — more, at any rate, than was set down in print.

In all probability, Felix Greve attended Lomberg's burial on November 22, as no report was made of his absence. Be that as it may, he must have been absent from Bonn one week later, shortly after Kilian's expulsion from the club. It is not known whether Greve was in any way involved in Lomberg's death. Yet his documented departure from Bonn after Kilian's expulsion and a *Journal* reference to him—referring to the still highly respected former leader of the club—seem to speak volumes. Dated January 19, 1901, the entry states: "Our erstwhile member Greve has been granted his request to leave the club."[24]

The entry is striking because of what it does not say. There is not a word of regret, no mention of his spectacular achievements for himself and the unprecedented recognition he had won for the club almost exactly a year before. The Lomberg affair had ended in sentimental funeral oratory. The mystery of his death was allowed to remain unsolved. It was as if all those in the know had formed a conspiracy of silence. Had there been an unwritten agreement—least said, soonest mended—to part ways with no damage to the reputation of either Rhenus or its three former members, easily the finest of the 1898 "foxes"? Of these, one was dead and two departed.

The sentence with which Greve's departure from the club was ratified, however, was not the last reference to him in the Rhenus files. "Nixe," the excellent athlete and admired leader of the club, would be mentioned again. His proper name, however, was hardly ever referred to and is found primarily in protocols, old membership lists and forgotten photograph signatures. He had left the closed world of the Bonn club to enter into a new, wider world. No further mention is contained in the Rhenus documents of the events of autumn 1900 or of Greve's fraud case of May 29, 1903, although there were Rhenus members active at the Crown Attorney's Office who were thus well informed. There is not a word in the Rhenus records concerning Greve's public disgrace. Indeed, his name is so extensively erased, he might just as well have died in February 1901.

♦ A LOOK BACK

That which we now know about Felix Greve's time in Bonn, that which is no longer enshrouded in darkness, conclusively proves that his early years were not merely a prelude to his development as a man of letters or his fraudulent behaviour regarding Kilian. The young man who allowed himself to be called "Nixe" was also—and not only in Whitmanesque terms—an excellent athlete and an extraordinarily gifted and efficient student with truly impressive intellectual abilities. As the principal member of a respected club, he showed the ability to create opportunities necessary to enter upon a promising career. In its depiction of his childhood and youth, *In Search of Myself* frequently resonates with more than mere flights of boasting and craving for status. The incredible physical and psychological strength that FPG was continually able to mobilize allowed him to slough off any setbacks which seemed to restrict further development. The figure of minor nobility Greve created for himself by fictionalizing his descent from the gentry also reflected a certain claim to "nobility of soul" that he wished to see based on his accomplishments, regardless of material success. By recreating himself in Bonn after leaving his youth behind in Hamburg; by recasting the Rhenus boathouse as a writer's "castle" and the Rhine as the Ohio and St. Lawrence Rivers; by using his Bonn friends Cappenberg, Kilian, Lomberg, Thiel and von Kraft in order to create a new family, Felix Greve developed the imaginative experiences of a needy, ambitious have-not who took for himself that which he desired of the world. In leaving Rhenus, he abandoned the professional and social status which his club membership and accomplishments had helped him to achieve. If the departure was in fact Greve's personal decision, then parallels may be drawn to Ernst Hardt who, in a similar move, "left the cadet school" in order to become a poet (Lepsius, *Ein Berliner* 176).

In terms of its relevance for FPG, the sport of rowing may easily be underestimated, especially when viewed in relation to archaeology, philology and literature. Thus it deserves to be made explicit that rowing was not simply a sport for the elite, but had also become an object of the fine arts. Works from the Anglo-Saxon world, such as the homoerotically allusive paintings by the American Thomas Eakins, himself a rower, make this clear. That such circles also had members with homoerotically coloured friendships has also been shown (see Cavell, "Felix Paul Greve"). As a student from anglophile Hamburg, the member of a rowing club at the "Prussian Oxford" would have been well aware of this.

Life in the Rhenus boathouse was also in many respects a phase in the trial and discovery of skills which Grove would require in Canada. Thus, for the narrator "obsessed with the study of nature," "the sharp crest-wave of snow spray" in the wilds of Manitoba appeared "like the wing-wave thrown to either side by the bow of a power boat that cuts swiftly through quit water" (OPT 160). In Canada he sees himself "threatened by nature" when his light wagon—he uses the term "cutter"—is compared with the "wind-tossed nutshell of a one-man sailing craft" (OPT 129). Curtains, the narrator reports, "emit that crackling sound which indicates to the sailor that he has turned his craft as far into the wind as he can safely do without losing speed" (OPT 156–57). Sound waves are quickly transformed into waves of water. Grove's first Canadian writings in particular feature these easy shifts in imagery. It is as if the author, living landlocked in Canada, loved to play with images from his earlier experiences on German waters. Such shifts subtly carry both author and reader into different realms of nature and reveal new sides of a person who felt equally competent on land and water.

"Oh, for the juggling of words!" Grove exclaims (OPT 166). To a lesser extent than Joyce, Greve played with his own name. We have seen how Felix became "Nixe." Elsewhere, we will witness how Greve will become Friedrich Carl Reelen, F.C. Gerden and—partaking less of Thurow and more of Thoreau—Konrad Thorer. These identities coalesced in the creation of Frederick Philip Grove, who invented Phil Branden of *A Search for America*. Finally, we may recall how somebody called von Kraft served him as a model for those powerful "family members" he was in search of— the "fathers" and "uncles" of his own making who carried both Young Felix and "Young Phil" away on tours of the world, both real and imaginary. These strong figures, often father figures, reappear in many of Grove's Canadian novels and stories, as Niels Lindstedt in *Settlers of the Marsh*, John Elliot of *Our Daily Bread* and Abe Spalding of *Fruits of the Earth*, among others.

3

ARCHAEOLOGY·AND
LITERATURE

Felix Paul Greve *ante portas*

AS FREDERICK PHILIP GROVE APPEARED TO SEARCH for
his lost youth in his autobiographical works, readers may have suspected that
the author, despite what he called his memory lapses, was attempting to
uncover and arrange the various layers of his past. And yet it is neither a solution to the enigma nor answers to our questions which Grove arrives at; in
fact, his autobiographical texts refer to their own omissions and gaps. The
textual record of Grove's life not infrequently suggests that the author
purposefully mystified portions of his past. This was not in an attempt to erase
all the clues from his earlier life in Europe, but rather in the manner of his
modernist contemporaries who deliberately wished to "make the visible a
little hard to see" (W. Stevens). As a student of archaeology, Greve would
have learned the methods with which he would later reconstruct the fragments of his own experience as an author "in search of himself." Through
his works he would become an important figure in modern Canadian literature and a chronicler of pioneer life in Canada.

It is of little wonder, then, that archaeology and philology would became
recurring metaphors in his writing. After initially following the data Grove
first offered him in 1945, Desmond Pacey later wrote that some "of the most
important passages in Grove's books are those in which he draws upon his
knowledge of archaeology" (Pacey, *Grove* 1970, 47). Despite this early infer-

ence, no information yet exists which might provide the dates and facts necessary to read these "most important passages" from Grove's works. It should be observed here that Felix Greve's literary and archaeological activity coincides with the "compatibility of the literary and monumental tradition" advocated by Adolf Furtwängler, his future teacher and a leading Munich archaeologist. On the basis of new evidence, I will first contextualize and then re-read Grove's reports and comments concerning his archaeological interests and studies. This will provide Grove scholars with a new reading of the autobiographical sources in relation to Grove's interest in archaeology. Of course this reading will not answer all the remaining questions. Nevertheless, it will henceforth be possible to close chronological and factual gaps and to fill in several missing areas from the map of Grove's life and his intellectual and literary career.

Little in the European parts of *In Search of Myself* indicates that the author strove for a career as writer. On the contrary, his school and university education would have suggested a career as a diplomat or, given his excellent knowledge of classical languages, that of an archaeologist. This would have corresponded to the wishes of his father concerning an appropriate future (ISM 176). A career as an archaeologist would also have advanced him in the eyes of his lover "Mrs. Broegler," the fictional wife of his Hamburg chemistry teacher whose first name he could not remember. Another lover, "Kirsten," whose last name Grove unfortunately failed to mention, would also have admired him in the role of archaeologist. "Would a professor of archaeology be an acceptable son-in-law?" young Phil Grove supposedly asked "Kirsten" in Room One of Munich's Pinakothek. A professorship would have provided him with a career which would have allowed him "to earn his daily bread." Unfortunately, after the sudden death of his father he was forced to earn his living "not as a professor of archaeology or comparative philology, but as a waiter in a cheap eating house on Yonge Street, Toronto" (ISM 171).

This pitiable expression of failed plans and missed opportunities comes at the end of the second of the four sections which form *In Search of Myself*. It is probably intended to conclude Grove's account of his European past and to provide a transition to the well-documented places in the author's Canadian life. However, rather than beginning with a description of his years in the United States and Canada in the third section, which his readers would have been eagerly awaiting given the success of *A Search for America*, Grove recounted episodes again dedicated to his experiences in Europe and to his interest in archaeology and philology (ISM 196–205). Surprisingly, the author now claimed to have spent time in Rome on two separate occasions.

The first visit involves a spectacular occasion, were Grove really to have experienced it. "Once having gone through France and Northern Italy at a leisurely pace, I arrived at Rome in December. It was the year 1899; I remember it by the fact that I was present, in St. Peter's, at the great millennial midnight celebration of January 1, 1900" (ISM 198). The accuracy of this claim has been doubted (FPG 59). As we know, Greve was in Bonn in 1899, preparing himself for another important occasion, the Imperial Birthday Celebration. Grove writes further that he was well supplied with money. He stayed in the expensive "Hotel de Rome." At the time, however, there was no hotel of that name in the Italian capital. Following evidence from a letter Greve later wrote to Wolfskehl in April 1902, however, it is possible that at least once he did stay at the Grand Hotel de Rome in Berlin, at 39 Unter den Linden.[1] In this context, and given Grove's reminiscences of his supposed acquaintances with leading French symbolists in Paris, it is of note that Stéphane Mallarmé lived (and died in 1898) in the Rue de Rome in Paris. Greve could have drawn reference from Klaus Mann's book on Gide, in which Gide figures in the circle surrounding Mallarmé (Gide 64–65). The possibility cannot be excluded that Grove read this book in memory of Gide. Klaus Mann was the son of another immigrant to whose father, Thomas Mann, Grove would present books in 1939 while himself writing In Search of Myself (still under the working title of My Life).[2]

In Rome's "Hotel de Rome" he is to have made the acquaintance of a certain "Lady X" who although "not...in her first youth...was not yet forty, either." She was divorced, and they quite conspicuously spoke French. "To this day," Grove emphasizes, "I am puzzled why she should have been speaking French in that crowded polyglot dining-room when she was as English as anyone could well be" (ISM 199). These pointed references by the author would seem to contain information for the reader. Did "Lady X" have anything to do with Mrs. Broegler, by now also divorced, whom Greve supposedly saw again in Berlin although he was unable to remember her first name (ISM 167)? Could they have met in the Berlin Grand Hotel de Rome and not in a hotel in Rome? Or did Greve have another "lover" in Rome, although not in a hotel? Grove writes further that soon, almost completely impoverished, he played the role of the paid cicerone for this lady and her acquaintances, leading them through the museums of the Vatican. Furthermore, he suggests somewhat preposterously that he could have earned a living conducting personal tours of Europe, had university professors not continually received the jobs instead of him.[3]

Clearly, these are the outlines of a palimpsest with many different elements: two, possibly three years (1899–1901), different cities (Berlin, Rome), different individuals (Mrs. Broegler, Lady X, Kirsten), different professions (tour guide, professor of archaeology or comparative philology) and a polyglot social environment. The palimpsest also incorporates the various dates and events from the second of Grove's reported trips to Rome. The first trip to Rome includes several additional components of the "Grove in Rome" palimpsest.

According to Grove, young "Phil" received his advanced education in Paris and Bonn, before he "landed, late in the summer," in Rome, where he matriculated himself as a student at the university. He at once "secured lodgings on the Capitol and plunged into hard work." As a prospective archaeologist, Phil Grove could not have found a more strategically appropriate place to live: "There was, above all, right in my neighbourhood—if I remember correctly, in the Palazzo Caffarelli—the Imperial German Institute of Archaeology where I spent six or seven hours daily in study, attending lectures, seminaries, and demonstrations" (ISM 164). It has been reported elsewhere that Felix Greve was never enrolled as a student at the university in Rome (FPG 59). On the other hand, it has also become evident that hardly any of Grove's statements fail to contain at least a kernel of establishable fact. This is likewise the case with Grove's various accounts concerning archaeology, Rome and professorial chairs. They all indicate that these things were of great importance to the author, even if in contexts and for reasons which were perhaps other than those provided. The specific reference to the Imperial German Institute of Archaeology suggests itself as point of departure for verification of this reference.

◆ MONTE TARPEO

The German Institute of Archaeology (DAI) was situated, as it still is today, on the Capitoline Hill. Its first address was the one given by Grove in the halls of the Palazzo Caffarelli, founded in 1836 as the "Istituto de correspondenza archeologica." During the year of its establishment, the DAI moved to the new "Knapp Building" at 129 Via Monte Caprino, across from the Palazzo Caffarelli. Another move followed in 1877 to the "Laspeyres Building," in which the DAI remained until 1915. The entrance was located directly across from the Palazzo Caffarelli. The new address, and the only one which FPG could have known, was 28 Via di Monte Tarpeo.

A narrative strategy is apparent in Grove's semi-autobiographical collation of fact and fiction. The generally verifiable name (Palazzo Caffarelli, Imperial German Institute of Archaeology) is mentioned with reservation and yet with such an obvious shift in time that the intervention functions both as a veiling of the actual co-ordinates as well as a reference point for renewed observation.

There can be no question that the events associated with Rome must have moved Greve deeply. Rome, as we have seen, recalled various episodes and associations. The impressions of his memory, which are bound to specific places in the itinerary of his life, are like pieces of a puzzle which need to be fit back into place. Here the obvious discrepancies between events are evident, in addition to the missing transitions in Grove's autobiographical texts and the proffered explanations and absences which together form the palimpsest. By 1927, the author uses a cinematic metaphor to characterize the functioning of a seemingly autonomous memory; impressions flash and are thrown against the screen of memory, swiftly appearing frames are connected to form the film which is viewed as a fast-paced sequence of frames for the viewer/reader. The author is describing nothing less than the transformation of fact into fiction in a manner which he also used in his second autobiography.

What were the features of the Imperial German Institute of Archaeology which Grove claims to have been familiar with? The building was situated in the Via di Monte Tarpeo in such a way as to offer a spectacular view of the Forum Romanum. The library formed the centre of the interior of the building. There were "guest rooms with a view of the city which were primarily intended for students but which were also available for visiting scholars" (Rieche, *150 Jahre* 58–60; 94). It may be assumed that Grove's room in the so-called "Hotel de Rome" was in fact a room for visiting scholars in the DAI. It is likewise possible that Grove's mysterious "Lady X" was another guest or occasional visitor at this "hotel." If she was not in a relationship with Greve, she was in the company of another visitor to Rome. Before her marriage to Endell, Else Ploetz was certainly in Rome during the same winter, precisely at the time of Grove's "great millennial midnight celebration of January 1, 1900" with the sculptor Richard Schmitz, brother to the author Oskar A.H. Schmitz: "With Richard I stayed for one and a half years, one year travelling—the other half having adjoining studios in Rome—on the Via Fausta before the Porto de Popolo...It was in the winter of the century-turn 1900" (BE 52). Else, incidentally, again spent time in Rome in the winter of 1903–04 when FPG was in a Bonn jail (BE 171). Apparently, Grove adapted an experience of his previous companion, just as he did as Greve in 1904 when he used Else's memories for his novel *Fanny Essler* (see Chapter Six).

Among the guests of the Institute that winter was another candidate for the role of Grove's "Lady X." This was Else von Hoesslin, the future wife of the young and highly promising archaeologist Richard Delbrueck. They had met in Athens. Else's sister Polyxena (or Polly) had been married since 1899 to Ernst Hardt, the poet, dramatist and friend of Graef, Vollmoeller and Wolfskehl—men who would soon also form important contacts with Greve.

Else von Hoesslin, who could well be the figure recognizable in a picture from "around 1900" in the library of the DAI, may have been the first Else to have played a role—perhaps imaginary—in the emotional life of the young "independent scholar" Greve before Else Ploetz, later Endell.[4] After a lengthy period of hesitation, Else von Hoesslin and Delbrueck were finally married in 1911 (Else had felt herself also attracted to Delbrueck's student and Greve's acquaintance from Munich, Herbert Koch).[5]

FPG's stay in Rome in the autumn and winter of 1900–01 was important not only for his private life but also for his career choice as an archaeologist. His preparations for such a career had begun in Bonn. Here, not only the university courses he took deserve consideration, but also the memorable 1899 boat excursion to Miltenberg. As a student of Loeschke, he would have been able to admire the remains of the limes in the historically rich land-scape, and, in the courtyard of Castle Mildenburg, the "Toutonenstein" with its fragment of a Roman inscription. He may even have had an opportunity to see the work being conducted by Professor Conrady, who worked in archaeology as a colleague and competitor of Loeschke. Grove confirmed his more than theoretical interest in archaeology before he went to Rome: "From an early age I, being thus taken over the face of Europe, evinced a special, almost passionate interest in the remains of antiquity, mostly Roman, of course" (ISM 84).

This interest was not unusual, when one considers that archaeology and archaeologists enjoyed considerable attention and respect at this time, and not only in the German Reich. It must also be said, however, that Greve's achievements as a student in the field were not particularly impressive, since he never advanced beyond introductory studies. Nevertheless, it can be assumed that his non-credit courses in the summer semesters also included practical work. Loeschke, then involved in tracing the extent of the limes, was working around Cologne and Bonn, while Conrady was active in Miltenberg and elsewhere. Greve's visit to Miltenberg showed he was an enthusiastic student who perhaps wished to advance further, if not as an authority in Loeschke's seminars, then perhaps as textual scholar and assis-tant at the excavation sites. At the same time, Wilhelm Dörpfeld, Heinrich Schliemann's assistant and the director of the DAI in Athens, had his hands full with excavation sites at Mykene and with the stream of ambitious young visitors who came to observe his work. Among these was the former Bonn student, archaeologist, dramatist and friend of André Gide, Karl Gustav Vollmoeller.[6] According to their student records, both Greve and Vollmoeller had taken Loeschke's courses "History of Greek Art," "Beginner's Course" and "Advanced Course" in the summer of 1900 and in the following winter semester. Vollmoeller was possibly a contributing factor in Greve's decision to travel to Rome.

◆ AMONG ARCHAEOLOGISTS

Like Dörpfeld in Athens, the Director or "First Secretary" of the DAI in Rome, Eugen Petersen, had more than enough to do with the throngs of visitors who turned to him and his colleagues with requests for help and accommodations. The tremendous respect accorded the Institute is evident in that the Kaiser, as patron of the central institute in Berlin, occasionally visited the DAI with his family. Certainly there was hope that promising young researchers could make a name for themselves, especially if they came from universities such as Bonn which already had a name in the discipline. The "high time of discovery and insight" in the world of archaeological scholarship was in no way over (Schuchhardt, *Adolf Furtwängler* 12). Grants were also available to young scholars who could spend as long as a year working at an excavation site in Rome or Athens. While there, they could acquaint themselves directly with the prominent figures in their field.[7] Loeschke's most talented student in Bonn, Richard Delbrueck, who in 1899 had completed his studies with a doctorate after only six semesters, received a DAI scholarship for 1899–1900 for research first in Greece and then in Rome.[8] Felix Greve, also Loeschke's student in Bonn, would certainly have known Delbrueck, who had matriculated two weeks after Greve on May 4, 1898. At the beginning of 1899, while Greve was still in Bonn, Delbrueck and Vollmoeller departed for Greece.[9] By late autumn of 1900, however, not only Greve but Delbrueck too left for Rome, to be joined later by Vollmoeller.[10] This may have been coincidence, although it is equally likely that each was drawn by the promise archaeology seemed to extend. "The standard autumn junket back to Rome," as it was described by Curtius and Delbrueck—both future directors of the institute—must have seemed almost *comme il faut*, even for the non-scholarship students interested in archaeology (Curtius, *Deutsche* 116).

Educational trips to Italy, Greece, North Africa and Asia Minor were absolutely essential for an ambitious student of archaeology and classical philology. It is not improbable that even before the "autumn junket" Greve had advanced beyond the archaeological activities led by Loeschke and, like Delbrueck and Vollmoeller, had travelled to Greece during the final days of 1899 to attend the twenty-fifth anniversary celebrations of the DAI in Athens. The earliest opportunity to undertake a journey not recorded in the Rhenus records would have been after his withdrawal from the activities of the club at the end of the winter semester 1899–1900—at the latest, that is, between February and April 1900. A more likely time would have been a period coinciding with Vollmoeller's stay in Bonn as a student in the summer of 1900. In fact, we recall, Schultess was able in September 1900 to respond to a question as to Greve's whereabouts, as he had not collected his Münden scholarship which was to be given out elsewhere: "Stud Greve is, I am told, in It[aly]." To this he added: "That he is suffering privation...I doubt." Schultess would have known this because Greve was obliged to maintain regular contact with his Hamburg mentor. Was Schultess concerned about Greve's absence from Bonn? He could not have failed to notice the progression of his pupil from philology to archaeology—a classic pattern since the time of Johann Joachim Winckelmann from a "Saul amongst the classical philologists" to a "Paul of the art historians" (Leppmann, *Winckelmann* 99).

Felix Greve's arrival probably coincided with the arrival of Delbrueck from Greece (and perhaps Vollmoeller), who as a scholarship holder received a room at the Rome DAI. Surviving records of the German Institute of Archaeology definitively document Greve's presence there.[11] Was Greve also able to occupy one of the rooms for visiting scholars? The fact that the next year he registered himself at the Munich Municipal Registry Office as "independent scholar" suggests that he may already have used such a professional designation in Rome. Life in the guest house was probably less than comfortable: "Beside me, in the rooms of the same corridor, lived German scholars whom I shyly greeted and who barely honoured me with so much as a glance. Never in my life have I spent a winter of such unusual loneliness as that Roman winter in a house that was intended by its founders for the noblest of intellectual communities" (Curtius, *Deutsche* 118). The intense competition would not have eased the situation. In regular meetings, the directors of the institute ensured that the research findings of its members and guests were publicly presented, debated and, if they found general agreement, published in the papers of the institute.

Greve is first on record at the beginning of the "Winter Meetings" of the DAI, the first of which always coincided as closely as possible with Winckelmann's birthday (December 9). They tended to end around the time of *Palilientag* (April 21). The winter meetings of 1900-01 began on December 7 with a lecture by the director, Petersen. Present were Pompeii researchers, Christian Hülsen, August Mau, colleagues from archaeological institutes from other countries, as well as visitors from Austria, England, the United States, Italy and Germany—among the latter the Imperial Ambassador to the Vatican and the Royal Bavarian Ambassador to Italy. There would not have been a better opportunity for young Greve to present himself, as he had at the Kaiser's birthday in Bonn, to an illustrious gathering of individuals. He followed a pattern of behaviour which had begun in Hamburg—namely, to avoid the daily drudgery of student life and the hurdles presented by exams by seizing opportunities for spectacular displays of his extraordinary talents. In contrast to Delbrueck, he had not been able to complete a university degree or receive a scholarship. He was required, therefore, to use the freedom and the time which his mentors in Hamburg had made available. Grove the Canadian described the situation as follows: "Within the university I did not find that enlargement of my horizons which I was looking for. Naturally, then, I soon sought it outside the university" (ISM 160–61).

Felix Paul Greve participated in three scholarly meetings from December 1900 until February 1901 for which attendance records have survived. During that period he may well have participated in the excursions led by Mau and others to various noteworthy sites: "It is true, I made many excursions; but all of them had a professional tinge; I went to Baiae, Naples, Pesto, Palermo, Girgenti—wherever remains of Greek antiquity demanded study." Since the DAI organized excursions for guests and visitors—and also for interested teachers—Greve himself could have led such trips—not only in the museums of the city and the Vatican, but also, as Grove claimed, in the "surrounding campagna, the Albani mountains, even the Abruzzi" (ISM 164–65). Had FPG in fact earned his daily bread as a tour guide, he would again have emulated another "independent scholar," the great Johann Joachim Winckelmann himself, no doubt pleasing the administrators of the DAI (Leppmann, *Winckelmann* 193).

In the meantime, the scholarly meetings were taking place. Greve's signature is the seventh, among several Anglo-Saxon names, to be found on the list of participants for December 21, 1900.[12] Delbrueck's signature is the tenth. Did Greve arrive with the group of Americans and British, whom he led during the day (ISM 198–201)? Greve, like Delbrueck, was among the regular participants in the meetings, and was also present during the last December meeting.

It is no longer possible to establish whether Greve left Rome and Italy at the turn of the year. According to the records, he did not attend the next meeting on January 11, 1901. Had he left for Bonn to submit his resignation from Rhenus on January 19, as the Rhenus *Journal* indicates, he would still have had time to attend a papal mass at St. Peter's Cathedral, an experience that Grove later claimed for the previous year. At any rate, he did not attend Richard Delbrueck's presentation on January 11, during the course of which hypotheses were advanced which were then challenged by Petersen. Delbrueck, in turn, answered them (*Mitteilungen* XVI, 94). The scholarly dispute would only have served to raise Delbrueck's profile and to direct welcome notice at him. Felix Greve would certainly have learned of his colleague's skill upon his return, for it is almost certain that the minor altercation would have been further discussed by the residents of the guest house.

On January 25, Felix Greve was once again present, along with Delbrueck. This time Ernst Pfuhl, another promising young scholar, spoke. Petersen responded to his lecture with agreement. On February 8, Felix Greve appeared early, for his name is the second on the attendance list. Delbrueck was again also present and directed the discussion to Pfuhl's lecture of two weeks previous. On this occasion, as on January 11, the discussion did not end with Petersen's comment; and yet it was not Pfuhl who replied to the challenge but another participant. The protocol reports with usual brevity: "In addition, Greve" (*Mitteilungen* XVI, 94). Apparently his comments were of sufficient weight to be noted in the widely read *Mitteilungen* of the DAI. A review of its pages from the same year reveals that not one guest offered a public response apart from the directors of the institute and the lecturers themselves. Greve, then, had dared to present himself as an authority in his role as independent scholar. Nevertheless, this auspicious beginning was also the end of Greve's stint as a fledgling archaeologist.

Delbrueck's and Pfuhl's papers were soon published. While Delbrueck's response to Petersen's commentary on his paper was also published, Greve's commentary on Pfuhl's published lecture was not mentioned. Pfuhl was three years older than Greve and Delbrueck's friend. They were such close friends that Pfuhl is said to have claimed of Delbrueck: "If I were my own sister, I would fall hopelessly in love with him" (*Archäologenbildnisse*, 192). This was possibly another constellation of male friends reminiscent of the one Greve had just left in Bonn.

Ernst Pfuhl, incidentally, received the coveted DAI scholarship in classical archaeology for 1901–02 (*Jahrbuch* 1901, 103) and departed for Athens, as did Delbrueck and Vollmoeller before him. Greve, his respondent, received nothing, not even official status, and was never again mentioned in the DAI annals.

The meeting of February 8 is the last one at which Greve's presence was registered. His absence from the following meetings on February 22 and March 8, 1901 could well be interpreted as the direct or indirect consequences of his comments on February 8. Given Greve's oft-repeated preference for archaeology, which needs to be distinguished from his robust condemnation of the discipline's professional representatives, a sudden development has to be assumed which would have caused him to leave the DAI and abandon his nascent career as an archaeologist. Other than his abrupt break in relations, absolutely nothing concrete provides a parallel with his similarly sudden departure from Rhenus. However, the beginning of a pattern seems discernible. In October 1902, he would just as precipitously leave Munich for Berlin; later, sometime in June or early July 1909, he would leave Germany altogether. As of 1901, however, Felix Greve only left Rome behind him.

It can be assumed that he travelled to Hamburg next to collect his scholarship monies personally before the beginning of the summer semester. Greve's departure from Rome was not yet an official break with archaeology, for in the autumn he would at least formally continue his studies with Adolf Furtwängler. Still, his attempt at establishing himself as an archaeologist per *coup de main* in Rome had failed. It had been an instance of Greve's typically brassy, courageous charlatanry—similar to that displayed before the members of the DAI, which even as late as 1938 must have moved Karl Wolfskehl to the rather hard-hearted characterization of Felix Greve as "that pseudologist of the early period" (Wolfskehl, *Briefwechsel* 261). And yet Felix must have felt himself close to the great archaeological names of his generation, whom Grove would later have so little positive to write about. Among these were Ludwig Curtius, Richard Delbrueck, Herbert Koch (about whom more later) and Ernst Pfuhl, as well as those who were already established at the time of Greve's contact: Hülsen, Mau and Petersen. Greve drew attention to himself, seized the floor and quickly fell back into anonymity. Vollmoeller alone found success in the leap from archaeologist to writer. Greve attempted a similar leap, although he was denied a comparative degree of recognition as either. Ultimately both of them would continue their careers in North America. Greve would not forget Vollmoeller and later mentions his name, albeit rather disparagingly (Grove, "Thoughts and Reflections" 318).

Greve too, however, was in no way forgotten. In a letter from 1904, Karl Gustav Vollmoeller recalled how Felix Greve had appeared, penniless and bedraggled, before the door of the DAI guest house on his way to Bonn to solicit more money from his friend Kilian (in April or at the beginning of May 1903, having left Palermo and, temporarily, Else). Evidently, it had been an address he felt he could turn to again:

> I'm sitting here again on Monte Tarpeo, melancholically enough in Delbrueck's old room. There was no other alternative, and I find it somehow odd, as most things human are.

> Our gaunt care-taker just told me of Greve, who stood before her door one evening, pale and shivering, and how she let him stay for the night and even made extra coffee for him in the morning. That was at the time when he left for Bonn. He claimed to have slept badly because he had left his suitcase unlocked at the station. And in it were his diamonds. (*Entre nous*: HE wrote me a very strange and aggressive letter at the time of his release, which I have kept).[13]

This "strange and aggressive letter" no longer exists, although it presumably contained something about the desertion of the "friends" whom Greve, then in prison, must have felt had callously abandoned him. From the letter, it would appear that Vollmoeller preferred not to spend the night in "Delbrueck's old room." The two had fallen out. Greve and Vollmoeller had travelled together to Italy in 1902 and for a while remained friends. At the time the letter was written, Delbrueck was confidently on the way to success. He was teaching in Berlin and was a regular guest at the DAI in Rome. Vollmoeller had published his drama *Francesca di Rimini* with Insel while Ernst Hardt continued his successful career as a dramatist which he would crown in 1907 with his Tristan play *Tantris der Narr*.

It seems probable that Vollmoeller, Hardt and others connected to the DAI exchanged correspondence (and warned each other to destroy the letters). Greve too probably would have written more than one letter of request, or of complaint and threat, to his acquaintances in Rome. It is precisely the absence of these letters—along with entries mysteriously missing or clearly cut out from diaries and memoirs from the correspondence which is conspicuous and should not be overlooked. Felix Paul Greve moved among a group of young men who were as ambitious as he, financially comfortable and provided with the best social contacts. Many were the sons of wealthy fathers. Vollmoeller, the son of an industrialist from Stuttgart, also belonged to the group. For Greve it would have been necessary to impute the existence of diamonds, which Vollmoeller ironically referred to, in order to be accepted. The moment the *financial* swindle became apparent, Greve's acceptance vanished. He must have failed to observe that these friends and acquaintances were, with the exception of Vollmoeller, only temporary bohemians, and that for all of their daring they would never imperil their essential respectability as future servants of the state. There would be escapades, but care was taken that no clues be left behind. Correspondence, especially as it related to "Gerden," was returned, as it was from Vollmoeller to Hardt ("F.C. Gerden" was the pseudonym under which Greve later published his Browning translations with Insel).[14] Felix attempted to form a career on the basis of his mental abilities, but only managed to keep up the façade of independent scholar for a short time. He must have clung to the belief that he could challenge the unwritten rules of wealthy society in Imperial Germany or elsewhere. The "diamonds" were to be Greve's stumbling stones, and he fell into an existential hole that must have appeared bottomless to him in 1909.

◆ WANDERINGS

Wanderungen, Felix Paul Greve's 1902 book of poetry, could well have been inspired by Greve's wanderings in southern lands, and perhaps not only in Italy. At first glance, however, there is little of interest in these precious, late-romantic texts with their medieval imagery involving the "cosmic" importance of the desert, also mentioned by the Canadian Grove in a different book (ISM 162). The transfigured knighthood of *Wanderungen* does coincide, however, with a passage from Grove's *Over Prairie Trails*, where he states that: "The Southern Cross is no strange sight to my eyes. I have slept in the desert close to my horse, and I have wandered in Lebanon" (OPT 90). It almost appears as if the title poem "Wanderungen" were recreated in the form of an idealized self in Grove's first Canadian book:

WANDERUNGEN
VON FELIX PAUL GREVE

Dem Freunde und Gefährten
HERMAN F. C. KILIAN

✳ *Felix Paul Greve,* Wanderungen *(1902), title page and dedication to "my friend and companion Herman F.C. Kilian"*

You were lured by sea-swept island-worlds
And coasts of song all wrapt in legend
Which hailed you in your dreams in bygone days
From a sun-lit land with its whitened tents...[15]

This is certainly nothing more than an echo, a vague evocation of a southern environment that may have recalled southern Italy and Sicily (if North Africa, then probably at second-hand). The only direct reference to "the south" is in a December 5, 1901 letter Greve wrote to the Hamburg publisher Alfred Janssen:

The author of the enclosed manuscript is a native of Hamburg and maintains close connections to the Munich circle of *Blätter für die Kunst.* He has spent a long time in the south and a fruit of these journeys, the earliest, is the little book which he is now offering to you for publication. The themes of this collection of poems, which is meant to form a unity, is the development from life-denying pessimism to a one-sided and yet strong affirmation of the future. The author's goal is to create a form of art which raises life with it to new heights.[16]

The "long time in the south" would include Greve's archaeological excursions in Italy in 1901. "And yet again you lure me, you Circe South" (W 26) he wrote in the same year, obviously as an Odysseus in Sicilian waters, who said of himself that he had listened to the ancient songs of "wild Ephesian remains,/of walls of temples and palaces." Undoubtedly this was all sincerely felt, though hardly original. When he writes of "coasts of song all wrapt in legend/Which hailed you in your dreams in bygone days" (W 17), is the author thinking of the white tents of the Berbers at, say, the Biskra oases in Tunisia across from Palermo? He may have read about them in André Gide's works or perhaps heard of them from Vollmoeller, Gide's friend, who was there with Gide and first mentioned him to the French writer. At any rate, Grove (evidently thinking of Gide) mysteriously wrote about a trip with a young Frenchman he claims to have taken "through the Sahara, above all, to go with him to Biskra which he knew well" (ISM 162).

The letter to Janssen permits at least two interpretations. Either Greve was familiar with Gide's life and writings, or he had been instructed about Gide's vitalistic approach to life elsewhere. In this context it may also be possible to accommodate the rather obvious cleft between Greve's romantic feelings, his stilted poetic diction in *Wanderungen* and his claim to Janssen that he had replaced a "life-denying pessimism" with forward-looking optimism. For it is precisely this transformation to a life-affirming outlook which characterizes Gide's *Les nourritures terrestres*. Greve's idea of "a form of art which raises life with it to new heights," as he termed it in his "pompous celebratory style," originated in his school days. It approaches Gide's understanding of life lived without limits, an ideal frequently expressed in the art of the time.[17]

Whether Greve was in Africa or not, then or later, André Gide had been there more than once, and Greve became his translator. We notice, again, that in *L'immoraliste* Gide has his narrator Michel celebrate his reading of Homer's Odyssey; Greve similarly searches out Greek and Roman settings in *Wanderungen* and chooses the persona of Odysseus for himself. Frederick Philip Grove takes up the image of a palimpsest and uses it to compare himself to one. In this, too, he follows Gide's Michel who compared himself "with palimpsests" and referred to "hidden texts" still to be uncovered. In his second autobiography, *In Search of Myself*, Grove mainly reveals the "younger text" — the Canadian text — which must be partially erased before the older text may be revealed — the text of the German life of the author. The older text under the newer writings was presumably "much more precious" to Grove at the end of his life, yet it appeared to him that he couldn't have the one without destroying the other. In writing his autobiographical "younger text," Grove simultaneously gives the reader the information necessary to excavate and raise a portion of his buried life. In the portrayal of his development from archaeologist to poet to translator to narrator, the Canadian Grove adopted thoughts from Gide's texts which Greve had once translated. Like "Phil Grove" and Felix Greve, Gide's Michel also described his association with archaeologists and philologists:

> A little less eagerly I again saw people of my own standing, archaeologists and philologists; to converse with them, however, was hardly more pleasurable, provided me with no more interest, than when I flipped through a good historical hand-book. At the very beginning I had hoped to find a more direct grasp of life from a few novelists and poets; yet if they had seized life, one must admit, they hardly showed it. It appeared to me as if most of them were not living, as if they satisfied themselves with an appearance of life and saw life as a restriction, an irritating impediment to writing (Gide, *Paludes: Die Sümpfe* 99).[18]

In his own writings, especially in his two German novels of 1905 and 1906, Greve devoted himself to a more intense experience of life. In Canada, Frederick Philip Grove presented physically strong characters in his novels whom he placed in the American and Canadian wilderness, on the prairies and in the marshes. He celebrates them (and himself) most successfully with a mixture of *élan vital* (in the Bergsonian sense), a family-directed sense of emotion in *Over Prairie Trails* and in a one-sided, modified Nietzschean form in the figure of Nils Lindstedt in *Settlers of the Marsh*.

Following his time in Bonn and southern Europe and after writing his first verse, Greve saw himself between two lives, two careers. Both are again intertwined in Grove's subsequent attempt to obscure without burying his true past while writing of his archaeological ambitions. At the end of his archaeological period, Greve turned toward a literary existence as a writer and translator.

4

A·POET·AND
TRANSLATOR·IN
MUNICH·AND
BERLIN

AFTER HIS ROME INTERLUDE and a long summer in the Mediterranean, Felix Paul Greve was not required to make up for lost time or any demonstrable interruption to his university studies. As Spettigue has indicated, the Bonn university administration retrospectively granted him a formal leave of absence for the second half of the 1900–01 winter semester and for the following summer semester (*FPG* 62). He seems to have presented his stay in Italy to his mentors in Hamburg and the administrators of his scholarships as relevant to his studies. These, in turn, seemed to have shifted significantly in the direction of archaeology and art history.[1]

Although still a student, he proudly registered his occupation with the municipal authorities as *Privatgelehrter* ("independent scholar") and *Schriftsteller* ("writer"). Greve indicated *Privatleben* ("private life") as the purpose of his stay on September 30 in Munich. Little concerned with concealing his true interests, he wanted to give the impression of a man of leisure. Obtaining a student identification in Munich was of primary importance because he was required to present it in Hamburg before receiving the last instalment of the Fischer Scholarship. Apparently, he had already

❋ *Members of Stefan George's circle: (l. to r.) Karl Wolfskehl, Alfred Schuler,*
Ludwig Klages, George, Albert Verwey, 1902
(Schiller Nationalmuseum/Deutsches Literaturarchiv, Marbach)

received a reminder from Hamburg, since a message from Greve informed
Schultess that he would not receive the required document "before October
18th." It would be November 5th before the certificate from the Royal
Bavarian Ludwig-Maximilian University would be sent to Hamburg. It was
Greve's last remaining letter of the period to Schultess.[2]

   Felix Greve's first apartment in Munich at 24 Amalienstrasse (today
number 45) was located a few steps away from the university buildings along
Schellingstrasse. It was a short distance from Hanna and Karl Wolfskehl's
apartment, which was close to the popular cafés along the famous
Leopoldstrasse. Upon arrival in Munich, Greve may have been able to count
on the help of friends from Bonn in his search for an apartment. A Rhenus
member lived in the neighbouring building at 22 Amalienstrasse. Once
established, Greve probably busied himself with befriending Karl Wolfskehl
and other members of Stefan George's famous circle, including the "master"
himself. Ricarda Huch, the writer and Beethoven biographer, has reported
how one could make the master's acquaintance on Sundays at the *jours*
organized by the Wolfskehls at their apartment, a popular meeting spot (Ott-
Pfäfflin, *Ricarda Huch* 166).[3] Felix Greve's extant cards and letters to Hanna

and Karl Wolfskehl, beginning that December, show that he once again introduced himself as a comfortably wealthy connoisseur. This practice served him particularly well in Munich. Frederick Philip Grove described how his alter ego Philip Branden went about forming useful contacts in this fashion:

> My reputed wealth opened every door. I sometimes think that some of the men with whom I linked up—or upon whom I thrust myself—men, some of whom have in the meantime acquired European or even world-wide reputation, must have smiled at the presumptuous pup who thought he was somebody because he threw his father's money about with noble indifference. It is a strange fact that they received me on a footing of equality and led me on; they had time to spare for exquisite little dinners no less than for the nonsensical prattle of one who gave himself airs. Of course, there was an occasional man who kept himself at a distance; but on the whole I cannot avoid the conclusion that these idols had feet of clay (SFA 4).

The same situation almost certainly applied to Felix Paul Greve.

Felix Paul Greve, a seemingly wealthy but unknown young man, presented Karl Wolfskehl, the wealthy heir to a fortune in Darmstadt and a well-known writer, with rare and expensive gifts: *Aubrey Beardsley's Later Works* and his *Early Works*, selected plates from the appendix to Professor Adolf Furtwängler's (out of print) *Vasenwerk* (*Book on Ancient Pottery*), as well as a "little something" for "your Christmas table" (Furtwängler 1885). He also kept Wolfskehl informed of the progress being made on his (and Kilian's) translation of Oscar Wilde's book of essays (*Intentions*), and in passing called attention to projects completed at an earlier time: "Incidentally, I recently found amongst my papers a translation of Dante's *Vita nuova* completed in 1898. I would like to inform you of this as something I don't consider at all bad. The Wilde project is coming along sprightly."[4] It is not possible to ascertain when the Dante translation could have been completed during the busy year of 1898 unless, in a striking parallel to Stefan George, Greve had turned his attention to Dante as a student at the *Gymnasium* (George, *Werke*, vol. x/xi 144). The immediate source of Greve's comment might well reside in George's ongoing interest in Dante's *Vita nuova* from 1900 onwards, as a letter to Friedrich Gundolf of January 28, 1901 would suggest (Boehringer, *George-Gundolf* 76). George published his Dante translations in *Blätter für die Kunst* during this period. Nevertheless, Greve could have presented his Dante translations to Wolfskehl along with an undated letter from the final days of 1901 or the beginning of 1902. He may have suggested that his linguistic efforts as a translator owed something to Wolfskehl:

> At the same time allow me to present you with nine randomly selected sonnets from my Dante translation. I'm almost ashamed to do so as they appeared to me rather flat and poor as I copied them out. My only excuse is that they were completed 3 years ago. In one place where it seemed to me I had completely missed the mark I even plagiarized you while copying it out (Sonnet 3).[5]

Could it be that Greve's Dante translations had just then been completed, following Wolfskehl's example? Or were these "randomly selected" sonnets all that could be presented for the time being from all of his "early" transla-tions? Perhaps Greve only intended to draw attention to his artistic proximity to Wolfskehl and to the spiritual harmony between the master George and the undersigned ephebe-to-be. He may have been taken aback when asked to produce all of the "early translations."[6] *This* could be one of the sources of the references—at the time still relatively good-natured—to Greve's Munchausen-like pranks by Wolfskehl. On February 4 he suggested to Gundolf that Greve was ill, when it was perhaps only an intense craving for admiration:

> I must mention something else to you and I ask you to be very careful and clever. It seems that our mutual friend F[elix] P[aul] G[reve] has shown signs of Munchausen-like behaviour to such an advanced degree that it must be allowed to inform friends how little confidence can be extended to him. He seems to have confused a great deal here and…Or perhaps he's sick? (Kluncker, *Wolfskehl* 151–52).[7]

Although Greve's health problems (among them surely a severe case of grandiloquence) would soon be a topic of discussion, Wolfskehl would have been thinking less of a weak lung than psychological or moral failings, although here too there is little concrete evidence. Whatever the case may be, Greve's reference to Dante would have appealed to the tastes of the George circle, which showed pronounced interest in classical literature. At the time it was not at all uncommon, for example, to dress up and present oneself wearing classical robes as Dante (Stefan George) or Homer (Karl Wolfskehl). In fact, at least one photograph remains of a costume party in the spring of 1902 showing those present in such dress. Greve's concerted attempts to ingratiate himself were also evident in the increased pompous-ness of his writing style, which had already been noticed during his school

✜ *Herbert Koch*
(Collection Rose String)

days in Hamburg. Greve reported to Wolfskehl not only that his work was advancing *rüstig* ("sprightly") but he also wrote *sich's die Mühe nicht verdriessen zu lassen* ("please do not unduly trouble yourself")—an excellent imitation of the stilted and occasionally old-fashioned style of letter-writing within the George circle. He wrote daily letters to Wolfskehl, noting only the day of the week. In his turn, he received a not particularly well-preserved edition of George's *Algabal* and translated, apart from Wilde, Walter Pater's essay on Antoine Watteau, *A Prince of Court Painters*.[8] Next he reported that he intended to take a trip to the mountains in order to "rest myself for one day from the strains of my excessive toil." At the same time, he sent along the first of his own works, the poem "Knight Errant." In another undated letter, in response to a request from Wolfskehl via another member of the circle, Franz Dülberg, he sent a "Hercules" poem.[9] He also mentioned the address of a new acquaintance, Herbert Koch, living in their vicinity at 75 Königinstrasse II.

❈ *Franziska zu Reventlow, 1905*
(Münchner Stadtmuseum)

Mention of Koch to Wolfskehl indicates that Felix Greve continued to use the university to expand his circle of acquaintances. Indeed, he was already providing sponsorship (as he had done during his days with Rhenus) as if it were a matter of course, although he also sought patronage for himself. He showed familiarity not only with prints from Furtwängler's *Vasenwerk*, but also made it clear that he was acquainted with the famous university professor, not only as a student but also personally.

Herbert Koch, one year younger than Greve, had (like Kilian) attended a *Gymnasium* in Dresden. He studied music, history, German philology and philosophy in Leipzig; he continued in Munich in German philology, archaeology, art history and psychology. He also took courses with Adolf Furtwängler and attended musical soirées held at Furtwängler's home. Whether Felix Greve met Koch at these musical events, which were also attended by Ludwig Klages, Friedrich Huch and Ludwig Curtius, will have to remain unanswered (Schröder, *Klages* 442–43). Greve could have met Koch via Friedrich Huch, another young but successful author who also associated with Furtwängler.

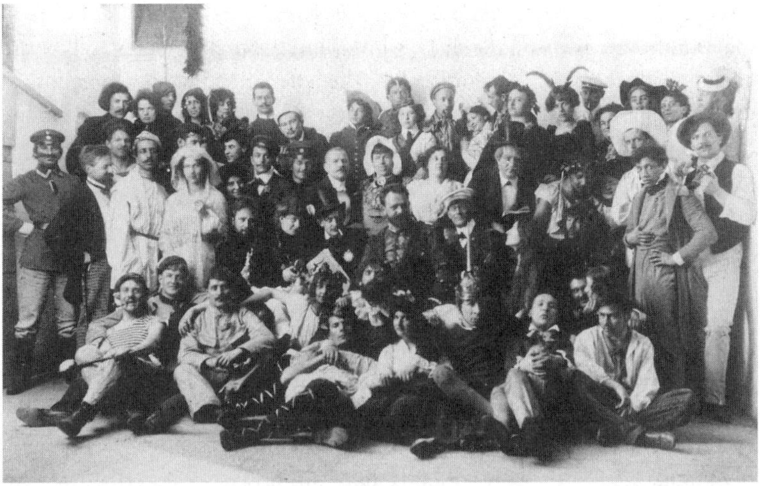

⌘ *Ball initiated by the cabaret "The Eleven Executioners," Schwabing* Fasching, 1903 *(Collection Rose String)*

Their shared interest in literature, archaeology and art history brought Koch closer to Greve, who could speak of Delbrueck, Vollmoeller and Rome, and also about Wilde and Beardsley, and even about his soon-to-be-published poems and translations. For his part, Koch made the acquaintance of Countess Franziska zu Reventlow, with whom he corresponded even after his time in Munich. Among other figures, Koch and Reventlow wrote about Greve, whose novel *Fanny Essler* the countess was later to read (Reventlow, *Briefe* 375; Koch to Reventlow, n.d. [ca. spring 1906]).[10] These young men seem to have formed a circle of young people close to the inner circles around George, Klages and Wolfskehl. Koch, Helene Klages, Roderich Huch (called "the sun-child"), his cousin Friedrich Huch, Wolfskehl and the countess seem sincerely to have enjoyed each other's company. The dramatist and art historian Franz Dülberg and the "Cosmic" Alfred Schuler also belonged to the circle. All of them appear to have associated not only with one another but also with the well-educated, tasteful and seemingly wealthy Felix Greve. Greve was a central figure, and not only for those mentioned here. Members of these circles met at the university, in various apartments and during *Fasching*. They appear to have got along quite well. Not for nothing did Koch write to Reventlow full of nostalgia after his time in Munich: "Dear Countess—Today I have spent the entire day going through letters—just now ones from Greve, Helene, Rodi, Fritz, you,

Wolfskehl and am now of course feeling so sentimental that I wish I were in the Mandstrasse lying on the divan with you in the rocking chair and it were already endlessly late."[11] Unfortunately, the letters Koch wrote are no longer extant. A photograph from the Koch family archive shows members of the circle of friends at a ball initiated by the cabaret "The Eleven Executioners" of 1903—Koch, Wolfskehl, Reventlow, Franz Hessel and others. By this time Greve was already on his way to Sicily.

The Schwabing world of literature and art that Greve entered at the end of September 1901 had dimensions entirely different from those in Bonn, although there were institutional parallels. Readings and theatrical productions were frequented by those invited from the worlds of art and academia—the Munich "Academic-Dramatic Club" (1891–1903), at Greve's time under the direction of Ernst von Wolzogen. Thomas Mann read on November 18, 1901 from his story "Gladius Dei" (Kolbe, *Heller Zauber* 58). Jacob Littauer's Book and Art Store at the Odeonsplatz, unmistakably described as "M. Blüthenzweig's expansive beauty emporium" in Mann's short novella, could not have failed to make an impression on Greve:

> Yet up there on Odeonsplatz…the people crowded around the wide windows and show cases of the great art store, M. Blüthenzweig's expansive beauty emporium…Luxurious display copies, triumphs of the new art of display, works by fashionable poets, enveloped in decorative and distinguished splendour….He saw the copies of the masterpieces from all the galleries of the earth, the expensive frames in their simple *Bizarrerie*, renaissance sculptures, bronze figures and decorative glasses, shimmering vases, book decorations and the portraits of artists, musicians, philosophers, actors, poets. [A]n abundance of colour, line and form, of style, wit, taste and beauty (Mann, "Gladius Dei" 156; 159; 162).[12]

The Drama Club also played a role in the story (198). Greve, familiar with its Bonn counterpart and also with readings and theatre productions, would not have failed to notice the club. "The Eleven Executioners" performed in the *Gasthaus zum Goldenen Hirschen* ("Golden Stag Inn"), located in Türkenstrasse parallel to Amalienstrasse. The editorial offices of the satirical magazine *Simplicissimus* (where Thomas Mann was a part-time employee in October 1901) was within walking distance. The editorial office of the magazine *Die Insel* was located at 4 Leopoldstrasse. It lasted until the double issue of September 1902 before yielding to the successful publishing house of the same name. Greve had already established contact with it and published a translation of a short Wilde piece in the magazine before it expired.

The better-known publishing houses of Albert Langen and Georg Müller enabled talented writers to work as translators. Countess Reventlow, for instance, earned an meagre income in this way. Felix Greve, the prospective translator, could have taken warning from her. In April 1897, she had for the first time "gone to Langen...I wanted to work, although he had to give me an advance immediately—Gave me a book to translate and 200 marks..." Later she wrote: "[They] all think that I live a quite normal life from my translations—good Lord" (Reventlow, *Briefe* 50; 104). It is essential to note here that Greve was not only part of a German literary avant-garde, but, more importantly, a member of a well-regarded *translation culture*. In this Greve joined the ranks of such individuals as Ernst Hardt and Karl Gustav Vollmoeller, and, still more importantly, Rudolf Borchardt, Rudolf Alexander Schröder and even Stefan George himself.

At the time, translation was expected to develop the linguistic competence necessary for the composition of verse; such verse (following Hugo von Hofmannsthal's example) would then lead to first attempts at playwriting (Soergel, *Dichtung* 1911, 854). And yet, despite the long-term cultural benefits of translation, the actual work of translating remained the most thankless form of "exhausting piecework": "To complete the immense quota, [Reventlow] must not infrequently work around the clock to the point of total exhaustion" (Wilhelm, *Münchner Boheme* 161). Greve himself would very soon be forced to perform such piecework.

Greve's Hamburg monies seem to have dried up completely by the end of the 1901–02 winter semester. Unlike Reventlow, though, he appears not to have translated as a means of supporting himself. His work as a translator was much more an opportunity to show his linguistic gifts, as his correspondence with Wolfskehl and George indicates. References to his Dante translations, his efforts with Wilde and Pater, the offer extended to Stefan George as translation critic, his request for advice from Wolfskehl concerning translation solutions, his own poems—these leave no doubt that Greve wanted to establish that he possessed the relevant knowledge and was himself poetically gifted. After all, George and Wolfskehl presented themselves as poet-translators who seemed to demonstrate that the one activity complemented the other. In fact, George had a formative influence not only as an author and aesthete, but also in the field of literary translation. His 1905 translations of contemporary English and French poetry in two volumes contained, apart from Wilde, such important authors for Greve as Dante Gabriel Rossetti, Algernon Charles Swinburne and Ernest Dowson. As in his own poetry, George was concerned with exemplariness above all. His renderings were, as he wrote, "occasioned by indignation over the distortions which were offered to us as reproductions of the venerated master" (George, *Zeitgenössische*

❈ *Alfred Janssen*
(Collection Heiner Stiebeling)

Dichter, 5). Greve's own volume of poetry, *Wanderungen,* initially turned down by Alfred Janssen in Hamburg, appeared for sale in Jacob Littauer's store at the Odeonsplatz in "decorative and distinguished splendour." It seemed advisable to Greve to regard this expensive and independently produced work as an abandoned trifle in order to make use of another well-known name, Oscar Wilde. Through activity as a translator he could advance further in his development as an author.

The behaviour is again unmistakable. In his efforts to gain recognition as a poet, Felix Greve sought out the famous names most worthy of support and patronage. This was analogous to the efforts he made to establish himself within archaeology and among archaeologists. Thomas Mann, incidentally, had thought the same, and in the magazine *Die Gesellschaft* (1899: 183), then under the direction of J.C.C. Bruns Publishers, had formulated in verse his "Dream of a Slender Crown of Laurels:"

And lost my spirit roams the land
And, reeling now, I grasp at each strong hand
I'm but a weak and childish dreamer;

And yet, deep within me, some hope stirs
That some of what I felt and thought
Should once with glory pass from mouth to mouth.

Softly, now, my name is heard throughout the land,
Yes, 'tis spoken of with accents of respect
By those of judgement and good intellect.[13]

Felix Greve's strategy of seeking support from well-known names—attempting to grasp a "strong hand" and to move among people of "judgement and good intellect"—became evident in his campaign to publish his first collection of poems. Here it is noteworthy that he did not attempt to place his book with one of the famous Munich publishers, such as Albert Langen or Georg Müller. Were such an attempt made, no evidence of it remains.

So what could have caused Felix Greve to offer his first work to the Hamburg publisher Alfred Janssen? It is true that Janssen's socially liberal publishing house was based in Greve's hometown, although it first had been established in Berlin. But was Greve's attention pointed in another literary direction? Greve justified his choice in characteristic manner in a letter of December 5, 1901 to Janssen: "The circumstance of your having just recently introduced a *homo novus*, Mr. Huch, with such great success provides me with the hope that I will not be presented with a negative response." Greve was referring to Friedrich Huch's novel *Peter Michel*. Huch, who moved in the circle surrounding George and Wolfskehl and who was also a friend of the children in Thomas Mann's household, was soon to move to Hamburg as a private tutor and thus had his own contacts.[14] His book was greeted with much praise in the November issue of the new weekly magazine *Der Lotse* (also published by Janssen). The reviewer was Ludwig Klages, one of the "Cosmics" close to George and for a time a close friend and lover of Reventlow—a member, in other words, of the "circle of the *Blätter für die Kunst*." Greve, in turn, wished to use his proximity to this circle and its journal to recommend himself to the publisher.[15] The suggested analogies were not unfounded. Greve was from Hamburg, where Huch was occasionally employed, and both were familiar with the same literary scene in Munich. Why shouldn't it be possible for someone else from this milieu—Wolfskehl, say—to do for Greve's book with Janssen what Klages had done for Huch's? Despite the strategic similarities, Greve's manuscript was not accepted for publication. Huch's novel had little of the style and pathos of the George circle and little of the contemporary taste for decadence. On the basis of a possible review by someone from the "circle of the *Blätter für die*

Kunst," Janssen could not print a volume of poetry which had nothing of Huch's realism and which was in no way similar to his book.

Indeed, it is surprising that Klages should have placed a review with *Der Lotse* at all, considering the difference between his artistic tendencies and those of the circle surrounding the magazine, a circle which included realist authors such as Detlev von Liliencron, Gustav Frenssen and above all Gustave Falke (Pieler, *Janssen* 71; 107). Greve had certainly dealt with Wolfskehl patiently enough that he could have justifiably hoped for a positive response. He had even acquired a camera and enthusiastically sent snapshots of himself, as did others. Friedrich Huch, for instance, wrote his mother in Dresden in 1899 that he would soon send "a photo of me" that "a Scotsman had taken." One can only speculate whether another Dresdener, Herman Kilian, was meant here (via his grandfather Lord Rutherfurd-Clark, also a Scotsman). At any rate, the Scotsman must have been as wealthy as Kilian, since, as Huch reported, the man had "purchased a camera for 240 marks."[16] It remains unclear whether Greve owned a camera before he went to Rome in 1900. If not, it would not have been the costs alone which held him back. In 1901–02 he may have been able to use one of Kilian's cameras or to buy one himself. A "travel camera" could possibly have come into question, one which folded together and could thus be carried like a handbag. At the Imperial German Archaeological Institute he would have had ample opportunity to familiarize himself with the techniques of photography, for it was a part of the daily routine at the institute. Danesi, the photographer responsible for the illustrations in the *Mitteilungen*, would have made an excellent instructor. In general, photography had become an essential component of archaeological documentation, as Furtwängler's example had shown (Schuchhardt, *Furtwängler* 10–11). But more than this, a portable camera was also a status symbol. Grove's alter ego Phil Branden, forced unwillingly into a journey through America, held a camera in his hand like a talisman upon arrival in Canada (SFA 15).

Greve was also very much at the height of fashion in the art of bookmaking. By choosing Otto von Holten in Berlin as the printer for his *Wanderungen* and *Helena und Damon*, he had turned to the printer who had already produced George's *Teppich des Lebens* (1899–1900) for the publisher Georg Bondi. With Littauer he chose a commission-based book store which displayed *Blätter für die Kunst*. Like *Teppich des Lebens*, *Helena and Damon* was printed in costly scarlet and black (the young George had already copied out two sonnets by Petrarch in scarlet and black; George, *Werke X/XI*, 144). No wonder that Wolfskehl finally recommended the book and its author: "Mr. Greve, whom you rightly praise, has now had his poetic work, occasional pieces whose grace and charming flow of verse no one can deny, printed in a most delightfully stylish manner and which is *proprio*, a little wonder in its three colours and old roccoco italic print set on thin Japanese paper" (Kluncker, *Wolfskehl* 158). Greve came so close to the master that a cutting review of *Wanderungen* by Otto Julius Bierbaum would, in a practically honorific way, be similar to a vicious review of the master: "Did you know that in the *Insel* of J[une], Ojb-Slimer visciously and ridiculously ruffled him up? And did you know that the same shameful publication dared in the last (June) publication to attack the master? Franz Blei is the name of the hack that this business was left to" (Kluncker, *Wolfskehl* 158). In the opinion of Wolfskehl the prophet, master and ephebe found themselves together. There was no disparaging talk of a "sick" Greve here. On the contrary, Greve was singled out for healthy praise. It wasn't until later that year that another incident instigated Wolfskehl to form a negative opinion. Only Else von Freytag-Loringhoven's refreshing lack of respect towards these arbiters of taste turned such judgements against their originators. It also casts a cooler light on the all-too-frequently self-referential commentary written in the Munich circle around George and Klages.

◆ KNIGHT ERRANT

As we have seen, Felix Greve was without question an accepted presence among the young men in Schwabing, with Countess Reventlow as their shared muse. This is again evident in a reference by Theodor Lessing, a once well-known writer and archaeologist:

> In the evening I said to Franziska Reventlow, the sole woman for whom [Klages] ever had a flame: "Today I showed Ludwig Klages how one seduces little goslings. He found me 'colossal.'"—And she sniffed: "He also finds me 'colossal.' When my hair flutters while dancing, he stands behind the column and despises. He despises Hentschel and despises Wedekind and despises Felix Greve and despises Ohaha Schmitz. In short he despises everyone who takes me and kisses me. For I am supposed to purify myself and fly with him. And I do want to fly. And as he is the only one with whom I can fly, I have to content myself with kissing the others.[17]

Did Felix "take and kiss" the countess, also known—less than delicately—as "Lais?" Who was her monk Paphnutius? Greve? As she could only "fly" with Klages, perhaps Greve had undertaken his first attempts at flight with others. We know little of Greve's heterosexual love-life in Hamburg, Bonn and Rome, insofar as there was one. There is, however, evidence of an affair

✷ *Else von Freytag-Loringhoven, ca. 1920*
(Whitney Museum of American Art, New York)

during Greve's sojourn in Munich which could have led to his abrupt departure for Berlin. Else von Freytag-Loringhoven, who in 1902 was still married to the *Jugenstil* ("Art Nouveau") architect August Endell, had taken particular notice of Greve, as she herself writes. Else was a smaller and more attainable Lais than Reventlow. She writes in her memoirs of a largely platonic relationship with Greve which was based less on the intricate seduction of goslings *à la* Theodor Lessing than on naïve exercises in courtliness. The cast of characters is given in her memoir: "Mr. Felix" (Felix Paul Greve) and "Dr. Phil." (Karl Wolfskehl). Only the identities of the "girl" and her "brother" from a small provincial city in northern Germany remain uncertain. A long excerpt is in order here:

> Mr. Felix—whom I shall now call Felix—for that was his Christian name—told me a story about a love affair he had had shortly before he had come to Berlin...that he had travelled with a girl I had once met at Dr. Phil's. It was very much made of her—I couldn't understand

why—I felt not only indifferent—I felt hostile towards her—she disgusted me! I saw through her!—How right my instincts are! ...

I had to hear that he had travelled—when I thought him "too good" for me—with this insignificant coward—in Italy—*not* as lovers—that was the exasperating circumstance—she travelled with him on his money but "she couldn't decide to let him have her!" He told me how he had waited her *final decision*—*waited before her door!*

To imagine this marvellously turned out young man—waiting before this little insignificant ninny's door—a "Knight Toggenburg"—

...But I couldn't get him again to talk of it—very cleverly. I felt an overpowering contempt for this girl...

This girl had come to him—begging money for her brother's embezzlement. I knew—such an affair was talked about at the time—I didn't care to listen. "For the sake of the girl to save the brother"—or for the sake of the "circle." It was quite a sum—10,000 Marks—and Mr. Felix had given it to her. He had fallen in love with her—making her a marriage proposal (nice for me to hear—about that sum of money too—for the pleasure of some virgin's criminal brother!) For that is what she was—and made her supposed charm—a virgin—having come to the *Munich artist circles* from a small town—her father a grocer—I think. *How* she came into that very exclusive circle, I don't know. Probably they got a fad suddenly on some pretty everyday girl's virginity—who cherished it for advertising purposes. Dr. Phil...was capable of getting a fad for anything—served in the right way at the right time—not to be short of something to *get* excited about—for that was his great purpose and business in life.

Well, this girl took the money—but she did not feel obliged to do something for it. But just to "think the thing over" she agreed to travel with Mr. Felix. But she couldn't marry him, it seemed, nor part with her virginity. And now Mr. Felix was supposed to have "ruined the girl's reputation" in travelling with her. That is why he came to Berlin. Later the girl got an illegitimate child—probably by somebody with less patience and delicacy than Mr. Felix without giving her a cent...(BE 79–82).

❧ *Helene Klages, ca. 1902 (Schiller Nationalmuseum / Deutsches Literaturarchiv, Marbach)*

The references to the "girl" may establish a possible connection to Greve. Unfortunately, it is not possible here to establish her identity given the absence of conclusive documentation. Nevertheless, the probability of a relationship is high enough to warrant reference.[18]

Some time around the middle of 1902, Greve wrote to Wolfskehl for several reasons: to acknowledge the receipt of a "Machiavell," to announce his departure for Gardone (Northern Italy) and to forward the snapshots he had probably taken with a travel camera. He added the following in parentheses: "I have kept an ex[emplar] of your pictures for Helene Klages." Apparently Greve was already acquainted with Ludwig Klages's sister. As an earlier note from Dülberg to Ludwig Klages reveals, Felix Greve played a highly important role for both the Klageses during this period. Indeed, Greve appears to have been more than a mere outsider; in fact, his arrival was often the cause of get-togethers with the siblings: "Dear Doctor! As Mr. Greve has informed me that he will again be in Munich on Friday, might I invite you and your sister to my modest home as guests this coming Monday at 8 o'clock?"[19] That this note was found in a bundle of handwritten drafts in the Klages estate arouses less interest than the far more curious fact that none of the correspondence concerning Greve, Dülberg or the Klages siblings is extant. Something appears to have happened which necessitated the deletion of Greve as a member of the circle. Theodor Lessing, who mentions Greve, sent all the letters he received from Ludwig Klages back to him (Lessing, *Einmal* 383).[20] Neither in Schröder's account of Klages's life and works nor in Klages's papers is Greve's name to be found in legible form.

Who then was Helene Klages? She had followed Ludwig from their parents' middle-class household in Hanover to Munich, where she and her brother lived in an attic apartment.[21] According to Theodor Lessing's statements, Hanover could have been considered a "small" city, in the sense Freytag-Loringhoven suggested in her memoirs.[22] Helene and the countess had decorated the Christmas tree at the Wolfskehl's in 1901, when Greve was forming contacts with Wolfskehl and George and was about to meet Reventlow (Reventlow, *Tagebücher* 376). In the spring of 1902, Klages visited Friedrich Huch in Poland, where the latter was working as a private tutor. Around the same time, he went to Lodz to secure money from the industrialist Richter. He needed money to support the countess with whom he was having a love affair. It is not certain whether Klages, as poor as he was, sought money for himself as well. His trip to Poland seemed at first a success, although the payments of 800 marks to Reventlow stopped in July. Klages's subsequent trip to Poland on the first of September, this time in the role of petitioner, would prove fruitless (Schröder, *Klages* 334).

Who supported Klages? Why is there so little mention of Klages's financial problems and so much of Reventlow's difficulties, which were known to others and about which she herself wrote and thus could not deny? From Theodor Lessing's comments it can be inferred that Klages and his sister indeed lived in terrible poverty at first. While Ludwig occupied his time with graphological reports, Helene's move to Munich appears motivated by more than artistic ambitions. It is apparent from one of Reventlow's letters that Helene's relationship to her father, the Hanover textiles merchant Louis W. Klages (the man referred to by Else as a "grocer"), was very poor: "What is Helene writing there? As long as I don't have to go home. If I were allowed to have my say I would advise her not to go home, for even the shortest amount of time" (Reventlow, *Briefe* 371). It may be assumed that Helene's (and perhaps also Ludwig's) relationship to her family was as irreparably damaged as Reventlow's to hers. There may well have been some grave, financially based source of ill will. At any rate, no financial help from home was forthcoming. Accordingly, the siblings shared similar financial worries, as both wrote to Friedrich Huch: "Living with Helene from hand to mouth and only manage to keep my head above water in that I write graphological diagnoses daily. (Helene writes novellas.)"[23] Helene, who had ambitions as an actress, obviously wrote fiction in addition to graphological reports. She also tried her hand at translation, as another of Reventlow's letters indicates. But the countess, who had a close relationship with Ludwig Klages and thus felt attached to Helene, refused to act as her mentor in translation:

> As far as translation is concerned, that, my dear friend, would mean double the work, for I am so well trained through so much practice that I only copy French out, especially when it's easy. You know, everyone has such a different style; I have often tried it with people I know, even people with practice in it and each time I've found that it is more effort to change the work of others than the usual scrawl. Helene should not misunderstand this and think that I don't trust that she could do it (Reventlow, Letters 358).[24]

Despite this refusal, the countess later offered "to give her a few hours of instruction." It is possible that Felix Greve, an equally inexperienced trans-lator, filled the breach and began to lead Helene's hand.[25] At the time Greve was busy with his translation of plays from Wilde's *Intentions*. He had already dedicated *Wanderungen* to his "friend and companion Herman F.C. Kilian" and had entrusted Kilian with the translation of "The Decay of Lying" from the Wilde volume (although he would later not mention him as a co-trans-lator). Thus the possibility cannot be discounted that under Greve's direction Helene translated one of the first plays that Greve sent to J.C.C. Bruns Publishers on January 8, 1902—and later replaced it with a new version.[26] In support of this hypothesis is an undated letter in which Greve refers to Helene in the context of Wilde: "Since Miss Klages will be dining with you today, might I ask you the favour of telling her, in the first chapter of Dorian Gray…"[27] Although Greve did not send the completed manuscript of *The Picture of Dorian Gray* to J.C.C. Bruns until July 17, 1902, immediately before his departure for Gardone, by 1902 he seems to have familiarized the Wolfskehl circle not only with Wilde's essays but also with his novel. Both works were appropriate given the climate of decadence. They were also easy to translate, which was important for Greve's relationship with Kilian and Helene Klages. Jorge Louis Borges, another writer familiar with Wilde's writing, has commented: "[I]n verse or in prose Wilde's syntax is always very simple. Of the many British writers, none is so accessible to foreigners. Readers who are incapable of deciphering a paragraph of Kipling or a stanza by William Morris begin and end *Lady Windermere's Fan* on the same after-noon" (Borges, *Wilde* 83). Thus Greve would have been able to shine as a translator in the "Cosmic" circle. This would also have earned him the appreciation of Kilian and the good will of Helene, who would now have her opportunity to work as a joint translator following the countess' refusal. Had Greve used translation as a means of developing his relationship with Helene Klages—which, according to Dülberg's invitation in April, seems to have worked—then the Schwabing *Fasching* celebrations of February 1902 would have offered further opportunity for mutual contact.

Although jealously supervised by her brother, Helene Klages also took part in the festivities. It would seem that her presence aroused considerable interest, for her distinctive contours were, according to Roderich Huch, commented upon with prurient interest in the *Schwabinger Beobachter* (*Schwabing Observer*). Although there is nothing which crudely suggests a formerly *fromme Helene* ("prissy Helene"), to quote the satirist Wilhelm Busch, there is nevertheless the self-declaration of a "former maiden Magdalena" who lost her virginity during the *Fasching* revelries: "In place of a special report: Yesterday one of my closest acquaintances robbed me of my most precious good." Huch is of the opinion that Helene Klages herself penned the text (R. Huch, "Erinnerungen" 44). If Helene had overcome her brother's restraints and if Greve had been the "acquaintance," it doesn't seem to have affected his relations with Klages, Dülberg, Huch, Reventlow and others, for his interaction with them continued for the time being. Nevertheless, the Klages papers collected and paraphrased by Schröder would suggest that she had indeed made a cult of virginity, as Freytag-Loringhoven claimed, such that the self-declaration ought to be taken as a hoax. This may have resulted from Klages's prohibition against "girls from the circle" associating further with the attractive Roderich Huch (Huch, "Erinnerungen" 43). For the strangest of reasons, it was becoming increasingly common for Klages to break with more and more acquaintances and friends, ultimately even with Theodor Lessing and Stefan George. Perhaps Greve was one of his victims. When it appeared that Huch had taken up with Busse's girlfriend "Bix," for instance, Klages and Busse reacted violently: "A fierce argument between us ensued and as I couldn't convince him that I had not the slightest interest in the girl, he declared that all contact with me was to be broken and demanded that I leave Schwabing and Munich and that if I didn't something terrible would happen. From Franziska Reventlow I learned that Klages was entirely on Busse's side" (Huch, "Erinnerungen" 41–42). Could a similarly violent conflict have been the cause of Greve's letter of October 10, 1902 to Wolfskehl, in which he announced that he intended to leave Munich? After all, he did burn all his bridges to Schwabing and Munich and left for Berlin. If Greve and Helene began an affair, would he have helped Ludwig Klages with 10,000 marks during the spring and summer of 1902, which in turn would have delayed the termination of the relationship? Was Greve in Helene's company while he completed his Wilde translations between the end of July and the middle of August in Gardone? Given her interest in translation, the relationship would have been convenient for both of them. In looking at the photographs Greve sent from Gardone to the Wolfskehls, informing them of his feats at swimming and the development of his beard and which show him in a boat either alone or with his Italian companion ("Might I introduce to you the noble Francesco, my friend and barcajuolo"), one feels compelled to ask who else was in the boat and took the pictures (cf. Spettigue 1992).

From this perspective, Greve's comments in the letter above take on added importance. In this letter Greve sent photographs to Wolfskehl in Darmstadt and in a postscript advised him that he was retaining copies of photographs for Helene Klages. Were the photographs intended for Helene in Munich or did he simply wish to create this impression before they travelled together to Gardone? Did Greve spend the night "waiting before this insignificant ninny's door" at the Pension Häberlin in Gardone, as Freytag-Loringhoven so jealously put it later? Was it the revelation of this affair (and not the enormous sum that Greve was to pay) which drove Greve from Munich? Still more suggests that Helene was the ultimate cause of Greve's departure for Berlin and that Else's sarcastic remarks about the future of the "ninny" indeed refer to Klages's sister. In fact, Helene must have met a less hesitant lover than Greve, "somebody with less patience and delicacy than Mr. Felix," for she moved "to Berlin in the late summer or autumn of 1903...for 3 months," although certainly not to meet with Greve who was being held under detention in Bonn. After her return on March 17, 1904, Helene bore an illegitimate daughter, Heidi (Schröder, *Klages* 446). In the meantime, Greve had begun his affair with Else Endell. When Felix published his novel *Fanny Essler* in 1905, making use of Else's excellent memory (as attested to in the memoirs written for Djuna Barnes), he was remembered by several of the people who had previously lived in Munich or who had remained in Schwabing. And when one considers the prominent role he played there, the subsequent silence about him is all the more striking. Herbert Koch alone seemed prepared to write quite openly from Munich to the countess (albeit in undated letters), raising the spectre of undesirable revelations which referred to everyone, including Helene:

Have you read F.P. Greve's novel? Neither we nor Helene Klages have come up yet—but given the con-man atmosphere of the last part I had to think back on the old days. Incidentally, Else Ploetz must have done a great job in playing to him the role of the affected people (Lechter, Endell and especially Ernst Hardt). By the way, it's quite without talent and somewhat nasty.[28]

With the comment on the "con-man atmosphere," Koch is thinking not just of Greve but of the time they spent together. It was a period characterized by possibility, of "more appearance than reality." Works of art in progress, for instance, many of which would never appear, were continually being referred to. Klages himself was not averse to making such hasty announcements, as Reventlow remarked in the *Schwabinger Beobachter*. Nevertheless, some members — Greve unexpectedly prominent among them — ultimately managed to realize their artistic inclinations in publications.

◆ A PUBLISHER IN MINDEN

Greve was encouraged by the appearance of his volume of poems in the artsy milieu he desired. When he offered his first manuscript of translations from Wilde's *Intentions* to the Minden house J.C.C. Bruns, he mentioned the Munich circle as he had done when approaching Janssen. This time, however, Wolfskehl's name was explicitly mentioned as a potential reference:

Dear Sir:

Allow me, in my name and in the name of my friend, Mr. H. Kilian-Rutherford-Clark, to make the following enquiry.

Together we have translated into German one of Oscar Wilde's most important books, his *Intentions*.

Would you be prepared to undertake the publication?

The book will undoubtedly be an exceptional success.

3 portions of the book: "the decay of lying and the critic as artist" are already prepared, the other 2 ("Pen, pencil and poison" and "the truth of masks") are to be offered only in parts, as they are less accessible to German.

Should you be prepared to undertake the publication, allow me the following suggestion: apart from a regular edition (with paper similar to that used in your Baudelaire edition, Latin print, Price 3.50–4 marks) to print a special edition on real van Geldern paper in ca. 60 copies at ca. 6–8 marks. For the latter I could assure ca. 20–30 subscribers (in the circle of *Blätter für die Kunst* where I have already read portions).

In awaiting a positive response, I remain,

Yours sincerely,
FELIX PAUL GREVE

(Potential referent: Herr Dr. K. Wolfskehl, Munich, 51.I Leopoldstr.)[29]

With this letter Felix Paul Greve began his new life as a "writer," the second time that he had done so. As Wolfskehl and George's favourite poet Dante had written, *incipit vita nova.*

This time, Greve would present himself to the literary market as the author of privately printed vanity titles. If it had been formerly possible to use stipends to finance his *Wanderungen*, the loss of his income from Hamburg must have confronted him with concerns about his future finances. At the same time, his letter reveals that he could still count on financial backing from Kilian, and thus he presumably felt no need to abandon his role as a well-situated and well-connected man of the world. Greve sought to establish his market worth via implicit references to his independence, content to play the role of well-to-do connoisseur.

Felix Paul Greve's letter to J.C.C. Bruns documents one of the few cases in the history of German literature in which someone presented a translation composed of individual pieces as a joint effort. When Arno Holz and Johannes Schlaf brought out their *Papa Hamlet* (1899) under the pseudonym Bjarne P. Holmsen, they presented themselves as a Norwegian author and thus appealed to the prestige associated with the Scandinavian naturalist dramas of Henrik Ibsen and August Strindberg. In explicitly naming his friend Kilian as co-translator, Felix Greve achieved two goals. By representing Kilian under the (falsely spelt) name of his Scottish grandfather, Lord Rutherfurd-Clark, he not only added something respectable to the commonplace name Kilian (which some people, such as Freytag-Loringhoven, found positively vulgar sounding),[30] but also managed to suggest that at least one of the two was (almost) possessed of fluency in English.[31] Greve probably entertained few doubts about his own abilities in English, despite translating "criticism" for the required word "critic" and misspelling the title of Wilde's book. Bruns would also have noticed that two *male* friends were offering their

❈ *Oscar Wilde*
(J.C.C. Bruns Archiv, Minden)

mutual translation of a work by Oscar Wilde, the Anglo-Irish aesthete who had died under tragic circumstances in December of 1900 and whose friendships with men were the stuff of rumour and, ultimately, of tragedy. Of particular note here is Wilde's notorious relationship with Lord Alfred Douglas, "Bosie," who, like Herman Kilian (Rutherfurd-Clark), was also of Scottish descent.

Greve's approach betrays his cunning. Presenting only a portion of the proposed translation would allow Greve to turn to another publisher in case of rejection. On the other hand, he was probably not in a position to offer much more, as was once previously the case. His suggestion that two editions be prepared was undoubtedly intended to indicate that he had commercial experience and that he could be of help in reducing the financial risks of publication. This, at any rate, could also be read into a letter to Wolfskehl in which Greve discussed prepatory work "for our prospective undertaking," the necessary "financial backing" and the "development of a brochure."[32] In the same vein, Greve refers to expensive "van Geldern" paper in his letter to Bruns, which he repeats in his next letter. Grove was later to recall this "Holland" paper while writing of his time as a book dealer among a group of hawkers and swindlers in America (SFA 212). Indeed, the novice went so far as to suggest book prices to the publisher.

From the very beginning of this new publisher-translator relationship, Greve wished to suggest that he was an experienced and in no way impoverished man of letters who enjoyed the best of contacts. He made explicit why he had approached J.C.C. Bruns ("your Baudelaire edition") and thereby managed to bring both of them into complementary proximity to George, who also translated Baudelaire. He also mentioned Karl Wolfskehl and *Blätter für die Kunst*, both well known, and alluded to his own unconventionality—Wilde and his friend with Scottish connections. Greve additionally indicated his insider knowledge of the publishing business: paper types, prices, subscription possibilities. Even more important was the tone of the gentleman scholar and connoisseur which he had practiced to perfection with the Wolfskehls. He was now, however, without his usual source of money from Hamburg, and precisely because of his developing dependence upon Kilian, it was imperative for him to play the role of the independent in order not to be taken for one of the many impoverished literati he had come to know in Munich. This façade, which was to be maintained, literally, at any price, determined his consciousness and his image in the eyes of others.

Although Greve had not yet established connections to Insel Publishers, the tone he struck with J.C.C. Bruns was already reminiscent of that adopted by the wealthy young patrons Alfred Walter Heymel and Rudolf Alexander Schröder. This pair had played a prominent role in financing *Die Insel* magazine and Insel Publishers, and had also distinguished themselves with their own literary productions. Kurt Wolff, who would later emerge as an influential publisher of the Expressionists, also counted himself among these rich, energetic and tasteful young men. Max Bruns in Minden, the publisher's son and a poet of approximately the same age, could also devote himself to literature for the love of it and not simply for money.[33]

At first, J.C.C. Bruns would have been impressed by Greve's approach, although he in no way allowed himself to be placed under pressure. The Bruns publishing house enjoyed a considerable reputation as an innovative and powerful presence in publishing circles and had issued many well-reviewed works. Among these were books by the poets Alfred Mombert and Paul Scheerbart, as well as the novelist Jules Barbey d'Aurevilly and several Americans, including George Washington Cable and Ralph Waldo Emerson. Most notably, however, the young Max Bruns, himself a well-regarded poet, had published the works of Charles Baudelaire just as the first volumes of the firm's ten-volume Poe edition were arriving in the bookstores. Greve's choice of the Minden publisher was clearly well timed. From

Reventlow's experiences he seems to have learned just how precarious the position of a prospective author was, and especially that of a translator who wished to offer his talents. He could not have known, however, how transparent the role of the financially independent, self-confident connoisseur of art had become for the publisher. The J.C.C. Bruns correspondence contains numerous examples of initially independent and proud young authors, editors and translators who quickly began making unrealistic demands after signing their first contracts.[34] Calls for advances and gifts, a willingness to conclude the most questionable of deals, repeated offers of work with no translation rights—all this was familiar to the Minden firm. It would be no different for Greve, as his Munich expenses were far beyond the means of his modest income. Decades later Frederick Philip Grove would write: "A rate of expenditure which one has reached is much harder to give up than it was to attain."

Thus the publisher had no need to hasten his response. Greve answered this silence with the utmost professionalism, writing to Bruns at the end of February as someone with so much to do that

> it would mean a great deal to me to have the book published in the spring, as, apart from a collection of my poetry which already appeared in February, I have a series of my own works which I want to publish although I would like first to conclude my Wilde project which is something of a preface to my own work.

In obvious misappreciation of the capabilities of the publisher, Greve's Wilde book was too optimistically construed as the prologue to his own writings—the translation that would lead him to his own authorship. What was to hinder him from going straight from his volume of poetry to his other texts? It would seem that the urgency and importance of the Wilde book was due in part to the participation of Kilian, whose support would not be acknowledged with this publication alone (*Wanderungen* had already been dedicated to "my true friend and companion Herman F.C. Kilian"). *Intentions* contained no such dedication (although Kilian is indicated in the table of contents of the book's first edition as the co-translator), nor is Helene Klages's hand to be felt. She was the anonymous addressee of the "dedication" in Greve's "Play in Verse," *Helena und Damon*, whose name he "respectfully avoided" even though he rather transparently included it in his title. Was *Helena und Damon* one of his "own works" which was to be accompanied by *Intentions*? At first blush, it appears as anachronistic as it is precious, although in setting his idyll during a "spring festival at the beginning of the 18th

❊ Felix Paul Greve, Helena und Damon (1902), *title page and dedication*

century," Greve may have had in mind Hugo von Hofmannsthal's re-imple-
mentation of the idyll genre. At the same time, however, the "play" about the
passion of a poet for his loved one is both rather private and somewhat less
than revelatory. We learn little new, especially with regard to the poet.

"Written in March" and "printed in May," or so it appears in *Helena und
Damon*. This is the timeframe between the end of the Munich *Fasching* of
1902 and Greve's journey with Kilian via Darmstadt through Bingen and
Cologne to Paris, with a visit to Stefan George on May 16. In Paris, he and
Kilian addressed a postcard to Wolfskehl which was written in the exclusive
restaurant Tour d'Argent on May 21.[35] Could this journey have been undertaken to allow his trifling in verse the opportunity to take its effect at home
in Munich—to allow Helene Klages to appear as the "crown of thorns" on
"my skin" (HD 39)? Anyone concerned not to diminish the importance of
Greve's work as a translator, but rather to see it in relation to his own work,
should give his second letter to Bruns the emphasis it deserves. It was not his
recent book of poetry, lavishly printed on "hand-made Dutch paper" for the
"most sublime connoisseurs of the circle," which was to be "the preface to
[his] own works," nor was it his "play in verse." Instead, Greve gave voice to
the Anglo-Irish aesthete in his translated German words. Wilde's *Intentions*
would simultaneously serve as a statement of his intentions and a "pronounce-
ment," as O.J. Bierbaum's fictive hack writer "Henry Felix Hauart" put it with

regard to the publication of his book of poetry, significantly entitled *Rosa mystica* (Bierbaum, *Prinz* 655–56).[36] Contained in Greve's letter to Bruns is an implicit proclamation that *Wanderungen* had been surmounted. This imitates Wilde's strategy of treating each new book as an achievement beyond the previous work, as a rejection, even a kind of "murder." This approach was also taken by Gide, who, according to Wilde's biographer Richard Ellmann, felt he had overcome *L'immoraliste* with *La porte étroite* (Ellmann, *Wilde* 340). Greve would later translate both these works. For the time being, however, he was occupied with the translation and rapid publication of *Intentions*. The volume also contained Wilde's essay "The Critic as Artist," the second part of which includes a detailed celebration of Dante (Wilde, *Intentions* 177). "The Truth of Masks," the last essay of the volume, succinctly states what must have sounded to Greve like the justification of his own development, namely that "the archaeologist is to supply us with the facts which the artist is to convert into effects" (Wilde, *Intentions* 243).[37]

The translator and critic Max Meyerfeld, a friend of Wilde's and an astute critic of his works, quickly and vigorously attacked not only Greve's collected Wilde translations, but questioned the translation of the supposedly unnecessarily qualified title: "Why, incidentally, *Fingerzeige*? Out of fear of the foreign word *Motive* ('motives')?" The choice of the new word was probably due to George's disdain for foreign words. Beyond that, however, the critic observed that Greve had omitted all reference to individuals and the original setting. If Greve had wished the translations to function as a "preface" to his own writing, then this approach too was understandable. For Greve was undoubtedly little interested in linguistic accuracy or in referring back to the text's origins in Wilde's time. Rather, his goal would have been a literary creation of the translator's own time. Meyerfeld further skewered a series of actual mistakes in the translation. In the first edition, for example, Greve wrote "James Henry" for Henry James and Mrs. Oliphant became "Mr. Oliphant." The critic also reproduced a series of printing errors in the source text and used the opportunity to bemoan the poor abilities of English translators in general (Meyerfeld, "Oscar Wilde" 542). Apparently Greve had good reasons for emphasizing the Anglo-Saxon background of his co-translator Kilian in his first letter to Bruns. And yet it needs to be stressed once again that Greve was probably little concerned with serving the interests of the English author and his text. Instead, his often lax approach corresponded to the common practice of treating the text with gusto in order to produce a readable translation. Abridgements, omissions and altered formulations were more the rule than the exception. This practice was confirmed by Franziska zu Reventlow: "You must realize that I treat the novels quite subjectively, shorten where I feel it is required (the last one…I shortened from 600 pages

⌗ *Max Bruns*
(J.C.C. Bruns Archiv, Minden)

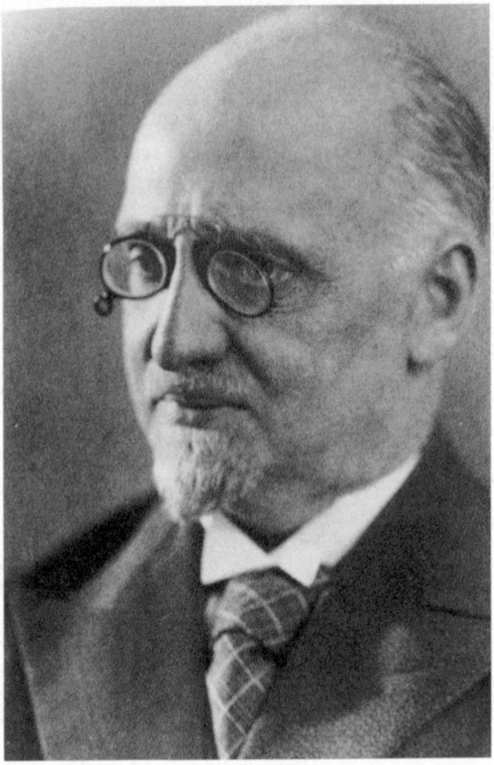

to 450) etc." (Reventlow, *Briefe* 358).[38] The new title for Wilde's *Intentions* was well considered: *Signs* had a faint aura of the prophetic; it suggested the occult knowledge of the initiated, as would be expected from the high priests of art who congregated in the circles around *Blätter für die Kunst*. A sign of fate was the goal, writing on the wall as if from "the fingers of a human hand," as the book of Daniel puts it (5:5).

One of the gods of the new art was Oscar Wilde. Greve girded himself for the task of being not only Wilde's German amanuensis but also his prophet. But he was not the only German translator of Wilde. There was also Johannes Gaulke, who in 1901 had produced the first German translation of *The Picture of Dorian Gray*. It was Greve's unusual luck that Max Bruns, unbeknownst to Greve, had harshly criticized a manuscript by Gaulke only a few months previously, rendering Greve's appearance more than fortuitous.[39] Bruns, who occasionally worked as an editor in his father's publishing house, had also indicated interest in Wilde in November 1901 and, after Greve's first letter of February 1902, had acquainted himself further with the author by means of Wilde's essay "Criticism as Art." Bruns noted the following: "Unquestionably an *homme grave*. Wilde is quite serious about his paradoxes; his is no easy task, that of raising himself above himself. And yet *what* he proclaims is truly a gospel worth hearing. The transformation of the artistic into critical creation."[40] As Greve presented J.C.C. Bruns with his translations, Max Bruns was already prepared to place Wilde's works alongside a series of works he greatly respected by Charles Baudelaire and Gustave Flaubert and which he had either already translated and published or was in the process of having prepared.[41] Bruns was thus in a position to publish Wilde and required little convincing, especially since the competition was already in sight. Hedwig Lachmann, a noted translator and writer who had participated in Bruns's Poe edition (which included her translation of Poe's poems), was preparing a joint translation of three plays by Wilde with her future husband, the writer and radical socialist Gustav Landauer. It would appear in 1904.[42] Their translation of Wilde's *Salomé* was already available in 1902 in a pre-print edition published in the *Wiener Rundschau*; it would be published by Insel in 1903. If J.C.C. Bruns was to profit from the developing interest in Wilde, then haste was of the essence.

Felix Paul Greve appeared as the right man for the task. Not only did he offer assurances in writing that he, "with authorization of the Wilde estate…was in possession of a general authorization for the posthumous works of Oscar Wilde," but further comments seemed to indicate that he was well informed of the conditions regarding both Wilde publications and English publishing practices in general. Moreover, he seemed to have the authorization of the copyright holders. His proposed translations would be based on five privately printed volumes published by the Ormond Press. A remark made to Bruns revealed not only his knowledge of financial conditions but also that small sums of money were important to him. This was in contrast to the wealthy Wolfskehl, to whom he had remarked: "For this authorization I have paid the sum of 5 pounds per volume."[43] For someone who no longer had a fixed source of income, twenty-five pounds sterling was not an insignificant sum of money. Greve undoubtedly indicated as much to the publisher not simply to demonstrate his authorization as a translator but also to seek compensation as quickly as possible. Unfortunately, the exclusive translation rights were not forthcoming, since English bankruptcy law dictated that Wilde's estate be settled by the courts. Thus it was up to the publisher himself to determine the required speed and reliability of the translation, as well as the desired literary quality. Basically, the books were available to anyone who wanted to publish them. The ability to go into production quickly became apparent in texts which were presented and contextualized before agreement had been reached: "Of these works, one has already been translated into German, 'Das Bildnis des Mr. W.H./The Portrait of Mr. W.H.' (a study of Shakespeare disguised in the form of an engaging novella). I intend to release it together with Oscar Wilde's aphorisms regarding art, poetry and the production of books in a volume of six sheets." And what of Wilde's other works already in translation? Greve refers to them immediately:

> Of the other works by Wilde to appear in German translation: Salome (well translated)[,] Dorian Gray (minus the excellent preface which is perhaps the most important thing Wilde wrote; very poorly translated; published by Max Spohr in Leipzig). A new edition of Dorian Gray would be important and desirable.

In short, Lachmann's translation of *Salomé* could not be hindered; besides, it had already received positive reviews. But perhaps he would attempt it nonetheless. Wilde's central work, *The Picture of Dorian Gray*, although already available, would have to be completed and given new life by Greve. To be on the safe side, he prepared an article on Gaulke's translation which would justify his new translation.

Firm of tone, precise in judgement and in possession of all the facts in his relations with Bruns, Greve had taken the initiative as if he were an editor for the publisher and not a translator in search of work. Market research, evaluation and production seemed to be united in him. A contract for five volumes, including *Salomé*, was prepared and signed.

◆ GETTING UNDERWAY

During the first months of intensive contact with his new publisher, Greve also continued in his Munich role as a protégé of George and Wolfskehl. He courted Helene Klages and undertook journeys both by himself and in the company of Kilian. Greve spent April of 1902 in Dresden where he underwent a "long examination by my doctor."[44] He wrote to Wolfskehl of a "festering wound" which was healing; he also stated that he had suffered this "condition" in the previous year but that "thanks to [his] otherwise perfectly strong and healthy constitution" was able to report "considerable improvement." It is never made clear precisely what the nature of this illness was, although he did state that it required "total abstinence from alcohol" and "continued moderation in his lifestyle." Apparently, young Greve had been not only preoccupied by high thinking but also by high living. While in Dresden, Felix stayed in the modern and expensively decorated Hotel Continental "vis-à-vis" the train station. Who was his doctor? Was it the senior medical officer Kilian, Herman's father, who may also have helped him to avoid military service? Did Greve take the opportunity to meet with Koch and Koch's parents? Whatever his movements in Dresden, he planned to see his "English tailor," who most certainly must have been Kilian's tailor, as is evident in the photographs from Bonn. So attired, as he wrote to Wolfskehl from Gardone on August 13, he could be taken for an Englishman; indeed, he might even be mistaken for Oscar Wilde himself.

That Greve also used the April 1902 journey to promote the publication of his books is apparent from the letters he wrote during the period. In Leipzig, he took the opportunity to acquaint himself with the centre of the German publishing industry and book market. He then travelled on to Berlin where he stayed in the Grand Hôtel de Rome. There, he visited August Endell and his wife Else in the suburb of Zehlendorf and dined with Botho Graef. Apparently Kilian had provided him with a considerable amount of money, and Felix made liberal use of it. During his trip, Greve made the rounds of "all the antiquarian and used book dealers in Dresden and Berlin," and wrote to Wolfskehl that he was bringing "the treasures of India to Munich — manuscripts and unbelievably rare books." They must have cost an enormous sum of money, for he was forced to wait "a few months with the furnishing of [his] apartment." It appears that Greve intended to establish himself in Munich for a longer period of time — in the expectation of marrying Helene Klages — and thus had given up his room, then in the Pension Gisela. It can be assumed that Greve's furnishings were as expensive as the books. It is not clear, however, whether he intended to rely on anticipated incomes as a translator alone. During this trip he occupied himself with business matters regarding publishing. He negotiated with Otto von Holten concerning issues of book production and was able to inform Wolfskehl that "[his] play [*Helena und Damon*] was going to be printed by him after all on expensive Japan [paper]," adding that "it's going to be a typographical work of art."

Greve was not concerned only with the formal appearance of his works, but also with a planned edition in collaboration with Wolfskehl (and perhaps others). For this, he was able to report, the Holten publishing house had produced an estimate of costs and a trial sheet for a prospective series of "monumental editions...without obligation on our part." The "artistic" design of *Wanderungen* and *Helena und Damon* may thus signal more than the imitation of the appearance of Stefan George's (or Max Bruns's) books. The "monumentality" of the proposed editions would also have been modelled in part on William Morris's production of expensive and aesthetically designed books, still very influential internationally. ("Masterpieces of

World Literature" would be the name of the J.C.C. Bruns series which Greve would help to develop two years later as an editor and translator of English and French authors.) This may have been the source of Greve's meeting with August Endell, a man also inspired by the famous English author and book designer. He had developed a reputation not only as an architect but also as an art dealer and the creator of such unusual, Nietzschean designs as the "Court-Atelier Elvira," Anita Augspurg's and Sophia Goudstikker's well-known "Photographic Institute" in Munich (Buddensieg, *Endell* 232; 239; Wilhelm, *Bohème* 115–23). Greve may have seen furnishings designed by Endell and presented at the Dresden Art Exhibition that spring. He may also have been familiar with the hall designed by Endell in Wertheim's huge Berlin department store and may have been interested in one of the designer's creations for himself (Reichel, *Endell* 116–17).

Despite all his activities in support of his own work and the work of others, Felix Greve still presented himself and his work in a manner advantageous to his reputation in the Bonn and Munich literary circles. To this end he would be greatly aided by brief proximity to Stefan George, who would soon declare that he was interested "now more than ever in translation," since he learned from language "that he had actually never created new words, but rather rediscovered old ones" (Seekamp et al., *Stefan George* 161).[45] From the end of March until the end of April 1902, George made his home, at times with his friend the Dutch poet Albert Verwey, at 15 Giselastrasse in Munich where Greve also lived. It is unclear whether George and Verwey lived in separate rooms on the fourth floor of the pension or stayed with Greve. As Greve was to be away on a trip for two weeks in April, he may have offered his rooms to George. At any rate, during the period before and after his journey to Leipzig, Dresden and Berlin, he could often have joined the gatherings of George, Verwey and the Klageses, as well as Schuler and the Derleth siblings, assuming they were not held in Greve's rooms. Dülberg's April 22 invitation to Greve and the Klageses, the day after Greve's return and George's return trip to Bingen, may have been part of this intensive exchange (Seekamp et al., *Stefan George* 123). Perhaps Greve was in attendance on April 8 with other members of the group during a reading of George's poems by the actress Ria Claassen in the Banquet Hall at the Bayerische Hof hotel (Seekamp et al., *Stefan George* 121–24). Whatever Greve's precise movements, increasing familiarity with the George circle is certain. In May, after his return, Greve corresponded with Delbrueck, his acquaintance from Bonn and Rome.[46] While in Bingen, he discussed an English translation of poems from *Teppich des Lebens* with the master. (George had sent the volume to England as "the fruit of his memories" of the Giselastrasse in Munich.) Lastly, during Greve's return trip from Paris to

Bonn, where he likely stayed with Kilian, he reported on George's proposed changes to the translation.[47] George learned that Greve's "stay in Paris was quite productive, despite its brevity." Unfortunately, the exact nature of this productivity is not recorded. On one occasion, as he wrote to George in June, he returned with, "among other treasures, a bout of pleurisy."[48]

Greve undoubtedly purchased expensive books in Paris, but we do not know whether he formed any literary contacts. Frederick Philip Grove reported that in his youth he was familiar with a number of famous French poets: "By that time I was more or less intimate with such people as Henri de Régnier, Jules Renard, Herédia, Mallarmé, and others. I was at least in touch with Verlaine and Rimbaud" (ISM 163). Of these, Herédia, Régnier and Renard were still alive in 1902. Whatever the actual purpose of his visit to Paris, Greve (like Thomas Mann's fictitious con-man Felix Krull) occupied a room in the luxurious Hotel St. James & Albany in May 1902. Grove would later proudly remember the luxurious European hotels he had frequented—the Hotel de Rome and the Hotel St. James & Albany, as well as several "Hôtels de l'Europe."

Back in Munich and still confined to bed, Greve sent Stefan George his "little wedding play" in early June, which had in the meantime appeared in its "capricious form."[49] The master's reaction is not known, although it couldn't have escaped the notice of some Munich readers that the author, who had already made plans for expensive apartment furnishings, had a liaison with a certain "Helena" in mind. While still a convalescent, Felix Greve continued work on his translation of Wilde's *Dorian Gray* and prepared a "pamphlet" in which he would attack Johannes Gaulke's unfortunate translation as a justification for his own. In a letter to Wolfskehl, Greve criticized Gaulke for quaintly translating the name "Prince Charming" as *Prince Lobesam*. Three weeks later he suggested *Märchenprinz* (an obvious solution) as the correct translation and asked Wolfskehl for his opinion. At the same time, he extended greetings from Karl Gustav Vollmoeller, who had just published his drama *Catharina* [*von Armagnac*], and promised on the following day to get around to doing some "photographing."[50] Everything seemed to be proceeding well. Greve appeared to have "arrived," with his future as a man of letters in the bohemian world of avant-garde Munich assured. His liberal investment in borrowed money had paid off rather handsomely.

Overall, the success of the period was characterized by excellent personal relationships with creditors, writers and publishers—so much so that Felix Greve would look back in October and refer to it as the "happiest year" of his life.[51] Greve's incredible ability to get things done seemed, at least for a few weeks, capable of contributing to the financial underpinnings of his future plans. On July 17, Felix sent "a package insured for 1000 marks with the manuscript ready for the printer" to J.C.C. Bruns. It was his translation of *Dorian Gray*. Around the same time, his pamphlet on Gaulke, which has not survived, must also have been sent to the Munich *Allgemeine Zeitung*, where he had published occasional pieces in the Sunday supplement since 1901 (see GG 194–95). With the assurance that printing would soon follow, Greve referred his publisher to the "prefatory remarks" which he had included with the manuscript, and which, he claimed, "justified" his work. At the same time, he requested that "final payment" be made to his account with the "Bavarian branch of the Deutsche Bank, Munich." This mundane detail is noteworthy because in his novel *Fanny Essler* Greve would also refer to his bank—evidence, as Herbert Koch suggested, of the all-too-thinly veiled (auto-)biographical revelations of that novel (FE 397).

Precisely half a year had passed since Greve's first letter to J.C.C. Bruns. A substantial portion of the Wilde translation was already in the hands of the publisher or was soon to be finished. It was now time for new plans, time also to turn his attention to his own writing and translation projects. Greve's pamphlet on Gaulke strengthened his resolve to try his hand at more criticism; he suggested to Bruns "a little volume of studies of English decadence (particularly Wilde and Beardsley) and their parallels in Germany." For this volume he could have used the expensive edition of Aubrey Beardsley's works which he had mentioned the previous year to Wolfskehl. Wilde could have been discussed in relation to the George circle and perhaps even Greve's own poems and his "play." Greve's approach was meticulously planned out and had its own inner logic. "[A] translation of the prose works of Ernest Dowson" would be undertaken which would have placed Greve alongside George as a Dowson translator. George, Greve reported, had translated poems by Dowson "and indeed excellently"; they were to appear "soon with the Bondi publishing house."[52] J.C.C. Bruns appears not to have been impressed by this suggestion, with its accompanying name-dropping, and declined the proposal. Greve's Dowson volume was soon published by Insel, in an elegantly bound numbered edition. Max Bruns, it should be added, had attempted as early as 1898 to publish his work in *Blätter für die Kunst*, although he then enjoyed as little success as Greve did in the summer of 1902.[53] In 1902 Bruns *fils* saw himself as a rival to George, if not exclusively as a poet, then as a translator of Baudelaire's works and verse by Mallarmé, Verlaine and Rimbaud (Martens, *Bruns* 23). Two and a half decades later, contemporaries of his would rank him together with Richard Dehmel and Stefan George.[54]

Felix Paul Greve then attempted to tie together an edition which would contain the one-act play *Salomé* and Wilde's "social comedies" in one volume. It could potentially be followed by "three additional" volumes. A "single volume" with the one-act play would also be possible. In making these suggestions, Greve emphasized his independence as he had done before. He made an offer and confidently proposed how to proceed in case of rejection: "Should my offer not be to your convenience, then I respectfully request the immediate return of my manuscript."[55] Whatever the fruits of these negotiations, Greve was going to have his hands full. He had manuscripts to complete and to send off and still others to begin; he was also pressed by preparations for his trip to Lake Garda, where he intended to reside from July 23 until August 14.

◆ GARDONE-RIVIERA

In Gardone, Greve took lodgings in the Pension Häberlin, perhaps, as previously discussed, in the company of Helene Klages. Given the typical layout of the Pension, it would have been difficult to share a room with her. Perhaps this is the reason why Greve had to wait before the door of his unmarried companion, as Freytag-Loringhoven somewhat gleefully reported later. Judging from his wide-ranging correspondence, however, Greve was not bored during this period, regardless of possible romantic involvements. While in Gardone he rushed letters to J.C.C. Bruns in Minden, Dülberg on vacation in Scheveningen, Wolfskehl at his parents' in Darmstadt and, for the first time, to the new Insel house in Leipzig.[56] And although he thought himself in need of rest, "as I feel very overworked," he took Wilde's plays along with him to translate. On August 2 he sent off the manuscript for *The Ideal Husband* and *The Importance of Being Earnest* (although in a letter to Wolfskehl the following day he reported that he was still translating what he then called the "Importance of Being Called Ernst"). He then announced the start of his work on two additional volumes of plays and the impending arrival of his prose manuscripts for Wilde's stories *The Portrait of Mr. W.H.*, *Lord Arthur Savile's Crime* and *The Priest and the Acolyte*.[57] At the same time he read the corrections and chose the paper for the special edition of *Intentions*. By the middle of August his publisher was in possession of five Wilde manuscripts in Greve's translation; a sixth, the second drama volume, was to follow.[58] There could not have been much in the way of rest and relaxation, given his "fourteen-hour work days." Yet Greve was not in Gardone to rest. He had other, more pressing interests.

Above all, his concerns centred on Helene Klages, his planned "furnishings" and perhaps the sum of money which was to be paid, or already had been paid, to others, possibly to Ludwig Klages. With the delivery of his manuscripts, Felix certainly had a claim to money; it would seem that he needed it badly. The nonchalance which he had thus far displayed was at an end. As he reported to Wolfskehl, pressure was being created not simply because he was "the victim of a *borsagnolo* or pick-pocket" who had stolen "his cheque book and approximately 200 lire." His financial needs appear to have extended beyond the return of this comparatively small sum.[59] As he wrote to Bruns:

> I would like to present you with an important request. Due to considerable losses to my modest capital, I find myself in a position where I will require a substantial sum of money by the 15th of September. Should all of my manuscripts be accepted, I would like to ask you to alter the contract regarding these five volumes (c. 70–80 sheets) such that I receive payment of 1800 marks before September 15 and the rest upon appearance of the final volume of the five. Were you able to fulfil my request I would be eternally thankful and in a position peacefully to continue my work on the Wilde translations.[60]

Even considering the costs of travelling on the North-South Express, the rental of pension rooms and the costs of living and further travel expenses, one thousand eight hundred marks was then a very large sum of money. And yet Greve seems to have needed the money desperately. Perhaps ten thousand marks (or even a less impressive-sounding figure) had already gone to the brother of "the girl." Occasional further expenditures were sure to arise as he had no intention of remaining anonymous in virtuous poverty. In Gardone he liked to be taken for an eccentric Englishman (likely in imitation of Kilian), indeed as Oscar Wilde himself to a naïve Berliner, maliciously reporting gossip about fictional figures such as "Schopenhauer's wife and Nietzsche's son." He sat "in the sole café and agitatedly discussed politics" and undertook a spectacular "nine-hour swimming tour across the lake and back." Inconspicuous he certainly wasn't. Despite his uninterrupted work, he no longer felt sick. Rather, he claimed not at all jokingly that one would have found it difficult to compete with his prowess.[61] Quite in contrast to his own occasional claims, Greve's boasts of health and strength are far less astounding than his habit of presenting himself as overly sensitive and even neurasthenic.

Excursions motivated by literary matters also took place during this holiday. The train trip to Gardone would have served for more than rest and uninterrupted translation work. One of the most highly regarded poets of Italian decadence, Gabriele D'Annunzio, was known to occasionally stay in Gardone. D'Annunzio's prose tragedy *La Città Morta* would certainly have attracted the attention of Greve and his friends. Produced first in 1898 in Paris and then in 1901 in Mailand (with Eleonora Duse), the play appeared in German translation the same year. *La Cittá Morta* was comprised of precisely that mixture of philological-mystical erudition, archaeological topicality, yearning for death and lyrically expressed sensitivity that attracted Ernst Hardt, Karl Gustav Vollmoeller and Felix Paul Greve—along with André Gide and his protagonists of the period. The play is set in Mycenae, which Schliemann had excavated (and where Dörpfeld dug), with Sophocles's *Antigone* providing the classical point of reference (in tune with the contemporary topicality of the story of the Atreides). Indeed, Greve felt that— perhaps because of classical allusions—an Italian translation of his *Wanderungen* would provide it with the necessary popularity back home. He may even have seen his "marriage play" *Helena und Damon* as part of the poetic theatre which D'Annunzio successfully produced with his next work, *Francesca da Rimini*. Staged in December 1901, it had just appeared in Mailand. Vollmoeller, known to Greve since his time in Bonn, would become the translator of the 1903 German version—possibly following a suggestion from George, who first had been approached by S. Fischer publishing house regarding the translation (Vignazia, *D'Annunzio* 297). According to a letter to Wolfskehl, Felix Greve visited Vollmoeller in Mailand during his vacation. The possibility that Greve also visited D'Annunzio and not just his translator cannot be excluded. Indeed, he may even have travelled with one or both to Verona.[62] Such a meeting would have brought together three authors, all of whom were interested in archaeology and philology. Vollmoeller's acquaintance with D'Annunzio and his translation of *Francesca da Rimini* was probably indebted to the appearance of his play *Catharina Gräfin von Armagnac* (*Catharina Countess of Armagnac*) in 1903. Again, the work of literary translation is closely related to the composition of literature. After his "wedding play," however, Greve himself no longer produced works in the style of poetic theatre but dedicated himself to the translation of drama.

Stefan George also translated D'Annunzio, so Greve's vacation at Lake Garda in northern Italy may have been a pilgrimage in the footsteps of the master. Following his return from Gardone, Greve finally felt in a position to make, via Wolfskehl as middleman, the decisive literary move for which he had so long been preparing himself. After making reference to several unfortunately unnamed "Italian products," he wrote:

> I would like to ask of you, when I ought to send my manuscr. to Mr. George in order to increase the prospect of seeing one or the other of my verslets in Bl[ätter für die Kunst]. This is <u>very</u> important to me. And yet my head is so full of other projects that I am putting it off as long as possible.[63]

Here too, Greve purposefully discouraged the impression that his poems were all that mattered to him—that recognition through publication in *Blätter* was his ultimate goal. He offered his Browning edition to Wolfskehl thus: "I don't need it anymore and will let it go cheap." He indicated in passing that he was having "a bit of a row" with Bruns and that he "was in the process of negotiating with three other publishers. Wilde he has for sure. Mi dispiace."[64] He led Wolfskehl to believe that the "row" resulted from the production quality of his *Intentions*, which was to appear at "the end of September." A row was not the only reason he had approached other publishers, specifically Insel, for his Dowson and Browning translations and Gose & Tetzlaff for his short book on Wilde. He offered his Dowson translations to Insel in a letter to von Poellnitz, the manager (until January 1905), before he had heard anything definitive from Bruns regarding possible payments. Besides, he had absolutely no hope of receiving the sizeable sum of money he so impatiently awaited from his publisher. On July 17, he had received four hundred and fifty marks from Bruns in Minden, money which probably allowed him to proceed with his trip to Italy. We also know that, according to his contract with J.C.C. Bruns, an agreement had been made whereby he was to receive 30 marks per printed manuscript page. When Greve so urgently requested the 1800 marks before September 15 on August 2, he estimated that the five Wilde volumes, comprising "ca. 70–80 pages," would earn between 2,100 and 2,400 marks. However, when one subtracts the payments already made from the requested advance of 1,800 marks, then the rest to be paid upon receipt of the final volume amounts to little more than 150 marks. Bascially, Greve had requested the entire honorarium owed to him by Bruns, even though he had not seen the galley proofs for *Intentions* nor yet sent the remainder of the translations, which were posted on August 7. While Bruns was occupied with proofreading the manuscripts and with calculating the payments, Greve was angered about not receiving the remaining payment immediately. Nevertheless, his abilities as a negotiator with Bruns enabled him to demand from Insel—and later receive—40 marks per page of translation, an unusually large amount.

Greve's financial obligations would become ever more pressing from the beginning of September onward. Regardless, he still hoped to earn money from the subscriptions for the special pre-publication edition of *Intentions*, for which he had prepared a special notice. The unspecified "number of pre-publication volumes on Dutch paper" would cost 12 marks per book. (Bruns's books usually cost between 2 and 3 marks, Insel books somewhat more, with only limited special editions going much beyond that.) The rather hefty price could be paid "via pre-arranged payment or upon delivery."[65] Since his beautifully produced *Helena und Damon* had been positively received by the

George circle, Greve hoped that he would also succeed with the pre-publication edition of *Intentions*, which displayed the expensive tastes he was counting on. Nevertheless, and despite the high aesthetic demands of his customers, he was clever enough in his tight financial situation not to sell to them on credit.

Looking back upon Greve's poetry and translations during this period, Else von Freytag-Loringhoven describes, in her usual, refreshingly penetrating manner, the way in which they were intended "to impress the 'circle' on the surface—but hitting it by stealth on the sore spot of its utter artificiality." That Greve had from the very beginning merely imitated the stylistic and linguistic features of this type of poetry, as Freytag-Loringhoven suggests, "to prove how easily this poetical sleight-of-hand game could be imitated by any apt, learned, linguistically gifted person with wit, intellect and rhythmical feeling" may be read as a later interpretation coloured by his subsequent separation from the George circle. At the same time, however, Greve's approach throughout 1902 clearly shows that he wished to use the favour of the circle to his own financial ends. Once again, an observation by Freytag-Loringhoven mercilessly captures the combination of extravagance, self-importance and conceit that was at play: "The most impressive part of this kind of poetry is paper, print and numbered privacy. It stood for the topnotch culture. Only who could afford it was truly cultured" (BE 161–62).[66]

In the days and weeks before Greve's return from Lake Garda, a combination of pressing matters led to a dramatic decline in his financial, professional and personal situation. This untimely confluence would eventually lead to a crisis and, in October, another flight from a difficult financial situation—his fourth after departures from Hamburg, Rome and Bonn. A pattern had emerged which extended back to his days as a student in Hamburg. He had orchestrated an impressive feat of labour in a short period of time to garner money and prestige. In this instance, however, the prestige was based on presumed or temporary wealth and was meant to ensure entrance into a literary circle. Once admitted, Greve could use his nonchalant industriousness to secure the status he sought as poet, critic and husband of the sister of a respected member of the circle. Greve was certainly correct in recognizing that it would be his financial "power" which would allow him entrance into the circle where he could then employ the power of his mind; and yet he still overestimated his ability to work and to earn. As the money came to an end late in the summer of 1902, many other matters also drew to a close. Freytag-Loringhoven correctly diagnosed the cause of Greve's failure in 1901 and 1902: "a poet had to have money—or his father had to have and indulge his cultured son—or he had to have friends with this precious commodity—or such whose fathers had—and flung it at the cultured disciple of the cultured word prestidigitator..." (BE 162).[67] It is quite possible that Greve's friend Herman Kilian, himself the son of a rich father, had stopped generously providing for his friend's material needs as a result of Greve's intention to marry.

For a while, however, the hope that everything would turn out well, that the goal would be reached and that the overdrawn resources would suffice after all, seemed plausible enough. J.C.C. Bruns transferred 1000 marks in partial payment of the honoraria for *Intentions* and *Dorian Gray* in time to meet Greve's deadline of September 15, as Greve confirmed in a letter on the same day. The day before, he had written that he was "at the point of suing Bruns." Bruns undoubtedly looked upon the matter with a cooler eye, for a review of the number of printed pages, according to which payment was to be made, had revealed that Greve had made a mistake in calculation to his advantage; he had used the smaller format of the English editions in making his estimate of costs. Unlike Insel, J.C.C. Bruns was not prepared to pay 30 marks per page for drama translations, the same fee Greve had received for Wilde's prose pieces. They agreed on 25 marks per page for the first 1000 copies, still a good price. In addition, Greve was to receive twenty percent of the net returns on all further sales as well as an advance of 150 marks from the base payment. All in all, this was a potentially profitable arrangement, although for Greve it seemed only just, for "precisely with the dramas" it was especially difficult "to translate into German the dialogue which was to a large extent comprised of epigrams." The greater time commitment, which the translator complained of, would at least be partially compensated for by the much smaller number of lines per page and printed sheet.

◆ GREAT EXPECTATIONS

Felix Greve was able to secure the amount he desired in this case. Even in his difficult financial straits, he appeared to have negotiated with particular success, since he had retained the stage rights and would therefore receive all the income from them.[68] The theatre seemed to allow him to win profit and prestige through his translations. The extent of Greve's hopes and expectations for the stage is apparent in a whole series of optimistic and increasingly excited announcements he made during the period. They are perhaps most evident in the context of a remark, both memorable and unintentionally funny, that he made on a postcard to Wolfskehl immediately after his return from Gardone and the completion of his drama translations: "This winter I will astound the entire world and still hope to be able to come to Darmstadt."[69] Whether Greve met Wolfskehl remains unknown, but the

Vom Übersetzer erschienen:
Wanderungen, Gedichte.
Helena und Damon, ein Spiel in Versen.
(Beides bei J. Littauer, München.)
Übertragungen (zum Teil in Vorbereitung):
Oscar Wilde:
Fingerzeige.
Das Bildnis Dorian Grays.
Salome.
Studien und Erzählungen.
Dramen. Band I: Lady Windermeres Fächer.
　　　Eine Frau ohne Bedeutung.
　　Band II: Der ideale Ehemann.
　　　Bunbury.
Ein Haus von Granaten (im Insel-Verlag).

OSCAR WILDE

DRAMEN

DEUTSCH
VON
FELIX PAUL GREVE.

*

BAND II:

DER IDEALE EHEMANN
BUNBURY

J. C. C. BRUNS' VERLAG
HERZOGL. SÄCHS. UND FÜRSTL. SCHWARZB.-LIPP. HOF-VERLAGSBUCHHANDLUNG
MINDEN IN WESTF.

⋇ *Oscar Wilde,* Dramen, *vol. II (1902), title page left and title page right*

attention of a larger audience could only be obtained via stage performances and public acclaim.

It cannot be said with certainty who provided Greve with connections to the theatre or who drew attention to his translations of Wilde's plays. It can be assumed, however, that the tremendous success enjoyed by Lachmann's fine translation of *Salomé,* of which Greve himself reported, was one of the sources for his optimism. Greve's acquaintance with the respected actor Robert Nhil could not have hurt; and August Endell, who built Ernst von Wolzogen's Kleines Theater in Berlin, was perhaps able to smooth the way. Felix himself seems to have suspected someone else of providing him with the attention—namely, Wolfskehl, to whom he had just announced that he would "astound the world" that winter:

Dear Doctor!

I completely forgot to inform you of the further events I have planned for this winter. For the last couple of days I have been besieged by half a dozen theatres regarding Wilde. I would like to know who put them onto me. They are all talking about me as the "known" translator and the "leading expert" (literally from Berlin!) on the writer. Io non capisco. Lei?[70]

If it was not Wolfskehl or J.C.C. Bruns who put the theatres onto Greve, then perhaps it was August Endell, Ernst Hardt or Karl Gustav Vollmoeller, all of whom had theatrical ambitions, although according to Greve's fictionalization of this period, Endell was more the protégé of Greve than the other way around.[71] Vollmoeller's *Catharina* was still waiting to be staged.

Whether there were really "half a dozen theatres" interested in Greve's translations can no longer be verified, although there were indeed at least two, as he wrote to Bruns: "In Hamburg and Berlin they intend to stage Wilde's drama [not *Salomé* but rather the social dramas], and thus have turned to me."[72] He requested the temporary return of his manuscripts so that copies could be made for the theatres, which could only "serve the interests of (their) project." Bruns complied with Greve's wishes. Greve nevertheless continued to report to Wolfskehl of "trouble with Bruns," with whom he "had to do everything himself at the last moment" and who, he claimed, caused him difficulties because neither the proper paper size nor sufficient type were in stock. In this Greve had in fact touched upon one of his publisher's weak spots. J.C.C. Bruns produced its books in its own printing and binding facility, which was often an advantage but also a disadvantage when the plant was busy with a job that brought in more money. Publishers such as Insel, on the other hand, were able to seek out printers with adequate facilities and time and which were thus best suited for any given job.

"Each theatre wants a new play to stage and requires translations of me," Greve complained. "Where am I to get them?" Unfortunately, these people seemed "so unbelievably unreasonable" that they "think I am able to translate a four-act drama in an afternoon."[73] Greve was not able to do this because he was not Oscar Wilde himself, as the Berlin tourist in Gardone had believed, and he was soon to tell the theatre people, "I do not know Wilde." In short, Greve was suffering from the torments of the successful and very busy. It is of little wonder, then, that he would soon try his own hand at drama, as the theatre had come to occupy such a central position in his life. By this time he had already become something of a literary institution. With pride he reported of "4 copyists" that he had "employed." At the same time, moreover, he was preparing a collection of poems for *Blätter für die Kunst* and directing his thoughts to other areas of activity: "If Mr. Koch and Mr. Salz were here, I would have them work for me."[74]

This time, Greve's rate of production was able to keep pace with his optimism. The Berlin premiere of *The Importance of Being Earnest* was on September 29 and he planned to attend.[75] *Intentions* was now ready.[76] The translation of *Dorian Gray* would also appear at the end of September and there was hope that Insel would issue translations of Dowson, Browning and Wilde's fairy tales, which Bruns did not want. J.C.C. Bruns would deliver

Wilde's plays and along with them a little book by Greve intended as an introductory essay to Wilde's "The Portrait of Mr. W.H.," but which would first go to press separately as *Randarabesken zu Oskar Wilde*. Everything seemed to be culminating perfectly. Greve's dry spell had ended. Now he was in a position to mention his publisher in Leipzig to Bruns in Minden and to demonstrate his growing independence. Indeed, now that "the excitement concerning these things was great," he could urge the publication of "all Wilde's remaining works," which would, of course, be offered first to Bruns—"always to you first." As the tone of his letters betrays, Felix now felt himself in a position where he could openly play his publishers off against one another; he no longer felt the need to negotiate in secrecy.[77] The prospect of money and publicity encouraged him again to plan excursions to Dresden ("to my tailor, as I'm going about in rags") and Leipzig ("because of the gentlemen in publishing") during his trip to Berlin, as he wrote to Wolfskehl, whom he now also informed that the trip to "Darmstadt was uncertain." Indeed, the prospect of earning money had him mentioning to Wolfskehl, only half-ironically in passing, that he was busy, not with proofreading, but with "transactions on the stock-market."[78]

The heady final days of August were followed by a dampening of prospects by the middle of September. He briefly noted that the "premiere of Wilde's *Importance of Being Earnest*" would not take place until "the first week of October in Berlin." Missing now is all talk of Hamburg or the other four theatres in Germany which, as he had claimed, had been clamouring for his translation work. Nevertheless, "a production of *A Woman of No Importance* was likely to take place on several German stages."[79] Clearly he was still expecting to enjoy numerous popular successes with Wilde's plays. Furthermore, he wrote to Wolfskehl that finally "4 entire comedies and tragedies by Wilde in at least passable translation by one Mr. F.P.G. were ready." This is the first example of Greve's self-stylization using his initials as a signature. This form of external self-address would later characterize the Canadian identity of "Mr. F.P.G."

In the letters which remain, Felix Paul Greve no longer makes specific reference to stage production dates, nor does he name any theatres other than the vaguely identified Berliner Haus (the Deutsches Theater?). He reported to Bruns that copies had been made of one of the plays there (probably *The Importance of Being Earnest*, which he referred to as *Bunbury*), before he returned the manuscript to the publisher. Upon the return of the Wilde translation, Max Bruns took the opportunity to comment on Wilde's style and those works by Wilde which had thus far appeared in Bruns's program or were in the process of being printed. Bruns observed their appropriateness for the house's new catalogue, noting that *Intentions* "at least read well" and that it showed "the aesthetic approach to art of Baudelaire=Poe and Flaubert." Like his translator Greve, he was less than assured of the success of the comedies as written texts. Rather, he emphasized the specificity of Wilde's particular tone and thus the critical importance of delivery during dramatic performance:

> Of the two comedies, I like "The Ideal Husband" only in some parts (and in some parts not)—"Bunbury" was made for the gallery...What empty sham in his dramas—and precisely there in "The Ideal Husband;" there where emotional notes ought to be felt, he completely fails...Wilde probably didn't speak any differently than his Gilbert. And yet what a difference between reading it and hearing it spoken with emotion![80]

◆ FEUDS AMONG THE LITERATI

Felix Greve also expressed himself as a literary critic during the last days of September. To Wolfskehl he wrote critically of Kuno Zwymann's study of George.[81] Choosing not to let the matter rest at that, he also added: "You know, I can't understand Klages's book either." Written by Helene Klages's brother, the book on George which Greve was referring to (dated 1902) had been in circulation since December 1901 (Seekamp et al., *George* 1901). Greve's criticism of Zwymann's book was exaggerated: "How is it possible to write a prose book in which only the verses"—George's—"are good?" The difficulties Greve had in understanding Klages's book came at an unfortunate time, as George himself had defended it against an attack by Hugo von Hofmannsthal at the end of August 1902. Hofmannsthal in turn used Zwymann's book against Klages's:

> And yet I have to admit that in Klages's book about you, the expression, the ability to embody inner perceptions seems obviously lacking in terribly important places. Metaphors are present which I am endeavouring to forget. I would almost go so far to say that I find the almost obsessively rigid method employed by Mr. Zwymann on your work to be more appropriate and useful (Boehringer, *George-Hofmannsthal* 169–70).[82]

Whether he liked it or not, Greve was united with Hofmannsthal in his criticism of the arrogant, philosophically minded Klages, criticism which was only intensified through comparison with Zwymann's conventional philological approach. In parody of Zwymann, Greve went still further.

Facetiously writing to Wolfskehl that he intended "to shake out his heart" (instead of pouring it out), he made statements which could easily be misinterpreted: "But please forgive my mentioning these gentlemen in one breath: Klages-Zwymann. George-Schiller. Nietzsche-Kant. Aren't they three lovely oppositions? Probably not very complementary, certainly not complimentary." Had Klages or George known of these sentiments, their amusement would have been dampened only by their timing; they coincided with the polemic with Hofmannsthal.

What could have provoked these ambiguous statements? Greve must surely have known that they would probably be passed on, just as all his previous requests to Wolfskehl for access to *Blätter für die Kunst* were likewise passed on. Greve's ultimate goal was undoubtedly to attract attention by having himself compared with the authors of other works on George. Here, Greve's quarrel was less with Zwymann than with Klages. Otherwise, Greve undoubtedly intended to promote his study of George—"my George article"—which he had just mentioned. His interests were certainly not in being "complimentary" but in placing himself in the limelight. This applies as well to Greve the translator, who in a letter to Rudolf von Poellnitz from the same period offered the only translation of Walter Pater's *Marius the Epicurean* while criticizing a book by Paul Ernst (who worked for Insel) as mercilessly as he had savaged Zwymann's.[83]

Following the imminent developments in Greve's correspondence, it is apparent that a whole series of factors confronted Felix Greve, each of which would bear different results. *Dorian Gray* was ready, the Wilde dramas were being printed and copies were in the hands of actors in Berlin. *Randarabesken zu Oskar Wilde* and *The Portrait of Mr. W.H.* were done. Greve's translations of Pater's *Marius*, Dowson's *Dilemmas*, Wilde's *A House of Pomegranates* (which Greve still referred to as *Ein Haus von Granaten* [A House of Grenades]) and small pieces by Browning—each with Insel—were all awaiting publication. In numerous newspaper articles he presented himself as a literary critic. He was indeed being praised, as Wolfskehl assured him. Secretly, Greve would have felt himself a respected member of the George circle. He was close to Helene Klages, was considering establishing a household and was even approached on occasion for professional advice by the master himself. Financially, it is true, things were not so well ordered, but this was of secondary importance, since he felt confident that more money would soon arrive from a variety of sources.

And then, just at the moment when he hoped to win wide acclaim with the publication of an important book, he received the first of several bad tidings. It reached him from Minden one week after his translation of *The*

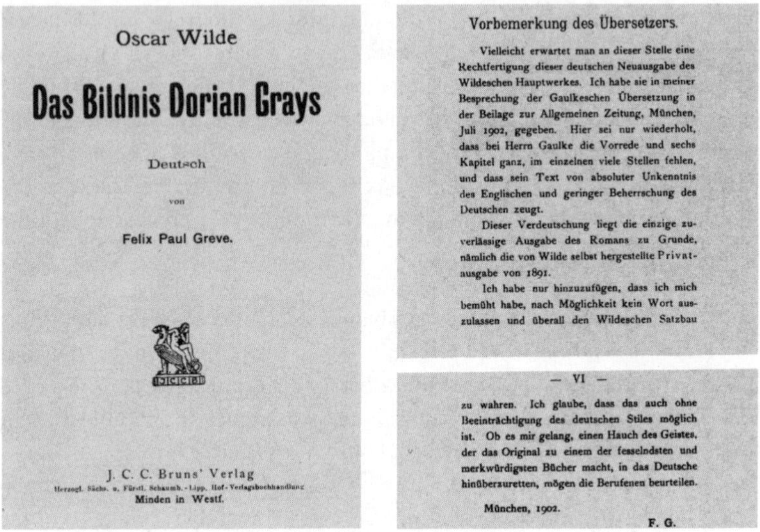

Oscar Wilde

Das Bildnis Dorian Grays

Deutsch

von

Felix Paul Greve.

J. C. C. Bruns' Verlag
Herzogl. Sächs. u. Fürstl. Schaumb.-Lipp. Hof-Verlagsbuchhandlung
Minden in Westf.

Vorbemerkung des Übersetzers.

Vielleicht erwartet man an dieser Stelle eine Rechtfertigung dieser deutschen Neuausgabe des Wildeschen Hauptwerkes. Ich habe sie in meiner Besprechung der Gaulkeschen Übersetzung in der Beilage zur Allgemeinen Zeitung, München, Juli 1902, gegeben. Hier sei nur wiederholt, dass bei Herrn Gaulke die Vorrede und sechs Kapitel ganz, im einzelnen viele Stellen fehlen, und dass sein Text von absoluter Unkenntnis des Englischen und geringer Beherrschung des Deutschen zeugt.

Dieser Verdeutschung liegt die einzige zuverlässige Ausgabe des Romans zu Grunde, nämlich die von Wilde selbst hergestellte Privatausgabe von 1891.

Ich habe nur hinzuzufügen, dass ich mich bemüht habe, nach Möglichkeit kein Wort auszulassen und überall den Wildeschen Satzbau

— VI —

zu wahren. Ich glaube, dass das auch ohne Beeinträchtigung des deutschen Stiles möglich ist. Ob es mir gelang, einen Hauch des Geistes, der das Original zu einem der fesselndsten und merkwürdigsten Bücher macht, in das Deutsche hinüberzuretten, mögen die Berufenen beurteilen.

München, 1902.

F. G.

⌘ *Oscar Wilde,* Das Bildnis Dorian Grays *(1903), title page and "Prefatory Remarks by the Translator"*

Picture of Dorian Gray was to have appeared. J.C.C. Bruns referred to a letter of complaint from Johannes Gaulke. At the very beginning of his business relations with Bruns, Greve had attacked Gaulke as a means of justifying his proposed new translation of Wilde's novel. This attack would now lead to troubled relations with Bruns. An additional cause of Bruns's wrath and Gaulke's outrage, which would cloud Greve's newly acquired prestige both commercially and publicly, is evident in the following remark from the first paragraphs of his "Prefatory Remarks by the Translator:"

> One might well expect here a justification of this new German edition of Wilde's central work. I have already offered it in my discussion of Gaulke's translation in the supplement to the *Allgemeine Zeitung*, Munich, July 1902. Here I only wish to restate that in Gaulke's translation the preface and all of six chapters have been omitted in whole or in part and that his text displays a total absence of knowledge of English and only limited command of German.[84]

Greve's daring and destructive comments on his predecessor would now come back to haunt him, regardless of how thoroughly he sought to justify them in letters to his publisher. Unfortunately for Greve, the article he had supposedly published in Munich's *Allgemeine Zeitung* was nowhere to be found: "For some reason unknown to me, my article, 'Translations from English' did not appear. I was expecting it as I wrote the preface to *Dorian Gray*." And yet that was in June and July. Was it believable that since then he had not noticed that his article had not appeared? During the reading of the galley proofs, he would have had the opportunity either to find out or to rewrite the preface. Thus a disastrous impression was left in the minds of readers and critics who had praised Gaulke's translation and who would now subject Greve to the very charges of carelessness and ignorance which he had so triumphantly pointed out in Gaulke. The repercussions would be felt as late as 1904 when the most important critic of the period was still drawing attention to the incident with biting censure:

> I must somewhat more thoroughly treat the case of the translator Felix Paul Greve. Bitterness moved him to take pen in hand—righteous indignation at Mr. Johannes Gaulke—who with his treatment of *Dorian Gray* had set a record in ignorance of English and mishandling of German. Thus Greve decided to offer a new and reverent translation of *The Picture of Dorian Gray*. Were style in German alone decisive in the evaluation of a translation—a view unfortunately adhered to by many a critic quick to speak—then one would not really have to censure Greve...A thorough sounding-out of Greve's knowledge of English, however, leads at times to very nasty disappointment (Meyerfeld, *Wilde* 542).[85]

Being lumped together with Gaulke must have resounded in Greve's ears. Unfortunately, Greve's "letter of self-justification" to J.C.C. Bruns contains passages—fortunately for him never publicized—which retain the distasteful stamp of opportunism. For Greve did not stop at merely emphasizing his privileged access to better source texts (which he purchased at great expense to himself):

> If Mr. Gaulke's translation has received positive criticism, this can only be explained by the fact that the rare and expensive original editions are as good as unknown in German (other than *Intentions*). I warned you of Mr. G. long before I even thought of translating Wilde...Worst of all, however, there are things in Mr. G.'s translation which are <u>not</u> in Wilde. For example, remarks which lead toward an emphasis on homosexuality, for which I could easily produce examples...Mr.

Gaulke's *Dorian Gray* translation, which appears to have been purposefully tailored for homosexual publication, was for me the first reason
to translate it myself.[86]

Gaulke undoubtedly was a cause of Greve's decision to translate Wilde. The
latter's image in Germany, insofar as he had one, was to a large part formed
by three of Gaulke's articles (1896, 1897, 1901) which preceded the translations of the novels. It would have been well nigh impossible not to take him
into consideration. It is nothing less than dishonesty on Greve's part—himself
emerging from a Munich literary milieu characterized by homosexuality—to
point out that Gaulke's translation of the homosexual Wilde were published
by Max Spohr's Kreisende Ringe house, in which books by homosexual
authors played a predominant role. It was Greve, after all, who first proposed
his Wilde translation to J.C.C. Bruns in collaboration with another man and
who emphasized his connections to the Schwabing literary milieu. Whether
Greve's vehement and public denouncement of homosexuals is to be taken
at face value or as a defensive posture remains open to question.

   This, however, was not the only bad news for Greve. Whether he knew it
or not, on September 3 George had already informed Gundolf that Greve's
poems would not be included in the sixth volume of *Blätter für die Kunst*.
Greve's selection "contained too little to serve as an introductory contribution" (Boehringer, *George-Gundolf* 120). Thus his efforts in the world of
poetry for almost an entire year were to end in vain. Greve's imitation of the
sumptuous language of George and his circle, the terrible expense of costly
paper, the luxuriously produced books—all this was simply "too little."
Perhaps in the end it wasn't original enough to distinguish him as an independent poet (and not simply a George epigone). He was, of course, no more
successful than other ephebes in emerging from the master's shadow to
display his own profile and gain the respect of George himself.

◆ PRIVATE PERFORMANCE

After Hardt and Vollmoeller had chalked up successes in the theatre, Greve
seemed assured of achieving something similar with Wilde. And yet during
the final three months of 1902, Greve's theatre project, which had begun so
promisingly, gradually lurched into difficulty. First the performances were
delayed, then they were threatened with cancellation. In the end, the publication of the two volumes of drama developed into an embarrassing and
expensive failure. It was soon apparent that the entire Wilde enterprise, as
promising as it had once appeared, was capable of extracting more emotional
and financial costs than could ever be returned. In his haste to succeed with

"his" Wilde against the competition presented by Gaulke, Lachmann and Baron von Teschenberg, Greve had not exercised the requisite caution with regard to the holders of the English rights. In fact, he had led his publisher to believe that he was in possession of the stage rights. In November, shortly after triumphantly announcing that he had "arranged" the distribution of *Bunbury* to the actors at the Deutsches Theater in Berlin, he assured the publisher—by now suspicious—that the question of authorization would soon be decided in his favour. J.C.C. Bruns certainly had reason for concern; the text editions intended for stage productions were already in print. In December, Greve was forced to inform his publisher that it was not he who had won the stage rights, but none other than Gaulke. The Deutsches Theater would be using Gaulke's translation.[87] Neither Greve's book version nor the stage texts were legal. The rights were in the possession of Albert Langen Publishers and the agent—the firm of Eduard Bloch—with whom Bruns and Greve would now have to negotiate. Perhaps the rights were still within reach. A deal might be struck with Bloch in the new year. A notice on the title page of the drama translations by Greve and published by Bruns indicated that the "stage rights in Germany" were to be "obtained from Eduard Bloch, Berlin, 1 Brüderstrasse." Despite this agreement, Langen nonetheless sold the publication rights not to Bruns but to Max Spohr's Kreisende Ringe house—the very publisher Greve had attacked for its supposed homosexual orientation. Thus the remaining dramas appeared with Spohr in von Teschenberg's translation.

But Greve's problems were still not over. His translation of *Salomé* would not be published either. With respect to authorization, Greve assured his publisher that he had been "the victim of an intrigue." With astounding *sang-froid* he went on to suggest that there would be no difficulties with *Intentions* or *Dorian Gray* and inquired whether Bruns would have any objections if he quoted passages from the novel in an article he was preparing on Wilde. Greve felt that this would provide excellent advertising; his publisher was less than enthusiastic.

On the contrary, J.C.C. Bruns felt betrayed. Two volumes containing four dramas and the individual stage editions were ready and yet would not be marketable for a long time or, at best, would only be sold after a delay and at a reduced profit. Accordingly, Felix Greve did not have to wait long for a response. Bruns's managing director, Heinrich Stiller, answered:

> Your letter of the 9th of the month concerning the question of dramas causes me deep regret, for a great deal of work has been done in vain. I miss in your letter any reference to, or suggestion regarding, how we

are to clarify the outstanding business between us. In this affair I have incurred expenses for both honorariums and the not inconsiderable printing costs and the matter cannot stand with your simple remark that the Deutsches Theater has answered negatively.[88]

What was to be done? It was unlikely that Greve would have had the money to repay J.C.C. Bruns. In vain he offered Bruns his translation of Pater's *Marius the Epicurean* as compensation, which Insel had already turned down (but finally published in 1908 in two volumes). Bruns kept the manuscript for a while as security. The firm simultaneously interrupted the typesetting of *Dorian Gray* and forced Greve, at least in this instance, to document his possession of the translation rights before completing the book. And since the publishing house was unable to sell the volumes of drama, Stiller coolly wrote to Greve informing him that they now belonged to the translator and that he could come by and pick them up. Greve thus found himself in a position similar to that of Henry David Thoreau, who said of himself that his library contained 706 of his own books (out of the thousand published copies of *A Week on the Concord and Merrimack Rivers*).[89] Greve, however, never stored his books in his room or attempted to sell them himself, as Stiller also suggested. While negotiating with the Deutsches Theater—ultimately in vain—Greve was nevertheless able to have *Bunbury*, along with a translation of *Salomé* (probably his own), produced for a private performance by the Kleines Theater in December. This had not been easy. In addition to Greve's many other difficulties, it appears that the police censor had voiced objections to the public performance of these plays, as is clear from Felix's performance invitation to Melchior Lechter, the illustrator, and, through him, to Stefan George:

> At three o'clock on Friday or Saturday afternoon of next week the premiere of Wilde's one-act play *Salome* and of the comedy *Bunbury* will take place at the Kleines Theater (44 Unter den Linden) for an invited audience.
>
> Would you and Mr. George give me the pleasure of attending? As I have to hand the list of my guests to the police (due to the censor's actions), I request your kind reply. I will notify you of the exact day of the premiere on one of the first days of next week.[90]

In spite of the censor, the two plays were performed. Max Meyerfeld discussed the reception of the Wilde translations in Germany in the *Litterarisches Echo*:

Two plays by the English writer were performed before a selected audience, behind closed doors so to speak, in the *Kleines Theater,* which more than any other theatre in Berlin seems to be displaying the greatest literary ambition: the inspired "Salome," a feat of incredible compression, and the profound-sophomoric comedy "The Importance of Being Earnest," whose stolid-stilted title, "How Important It Is To Be Earnest" I would have calmly avoided (the translator avoided the issue by supposing that "Bunbury" was the invisible hero's name and that of the hero's dummy). As ridiculous as it may sound, Oscar Wilde was discovered in the capital city of the German empire on that afternoon (Meyerfeld, "Wilde, Wilde" 459).[91]

There can be no doubt that Greve's anticipation of recognition could not have been completely disappointed, despite Meyerfeld's criticism. Still, Meyerfeld did direct his criticism in such a way that Wilde, and not his translator(s), received the laurels. In so doing, he aligned himself with those innumerable critics who, to this day, happily praise the "original author" when the translation is good and thrash the translator when they think the work a failure. When Wilde was discovered in Germany, he was discovered in the language of his major translator, Greve. The supposed "ridiculousness" of the means of discovery is not at all evident, although the attitude of the reviewer is more than apparent. What has truly remained ridiculous until the present are the grotesque contortions of some foreign literature critics. They propose to praise the foreign-language work when it is the work of a translator which is the true source of their familiarity and the sole object of their reading.

Greve undoubtedly intended the high point of his Wilde campaign to have been different: much greater publicity, more lucrative and much longer-lasting. Now he was forced to compensate J.C.C. Bruns for all the accrued costs or at least to do as much as possible to reduce his debts to the publisher. At the beginning of 1903 he was in that very position of dependence upon a publisher which he had seen with Franziska von Reventlow. It was precisely this role as a literary drudge that he had sought to avoid while adopting the persona of an informed, independent and successful man of letters one year before, at the beginning of his business relations with Bruns. His attempts to garner material success and to achieve literary renown as a member of the *Blätter für die Kunst* circle had come to nothing. There was little left but to make a new attempt, to break out and to begin anew. Such an escape would be Greve's second new beginning in three months.

5

OFF·TO·AFRICA·AND
INTO·THE·DESERT

BEFORE TURNING TO GREVE'S FLIGHT in the second half of 1902, it is necessary to examine the same period in the light of the young writer's complex private life. On October 8, 1902, Karl Wolfskehl received a dramatic letter from Felix Paul Greve:

Dear Doctor!

I am about to write you something *for reasons I implore you not to ask about.* You are soon going to miss me in Munich. I am leaving. Where I will go, I am not yet sure. For the time being, I may go to Berlin until I have everything prepared for my departure from Europe.

I would like now, however, to take the opportunity to say something to you and your dear wife—something which one shouldn't have to say, something a handshake ought to be enough to convey. It is as follows. This last year has been the happiest in my life. And so much of this I owe to you. Allow me to say everything with one word: I thank you and your wife. That this year was at once the year of my greatest hopes and the year in which these hopes were shattered may cause my destruction. I ask you once again not to question me. Rather than anything else I would like to present you with a few poor lines of verse:

Life is the bitterest satire
On all the stages, a brightly mottled state:
Trying not to freeze, one feeds the fire
With the sprouting seed of one's breast.

I am selling my possessions. As soon as I have done so, I am leaving...[1]

Given Greve's rather execrable verse, it would seem that he was finished with more than the "brightly mottled state" of the stage, and that he had settled his accounts in more than one way. Helene Klages had definitively decided against him, leaving his hopes of establishing a household with her "shattered." Her decision must be seen as a result of the remarks Greve made to Wolfskehl regarding her brother's book on George. And yet Greve may have himself ended the affair for other reasons. Were he still to have retained the hope of having his work published in *Blätter für die Kunst*, he now had the opportunity to meet the master outside of Munich; for during the autumn and winter of 1902, Stefan George was repeatedly in Berlin for extended periods of time. Thus there may have been more than one reason for Greve to travel to Berlin. Ultimately, however, Greve's "gentlemanly withdrawal" from his relationship with Helene seems to have been the primary reason for his dramatic flight from the "happiest [year] of my life."

Regardless of the bathetic state of his private life, Greve maintained a cool head with regard to his business dealings. The day after presenting Wolfskehl with his dramatic letter, Greve sent von Poellnitz the first part of his translation of Pater's *Marius* and announced delivery of the second for November. At the same time, he would send along the first of his verse translations of Robert Browning's short dramatic work *In a Balcony*. On the basis of this work, which had not yet been accepted with certainty and which was only one-third completed, Greve made the managing director of Insel an astounding offer:

> Now I have a substantial, somewhat unusual request. Just recently I
> was offered a collection of very rare works of English decadence for a
> relatively good price. As I am reluctant to withdraw from my modest
> savings, which are meant to ensure my independence, I wanted to ask
> you whether you would be willing, were my *Marius* to be accepted, to
> give me an advance in the amount of c. 800 marks for the three
> volumes which would then be yours. This money would allow me to
> make a purchase which would be very important for my studies.
> Assuming that you are willing to grant this request, I would like to ask

you to respond immediately as I have the books reserved until Sunday morning only. Otherwise, they will pass into other hands.[2]

Only a few weeks previously Greve had offered Wolfskehl his Browning works "because [he didn't] need them any more"—this, though he was unable in October to deliver two of his Browning verse translations. Thus the sale of his Browning collection and the sudden offer to buy "works of English decadence" take on new meaning in relation to his departure, for which he was going to need money. With the reference to his "modest savings," Greve sought, as before, to draw attention away from his dire financial straits. He had already been adversely affected "by considerable expenses" in Gardone, as he wrote to Bruns on August 2 in connection to a request for money. It would seem that Greve intended to make up for the losses caused by his failed relationship with Helene Klages and her brother, and to prepare for the costs of his imminent departure from Munich. The plans entertained for this move seem to have been far more extensive than simply taking a train from Munich to Berlin. This is evident in a letter to Wolfskehl which followed immediately upon the one quoted above and which seems even more breathless:

> Today, I am already writing you from another apartment. I have struck all of my tents. On Sunday I am travelling to Berlin to organize my final arrangements. Soon I will board a German East-Africa steamer in Hamburg. I have a ticket for a half-year journey around Africa. Thus I will be able to stay where it pleases me...I am in such a state that I fear I could collapse at any moment...I will always think of your home as one of the few places where I experienced hours of total peace, complete happiness and cheerful enjoyment. A less complicated person might, despite everything in Munich, attempt to hold onto your home. My wanderings are not yet over and I must move on. Believe me, it feels as if my roots were being cut away. Munich was the first place in a long, long time that I stayed for more than a year. I feel that I matured there to some extent and thus feel an emptiness in front of me. It would probably be a good thing if I were to do physical work.[3]

Munich was in no way the first place "in a long, long time" where he had stayed for an extended period of time. The theatrically gifted author of *Wanderungen* stylized himself as a wanderer in the manner of Stefan George, who had perfected the role. In so doing, he explicitly fictionalized his persona in a way which foreshadows the self-depiction of the narrator in *A Search for*

America, for whom physical labour as an itinerant worker was a blessing. And yet what was the role of Africa in this self-dramatization? Had he been there already, or did he intend to follow the example of Vollmoeller's journey with Gide? The phrase about "striking his tents" would point in that direction. One thing, however, is clear. After the letter to Wolfskehl he definitely did *not* travel to Africa. Assuming Greve actually intended such a trip, the question remains how he intended to finance it. Greve was used to receiving sums of this sort from Kilian, who was already getting ready to finance him for his supposed journalism with a similar sum. Upon his departure from Munich, Greve could very well have considered leaving Europe completely. At the same time, however, "Africa" may have been related to Greve's presumed separation from Helene Klages, whose brother he may or may not have given "ten thousand marks." Neither of these actions would have hindered them from sending him, metaphorically speaking, "into the desert."

Apart from remaining letters, Freytag-Loringhoven's spotty and understandably prejudiced recollections and Greve's first novel, *Fanny Essler*, little remains to document Greve's movements during this period.[4] Nevertheless, Greve's novel, as has often been indicated, contains so many exactly rendered details that it may be possible to use the relationship among Fanny Barrel, Eduard Barrel and Friedrich Karl Reelen (i.e., Else and August Endell and Felix Paul Greve) as a kind of guidebook to Greve's maneuvers. The undeniable malice in the depiction not only of August Endell but also the Wolfskehls and their Munich circle of acquaintances (the master Stefan George is referred to with respect) can undoubtedly be traced back to Greve's bitterness during his imprisonment in Bonn at the time of writing. In little more than a year after his painful departure from Munich, Wolfskehl's household of "complete happiness" and "cheerful enjoyment" would become the house of "Dr. Katzwedel," the servile centre of a circle in which "all sorts of nonsense and idolatry would be conducted with the second 'master,' the poet" (FE 41).[5] The primary audience for the novel—Delbrück, Hardt, Koch, Wolfskehl, Reventlow, Vollmoeller and others with inside knowledge— would certainly have noticed all this as they anxiously read the 1905 work. According to the novel, the Barrels attended the Katzwedel's *Jour* in Munich where they met Reelen, whom they would again meet on subsequent Sundays. That would have been in March 1902. Later in the book, Barrel's acquaintance with Reelen in Florence is described: Reelen "was involved in archaeology and was very useful to me." This would suggest that Endell and Greve already knew each other in the spring or summer of 1901, after Greve's departure from Rome. Accepting the middle of April as the relevant point in time, the reference to the early summer of 1902 also seems correct: "At the

✸ *Nordsee Sanatorium, Föhr Island, ca. 1900 (Stadt Wyk/Föhr)*

beginning of May, Mr. Reelen was already in Berlin" (445). Ultimately, the Barrels moved back to Berlin and on June 15 "took up lodgings that evening in the Pension Queen Augusta" (448). Greve's first address in Berlin, on Queen Augusta Street, was first indicated in an October 19, 1902 letter to von Poellnitz in which he mentioned that he had "personally returned to Berlin" in order to buy "works of English decadence" apparently still available.[6] Greve's arrival is confirmed by the author of *Fanny Essler*. The reader also learns of Reelen's travel plans, which were the actual plans of the author at the time, even if they were ultimately to be changed. Acknowledging past intentions was undoubtedly meant as a means of retrospectively confirming Greve's integrity to the many initiated readers of his *roman à clef*. The following passage, for instance, falls into this category: "And then in October the year before last, Eduard arrived home with the news that Friedrich Karl Reelen was back in Berlin, although only for a few weeks before he wanted to undertake a long journey to Africa" (454). Fanny learns an additional detail of Reelen's/Greve's wanderings during a conversation with Reelen: "For the time being I have reserved a ticket to Kapstadt. I'm going to go on a bit of an adventure..." (455). Greve's itinerary may well have been inspired by Wolfskehl's independently formulated travel plans, which originally foresaw a "journey to the orient" for February 1903 but which had a precipitous and disastrous end (Seekamp et al., *George* 133).

Greve would remain in Berlin until the end of January 1903 and then board a ship. In the meantime, he courted August Endell's wife Else. He corresponded with her during her stay throughout November and December at the *Jugendstil*-ornamented Nordsee Sanatorium, headed by Dr. Karl Gmelin—"Dr. Koslin" of the novel—and built in 1898–99 by her husband. Else, in turn, fell in love with Greve.[7] Thus his journey to Africa was also cast in doubt. In the novel, the following happens on December 23, 1902: "Mr. Reelen told me that he would be leaving on Thursday for sure, although it was no longer certain whether he would be going to South Africa. He said that something else had come up in the meantime" (500–01). What had "come up," of course, was the disastrous failure to secure authorization for the Wilde comedies, which in turn scuttled his hopes for earning the money necessary to carry out his plans.

◆ HIGH STAKES AND OPULENCE

Something else happened as well. In the days following his arrival in Berlin, von Poellnitz returned Greve's Pater manuscript unread, along with a coolly formulated letter in which he made it clear that he would not submit to pressure and that he now regretted his decision to publish Wilde as "overly hasty." In conclusion, he expressed the hope that Greve would be able "to offer this manuscript to someone else," and, incidentally, that he did not believe that the book designer Marcus Behmer would be able to do much with Greve's Dowson translation.[8] Greve's shock can be imagined. He answered that the disappointment caused by this turn of affairs "sapped his strength and would render him unable to work for a long time," and requested an explanation for the rejection. After all, he could not afford "to work for months for nothing…especially as [he] had things of his own to do which [he] had completely put aside." He once again referred to such "discriminating individuals as Karl Wolfskehl" who had praised his translations.[9] It speaks well of Greve's appeal and usefulness that the Insel manager ultimately agreed to tell him the reasons for his reservations:

> In May, when we saw each other for the first time, I explained to you that I was very positively predisposed towards your proposals but that I was not in a position at the time to begin work with your manuscripts. I wanted to introduce Dowson and Wilde in the spring, Pater later. You told me that you were not in a hurry and a few weeks later requested of me an advance on precisely this manuscript. At approximately the same time as our exchange of letters, several acquaintances from Munich and Berlin told me a wondrous story of an unbelievably opulent dinner to which you were to have extended the invitations. It was further suggested that Insel Publishers would be publishing a large

number of your books. All these statements were said to have come from you personally, and even when I made allowances for the usual exaggerations, I was nevertheless left with a story which left me less than comfortable.[10]

Greve did not reply by return mail. When he did write, he reacted less to the specific criticism as to the uncomfortable impression left by the story; he suggested that although rumours had indeed circulated about him, he was in a better position to confirm them than von Poellnitz. It would appear that Greve knew the source of the "exaggerations" but nevertheless requested to know which of the "acquaintances from Munich and Berlin" had spread the story. Greve's interest was probably all the greater, as he had just departed from Munich rather hastily and settled in Berlin. He must have truly felt that he was being followed and that someone had an interest in "passing off on me the most unbelievable statements and actions." Upon returning from his first visit to Insel in Leipzig, Greve admitted that he may have, "during a moment of exuberance, described his visit [to von Poellnitz] in the suggested manner with grotesque exaggerations."[11] The opulent dinner ascribed to him must have taken place during the last week of August 1902, when Greve had high expectations for his numerous forthcoming publications and the theatre productions in preparation. This is the same time at which Greve suggested to Bruns and Wolfskehl that he could employ four copyists and that he was even considering certain "stock-market transactions." But some particular indiscretion must have been behind reports of Greve's exuberant boasting, which was delayed until after his Munich departure and his first few weeks in Berlin. In the social and literary circles to which Greve belonged in Munich and Berlin, however, such rumour campaigns were anything but rare. Thus Roderich Huch wrote in consternation to Ricarda Huch: "Thanks to Lepsius, I hear almost daily some disparaging statement made about me [such that] Munich now seems to me a den of vipers…Everyone seems to be under Klages's influence, who tries to do whatever he can to harm me."[12] Although no innocent *Sonnenknabe* himself, Greve undoubtedly also suffered as a result of the duplicitous practices of the group.

During this time, not only Greve but other "acquaintances from Munich and Berlin," known both to Greve and von Poellnitz, were also in Berlin for extended periods. On September 30, a Melchior Lechter exhibition, which would run for several weeks, opened at Keller & Reiner's Gallery with George in attendance (Seekamp et al., *George* 130). As late as 1941, Frederick Philip Grove would recall this gallery, referring both to it and a local pub much frequented by artists, Ewest's. This establishment was also possibly the location for Greve and Else Endell's private rendezvous (ISM 168). In the middle of October, Gundolf was in Berlin, as were the Wolfskehls and Stefan George, who was to hold a semi-public reading for the first time in the rooms of his publisher Bondi on October 22. Ludwig Klages's visit on November 9 for only one day must have occasioned surprise. On November 14, Wolfskehl sent unspecified "warnings" regarding Greve to Gundolf, who replied that he saw "F.P.G." infrequently. At the same time, George pressed Gundolf for information from Munich which might have been related to his looming break with Hugo von Hofmannsthal. This may have been the result of a dispute similar to Klages and Zwymann's, which was caused by different studies of George (Seekamp et al., *George* 130–32). As would be revealed in 1907, Greve remained in contact with Hofmannsthal to the further displeasure of the George circle. It seems more than plausible that after Greve's departure from Munich, Klages followed him to Berlin as a form of personal nemesis to "enlighten" George, Wolfskehl and other members of the circle about him. Similarly, the not-so-good friend Wolfskehl began again to "warn" of Greve, as he had at the beginning of the year. Some of these rumours reached von Poellnitz at Insel in Leipzig. Although Gundolf had been warned by Wolfskehl, on George's behalf he would request a meeting with Greve regarding the translation of Browning's *A Blot in the Scutcheon*. Greve declined, although he did use the opportunity to have a "Van-Geldern copy of *Intentions*" sent to George, whom he still revered.[13] The matter would not rest there, however, for even more was reported about Greve. In his detailed response to von Poellnitz's criticisms, Greve made the following unprovoked statements:

> And I am to have spread the strangest of rumours about other acquaintances of mine, whose names I wouldn't dream of mentioning. And my friend August Endell informs me that the most impossible rumours are circulating about me. It is said that I spend my evenings in a disreputable hotel where I indulge in gambling, etc. I'm telling you all of this so that you will be better able to evaluate the rumours that you hear.[14]

By announcing even further rumours circulating about him, Greve did little to invalidate those which had already reached von Poellnitz. Indeed, his defence of himself sounds more like a playful attempt to diminish the criticism by in part acknowledging it. But what is to be made of his "evenings in a disreputable hotel" and gambling? If he had already received the ten thousand marks from Kilian, he would have had the necessary resources to gamble. He could have seen it as an escape from his precarious financial situation. Nor would he have been alone in granting himself this illusion. On the one hand, he attempted to impress von Poellnitz with his "friendship" with Endell, who was just getting to be well known, just as he had previously made use of Wolfskehl for similar ends. On the other hand, he was doing all he could to impress Else Endell with his manners, his knowledge of the world and his wealth. Greve was also undoubtedly drawn to the high-stakes, all-or-nothing persona of the gambler and gambling as dramatized in Dostoevsky's novel *Igrok* (*The Gambler*). He had already demonstrated such an attitude in other parts of his life.

It is important to note here that forty thousand gold marks would be referred to in Greve's court proceedings nine months later. Greve could also claim not inconsiderable monies from scholarships and translations. Even subtracting for his extravagant tastes in boats, books, clothing, journeys and his generous support of the man referred to by Freytag-Loringhoven as the "brother" of the "virgin" Klages, Greve still had a sizeable sum of money that he could cart off to the casino. He could also have followed the example of his Minden publisher Gustav Bruns, a truly wealthy man who took to the tables in Wiesbaden and a few years later left his son a publishing house with a debt of one million gold marks (Martens, *Bruns* 25). It seems clear enough that in the final months of 1902, Felix Paul Greve repeatedly sought compensation for the series of setbacks he had experienced despite months of promise. A combination of factors could well have enhanced the allure of the tables: the absence of a single, decisive financial success; his failure to achieve public acclaim as a poet and translator; his disappointments in his private life and the related inability to settle down in an stable household. Hence the bravura, the gambling, the planned escape, the wish finally to be "off to Africa" in whatever shape it would take.

◆ ESSENTIALS

Greve was now in the process of changing his life's plans. Else Endell, as he declared to her husband, would be travelling with him. It now seemed as if nothing more than physical appearance and sexual attraction mattered. Greve's all-too-gentlemanly behaviour around Helene Klages may have concealed more basic needs in himself. Else Endell also claimed to have grounds for complaint, as a kidney disease had supposedly rendered her husband impotent. Greve described the contrast in physical appearance between Greve/Reelen and Endell/Barrel from the perspective of Fanny Essler with the barest of restraint. According to this description, Barrel/Endell

❀ *August Endell, ca. 1900 (Collection Dorothee Pfeiffer)*

was a long, gaunt person of brooding, gangly movements and slightly stooped composure…On his head he wore a large floppy hat. Behind his gold-rimmed glasses [she saw] unusually large and round dark eyes, and under the brim of his hat rather long, ash-blond hair. His head [seemed to her] remarkably similar to that of a bird; perhaps the resemblance lay in the paleness of his face (FE 402, 407).[15]

Greve's alter ego Reelen, who meets Fanny at the Katzwedel's, is described somewhat differently:

She noticed only one new figure, a strikingly tall and slim, strikingly blond, strikingly elegant man of about thirty. When spoken to he responded with such obliging courtesy that all in the circle were reduced to embarrassment. It also seemed as if only a scant few dared to speak with him. His external accuracy of dress and style seemed to intimidate the others. And all the while he looked off into the distance, regardless whether he was silent or laughing kindly, with the same almost naive light blue eyes. His mouth, after the English fashion, was hidden behind a drooping reddish-blond moustache. His large nose receded directly back into his forehead and lightly flared without being stubbed. His carefully parted hair, and his two medium-sized eyebrows were of such light blond colour that his whole head seemed expressionless in the lightness. And he towered above even Eduard by a head (FE 441).[16]

Now that was a man. Unlike Eduard Barrel, Fanny would not accuse him of impotence, or "sexual torment" as she termed it (FE 438). The same element of self-promotion is also evident in FPG's later works. The description of Reelen recalls the self-satisfied self-description of Grove's narrator Phil Branden upon his arrival in Canada:

I was six feet three inches tall, with a waist-measure of twenty-six inches. Hands and feet were narrow and long; my shoulders had begun to stoop. My hair was exceedingly fair — of that ancestral Scandinavian fairness that makes me to this day appear like a much younger man than I am. My eyes were blue, arched over by bushy, yellow brows, and set rather deeply in a long, narrow face with a somewhat receding chin.

Add to that a certain diffidence in demeanour — the diffidence of him who is on familiar ground — and the considerate politeness of the man who is used to look upon most of the people he deals with as socially his inferiors — as to be treated with kindliness because they must suffer from the mere fact that they are what they happen to be — none of their fault of course (SFA 15).

This is probably the best example of Felix Paul Greve's role-playing. He was able to create for himself a single, composite persona of universal appeal, one which, as the passage above would indicate, incorporated an international ideal of masculinity. It also combined both attractive physical appearance and perceptive intelligence. The actual person behind the persona was unimportant. August Endell, unlike Greve, had placed his imagination at the service of his profession after the completion of his studies and the publication of a volume of poetry in 1896. He was not financially successful, although he was well respected professionally. While Else felt attracted to Greve and in admiration sought close proximity to the seemingly wealthy man, Greve for his part undoubtedly felt drawn to Endell, the successful architect who, apart from associating with members of the George circle — including the writer O.A.H. Schmitz — had also been connected to

Rainer Maria Rilke and Lou Andreas-Salomé since at least 1897. "My friend August Endell" was thus a useful acquaintance whom Greve would keep for the time being; Endell, likewise, felt the same about him. Else attended to her own needs.

It is revealed in the course of *Fanny Essler* that Reelen continually postponed his departure to "South Africa" because something else had "come up" (500–01). The many unsold copies of Wilde's dramas at J.C.C. Bruns's, which now belonged to Greve and had to be paid for immediately, come to mind. Greve even suggested attempting to sell the copies which could not be sold in Germany in Switzerland, where different copyright laws were in effect.[17] Nevertheless, Reelen celebrated Christmas Eve together with the Barrels. They enjoyed a festive meal at a "Hôtel de Rome" (yet again), and various Christmas gifts were distributed in Fanny's salon. On Boxing Day, Reelen declared his love for Fanny and on that very afternoon "two wagons heavily loaded with luggage halted in Hamburg in front of the Hôtel de l'Europe...Friedrich Karl Reelen, Mrs. Fanny Reelen...and a servant" (510). Like Greve, Reelen was intimately acquainted with Hamburg, especially with the *Scheunenviertel* (the city's "skid row"). As this was the city of Greve's youth, Reelen was able to demonstrate his intimate knowledge of Hamburg to Fanny. Since both Fanny and Else Endell were once actors, "Friedrich Karl and Fanny visited the Ernst Drucker Theatre at St. Pauli's Spielbudenplatz" (520–21). In *Fanny Essler* the pair travels further to Paris, where they learn that Eduard Barrel has shot himself. Fanny and her "northern god" (514) then travel on to Antwerp to board "a steamer of the German-East Africa Line" that would take them to Lisbon. Soon thereafter, Fanny dies an early though peaceful death in Lisbon.

The remaining letters of Felix Paul Greve, as well as such sources as Freytag-Loringhoven's memoirs, provide little direct information about this period. Yet because of significant divergences in detail provided by these separate accounts, each is in its own way illuminating. On December 27, 1902, Else wrote her previous lover, the book designer Marcus Behmer, a postcard showing "Dr. Gmelin's North Sea Sanatorium" on the island of Föhr, where she had apparently spent Christmas (in contrast to the account in *Fanny Essler*).[18] A few words regarding the island sanatorium are in order. Karl Gmelin, who came from a well-known family of botanists and chemists, had practiced at Dr. Lahmann's renowned sanatorium in the Dresden *Weisser Hirsch* ("White Stag") district, before deciding to found a new sanatorium on Föhr with a merchant and philologist.[19] The brick sanatorium, built to international standards by Endell near the hamlet of Boldixum, lay "150 metres from the coastline, surrounded by gardens with playgrounds and wind-protected spaces and in the middle of which was an atrium for taking in the sea air." Apart from this, there were so-called "airing cabins, used to great affect by patients suffering nervous ailments." Rooms equipped for "thermal treatment...light treatment, massage and physio-therapy" were located on the second floor of the so-called "Kitchen House," the first edifice built along with the "Main Building" (*Nordsee-Sanatorium*, 3–6). The rooms were provided with simple wooden furnishings designed by Endell.

The Atelier Elvira in Munich and this sanatorium were Endell's main projects at the time of his marriage to "Else Ti Endell, *née* Ploetz" in Berlin-Zehlendorf in the autumn of 1901. The marriage announcements distributed to their friends displayed a stylized "T" under the cross-beam of which two symmetrical "E"s faced each other, separated and connected by the vertical axis of the "T." This was their mutual symbol which, in keeping with their nicknames "Tse" and "Ti" (pronounced "Tee"), approximated a Chinese character. Within a year, however, the unity symbolized by the sign had been rendered asunder. During the winter of 1902, Else was sent to the island sanatorium, and not just for the benefits of the excellent air. As von Freytag-Loringhoven would recall a quarter of a century later:

> Later on—my husband sent me to a sanatorium at the shore of the North Sea—to be away from him and to have by-the-way, my womb massaged for his impotence...So here I was—installed in a sanatorium having my womb twiddled by a very married bourgeois doctor—who for business' sake with the silent consent of his spouse—silently suffering himself to be the more or less openly expressed desire for many a waning young lady's erring sex call—that was under his care (BE 60–61).

It was an accepted form of treatment to diagnose the complaints of women whose sexual needs and behaviour were—after extended denial—deemed "impertinent" and "hysterical" by their husbands and families. "Disturbances of the sexual organs" were to be "treated locally;" "water treatments, sojourns by the sea and bathing in the sea" were considered medicinally useful (*Meyers Lexikon* 1924, 729). Under pressure from the demands of his wife, Endell allowed her to be submitted to treatments conducted in parallel with the newest findings of Freud and Breuer. He likely discussed Else's "problems" with the resident doctor while furnishing the sanatorium. Thus Endell attempted to conceal from himself his own neuroses and impotence. The normal needs of his young and sexually unsatisfied wife thus needed to be diagnosed and treated as "abnormal."[20]

The treatment had little effect, as became clear following Else's return. Now, without further hesitation, she turned closer attention to Greve, who had "provided company" to her husband during her absence. Endell, who had thrown himself at her feet, having suffered her liaison with Greve out of helplessness and in the hope that his beloved wife was not Greve's "type," could now do nothing to hinder her as she turned fully to Greve, willingly consenting to travel with him to Italy. He abandoned all pride and accompanied both as far as Naples after borrowing money from Greve for his travelling expenses (thus Endell in *Fanny Essler* was maliciously transformed into the "servant"). "Not only did you leave me," Endell is to have said to Else during their trip, "you even stole my friend" (BE 86–87). In Naples, after a night in the Grand Hotel, Greve put his friend up in a pension, although not without indicating the costs which he knew Endell could not meet. According to Else, the pension was then apparently the scene of an obviously faked suicide attempt by Endell. Thereafter, the "thoughtful" Greve bought him a bicycle so that Endell "could get a little exercise and sent him to Ischia to regain his balance or to break his neck." The lovers then travelled on to Sicily and Palermo. All this is according to Else von Freytag-Loringhoven (BE 89–90).

Unlike the fictional Eduard Barrel, August Endell's life did not end with suicide. After further work as an architect and designer, he remarried and eventually became a respected professor of art and architecture in Breslau (achieving what Greve, according to Grove, had planned for himself). He died young in 1925. This much is known. The fateful year 1903, however, remained absent from all accounts of his life. Even the now-accessible and occasionally vivid correspondence conducted with his better-situated cousin Kurt Breysig contains only a few details touching upon the catastrophe in his life, although the torment caused by his wife's abandonment and friend's betrayal is evident. At the end of January 1903, he wrote: "I can't take it anymore. I'm exhausted. It came faster than I thought. I'm very sick. Perhaps forever. I'm going away for several months. Adio…"[21] It would appear that after his little intermezzo in Naples in early March, Endell retired to Ravello for the rest of 1903, to a vacation resort close to Amalfi, well known to him and his friends Vollmoeller and Wolfskehl. From there he sent a long, torturous letter to Breysig requesting financial help. One of Endell's letters to Breysig contains a previously unpublished assessment of the events in Berlin and a judgment concerning Greve and Else. It deserves citation as a contrast to the pitiless depiction in *Fanny Essler* and the equally harsh recollections of Endell's former wife. Endell resisted discussion of "intimate details" with his cousin and suggested that his failings, which led to the marriage crisis, were a result of professional misfortunes that had robbed him of all hope. Ultimately, he hadn't had "the strength to offer her anything:"

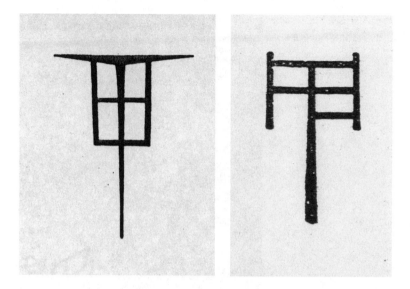

※ *(left) Symbol from the marriage announcement of Else and August Endell, 1901 (Staatsbibliothek Preußischer Kulturbesitz, Berlin); (right) Symbol from an advertisement in Die Zukunft for August Endell's "School of Design," 1905*

I had lost all sense of confidence. In Munich this would not have happened, for I would always have had help and it wouldn't have been able to go so far. In Berlin I had no one other than that half-crazy being who betrayed me and caused me even greater confusion by continually boasting about his strength and capacity for work and by increasingly making me feel my weakness [and] incompetence through thousands of tricks. And all this under the appearance of wanting to help. I finally felt myself the most pathetic [and] worthless being imaginable and allowed others to do with me what they wanted without noticing or resisting. I *was* at the edge of madness. And with time my agitation increased. The man was a malicious swindler and the woman, whom I loved more than anything—and she was worth more than you think—in despair. Me, without strength or hope with no way of doing anything. The situation *is* critical, very critical.[22]

Apart from a brief interruption during the erection of the Wolzogen Theatre, Endell probably returned to Berlin for good in the summer of 1904. Once in Berlin, he founded his "School of Design" which lasted until 1914. The education and training offered by the school corresponded to his own tastes

✖ *O.A.H. Schmitz*
(Collection Margarete Schirmer)

and background. "Copying other works, either past or contemporary, is prohibited as a matter of principle: Free Invention in Colour and Form is the Goal." Students were meant to strive for "harmony of form, an aesthetic geometry."[23] He placed announcements in Maximilian Hardens's journal *Die Zukunft*—where Greve would be published in the same year—which attracted attention with his *Jugendstil* monogram and an advertisement which read "AUG. ENDELL. School of Design, Architectural and Design Trade for Men and Women, Berlin, 43 W. Fasanenstr."[24] Previously published research on Endell remains somewhat taciturn regarding the period from 1902 until 1904. It has been claimed, for instance, that it was reported in 1905 that Endell had "again returned to Berlin" after a "long sojourn in the south due to illness," for which neurasthenia was mentioned. It says later that this sojourn must have been "Endell's journey to Italy in 1903" (Reichel, *Endell* 74). Elsewhere it has been reported that in January 1903 Endell suffered "a complete physical breakdown" (Buddensieg, *Endell* 142). And yet far more expressive than any words is Endell's altered monogram as it appears in the brochure for his school. Essentially the monogram is the same as Else and August's marriage symbol from autumn 1901. Now, however, the "E" placed on the left-hand side of the vertical shaft of the "T" has lost its bottom bar and become an "A." The stroke which had formed an "E" and provided his world with symmetry had fallen—like the ground beneath his feet—from both his name and former life.

It remains unclear under what circumstances Else's divorce from Endell took place and whether she ultimately married Greve. Municipal registry documents pertaining to Endell from late autumn 1905 indicate the following: "Wife: presumably residing in Switzerland," which suggests that her current address with Greve in Wollerau by Lake Zurich was no secret. A diary entry by Oscar A.H. Schmitz, who had apparently become close to Greve and who was himself undergoing a divorce, makes clear that Schmitz was unable to draw any explicit conclusions from Greve's report concerning the divorce in November 1906. In this diary entry, there is even unspecified talk of blackmail:

> I then took [Greve] with me into the city to get an explanation of the Endell situation, but learned nothing definitive. I can find nothing which speaks seriously for him and just as little for Endell. The issue of blackmail is explained as follows. Endell owed him approximately 3000 marks and at first gave him back 1500, which was to provide for a wedding in England, which Endell had made impossible in Germany by using his wife's infidelity as the basis for divorce out of revenge. Greve was thus to have threatened to appeal the decision to demonstrate the mutual guilt of the spouses and thus to remove all marriage hindrances. This the opposing side took to be blackmail. At any rate, the whole situation is unclear. Endell told me two years ago in Munich that he was the one who wanted to avoid the use of infidelity as a grounds for divorce but was hindered by the maneuvers of the opposing party. Whatever happened, Endell must have been extremely neurasthenic; he apparently followed Greve crying and threatening everywhere, even as far as Naples, because he couldn't live alone etc.[25]

For her part, Freytag-Loringhoven reported that Endell did in fact claim infidelity as the cause of divorce and that he placed all blame on her and Greve, depicting himself as an innocent victim. She supposedly had to sign a statement attesting to these charges before money from "Tse" would be returned to Felix. The whole matter was indeed "unclear," although Schmitz, who acted along with his brother Richard as a kind of intermediary between "the Greves" and Endell, was in a better position than anyone to know the details. It is only from Endell's previously unconsulted correspondence with his cousin Breysig that it becomes clear that Endell, who was continually required to request amounts of money as small as fifty marks from his relative, was in no position to repay the indicated sum of money to Greve or Else. It is also highly questionable whether Else and Greve were ever married. They certainly were in England in June 1904 and once again in the summer of 1905 for Felix's negotiations with H.G. Wells, and yet despite intensive investigation there is no evidence of a wedding from the period of their residence in Europe.[26] Indeed, the divorce from Endell was not yet completed as of November 1906. In 1904, Endell had already met Anna Meyn, whom he would marry on January 3, 1909.

However, just a few weeks after his walk with Schmitz in 1906, Greve invited his surprised acquaintance to a "wedding breakfast." Apparently, Greve was "on the point of resolving all hindrances to legalizing his marriage."[27] And yet both seem to have drawn premature conclusions. Endell's second marriage in 1909 seems to suggest that a solution to the legal complications was not reached until just before Greve's final departure from Germany in the same year. Is this departure connected to a subsequent legalization of Else and Felix's difficult union on a farm in Kentucky and Greve's ultimate refusal to continue living with his partner? Did Greve forestall her with various maneuvers until his first flight (from Germany) saved him from honouring his promise? And did a second escape (from Kentucky and the United States to Canada) release him from the relationship, by then doubly undesired? Was Else, isolated on a farm in Kentucky, driven to "concubine-like" behaviour (Schmitz, "Diary") out of a need to improve her financial position and to escape her loneliness? Or did Greve ultimately marry her only to leave her again soon thereafter? "Mrs. Vogel" and "Nils Lindstedt" from Frederick Philip Grove's novel *Settlers of the Marsh* could very well contain, as has been suggested, traces of Else and Felix's life in Sparta, Kentucky. "Mrs. Vogel" would require little more than casting in softer shades and "Nils" substantial deletions from his noble naïveté. Perhaps it was his pride and energy that led Greve to push his scandalous relationship with Else to the point of legalization—to the point where all obstacles had been removed and he could render Else "honourable" by marrying her, only then to leave her. Were this the case, then what he perceived as her "concubine-like" behaviour as "Mrs. Greve"—which may in fact have supported them in Kentucky and Ohio—could have provided him with a reason to escape to Canada. But a short time later he would marry the young and honourable teacher Catherine Wiens (the "Ellen Amundsen" of *Settlers of the Marsh* in this scenario). Following this further, the new "Mrs. Grove" would replace the previous "Mrs. Greve," who no longer deserved the honour and esteem due a newly appointed Canadian schoolmaster. Grove continued to adhere to a romanticized ideal of virginal purity which had first manifested itself in the figure of Helene Klages.

◆ WITH CIRCE IN THE SOUTH

In assessing the real and fictionalized events of spring 1903, Greve's correspondence with J.C.C. Bruns sheds further light on the various versions of these events as presented by Greve's narrator Fanny Essler and Else herself. Mrs. Endell's lover did not for a moment neglect his business arrangements, maintaining a steady flow of letters to his Minden publisher.

His first priority was to relieve himself of financial pressures and responsibilities—above all the unsaleable Wilde dramas—without causing too much damage to his important business contacts. Greve soon found a solution not untypical for him. At first, as is evident from *Fanny Essler*, he began by increasingly identifying himself with his "friend" Endell, not only adapting that man's emotional role with Else but also ascribing to himself Endell's nervous condition. This is apparent in a letter to J.C.C. Bruns from the Hamburg Hotel toward the end of the month. It implies that Greve's departure from Berlin and his stay in Hamburg must have lasted longer than depicted in *Fanny Essler*. Bruns was probably surprised to read that Greve was all of a sudden "completely unable to work as a result of a nervous shock" and that he simply had to take "a journey to the south in order to recuperate."[28] In this, one almost hears the voice of the much-tormented Endell. In reality, however, Greve was not only Else's "healer"—far more successful than Dr. Gmelin—but also the vigorous husband August never was.

The situation was even more complicated. In claiming to have suffered a "nervous shock," Greve adopted the highly fashionable condition of neurasthenia, an illness suffered by August Endell and which had attained almost epidemic proportions in the hypersensitive literary circles of Munich and Berlin. Indeed, as Greve would later learn, the publisher's son and poet Max Bruns would also soon retreat into the same condition. In claiming to suffer from neurasthenia, Greve became identifiable as a contemporary avant-garde author; he was now recognizable as the sensitive kind who belonged to "the most recent artistic movement." At the same time, he managed to appeal to Else/Fanny as a vital man of action and not, like her husband, one of those repulsive, bloodless artists she had met in Munich and Berlin. Greve's account of her estimation of him in *Fanny Essler* shows that she continued to adhere to this aspect of his role-playing (which is curiously anticipatory of Freytag-Loringhoven's tone in her later recollections of the period, and testament to the extent to which he used her as a model in his writings):

Herr Reelen...yes, that was an athlete, you could see it in him. He rode and fenced and swam and played tennis. He was no artist! How she despised artists. Those half-men who took themselves to be the crown of creation!...The gods of dreams. Gods in their dreams, for they were incapable of real life! (FE 473)[29]

Before their departure for Italy, Greve requested the return of his Pater manuscript from J.C.C. Bruns in order that Insel could print it. He made reference to ongoing negotiations regarding "the question of the dramas." His luck seemed to have returned. He had exchanged unattainable love for an attained lover and felt prepared for clear sailing with his publisher. Finally, his *Dorian Gray* and further Wilde texts seemed ready for publication with Bruns, while his translations of Wilde's fairy tales and perhaps also the Pater and Browning texts would be coming out with Insel. The less glamorous work of proofreading could easily be delegated to others. He also instructed Bruns to send the proofs for *Dorian Gray* to an assistant, Herbert Koch in Munich, whom he had already once thought of employing along with Arthur Salz.[30] For a moment, in late January of 1903, Greve felt on top of the world as a sensitive artist, literary entrepreneur and man of the world.

J.C.C. Bruns was less than impressed. The publisher did not feel that his difficulties with Greve had been overcome. In a manner similar to von Poellnitz's in November 1902, Bruns observed with irritation the breezy way in which his debt-laden translator cheerfully issued telegraphed instructions from an exclusive hotel and made unspecified plans to move elsewhere. A telegram from Greve's publisher was insufficient to hold him back. Nervousness undoubtedly reigned in Minden as the Hamburg Hôtel de l'Europe responded, also by telegram, that the message sent by Bruns to Greve could not be delivered and that he had checked out of the hotel. The request for further information revealed "that Mr. Felix Paul Greve had left by ship on January 28, 1903 to travel via Rotterdam to Naples" and that his address there was to be the "Grand Hotel."[31] Around the same time, Bruns received an offer from a well-regarded author calling herself "Bertha Franzos." She informed Bruns that she had for a long time maintained good contacts with "excellent" British writers, among them Edmund Gosse. She offered Bruns what he thought he was soon to have from Greve:

...given the lively interest now being shown for the English author *Oscar Wilde*, allow me the opportunity to request whether you might in principle be interested in acquiring the volume of his unique "Essays," *Intentions* for your publishing house?...I have from *Oscar Wilde* himself the authorization for *this* work; furthermore, I am in possession of the translation rights from "Fortnightly Review" for "Poem in Prose"…[32]

Such an offer, coming as it did during the firm's ongoing difficulties with the Wilde dramas and the still-uncorrected proofs for *Dorian Gray*, must have once again sorely shaken Bruns's faith in Greve's competence. This time, however, Greve was better informed than "Franzos." The deceased author's verbal authorization carried no legal weight whatsoever.

Finally, Greve could be reached in Palermo four weeks after his departure with a letter posted on February 21. In his reply, the "convalescent" Greve quietly expressed his regret that all attempts to settle the issue concerning the plays had failed. He also remarked, apparently in response to Bruns's protests, that the *Dorian Gray* corrections would be "promptly taken care of in Munich."[33] Hamburg, Munich, Berlin, Leipzig, Minden—they all seemed so far away from Italy's more pleasant climes.

Else von Freytag-Loringhoven reports that in Palermo she and Greve lived in a small pension at 83 via Lincoln. In the mornings, Felix worked on his texts. They went riding and some afternoons went for rides with a horse and carriage. The rest of the time they were occupied with ridding Else of her inhibitions and in helping her attain sexual satisfaction. Often, Else wrote, she was subject to hysterical attacks of desperation; nevertheless, Greve's stamina helped him ultimately to achieve that which his predecessor never did. After two months, at the end of April, he left his beloved behind in Palermo under the pretext of returning to Bonn to look after some "investments" that he claimed to have made in a "failing bank" (BE 91–93).

◆ ONE PFENNIG

On the lonely trip home, which he must have undertaken almost penniless, Felix spent the night in the guest house of the DAI in Rome, as attested to in Vollmoeller's reminiscences quoted above. The caretaker had told Vollmoeller how Greve had stood "pale and shivering before her door" and that she had allowed him to spend the night free of charge and given him his morning coffee the following day. Vollmoeller's otherwise incidental recollection lends credibility to the report of Felix Greve's surprising arrest, which at first sounds anecdotal and exaggerated with its reference to his financial destitution: "Greve was arrested by the police at the Bonn train station; in his pockets was but one pfennig."[34] Although Kilian had instituted legal action for fraud against Greve, the court proceedings before Bonn's criminal court do not sound as if Greve's erstwhile friend was particularly interested in seeing Greve punished. Kilian was the recipient of the dedication in Greve's

⌘ *Article in the Bonn newspaper detailing the court proceedings against Felix Paul Greve (galley proof), May 29, 1903*
(J.C.C. Bruns Archiv, Minden)

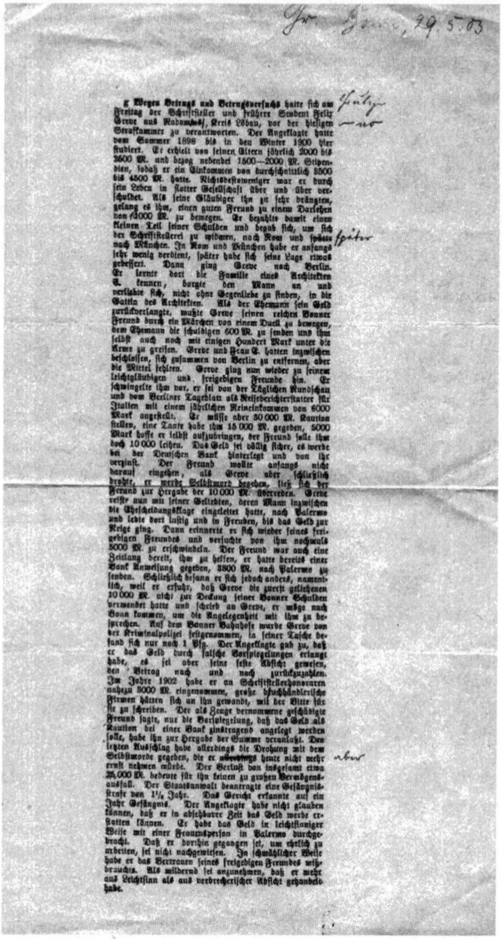

g Wegen Betrugs und Betrugsversuchs hatte sich am Freitag der Schriftsteller und frühere Student Felix Greve aus Radomno, Kreis Löbau, vor der hiesigen Strafkammer zu verantworten. Der Angeklagte hatte vom Sommer 1898 bis in den Winter 1900 hier studiert. Er erhielt von seinen Eltern jährlich 2000 bis 2500 M. und bezog nebenbei 1500—2000 M. Stipendien, sodaß er ein Einkommen von durchschnittlich 3500 bis 4500 M. hatte. Nichtsdestoweniger war er durch sein Leben in flotter Gesellschaft über und über verschuldet. Als seine Gläubiger ihn zu sehr drängten, gelang es ihm, einen guten Freund zu einem Darlehen von 10000 M. zu bewegen. Er bezahlte damit einen kleinen Teil seiner Schulden und begab sich, um sich der Schriftstellerei zu widmen, nach Rom und später nach München. In Rom und München habe er anfangs sehr wenig verdient, später habe sich seine Lage etwas gebessert. Dann ging Greve nach Berlin. Er lernte dort die Familie eines Architekten E. kennen, borgte den Mann an und verliebte sich, nicht ohne Gegenliebe zu finden, in die Gattin des Architekten. Als der Ehemann sein Geld zurückverlangte, wußte Greve seinen reichen Bonner Freund durch ein Märchen von einem Duell zu bewegen, dem Ehemann die schuldigen 600 M. zu senden und ihm selbst auch noch mit einigen Hundert Mark unter die Arme zu greifen. Greve und Frau E. hatten inzwischen beschlossen, sich zusammen von Berlin zu entfernen, aber die Mittel fehlten. Greve ging nun wieder zu seinem leichtgläubigen und freigebigen Freunde hin. Er schwindelte ihm vor, er sei von der Täglichen Rundschau und dem Berliner Tageblatt als Reiseberichterstatter für Italien mit einem jährlichen Reineinkommen von 6000 Mark angestellt. Er müsse aber 30000 M. Kaution stellen, eine Tante habe ihm 15000 M. gegeben, 5000 Mark hoffe er selbst aufzubringen, der Freund solle ihm doch 10000 leihen. Das Geld sei völlig sicher, es werde bei der Deutschen Bank hinterlegt und von ihr verzinst. Der Freund wollte anfangs nicht darauf eingehen, als Greve aber schließlich drohte, er werde Selbstmord begehen, ließ sich der Freund zur Hergabe der 10000 M. überreden. Greve reiste nun mit seiner Geliebten, deren Mann inzwischen die Ehescheidungsklage eingeleitet hatte, nach Palermo und lebte dort lustig und in Freuden, bis das Geld zur Neige ging. Dann erinnerte er sich wieder seines freigebigen Freundes und versuchte von ihm nochmals 5000 M. zu erschwindeln. Der Freund war auch eine Zeitlang bereit, ihm zu helfen, er hatte bereits einer Bank Anweisung gegeben, 3800 M. nach Palermo zu senden. Schließlich besann er sich jedoch anders, namentlich, weil er erfuhr, daß Greve die zuerst geliehenen 10000 M. nicht zur Deckung seiner Bonner Schulden verwendet hatte und schrieb an Greve, er möge nach Bonn kommen, um die Angelegenheit mit ihm zu besprechen. Auf dem Bonner Bahnhofe wurde Greve von der Kriminalpolizei festgenommen, in seiner Tasche befand sich nur noch 1 Pfg. Der Angeklagte gab zu, daß er das Geld durch falsche Vorspiegelungen erlangt habe, es sei aber seine feste Absicht gewesen, den Betrag nach und nach zurückzuzahlen. Im Jahre 1902 habe er an Schriftstellerhonoraren nahezu 8000 M. eingenommen, große buchhändlerische Firmen hätten sich an ihn gewandt, mit der Bitte für sie zu schreiben. Der als Zeuge vernommene geschädigte Freund sagte, nur die Vorspiegelung, daß das Geld als Kaution bei einer Bank zinstragend angelegt werden solle, habe ihn zur Hergabe der Summe veranlaßt. Den letzten Ausschlag habe allerdings die Drohung mit dem Selbstmorde gegeben, die er allerdings heute nicht mehr ernst nehmen würde. Der Verlust von insgesamt etwa 25,000 M. bedeute für ihn keinen zu großen Vermögensausfall. Der Staatsanwalt beantragte eine Gefängnisstrafe von 1½ Jahr. Das Gericht erkannte auf ein Jahr Gefängnis. Der Angeklagte habe nicht glauben können, daß er in absehbarer Zeit das Geld werde erstatten können. Er habe das Geld in leichtsinniger Weise mit einer Frauensperson in Palermo durchgebracht. Daß er dorthin gegangen sei, um ehrlich zu arbeiten, sei nicht nachgewiesen. In schmählicher Weise habe er das Vertrauen seines freigebigen Freundes mißbraucht. Als mildernd sei anzunehmen, daß er mehr aus Leichtsinn als aus verbrecherischer Absicht gehandelt habe.

Wanderungen, was the co-translator of *Intentions*, the probable financier and travelling companion on Greve's trips to Paris and elsewhere, and the chemistry student certainly in love with Greve. Moreover, as he testified at trial, "the loss of all together 25,000 marks meant no significant reduction of income for him." How could it have come to such a sum, an amount of money which would be worth ten times as much today? The report filed in the *Bonner Zeitung* detailed the payments. "Thanks to his life in high society," wrote the court reporter, Greve had already received a loan of over ten thousand marks in Bonn from his friend to help pay "a small portion" of his debts. Claiming that he was required to pay a deposit of thirty thousand marks in his function as a "travel reporter" for two well-regarded newspapers, the *Tägliche Rundschau* and the *Berliner Tageblatt*, Greve stated that he had been able to borrow fifteen thousand "from an aunt," "hoped" to be able to raise five thousand himself and had attempted to convince Kilian to lend him the remaining ten thousand. According to Kilian's testimony in court, Greve had threatened suicide in response to Kilian's hesitation to lend him the money. This was to have taken place in January 1903. Thus, during that period Greve was required to travel not only between Berlin and Hamburg, but also between Bonn and even Dresden, Kilian's home city, in order to raise the money for his journey with Else and August Endell. His own threat to kill himself could only have made him less receptive to Endell's equally ineffectual threats of suicide in Naples.

According to the court proceedings, Greve used the final ten thousand marks he had received in Palermo to live "cheerfully and in pleasure." Taking Freytag-Loringhoven's description of their stay in Palermo into account, it is difficult, apart from a little riding and a few excursions in horse and carriage, to characterize their lifestyle as particularly rich, still less extravagant enough to explain the expenditure of so much money. Was Greve the victim of failed acquisitions or speculations, as Vollmoeller's derisive comment about Greve's "jewels" might suggest? In Sicily there was always the temptation to buy unstamped precious metal at a much lower price than was possible in Germany. Whatever happened, Greve was out of money and requested another five thousand from Kilian. Apparently Kilian had already forwarded instructions to his bank to transfer three thousand eight hundred marks to a bank in Palermo when he discovered that Greve had paid back none of his debts there. Basically, he had defrauded him of the first loan. Kilian then wrote to Greve asking him to come to Bonn to discuss the matter and set the police upon him at his arrival.

Greve's apparently unbounded faith in Kilian's willingness to pay and in his own power over his friend seems naïve. Kilian may have been the first to succumb to Greve's appearance, his great charm and his aura of success and superiority. The drowned Lomberg would have been the second. It is quite possible that he was unable to tolerate the rivalry with Kilian and that he sacrificed himself to it. This, in turn, would also help to explain Kilian's absence during the burial. Again, an intense feeling of sexual jealousy for Greve's attentions may have had a basis in sexual practice, yet it may also have been wholly platonic. Dependencies there certainly were. A later auto-biographical statement by Frederick Philip Grove may be of relevance here:

> I went through one strange experience. A young man, very slightly my
> senior in years, was, in certain small circles, already regarded as a

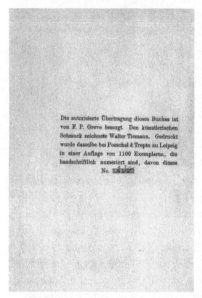

Die autorisierte Übertragung dieses Buches ist von F. P. Greve besorgt. Den künstlerischen Schmuck zeichnete Walter Tiemann. Gedruckt wurde dasselbe bei Poeschel & Trepte zu Leipzig in einer Auflage von 1100 Exemplaren, die handschriftlich numeriert sind, davon dieses No. 697.

❊ *Ernest Dowson,* Dilemmas *(1903), title page left and right*

❊ *Robert Browning,* Die Tragödie einer Seele *(1903), title page left and right.*
Translated by "F.C. Gerden"

coming light. While first avoiding and even discouraging my advances, he suddenly veered around and, incredibly, subordinated himself to me. It is true, in public he acted more or less as my mentor; but in private life he confessed that he was nothing, I everything (ISM 161).

This may be a thinly veiled admission of a homoerotic relationship in which Greve had the upper hand. It would have been this trust in his irresistible sexual power over Kilian that led him to believe that, upon their meeting in Bonn, he could not only win his friend over to his side again but that he could acquire more money from him. Letters from the month before his sentencing in May 1903 clearly reveal that, despite his arrest on account of Kilian's accusations, he could not believe that his friend would allow him to fall. Grove would later describe his "strange experience" in his 1946 autobiography. Although such hints of a homosexual relationship may have been daring, we cannot be sure exactly who was meant—Kilian, Lomberg, Hardt, Vollmoeller or Gide. The passage is as vague as it is suggestive.[35]

For the time being, in the spring of 1903, it was still "business as usual" for Greve. He thanked the Insel manager von Poellnitz for the payment of an honorarium, for he was "provided with rather little money for his travels." He promised to send the verse play by Robert Browning, *In a Gondola*, which he had intended to deliver to Leipzig personally, as a telegram from Palermo reveals.[36] He remained generous, however, allowing von Poellnitz himself to decide upon the appropriate payment for the text, as if he could afford it. He again offered *A Blot in the Scutcheon*, which he had asked George to assess for him the previous winter, writing that he hoped to be able "to conquer the stage for Browning"—in other words, to succeed with Browning where he had failed with Wilde. At the same time, he requested copies of Ernest Dowson's *Dilemmas*, which had not yet appeared. He desperately attempted to conceal his situation from his Leipzig publisher and possibly even himself—he was, after all, in jail awaiting trial.

His requests for copies of Dowson from Insel and his own translation of Wilde's *Dorian Gray* from Bruns indicate that he was preparing himself for his upcoming court case, in which he would have to prove that he was an author. For example, he would have to prove that he was not simply playing the idler in Palermo, indulging in an affair with another man's wife, but working in his profession as a writer, as he had suggested to Kilian upon receiving the loan. Unfortunately, only his translation of *Intentions* had been published, a book from the previous year. The Wilde plays had been printed but were unavailable in bookstores. Nothing else had been delivered yet. Most of his translations were still in the process of being proofread or still only in manuscript form. This was the case for a translation of letters by Elizabeth Barrett-Browning and perhaps other works which he had left behind in Palermo. Still, it would have wounded his pride to be apostrophized throughout the court proceedings as "writer and former student," although his attorney, Dr. Moosbach, would have undoubtedly expected more from the academic designation than the literary one. Greve did ultimately receive more translation deals—Robert Browning's *Paracelsus*, for instance—but these small and difficult texts brought him too little money, precisely at a time when he desperately needed larger sums to document his ability to work and to repay his debts.

Asked by Insel to produce advertising copy for the Dowson translation, Greve sent von Poellnitz a paragraph from his prison cell containing a collection of key terms. These apply equally well to himself and his situation, aside from the hardly apt physical description:

> Of Dowson I don't have much to say. His appearance: Bohemian—café life—permanent desperation. Held just above water by cheques from his publisher (Smithers). Paris: Latin quarter, London: Soho-Square. Drinker of absinthe. Constant smoker of cigarettes (120 per day, it is claimed). Died very young (I think at 27) of consumption. Visited Wilde in prison. As an artist: fine poet, very delicate, diaphanous, often sparse, seldom over-powering, and then openly startling. Influenced by Verlaine. Permanently exhausted, yet of a final, beautiful state of exhaustion. As prose writer, more or less the same applies. One tendency, to describe the *endings* of lives.[37]

For someone threatened with the prospect of imprisonment, who had translated Wilde, indeed who identified with him in many ways; who smoked and distributed many fine cigarettes, who was barely able to keep his head above water with cheques from his publisher; who had threatened suicide and who would in the future be forced to live a bohemian's life, these defining terms are nothing less than a form of macabre self-description. They were quite probably the unconscious product of rising desperation in the face of a seemingly hopeless situation. Here it is highly ironic that at precisely this time, when Greve thought he had found happiness and was prepared to undertake the troublesome task of translating Browning's poetry for little pay and in limited numbers to serve his artistic calling, the work brought him too little money in his desperate need to provide for Else in Palermo or even for himself. At first he requested that Insel double the one hundred-mark payment for his *Paracelsus* translation, as the size of this work was "almost four times that of the two other plays together." Von Poellnitz agreed. He also decided to double the printing to a thousand copies and to raise the price of *In a Gondola* and *A Blot in the Scutcheon*.[38] Payment, however, was slow in coming. In the middle of May a pressing letter reached von Poellnitz in Leipzig in which the imprisoned Greve offered his services without any attached conditions or feigned nonchalance:

> As you know, I am responsible for the care not only of myself, and thus pecuniary concerns occupy my foremost interest. I would be willing to undertake any task that I can manage in order to earn money, even if such tasks are not immediately comparable with others I have completed. Apart from German, I am totally fluent in three languages: English, French and Italian...That the work I deliver leaves nothing to be desired regarding care and precision, I need not emphasize. As a former student of classical philology, I would gladly undertake translations from classical languages.[39]

To his credit, Greve's initial goal was to provide Else with immediate and long-term support, since his defence counsel would certainly have given him little hope of emerging from the affair unpunished. In the end, the prosecuting attorney was to demand a sentence of one-and-a-half years imprisonment. It was now important for Greve to obtain new contracts before he was faced with a worse position from which to begin negotiations. His translation of Pater's *Marius* was still not out, leading him to complain that he had worked nine months for nothing. Two volumes thus lay fallow. Greve then offered Flaubert's *Contes* to Insel and referred to "Wells, who in England and France plays an important role along with Kipling." At the same time, Greve indicated a stylistic about-face, and not solely with his reference to Flaubert, Wells and Kipling. His suggestion to now translate novels by Giovanni Verga, which would find a readership because Verga "was the antipode of D'Annunzio and far beyond him in actual importance," firmly established his own course in the direction of realistic writing.[40] This would correspond to a statement he made in his next letter that he wanted to be finished with the Browning translation soon, "as a novel makes use of all of my strength." He made this statement in a letter from May 28, 1903, the day his sentence was delivered in the Bonn courthouse. He was lucky despite his misfortune, since the court decided for a sentence much shorter than the one requested by the prosecuting attorney. Greve was sentenced to one year in prison. According to the *Bonner Zeitung*, the court ruled that the accused

> could not have believed that he could pay back the money in the near future. He had made frivolous use of the money in Palermo with his

female companion. It was not proven that he had gone there to work. He had, in an ignominious manner, abused the trust of his generous friend. As a mitigating factor, it was to be concluded that he had acted more in negligence than in a consciously criminal manner.[41]

It says something of Greve's self-confidence and courage that the day of his conviction was immediately followed by an attempt to come to terms with his past in fictional form. Sublimation became novelistic fictionalization. If Else was the cause and occasion of the crisis in his relationship to Kilian, then she might also be the object of his emancipation as an independent author. As a lived fiction, the role of a rich young man of exclusive taste which he had previously played—a second Kilian or even Alfred Walter Heymel (the founder and major financier of Insel) or Count Kessler—had led him to ruin. In the novel *Fanny Essler*, which he was now about to begin, the former relation of life to fiction would be reversed. At the same time, he sought to finance the composition of his novel under a pseudonym that would help to raise the money that belonged to his debtor Kilian. Combining the initials from the first name of his pseudonym "F.C. Gerden" and those of his fictional alter ego "F.K. Reelen," he took the initials of Herman F[riedrich]. C[lark]. Kilian like a talisman into his new, impoverished life. They had once seemed to bring him luck.

◆ BONN GAOL

During the trial, Felix Greve made statements concerning his sources of income which he knew to be inaccurate on at least two counts. Although he exaggerated in claiming that his scholarships amounted to from one thousand five hundred to two thousand marks per year, this was not far from the truth. False, on the other hand, was the claim that he received a yearly income from his parents of between two thousand and two thousand five hundred marks. The court seems not to have checked the accuracy of his personal data. Thus the death of his impoverished mother and the financial state of his father, still living and who earned barely half that sum per year, remained undisclosed. Apparently Greve was able, at least in part, to maintain the fiction that he was assured a certain income from his family. He was also anxious to protect tangible sources of income—from Schultess, for instance—or others mediated by him. Greve was also, as Freytag-Loringhoven reported, able to save ten thousand of the twenty-five thousand marks required of him by the court. Contrary to the report filed in the *Bonner Zeitung*, it was not Endell who had lent money to Greve in January for their trip, but rather Endell who had requested and received money from his rival.

⁂ *Bonn City Gaol, 19 Wilhelmstrasse, ca. 1900* (Collection Bruno Klein)

Under certain conditions, the money, for which Greve was in part sentenced, could now be repaid to a certain extent by Endell to Else. This was done privately.[42]

The air of wealth Felix radiated, along with his fine physical appearance and composure, must have aided him in the courtroom despite the accusation of fraud. More importantly, Greve's disposition would have helped to protect him from a descent into psychological and social ruin in prison. Since the transcripts of the court proceedings and the prison files are no longer extant, there are no details regarding the conditions in the Bonn jail. There is no question that behind the sandstone walls and tiny barred window of the Bonn prison, watched by sentries from without and prison guards from within, Greve found himself in the company of men who he thought he had risen far above. In a supplement to the *Deutsche Reichs-Zeitung* that also reported on Greve's case, interested readers were informed of more upcoming cases involving a "maid accused of misappropriation and the falsification of documents;" "a drover charged with slander and obscenity;" and other cases against a "drover for attempted rape," a "day labourer" and an "occasional labourer...for sexual offences." They would all share the prison with Greve. He could soon expect, as the notorious expression had it, to be "humbled." Ironically enough, in May, the month of Greve's sentencing, Max Bruns would pen the following, after being deeply moved by his reading of Robert Sherard's biography of Oscar Wilde:

Awful reading! What a cruel country, this homeland of the puritans! The land of teetotalers and speculators. It's terrible the way Wilde was made to suffer. A German critic I read recently allowed that he had been thoroughly humbled because he was so arrogant, rather than god knows what else…Wilde's deficiency is in part the correlate of his strengths, his brilliant style and his nimble intellect; this deficiency—or to put it differently—his deficiency is the use of careless rhetoric in places where deep passion ought to be called forth.[43]

These observations have parallels not only with Greve's imprisonment, but also with his stylistic deficiencies which, given the increasing pressure to produce translations with increasing speed, were unavoidably the result of carelessness. In contrast to Wilde, Greve was concerned not to succumb to self-pity nor to allow himself to be "humbled." It was important for him to provide for Else and himself with as much work as possible and to maintain his contacts with various authors and publishers. Any expected monies would serve first to free him from the uncomfortably close contact he had to his fellow inmates, since everyone worked together performing the menial tasks meted out to them. He could free himself from this toil if he had the money to cover the costs of his maintenance. The following excerpt from a letter to Insel speaks eloquently of this:

[I would like] to add a further request, as I don't know who else I am to turn to. It concerns possibilities for further self-employment for me for which I have to pay. As my other credit has been extended to the very limit, I would like to ask a favour of you. I still have outstanding the honorarium for In a Gondola, the rate of which I left to your discretion. If that should be not enough, perhaps you could extend a small advance for Paracelsus which will be ready in a few weeks (it's already in draft form). The sum of money required is 60 marks. If you were willing to attend to my request, I would ask for the greatest haste possible. I would be extremely thankful to you.[44]

A handwritten remark on the letter reveals that Greve's call for help was heard. Insel paid on the very same day. As a result, the prison warden, the ominously named senior administrative inspector Krätke, was able to delegate one of the 118 single cells to the prisoner—in size between a small (18.4 square metres) and a large (43.3 square metres). Greve was no longer required to share one of the forty common cells (Rick, "Strafvollzug" 71).[45] Three weeks later, von Poellnitz received the translation of *Paracelsus* as promised. Along with his *Paracelsus*, Greve also sent an offprint of his translation of James McNeill Whistler's "Ten O'Clock" from the *Neue Rundschau* and suggested having it printed in book form. He now wanted to offer his Pater translation to Reclam. He also offered a translation of Thomas De Quincey's *Murder Considered as One of the Fine Arts*, although he claimed he had "another publisher for sure" for this translation. As is apparent in a letter to H.G. Wells, it would appear that he had already at least begun the translation.[46] Did he, however, actually offer it to J.C.C. Bruns or Insel? Neither was publishing De Quincey at the time, although Bruns did eventually publish a translation of the book in 1913. The translator's name was Alfred Peuker, which was not one of Greve's pseudonyms (Martens, *Bruns* 172; 193).[47]

Other letters make it clear that Greve had to pay thirty marks a month in order to continue work of his own. This regular payment impelled him to search for even more work. The prospect of being forced to perform such drudgery hung over him like the sword of Damocles during his first months in prison. Each delay in payment occasioned terrible distress:

Dear Mr. von Poellnitz,

I sincerely regret once again having to approach you with an urgent request and ask you not to think poorly of me as a result.

Your letter of VII 15 informed me that I could soon expect the honorarium for the translation of *Paracelsus*. I have made firm calculations on the basis of this payment and am not in a position to raise the money I require elsewhere. Considering this, do you think you could help me out of the difficult situation I find myself in? Otherwise I will be placed in a most uncomfortable position. Even if you were at first to send a portion of the payment, assuming you wanted to calculate the honorarium according to the size of the work, as I concluded from your last letter to me…With my repeated request that you not think poorly of me because of my urgency, I remain with the greatest respect

Your very devoted FELIX PAUL GREVE[48]

The hours Greve spent working in prison were probably not the break he had longed for after the wanderings of the preceeding years. It is true that he was not in Oscar Wilde's position, who had no comparable exemption from the awful drudgery he performed in Reading Gaol. Greve probably did not have his head shaved and may have been able to receive better food, assuming he had the money to pay for it. He was also able to write and receive letters and keep books, such as the recently published *Dilemmas*.[49] Nevertheless, prison life was anything but the previously apostrophized life in Munich, involving "hours of total peace, absolute happiness and cheerful enjoyment." After Wilde was discharged from prison, he vegetated alone in seedy hotel rooms, impoverished, despised and abandoned by former associates. In order to avoid the same fate, Greve remained on the offensive and planned for the future. Although he would seek refuge at a French seaside resort after his discharge—perhaps inspired by Wilde's example at Berneval—he was intent on making the financial preparations necessary for the realization of his goals (Ellmann, *Wilde* 502–14).[50] He would not be dependent upon others.

Greve's position was in no way easy. Although Else later made it appear as if his life in prison had basically been a success story, he was now an indentured author, the slave of his publishers, who were free to treat him at their discretion. Should Greve not comply with their demands, he could easily be left to his own fate in prison. Even if he were able to earn large sums of money, the loan collectors commissioned by his previous friends would be waiting for him at the prison gates upon his release. Furthermore, by this time notices of impending property seizure had already reached J.C.C. Bruns and Insel; this would affect any outstanding honoraria. The use of pseudonyms would not be enough to evade their demands. It would be necessary to use cash and to devise ways of countermanding a pocket seizure by the authorities when the time came.

The urgency of Greve's letters to Rudolf von Poellnitz in the summer of 1903 needs to be seen in direct relation not only to the apparent silence of others, but also the total absence of any form of aid from former friends and acquaintances. Where were Greve's former rowing-mates from Rhenus, one of whom, Renatus Schmidt-Ernsthausen, was employed by the office of the Bonn crown prosecutor? Where was Thiel? What had become of Schultess, and how did he react to the arrest and imprisonment of his favourite student? Where were his fellow archaeologists, and Delbrueck and Koch, all of whom still maintained excellent connections to Bonn? Or his professors, Usener and Loeschke and Usener's son Walther? What about Hardt and Vollmoeller? What did George, Wolfskehl, Reventlow, Helene Klages and Dülberg think or undertake? Felix need not have been left alone to endure Kilian's revenge, had others cared to concern themselves with him. In his cell Greve must have felt walled in by the deafening silence of all his former companions.

Apart from his publisher, it appeared as if no one was prepared to offer the least help. Oscar A.H. Schmitz alone appears to have written at the beginning of 1904. The opulent dinners, the expensive gifts, the financial help and the laborious efforts to develop social contacts—all of this seemed to have been for nothing. Against this backdrop of desolation and abandonment are the bitter notes of an ageing Frederick Philip Grove, from the first book of a work entitled "Of Nishivara the Saint," unpublished and unfinished by the author. He writes in the epigrammatic manner of Nietzsche's *Also sprach Zarathustra*:

4) One day, while still a very young man, he had a great shock.

5) For it came to pass that he found himself entangled in sin and shame; but he bowed his head and spoke to himself,

6) I have done only what others do; but being myself and not they, I did it more fearlessly and without restraint ("Nishivara" 83–84).

Grove's reference to Greve's time in prison seems inescapable. Of relevance here too is the condemning letter that Vollmoeller claimed to have received after this period.[51] Greve's friends distanced themselves from him rather quickly. Koch alone, as we have seen, wrote nostalgically to Reventlow from Berlin in December of that year. Was he able to do more for his mentor and temporary employer than sort through the correspondence of his youth? It would appear that Koch, along with everyone else apart from Wolfskehl, destroyed all correspondence either to or from Greve. This may have happened at the time of Koch's letter to Reventlow. Indeed, it is quite possible that no one wished to be drawn into the vortex that seemed to have consumed Greve and led to his downfall.

One of Frederick Philip Grove's German poems written in Canada, *Kopfschmerz* ("Headache"), treats of the trauma from his months in prison. It addresses the accompanying feeling of abandonment in a sentimental though moving manner:

Blood-red leaves of paper like fresh scars—
To the mirror, that slopes slanting to the wall,
I raise my eyes
From my head a flower rises—

The leaves of paper strung like fragments in a wreath
Are covered with brown dust and swing
Like sedge courted by the wind—
A haze descends, my thoughts swirl

And while the vision drowns in nothingness
And my head swims in the pillows dizzily,
A noise, like a clinking door,
Breaks into my heart—like canvas, that ripped—

And thundering, then, like iron bars screaming,
That through empty cities and forsaken streets
Trucks haul over dumb stone...
Damned, they who forgot me in my pain![52]

The productivity required for his own work would have saved Greve from destructive thoughts in prison. His projected novel *Fanny Essler*, with its malicious character portraits of those whom he had counted among his friends, would also have served as an outlet for emotional tension, as would several drafts for satirical plays at different times (and under varying titles). A play entitled *The Bloodbath in the Bavarian National Museum*, which was later announced but has never been discovered, may even have been ready for the stage. Assuming such a play existed, it may have been another satirical treatment of *Tempelkunst* ("temple art") by Greve's former friends in Schwabing's bohemian world.[53] Here, too, the actor Robert Nhil, a shareholder in the Deutsches Theater in Hamburg, may have attempted to promote Greve's ambitions in the theatre. After all, Hardt and Vollmoeller had achieved spectacular successes with their plays, so why not Greve?

6

FELIX·PAUL·GREVE, LITTERATUS

AFTER ESCAPING THE CRAMPED CIRCUMSTANCES of his family through a tremendous effort of mind and body, Felix attempted to enter those circles of money, art and education that seemed to promise advancement in the world. He had perfected the art of social mimicry and seemed to have succeeded until his naïveté, sheer bravura and callousness brought him down. His fall coincided with the discovery of his own heterosexuality and thus an implicit rejection of the many young men close to the master. Like Roderich Huch, it is possible that Felix had decided not to continue as George or Wolfskehl's plaything and sought different friends, emphasizing his own sexual and creative powers. He had grown tired of the "heavy liqueurs" of the homophile circles he had formerly enjoyed, or at least had pretended to embrace.

Of course another view is possible, one based on a late remark by Stefan George concerning the young men in his orbit who afterwards went their own ways "to Java to plant tobacco [like Dauthendey], to produce literature or to spend their lives with whores." George's caustic remark not only indicates his habit of holding on to the young men in his orbit "at the moment of the height of their lives," but also his resistance to their moving on. He liked them only during their time with *him* and he alone determined the time of their departure (Landmann, 183). This was certainly the case with Felix and Else, whom George seems to have had in mind. His remarks were clearly made with an eye to the future. Maximilian Dauthendey, Friedrich and Roderich Huch and Karl Gustav Vollmoeller were among those creative individuals who chose to go their own ways and on their own terms. Oscar A.H. Schmitz, who had been a member of the circle and who had dared in 1900 to criticize Melchior Lechter in the influential *Wiener Rundschau*, had this to say about George: "He never pardoned that I, like most of his disciples, had descended 'from the temple into the alleyway,' i.e., that I wrote for unsanctified newspapers and magazines and dealt with many a profane thing" (Hemecker, "Schmitz" 74).[1]

In his new station among society's undesirables in prison, where he could easily slide into the gutter, Greve learned to produce "profane things" for the marketplace. He was soon recommending realist authors to his publishers, among them such greats as Gustave Flaubert, but also popular authors with socialist leanings such as Herbert George Wells, who produced sensational works for mass consumption. Adjusting further to his new situation, Felix now also used his own writings to turn against George's aestheticism. If George may be termed an Anti-Naturalist, then Greve now became an Anti-Anti-Naturalist and his novel *Fanny Essler* a sharp parody of the George school. As an indictment, it was of a harshness that not even Franziska zu Reventlow in her novel and her *Schwabinger Beobachter* had risked, then or later.

Felix's sources of easy money had dried up. Worse, he was due to pay back his debts plus interest. Suddenly he was bound to play the role of the harried and overworked translator in constant need of funds of which Reventlow had become a pitiful example. According to her diary, "she earned a livelihood for herself and her child, in day and night shifts, often malnourished, in terrible health, producing 5722 pages of translation for the publisher Albert Langen" (Reventlow, *Briefe* 5). Although Felix and Else were not married and had no children, Greve still had to help finance Else and satisfy his creditors.

J.C.C. Bruns soon reminded the prisoner that they were still in business together. Like Insel, Bruns had abstained from suing Felix for outstanding debts. The publisher had been informed of the suit and subsequent verdict by a colleague from the *Bonner Zeitung*, a friendly newspaper. Greve quickly assured the firm that future fees would be applied to whatever might be outstanding later. This was the reason, Greve wrote, that he offered Bruns the Browning books first, although Insel and S. Fischer were certain buyers. He then reiterated an earlier promise that Bruns would have first refusal of any manuscript he produced on his own initiative. He added that two Pater volumes, translated but still unsold, each about 30–32 sheets, would almost balance his account. This allows us to estimate his debt to Bruns at about 1000–1200 marks. In addition, Greve wrote optimistically from prison that if the existing or forthcoming Bruns volumes sold well, money might even be credited to him.[2]

But Felix Greve was in a difficult situation. Despite the optimistic overtures, Bruns was not excited by Greve's proposals, although the firm did ask to see one of the Browning translations (which it later turned down). At Greve's request, Bruns sent copies of *Dorian Gray*, which the translator had not yet seen, to the Bonn jail. Although Greve had just claimed that he would offer anything new to Bruns first, only nine days later he mentioned new work on George Meredith to Insel; in fact, he offered to send *The Tragic Comedians* and *The Ordeal of Richard Feverel* by the beginning of October. After two weeks without a response from Insel, Greve offered Bruns the Meredith novels, keeping his promise of an exclusive offer with another author he now also considered translating, H.G. Wells. All of a sudden he staked most of his hopes on Bruns, hoping to substantially increase the comparatively meagre income from Insel:

> Apart from the work on Browning [for Insel], I am translating some books by a contemporary English author, *H.G. Wells*, who seems to promise successful sales. Perhaps you will take the opportunity to read a manuscript when convenient. Regarding the authorization I will negotiate with the author himself. Several volumes—as many as three—should be done, since they hang together.

> Further to this, I should like to edit a series of the most important English novels of the last quarter of a century. Of this series, I could offer you the first work: George Meredith, *The Ordeal of Richard Feverel* in the course of the next month.[3]

This letter from prison stirred J.C.C. Bruns into action, and in the long run the publisher profited from Greve's suggestions. In fact, Greve's idea for a series of novels would later give rise to Bruns's successful *Meisterwerke der Weltliteratur* ("Masterpieces of World Literature") series—a forerunner to similar series from other publishers. It appears as if Greve was ready to help Bruns plan a major part of its publishing program. No wonder, then, that Greve's next suggestions regarding three novels by Wells and Meredith's *The Ordeal of Richard Feverel* produced cautious agreement on the part of the publisher. Greve's advice to publish *Beauchamp's Career* was not heeded.[4] Caution, as will be shown, was exercised with the translator, although Max Bruns would soon write enthusiastically to his father about Greve's suggestions. Unfortunately, in private Max Bruns was less than delighted with Greve's work. This proved to be the case with Greve's introductory brochure for Wilde readers, the rhapsodical *Randarabesken zu Oskar Wilde*, separately published but meant (and later used) as the introductory essay to Bruns' and Greve's edition of Wilde's *The Portrait of Mr. W.H.* Max noted:

> The author of this little brochure, meant to introduce Wilde to Germany, has chosen the tasteful title "A Propos d'Oscar Wilde." I succeeded in preventing this nonsense. The booklet itself? Chatter. Long-winded and short in sense. The style hardly palatable. The affectations of a man completely devoid of affects. This booklet deserved a put-down by the critics (who will possibly ignore it).[5]

Although this dyspeptic judgment did not prevent the booklet from appearing, Max Bruns's low opinion of Greve's talents as a writer was sure to affect their relations. As Max's influence in the firm grew after 1907, a harsh tone entered their increasingly infrequent correspondence. In 1903, however, Greve's importance for the firm's list—not only as a translator but now also as an author and adviser—must have aroused Max's jealousy. Felix Greve was busy carving out a role for himself in English-language literature that was similar to Max Bruns's own role for French-language authors. On the other hand, of course, Greve was trying to compensate for the loss of trust in his financial transactions. Only through increased production could he regain his personal honour and reliability. Among other texts, Max Bruns read the first Meredith manuscript. Greve, sensing both J.C.C. Bruns's interest in the new books and the firm's hesitation, now hastened to remove any doubt as to his rights to Wilde's essays. He also immediately totted up an account, allotting himself 20% of future sales. In hopes of soon seeing himself free from debt, he praised the new authors he had recommended to Bruns in extravagant terms:

> Now I have to ask your attention concerning a discussion of further publications. You now have a volume each of Browning and Meredith. For both I have been doing my utmost. Presently there is vivid interest in Browning. Ellen Key published a book about him and his wife with Fischer. I am probably going to publish studies about him. A few trifles for which I could not find space in my larger volumes are to be published by Insel (I am soon going to present you with copies). I am the editor of his correspondence for Fischer. For five years, Meredith has been continuously talked about in Germany. One knows that in England he is regarded as a Shakespeare in prose. Everybody is talking about him with secretive awe and nobody knows him…It will not be necessary to do everything by Meredith in German translation

(although the English originals about whose immense linguistic difficulties Wilde speaks in *Intentions* may hardly be considered as rivals. The same is true of Browning), but surely about two or three more volumes, one of which I hold here in readiness.[6]

Greve cleverly played up to the firm's tendency to develop a homogeneous program. In this context, it was just a short leap for Bruns from Wilde, who had mentioned Meredith in *Intentions*, to the new author. Greve also proposed a small series of books which might prove useful should Meredith become a success. Of particular interest is Felix's remark about originals, their translation and their respective markets in the target country. Reference is clearly to the ready availability of foreign-language texts, mostly in English and French. Original-language editions and their translations were often published more or less simultaneously in the famous Tauchnitz or Reclam series in Leipzig. This, too, is a factor to consider when we judge translations as philologically faulty, much as Meyerfeld had so high-handedly judged Greve's. Source-language versions of texts were available to those who could read the language. For those who either wanted to admire the translator's art or who simply needed assistance, the translation facilitated access to the work of a foreign author. Although English was taught and spoken by the book-buying classes, knowledge of the classical languages and of French was much more widespread. Greve's own schooling at the Johanneum and his field of concentration at Bonn University reflected what could be expected of many of his educated readers. Greve would have earlier striven for a translation addressed to the *cognoscenti* in George's circle. The translations he now suggested, by contrast, were meant for a much larger audience.

Accordingly, Greve then went on to praise Robert Browning and Giovanni Verga, "the antipode of D'Annunzio, after whose novella was fashioned the script for [Pietro Mascagni's one-act opera] *Cavalleria Rusticana*." For the authorizations, he claimed to be in contact with Wells (correct) and Verga (no trace could be found). In fact, he was first compelled to deal with Wells's London publisher W.H. Heinemann before he was allowed to contact Wells directly.[7] Then he explained the very real and pressing purpose behind these offers for translation and publication:

> But now I come to my point. Next summer, approximately in June, I shall be in need of larger sums, and I have to arrange for them now. Should you also accept the Verga, and if nothing is published by summer, I would have to count on an advance from you at the said time (I am going to need several thousand marks—say, 3000).[8] Of course this advance would have to be below the amount to be expected

for the books, since I do not wish, as you can imagine, to come again into the uncomfortable situation of having a deficit in my account. I am telling you all of this in advance so that you may have a clear view ahead, and I also want to tell you the reason: I intend to get married. I therefore beg you, should my suggestions not be too much for you or if you were not so inclined or not in a position to help me in the manner indicated (until the summer I probably will not have to draw any money from my account, with the exception of a few small sums, even in the case of a larger plus in my account) to be kind enough to notify me, since, as of recently, a number of other publishers are available to me. I hope you are not going to misunderstand and to forgive me for bothering you with my personal affairs. For me, more than ever, it is a matter of life to order my finances in such a way that I may count on fixed sums for a sufficient time in advance.[9]

It is a well-planned and moving letter. No *cri de coeur*, to be sure, but it is the most rational and frank-sounding letter he could have written in his unfortunate circumstances. His financial situation had indeed become a "matter of life," for it concerned the question of a future with Else, whom he had left destitute in Palermo and who had a difficult time fending for herself in Italy. He also would have assumed that Endell had already sued for divorce (although he hadn't yet). His situation had to be dealt with rationally. He had much to offer his Minden publisher. He promised Bruns financial compensation and considerable future earnings. More, he now guaranteed security. Since he did not need the money for the time being, the publisher ran no risk of losing his investment. Maybe even more importantly, he made it implicitly clear that he was not unmoved but unbowed and in full possession of his powers. Indeed, his offers show that he would put his imprisonment to good and productive use—like a monk living a monk's industrious life.

On this occasion, Greve's repeated pleas for regular payments were crowned with success. Although both J.C.C. Bruns and Insel eventually turned down the Verga manuscript,[10] the publisher had no serious objection to the proposed pecuniary settlement. First, however, accounts had to be squared; the Wilde tales and the *Randarabesken*, Max Bruns wrote, were a beginning. Clearly the firm did not want to discourage Greve. Nevertheless, it would proceed with excessive caution and no money would be paid in advance. Most notably, the firm wanted to be kept informed about authorizations and be permitted to "look at agreements concluded with the author." It is thanks to such precautions that some of the agreements reached have survived among the Bruns papers.

Greve's role as the gentleman-translator and connoisseur had, for the time being, come to an end. Not only did he have to lay open his life to public scrutiny during the trial, but he even felt he had to comment on his private plans. Worst of all, the publisher would now monitor his translator's transactions with the foreign author. Greve was not only in prison but he had effectively ceased to act as a free agent in the literary market. If von Poellnitz's tone had already become cool and uncompromisingly businesslike, Max Bruns too felt no qualms about rebuking Greve in the tones of a pedantic and querulous schoolmaster:

> And on this occasion we would like to ask you to take to heart the reminder that you take special care to assure the good readability of your manuscripts. The handwriting in your translation of "Richard Feverel" is so crabbed and convoluted that we shall not be in a position to inform you about our final decision for another three weeks. Apart from the fact that the reading costs both of us much time, the reader finds it hard not to have that tiredness which overcomes him during the reading influence his judgment of what he has read.[11]

In spite of the optimism it was meant to inspire in Greve, this letter must have been painful reading. It still is. Bruns, it seems, was attempting to get back at Greve for his feigned neurasthenia at the beginning of the year, when he was purportedly leaving for Italy to recover and having somebody else—Herbert Koch—correct proofs for him. Max Bruns's intention seems obvious when he mentions that "our reader has for a long time now been ill with neurasthenia and must not be bothered with too much strenuous reading." In this case, the reader was Max himself. Bruns intended to chasten Greve and return in kind what Greve had given. Not surprisingly, in a note from December 2 addressed to von Poellnitz, Greve indicated that he had fallen ill.

Unbeknownst to Greve, Max sent glowing reports to his father on the new manuscripts. "I am reading Meredith on the side and find him superb. This year, the firm will attain an excellent position in the book market." He was right, but not because of Meredith. Although Bruns proceeded cautiously and initially published *Richard Feverel* in three separate volumes—thus carefully testing the market without investing too much—the initial sales figures were disappointing. In the long run, however, there were small but steady sales which allowed the publisher to keep the books in print for over two decades.[12] This was certainly attributable to Greve's translation since another publisher's edition appeared at the same time. Greve and J.C.C. Bruns also took a risk by translating and publishing Meredith's not unproblematic novel

Diana of the Crossways. Felix commented on the stylistic peculiarities of the book in his introduction, probably aware that both his and the author's work were ahead of their time and that a success with the readers would be nigh impossible.[13] Introducing the book, Greve took the bull by the horns and admitted that the critics had already attacked the first volumes of the Meredith edition. He then proceeded to give the reader a few (self-referential) "pointers," casually quoting Meyerfeld, his old enemy from the days of his first Wilde translations:

> A really exact translation of the "cliffs of the original" with its "daring diction, bold neologisms, superabundance of images and linguistic rapes" (Max Meyerfeld in the *Zeit*) must appear from the first an impossibility…it would take a Jean Paul as translator. Every translation is a compromise. The lover of literature reaches for the original. The reader from a wider audience desires mediation between himself and a mind of foreign nationality. Accordingly, the editor who had formerly thought it his duty to lessen the compromise as much as was in his power, substituted paraphrase for verbatim translations in the present work in the case of a number of particularly difficult or dark passages. Still, in spite of this he tried to fit his language snugly to the complications of the original. How far he may have succeeded in this compromise is not his to decide. Only one demand he wishes to reject right away—the demand for an elegant, fluent style.[14]

With this clever *apologia*, Greve killed two birds with one stone. He called upon his critic Meyerfeld, who had formerly crucified him for mistakes and inaccuracies, as a witness to the "cliffs" of the English text, and used this to forego a seemingly impossible precision which he—ever the radical—had consistently called for. He thus justified his somewhat loose translation while emphasizing his masterly command of language (placing himself near Jean Paul Richter, the Romantic novelist famous for his intricate style). The passage is a wonderfully covert polemic with its apparent readiness to compromise with his critic. Felix had obviously learned a lesson from the Gaulke controversy. At the end of his "Introduction" he pointed to the "well-known new forces" which the publisher had succeeded in winning for the Meredith edition, meaning, in short, that he would not continue working on the edition. In spite of his great efforts and the defence of his method in *Diana*, profit in money and reputation must have been low. The fourth novel in the series, *Rhoda Fleming*, was translated by a new talent, Sophie von Harbou.

Perhaps Felix Greve had dropped the Meredith project in order to have his hands free for the more promising work he had already begun. By now,

he had transformed his Bonn prison cell into a veritable workshop for translating and introducing new English and French literature to German
audiences. The prisoner was busy working on Meredith and establishing
connections with André Gide; work on Gustave Flaubert was to follow. H.G.
Wells, however, came first.

◆ THE ISLAND OF H.G. WELLS

As an occasional editor in his father's publishing firm, Max Bruns sought a
maximum degree of aesthetic coherence among the authors chosen for the
Bruns list. Max was striving to fashion J.C.C. Bruns's program into a kind of
Wagnerian *Gesamtkunstwerk*. Such a plan must have seemed obvious to a
poet and editor who was also an accomplished musician and a member of a
firm which had published writings on Wagner. Although Meredith seemed
a difficult fit, Max convinced himself that the novelist was somehow close to
Wilde. He promptly discovered in the latter, as he wrote in his reader's report
on *The Ordeal of Richard Feverel*, a stylistic receptivity showing the

influences of "Balzac, Flaubert, Baudelaire, Poe, Meredith, and even Maeterinck."[15] Until Greve started working for Bruns, only the Poe and Baudelaire editions had begun to appear in Minden. Greve's suggestion that Wilde, Meredith, and even Wells be translated and published—curious as this choice of literary bedfellows may appear today—seemed quite in line with Max's own plans for developing a list out of Poe and Baudelaire, the foundations of the firm's reputation as an innovative publisher. As will be seen later, their intentions converged only for a moment when Greve supported Max Bruns's long-standing plan to publish a Flaubert edition.

Far more profitable than Meredith, it was hoped—and certainly much more than Flaubert or Gide—were the works of H.G. Wells. In fact, all talk of a *Gesamtkunstwerk* along the lines of French aestheticism took second place to the money-making potential of an English bestseller. A place was quickly found for Wells among the fantasy writers whom the firm also published (E.A. Poe and Paul Scheerbart). Thus a semblance of programmatic coherence was preserved. Max soon praised the author Greve had recommended in a letter to his father (Greve had first contacted Wells by letter of November 9, 1903):

> Dear father—With the exception of a small portion I have now finished reading "Moreau's Island." It is a grandiose parody on being creative, on being human, on being...Even though Wells is a nervous hack, he remains artist enough in the dreamlike way of his visions... even when finer minds are going to turn less to the at times somewhat crude outer apparatus than to the "spiritual band" that weaves through this prestidigation. It appears to me, then, that a large circle of readers will get their money's worth with Wells: I think it entirely possible that, should another publisher throw Wells's book on the market, we would with envious regret take cognizance of the large numbers of copies sold. Something can be done with such books, there is no question about it to me. Wells is much more gifted with imagination than Scheerbart...he is a somewhat coarsened Poe with all the marks of a fluent raconteur (and to the vast mass he will be *nothing* else).[16]

Max's business instincts were telling him that Wells would undoubtedly turn out to be a popular bestseller. Better still, publishing Wells would not be wholly without literary merit. Best of all, J.C.C. Bruns's risk would be negligible: "If the publisher Heinemann wants to get a percentage of the printings (and *thus* I recall Greve's letter), I don't see why our taking on this work should be such a great financial risk." The firm, Max suggested, would do well to start with a (then) sizable first printing of three thousand copies.[17]

Only now, when Bruns's consent had been secured, did Felix establish direct communication with the English author, after first dealing with him through his agents. He first contacted Wells from prison via Heinemann in March 1904 (asking his correspondents to send mail to him care of the firm in Minden, thereby affirming his new trustworthiness to Bruns). Like Bruns, Heinemann had been careful and had first demanded a sample translation from Greve before allowing him access to the author. The translation sample turned out to everybody's satisfaction, as Sydney Pauling of Heinemann assured H.G. Wells: "The specimen of translation has been most carefully examined, and is reported upon most favourably. I am therefore writing to the translator to give him, as Mr. Heinemann suggested, a three months' option on the two books 'Dr. Moreau' and 'The Time Machine' in Germany."[18] The publisher soon revoked this limitation and prepared a contract. It granted exclusive translation and publication rights for *The Time Machine* and *The Island of Dr. Moreau* in the German-speaking world (Germany, Austria, Switzerland, Austro-Hungary). William Heinemann signed and J.C.C. Bruns countersigned for sums of twenty and twenty-five pounds (or 409 and 510 marks), respectively.

Shortly after his release from prison, Felix used some of the money Bruns had promised to travel to England and meet Wells himself. He booked a room for the weekend of June 24–27 in London at the Arundel Hotel, and visited Wells at Spade House in Sandgate, near Folkestone.[19] Only recently built, Spade House spectacularly crowned "the cliffs ninety feet above the sea," with its "pergolas and lawns sweeping down to the beach" (Dickson 82). In its seaview splendour it may have impressed Greve as yet another possible model for Grove's fictional boyhood home "Castle Thurow." Felix gained the trust of both the English author and his wife, who acted as his business manager. All concerned seemed to have firmly believed in the success of the venture. A first contract was signed July 2, 1904, comprising all German-language rights.

Five months later, as a result of Felix's first visit, Heinemann, Bruns and Wells signed a second contract for *The First Men on the Moon* and *The Food of the Gods*. The terms were the same as before, only Wells now settled for no less than almost double the sum he had received before, that is, forty pounds for each of the two new books. Greve and Bruns convinced Wells to allow publication of the translation of *The Food of the Gods* at the same time as the English edition—a signal success which Greve would repeat with the translation of Gide's *La porte étroite* five years later. Wells promised "to send a typewritten manuscript or a full set of proofsheets to Mr. Bruns's translator, Mr. Felix Paul Greve, so that the work may be published simultaneously in German and in the original." Bruns was also assured of the right of preemption for most of Wells's other works still unsold elsewhere. In order to specify what was meant by "other works," Wells wrote directly to Bruns from Sandgate three days later:

Dear Sir,

…It is understood between us that the works which may be acquired by you during the specified time on the same terms as you have agreed for, are the following:

The Wonderful Visit.
The Sea Lady.
Love and Mr Lewisham.
The Wheels of Chance.
Anticipations.
Mankind in the Making.
When the Sleeper Wakes.
Tales of Space and Time.
Twelve Stories and a Dream.

Any of the stories from "The Stolen Bacillus" and "The Plattner Story" which have not already been translated into German.

This list excludes my books The War of the Worlds, which was published in Germany some years ago, and The Invisible Man, which as I explained to Herr Greve, is already under negotiation, but which I think will very probably be in my hands again shortly (Wells to J.C.C. Bruns, July 5, 1904).[20]

Wells was delighted by the arrangements. He was hopeful for the success of Greve's translations, pleased by the sums received and flattered by the attention from his German translator and the Minden publisher. Although J.C.C. Bruns and Greve eventually were content with publishing only *When the Sleeper Wakes* and *Anticipations*, in addition to the four others on the list, Wells must have been quite satisfied with the deal. He readily agreed when Bruns and Greve asked for an extension of the option on Wells's books in 1905, and he volunteered information on his new book, *A Modern Utopia*, in the hopes of getting it published in German translation.

Against the expectations of all involved, however, the venture fell far short of the desired financial breakthrough. Although Bruns praised the author as

✸ *Advertisement for Wells, "The English Jules Verne." Pages one and two. "All three works rendered into German by Felix Paul Grove."* (*J.C.C. Bruns Archiv, Minden*)

✸ *Pages three and four* (*J.C.C. Bruns Archiv, Minden*)

der englische Jules Verne ("the English Jules Verne"), Greve had to inform Wells that, as of October 1905, the German sales had not exceeded a meagre 288 to 440 copies of the books already published.[21] Wells himself would not have been surprised, since his recent books, *The Food of the Gods* included, had not sold very well in the original. "My reputation is out of all proportion greater than my book sales," he wrote in 1905 (Dickson 143). Greve did not know this, of course. He blamed neither author nor translation but accused the German publisher of stinting on advertising. This was not quite fair, for Bruns had invested heavily in large ads in leading magazines. When, due to the small sales, the Minden firm refused to accept *A Modern Utopia*, Greve felt free to approach other publishers. Wells had recently made a similar move by contracting with Macmillan, pushing hard to have the new publisher take over the rights to all of his previous books (Dickson 138f.).

As it turned out, neither Greve nor Wells nor Bruns were to blame. At Greve's instigation, they had undertaken a pioneering venture which would only pay off much later—too late for Greve and Bruns. In the 1920s, after Max Bruns had sold his superannuated stock and the rights to his books to other publishers, the young Viennese publisher Paul Zsolnay bought all the rights to Wells's works, invested enormous sums in advertising and succeeded in establishing the author in the German-language market. Zsolnay, incidentally, had worked for Heinemann in London and enjoyed excellent relations with the firm. Greve's Wells translations remained in print even after Carl Hanser Publishers of Munich purchased Zsolnay in the late 1990s.

In 1929, Max Bruns wrote somewhat sadly that he had once counted upon selling two thousand copies of Wells's novels whereas Zsolnay was now used to printing editions of twenty thousand and more.[22] One can only wonder whether Frederick Philip Grove in Canada ever heard of the sensational sales of Wells's books in the 1920s, which caused the English author to go on a triumphant tour of Germany (cf. Vallentin, "Wells" 1). The world economic crisis of 1929, however, ended all that. The Nazis, moreover, were not inclined to promote an English author with socialist leanings, translated by a long-forgotten German author.

Regardless of its financial success, the Wells venture had given Felix a chance to visit England for the first time and to test his English proficiency. After the joke in Gardone, he wanted to see whether he could in fact pass for an Englishman or at least somebody who would not immediately strike an Anglo-Saxon person as foreign. He seems to have passed the test. He also appears to have succeeded in dealing with the famous H.G. Wells as a colleague, possibly also picking up hints on how to lead the life of a writer in, say, Canada. At the same time, he may have recognized in Wells, who had also come up in the world by industriousness and self-acquired *Bildung*, a kindred soul and a career to emulate. Twenty-five years later, however, when he seemed to have achieved a considerable degree of eminence in Canada as Grove, he claimed—recalling "a long walk on the chalk cliffs of Dover"—to have been amazed at the obedience of an (unnamed) English writer of "potboilers" to his publisher's wishes, thus missing the high watermark of "what he was capable of." FPG himself had never been innocent of the ways of publishers (or authors), and he certainly had hoped to achieve for himself the "little immortality" Wells did achieve (NS 10–11). In Canada, though, the moral high ground Grove took suited his new role as a herald of high culture.

The Wells connection and the surviving correspondence between the English author and his translator is invaluable because it provides additional glimpses into Felix Greve's busy life on the French coast. More often than not, this came to stand in the way of subsequent visits to his English "neighbour" across the Channel:

> I beg to excuse me: all through this summer it has been—literally—impossible for me to be absent a single day. Whenever the postman passed, he had a numerous [sic] "couvrier" of proofs for me—proofs that had to be returned within a few hours. I am sure you cannot imagine a busy life like mine. In spite of enormous activity as author (I am publishing the result of about 8 years of continual work), I had to continue translating half a dozen French and English authors because I don't wish to rely prematurely on what my own works MAY yield me as an income (Greve to H.G. Wells, October 6, 1905).

He was working incessantly, utilizing his past experiences as an author—although not of "about 8 years." Greve had hardly had a chance to rest during the period. Life, writing, translating—each must have seemed like the same endless, tiring work.

At the end of his prison term, by the last day of May 1904, Felix Greve had largely succeeded in achieving one of his financial aims. His work on Meredith and Wells had contributed to balancing his account with J.C.C. Bruns and he could confidently expect additional fees. Unfortunately, he also had to expect his major creditor, Kilian's Bonn lawyer Dr. Schafgans, at the prison gate to confiscate any money he might have on him or could expect to receive. It was of the utmost urgency to make arrangements that would offset the efforts of his creditors to strip him down again to his last pfennig, the condition he was in when arrested. If Kilian could lay his hands on him, the enormous amount of literary work he had undertaken would have been for nought. J.C.C. Bruns was his major source of income. To Bruns his creditors would turn first. As it happened, in spite of their existing and future disagreements, Bruns stood ready to help Greve in his need.

Upon leaving prison he was greeted by Else. She had spent the interval in Palermo and Rome, supported by what little sums Felix could send, what August Endell provided and whatever three lovers and friends could contribute. Freytag-Loringhoven's words would later testify to this (BE 136–37). The pair did not have to remain in Bonn to be stared at by former friends and acquaintances. It was probably Else who rented quarters for them at the rooming house of Frau Sachsenröder in the somewhat derelict old quarter of nearby Cologne (37 Albertusstrasse). They stayed for most of June. From then on, Greve would live again and again in such places. There were certain advantages: one did not have to fix one's own meals, a small measure of service was offered and the most important commodity—anonymity—was free and abundant. Such were the accommodations he sought for himself, from Via di Monte Tarpeo in Rome to Königin-Augusta-Strasse in Berlin to the Via Lincoln in Palermo to hideouts in Wollerau, Paris-Plage and elsewhere. Each seemed to repeat a pattern begun in his mother's rooming house in Hamburg.

In May 1904, Bruns's manager, Stiller, answered an official inquiry by Dr. Schafgans in partially good conscience. It concerned the attachment of money owing to Greve; Bruns claimed he owed Greve nothing but that Greve owed them (Bruns to Schafgans, May 31, 1904). There had been no long–term contract between Felix and his publisher. They had primarily acted on trust (which Bruns occasionally had reasons to regret), and thus there were no records. Now even Greve's former mistakes could be used to his advantage. Since a considerable number of works translated by Greve were forthcoming, however, a solution had to be found, and found quickly. It would have to safeguard the publisher's new books, which had already been advertised, and the income urgently needed to ensure the translator's continued productivity. Stiller wrote to Greve in Cologne and suggesting a meeting "here," since written messages were best avoided. "Here" meant not Minden but Wiesbaden, the fashionable watering-place of Gustav Bruns, the owner of the firm. Else, in Felix's place, sent a telegram consenting to a meeting. Probably realizing that he would have to have something new in hand to offer the publisher, Felix followed this up with a few lines suggesting that they meet in Wiesbaden at the end of the week, after a "rendezvous with a French author" in Paris. The French author, of course, was André Gide, who had consented to meet Felix on the first Thursday of June, two days after his release from prison. From Paris, Felix returned with Gide's consent that he become the translator for two new works. In the meantime, Stiller and Gustav Bruns must have discussed ways out of their common dilemma. One solution involved Greve giving his current and future income from Bruns to Else, whom he had mentioned to Bruns as his "wife" but to whom Stiller in a telegram to Wiesbaden referred to as Greve's "bride." The firm was not easily deceived:

> greve matter will not work this way, donation can be contested according to paragraph three contest law. contested would also be sale through the hands of the bride to us, since intention greve thus to take away the fortune from his creditors to their loss cannot said to be unknown to us, all the more if there is payment to bride. possible way out to buy directly from greve, however, greve must see to it that he receives the money quickly to provide for the case that, in case of an unfortunate coincidence, money may not be taken from him by court order. donation to bride not permissible, direct acquisition from greve by us possible, because the present court order does not extend to new business deals.[23]

This is how it was done. It explains Greve's increased activity, for money would be paid directly to him in the future (probably on delivery of the manuscript), and not into an account. Felix had reason to be grateful to his publisher. The Wiesbaden meeting was probably a good occasion to present Gustav Bruns with inscribed copies of his two small Browning volumes, then already published by Insel, which are still extant in Bruns's private library. One likes to imagine the meeting between the rotund old publisher, face half-hidden behind his enormous, full grey beard, and the elegantly clad Felix Greve, exceedingly tall and thin like a "slim pine," his "unbelievable hair of the texture, colour, glossiness of spun yellow glass," terribly pale "as if passed through chloride."[24] Did Bruns keep the young man at a distance or did he invite him for a walk through the hall of the famous *Kurhaus* and along the white gravel walkways of the public garden? Did they take a glass of the invigorating waters together or did they take a drink of more potent spirits and observe the gambling going on in the casino? Did the publisher also receive a draft of the *Fanny Essler* manuscript, eventually published elsewhere the following year? We do not know. But we do know that they talked about two manuscripts by the author whom Felix had just seen in Paris, André Gide.

❋ *André Gide*
(*Collection Catherine Gide*)

◆ ANDRÉ GIDE

Gide's importance for Grove was recognized in Canada from an early date. The reverse has not been true. In the wake of Spettigue's discovery of Grove's German birth and facts about his life there, Desmond Pacey was, it appears, the first to track down a letter of Greve's to Gide in Paris.[25] The title of Grove's eighth Canadian book forty years before, the novel *Fruits of the Earth* (1933), must have appeared to those in the know as a reference to a Greve translation of a small Gide work called "Menalkas"—an excerpt from Gide's *Les nourritures terrestres* which, in English, is entitled *Fruits of the Earth*. Grove must have enjoyed the little in-joke.

Ten years later, Grove again barely disguised the Frenchman's identity in recollections which were to form the preface of *In Search of Myself*. Here, the narrator describes an arduous car ride through a dreary-looking area. It is rocky and full of occasional patches of swamp between lakes Erie and Ontario, not too far from Simcoe where the Groves then resided. Suddenly, the car gets stuck in a large "watery mud-hole" and the narrator-driver, deeply tired and depressed, remains in the vehicle waiting for help from a nearby house. His depression is caused less by his present situation than by news from the night before. A friendly librarian (Grove's friend Richard Crouch) had brought a book that turned out to be the "biography of a Frenchman, still living, who in my early days had been one of my intimates." The narrator mentions no names but continues mysteriously: "At the time, this young Frenchman and myself had been aflame with a great enthusiasm for life and art." He then remembers the "anecdotes of our ardent association" that he had told the visiting librarian, about his "unbounded youthful admiration for the young Frenchman who, a year or two older than myself, had been one of the determining influences in overcoming my own immaturities" (ISM 3). Now, with his car lodged in the muddy earth, he is struck by the devastating awareness of the difference between them. "[E]ach had gone his way"—he in the crowded capitals of Europe, "I on the lonely prairies of Western Canada." Looking at the biography of his former friend (most likely the one published in 1938 by Jean Hytier), the Canadian drew a bitter conclusion:

> Like a flash of lightning it had struck me that, to earn the distinction of seeing his biography published within his lifetime, he must have achieved things which had focused on him the eyes of a world, a living world as full of fire and enthusiasm as any world that had ever been— whereas I, only slightly his junior, in spite of often titanic endeavour, had lived and worked in obscurity, giving expression, at the best, to a few, a very few mirrorings of life in the raw such as it had been my lot to witness (ISM 4).

The Frenchman's "life of art" is effectually contrasted to the narrator's "life in the raw." In his own art, however, Grove more often than not shied away from such rawness. He preferred putting it in parentheses, at least in its collo-quial expressions, in his carefully written, somewhat formal English. The gap between the Frenchman and himself, the narrator indicates, had grown wide indeed. Apart from the existing cleft, the narrator recounts how a gap between them had developed as early as one of their meetings back in Europe: "We had dinner together in one of the great, famous restaurants of Paris; and tragically, we had found that we had nothing any longer to say to each other" (ISM 5).

Since Pacey and Spettigue, readers of Grove know that the Frenchman in question was Gide, although the difference between them in age was ten, not two years. That Grove's narrator was flooded by the memory of Gide when his car was stuck in a morass should not surprise us. Grove always fash-ioned the palimpsest of his fictions and biographies carefully enough. We now know, after all, that Greve had not only translated Gide's *Les nourritures terrestres* and *L'immoraliste*, but also *Paludes* to which he had given the German subtitle *Die Sümpfe* (*The Swamps*). As to the facts of their meetings, we also now know that the two met only twice. Between their memorable first meeting on June 2, 1904 and the last one, on May 31, 1905, a little less than a year had passed, with the latter meeting being the disappointing one mentioned by Grove. More important than the actual meetings, however, is their much longer, much more intense relationship as writers, which resulted in a five-year correspondence. After the disappointing last meeting "in the flesh" (which, as far as we know, was in no way "fleshly"), the meeting of their minds in their letters documents the escalating interest in each other. It is essential to note that Greve's importance for Gide was at least equal to that of Gide for Greve. Further, it remained important for decades after their last encounter, as not only Grove's introductory essay to his autobiography of 1946 but also Gide's notes in his published *Journal* of 1931 make abundantly clear. Somewhat nostalgically, *Gide* refers to the supposedly deceased friend of his youth as his "disciple" and again, in what looks like a revisionary discussion of their 1904 meeting, attempts to explain the German's continued hold upon him. What was it that André Gide had explained about himself to Greve in 1904?

> No, I finally said [...] action only interests me in terms of the feeling it gives me, and what follows without anything held back. This is the reason why, in order to passionately interest me, it interests me even more when done by somebody else. I am terrified — understand me — I am terrified of compromising myself, of being constrained by what I do, by what I might do. To think that because I have done *this* I will no longer be able to do *that*, that is intolerable to me. I would rather *cause action* than act myself.[26]

In the course of the conversation, Felix called himself "terriblement fort" ("terribly strong"), revealing himself as the active one. Strangely, though, he immediately calls this statement into question when he poses as a habitual "liar." Apparently, neither wanted to exclude for himself the (opposing) traits he perceived in the other. They moved in a field of latency, a kind of limbo between life — sex? — and art. In 1931, with Greve supposedly long dead, Gide again reflected on the phrase he used in reference to Greve and its implications: "J'aime mieux faire agir que d'agir" ("I would rather cause action than act myself"). The conversation, "Grève" and the roles both played still haunt him, painfully, twenty-seven years later:

> No, this sentence has not "escaped" me. Think to whom I have said it, who I was in Greve's eyes, the circumstances, etc. If I found myself

in the same situation, I'd be unable to say anything different; at the most, I'd be able to explain it a little better. The astonishing thing about it is that Greve, in his reply, merely quoted the sentences of my *Nourritures*. By assuming my role he pushed me to the right. In short, I slunk away.

"Should my teachings be conducive to crime, however, I would prefer that you committed it." This is what I wanted to express with my sentence. Before me, Greve played the role of the helot. From pride I sought to save my face; I felt, though, that he had the upper hand and won over me. I was conquered by my "student" and retracted my ethic, if that's what it would lead to. The conflict of emotions, it seems to me, was too complex here for somebody to have drawn proof from my sentence. To find in this rear-guard action a thesis, a statement of belief, the declaration of an ethic, would be risky at best. The critic is free, however, to view my declaration as an "involuntary confession."[27]

This is the late Gide. Clearly he was previously as much interested in Greve's vitality as in the indecision and self-fictionalizing ("lying") he knew all too well in himself. Greve, then a Gidean immoralist, had after all suffered for committing the crime of fraud. Gide could not act out a crime in reality, but preferred to observe it in another—and write about it. Gide asserts in hind-sight that Greve acted as a catalyst to bring out in himself what he had tried to hide. Gide recognized that he had then employed what he knew to be his greatest gift: "mon meilleur gît dans un don de sympathie profonde," the gift of profound empathy, of becoming the other. This was the very gift, Gide had to acknowledge, that Greve had employed during their first interview by adopting the face of the other Gide had used in *Les nourritures terrestres*. Such deep understanding required distance to be sustained. It also meant a renunciation of intimacy and bodily contact. Mediated contact in the form of correspondence had to take the place of a more immediate relationship. Gide especially felt danger in prolonged immediate contact with "Grève." Still, he clearly wanted to use these experiences in his literary work, much as Grove was to use Gide in his Canadian autobiography.

Looking back from the *Journal* entry of 1931 to the diary summation of their interview of 1904, it becomes clear (and it must have become clear to Gide in 1931) that from the beginning the extreme stylization of the Greve-Gide relationship already contained in embryo a sketch of later literary creations. These were Julius de Barraglioul, the author, and Lafcadio Wluiki, the criminal of dubious origin, in Gide's novel *Les caves du Vatican* (1914). Not unlike Felix, Lafcadio is the one acting "immorally," the one who also wishes to attach himself to Julius (Grove's narrator, remember, was to speak of himself and the Frenchman as "inseparable"). Not unlike Felix, Gide's Lafcadio, impecunious and desperate, is ready to do Julius's bidding as an amanuensis for money. Lafcadio's frightening self-discipline and his terrible capacity for self-punishment—to the extent of inflicting pain on himself— may strike the reader conversant with Greve's 1904 role as not unfamiliar ("I feel terribly strong"). Readers familiar with Grove's autobiographical works and with *Les caves du Vatican* may find it hard not to detect "correspondances" to scenes rendered by Grove. Consider the narrator looking over Julius's shoulder as he secretly gazes at a photograph of young Lafcadio and his parents:

> At their side, behind a *flacon* of mint liqueur, a photograph which disquieted him not less: on a sandy beach a woman, not quite young anymore but unusually pretty, at the arm of a man of a decidedly English type, elegant, slender, in a leisure suit; at their feet, sitting on an overturned canoe, a strong child of about fifteen years of age with thick, blond, tousled hair and arrogant mien, laughing and completely naked.[28]

One is struck by resemblances to Grove's life and writings: his role as an English gentleman, his fictive parents (the mother Scots, the father Swedish), living at "Castle Thurow," Greve's proclivity for rowing, Else, homoerotically coloured friendships with Kilian and possibly Lomberg, the preference for "beaches." There are many such echoes and textual cross-references. "Proof," unfortunately, there is not.

Something else. Gide began to sketch the outlines of Lafcadio's character on his visit to Berlin in 1907, when he so curiously did *not* meet with Felix. As with the discontinued meetings in Paris and the correspondence that took their place, this may be explained as tacit acknowledgment of Greve's strong presence. It is possible that Gide worked all the more strongly thanks to a displacement that made the Gidean *sympathie* come creatively alive. How else to explain the strong emotional presence of Greve in Gide's thoughts:

> Do you not feel that I am in need of a word from you letting me know that my last letter has cured you of the bad opinion you had of me? Do I still have to insist, do I still have to assure you that I am not only not trying to pull away from you but that, if you would withdraw now or force me to assume towards you a less friendly tone, this would be one of the sorrows of my life.[29]

This impassioned cry—a reaction to Felix's coldness after he had learned that Gide had been to Berlin without coming to see him—is sufficient proof that Grove's words about his "ardent" relationship with the Frenchman in the preface to *In Search of Myself* were, quite simply, the truth. As in Felix's relation with his other ardent admirer, Kilian, however, the ardour again appears to have been mostly one-sided. In fact, since the first meeting between Gide and Greve, and Felix's vain attempt to resume his former friendship with Kilian (which he told Gide about), Gide may have replaced Kilian in Greve's life. For his part, Gide would soon realize the role Greve played for him in his creative life, when he again reassured his correspondent:

> Of all the figures I have met you are one of those who interested me most (I wrote down in detail, after returning to the country, the conversation we had in Paris), but when I saw you again in Paris, we had nothing to say to each other anymore. You interest me just as much as you did on the first day and this is, if one may put it like this, as much an interest of the heart as of the head; however, if it is not a matter of penetrating deeper into your life, I do not feel the need to see you again. And still, when I will return to Berlin, I am going to give you my hand with joy—once I know that you will gladly give me yours. But you can imagine only with difficulty how I feel because of the *causes*; here, I am becoming from month to month more immovable, and this develops into a real strain for me.[30]

Gide would remain (as he once signed himself to Felix) "votre écouteur passionné" ("your passionate listener," June 11, 1904). There can be no doubt of the central importance the meetings and correspondence held for both writers. But are we to believe Grove after he, as a Canadian noting the Frenchman's fame, had established such a stark contrast between the honours Gide had reaped and his own obscurity? Between 1940, when the preface first appeared as an essay, and the publication of his autobiography in 1946, Frederick Philip Grove was rather well known in his adopted country. Of course he had never regained the eminence he had known in the late 1920s, when a small and useful "scandal" based on the supposed immorality of his novel *Settlers of the Marsh*, along with his bestselling novel *A Search for America* and extended lecture tours throughout Canada as a literary and political pundit, had made him a public figure. Since then he had received the Lorne Pierce Medal of the Royal Society of Canada (1934) and had been elected a Fellow of the Royal Society of Canada. After the publication of *In Search of Myself* he was to receive a D.Litt. from the University of Manitoba and an LLD from Mount Allison University. Finally, in 1947, he received the Governor General's Award for non-fiction for his autobiography. This laurel came in the same year that saw the Nobel Prize for Literature awarded to André Gide. Most of the honours Canada could bestow had been conferred upon Grove. As early as 1939, *A Search for America* had been available as a school book. His books had been printed not only in Canada but also in England and the United States. In short, it seems unlikely that the absence of money or *honours* caused Grove's bitter remarks when he compared his reputation to that of the Frenchman's.

It would seem more likely that, by the end of his life, Grove's estimation of his impact on a culture that was still in some respects marginal was excessive in view of his actual career there. A certain sense of marginality was shared by many cultured Canadians (not least by Margaret Atwood, who would underscore it in her treatise *Survival*). But another matter troubled Grove. There is little doubt that he craved more than Canadian recognition. He carried a "literary" chip on his shoulder: his still-unknown European career. His autobiographical reckoning of the 1940s can be interpreted as a final rebellion against his portrayal of only one life as if it had been the complete life he had led. For better or worse, the second half of it involved partial anonymity. He now sought recognition for his whole life. At the time this must have seemed an impossibility, since he may have feared the opprobrium revelation could bring. Thus the troubling impact of Hytier's Gide biography on Grove was less a result of the Frenchman's worldwide reputation than simply the absence of his, "Grève's," life in it. If his former existence had been erased from the world in which he lived, then not even discovery (or rediscovery) would be possible. A major key to his whole life would have been lost. "The "search" that Grove had started for "myself" would have been in vain.

♦ LIFE IN LITERATURE

During their first meeting, Felix Paul Greve memorably insisted to André Gide that his life was "bien supérieure à celle de la littérature" ("far superior to that of literature"). Although we might easily settle with the fascination of both, it would become clear that their real-life fascination for each other came first, proceeding to be memorialized in the literature each would compose afterwards. It also forms part of the following observations concerning a literary feud, which is revealing in the light it casts on the vicissitudes of introducing Gide to Germany and the plight of Felix Paul Greve, the overworked author and translator.

❇ *Anton Kippenberg*
(Schiller Nationalmuseum/
Deutsches Literaturarchiv,
Marbach)

The literary and emotional importance of Gide and FPG for each other during the six years of their acquaintance can hardly be overestimated. From the outset Gide was profoundly impressed by Greve's looks and his self-stylization as a man of masks deliberately playing the Nietzschean literary roles he had invented in his early writings. Felix had in fact written a short piece on Nietzsche for the *Münchner Allgemeine Zeitung* in 1901, and, in his rhapsodic *Randarabesken zu Oskar Wilde* (1903), he had improvised on, among other texts, Wilde's essay "The Decay of Lying." This piece emphasized lying and masking: "The pose, however, became reality for [Wilde] and reality paled beside it; and where it was not pale, he mistook the dream for the objects, and life took revenge for this" (Greve 1903, 36).[31]

There are probably several reasons why there has been not merely a striking neglect of Grove in Germany but a certain amount of resistance to learning more about his life in Germany as Felix Paul Greve. Even if the impressive Canadian career of Frederick Philip Grove had not followed, a little less than a decade of feverish and incredibly productive literary activity in Germany should have earned him a small but secure place among the literati of the first decade of the twentieth century. The poets, editors, novelists, writers and journalists of the day—Oscar A.H. Schmitz, Julius Bab, Franz Blei, Otto Julius Bierbaum, Siegfried Jacobsohn and others—are still remembered today. So, too, are the publishers, who often served as poets and translators such as Max Bruns or immensely influential literary brokers such as Anton Kippenberg, the manager of Insel from 1905.

The interested reader, familiar with the Munich, Berlin and Vienna literary circles of which Greve was a part, will find scant reference to him in the existing literature. Even the meticulously edited and researched volumes published by the Deutsches Literaturarchiv, which cover influential turn-of-the-century literary figures and literary movements, contain hardly any reference to Greve. Was this deserved? Felix Paul Greve had translated more than sixty literary works in all, many still—or again—in print. He was not, it is true, an original author of central importance, having only two unsuccessful novels, a book of poetry and a (lost) play to his name. But he certainly was a pivotal figure—a prolific editor and translator in the literary business of mediating foreign authors of the first order. In view of the important role he played and in view of his ubiquitousness in circles of writers and publishers, one wonders what could have happened that his name was later cast into such lasting obscurity.

The striking lacunae regarding Greve in Germany seem to imply much more than the simplistic claim of Greve's supposed marginality. In fact, almost the reverse is the case. Even Freytag-Loringhoven, who—after being deserted by him in the United States—had no reason to sing his praises, wrote of his "rapid progress in name, income and fame" between 1904 and 1909 (BE 116). Did the dominance of his translations over his original writings count for little in the eyes of literary historians? This would have been strange in an age when translated work was included in literary histories. Was it his prison sentence that made association with him a social liability? Was it his eager and careless wrangling for attention? Or his no-holds-barred, all-out advocacy of the causes and authors he mediated, like Gide? His tone and attitude tended not only towards the proprietary but also the belligerent: "If I do anything at all, it will be a...revolution" (GG 140–42). He also informed Gide proudly: "I have fought a battle for you" (169–70).[32] By battling and slugging away he made powerful enemies. Even his time in prison and the scorn he poured on the heads of his former idols in his novels (who had dropped him like the proverbial hot potato after he had eloped with Else and had been convicted for fraud) do not explain his later neglect and the enmity he would encounter during his life as a writer in Germany.

How did Felix Greve first happen upon André Gide? Until well into the 1920s Gide was far less known to a general audience than Wilde, Wells or

Meredith and certainly much less than Flaubert. His works promised only small sales and little money for the imprisoned translator who was desperately in need of an income. Because of his contacts with Insel, Greve would have been aware of earlier efforts at translating Gide. As a former ephebe of Stefan George, Greve most likely would have known about the master's writings on Gide's *Les nourritures terrestres,* concentrating, as Felix was soon to do himself, on the chapter called "Le récit de Ménalque" and on "La ronde de la Grenade" (George 1897/Gide 1927). Whether George's estimation of Gide was then different from the one mentioned to Gundolf in 1916, when he had called him merely "an imitator of Oscar Wilde," cannot be said with certainty (Böschenstein, *George-Gundolf* 83).

By the end of 1903, when the imprisoned Greve first established epistolary contact with Gide in a letter dated December 27, 1903, two German rivals for Gide's works came into play. They cannot have expected any obstacles to the overtures they made to the French writer. One was the well-respected writer and friend of Rilke, Rudolf Kassner, who, as early as 1901, had published a version of Gide's *Philoctète* in the influential Austrian literary magazine *Wiener Rundschau* (also a source of inspiration for Max Bruns). He became a lifelong (although not very close) friend of Gide (cf. Bohnenkamp/Foucart, *Kassner-Gide* 83–84).[33]

The other, Franz Blei, an occasional collaborator of Kassner, was a much more active and serious contender. He commanded impressive resources, had excellent contacts and would fight Greve for André Gide even after Greve's disappearance from Germany. He may have contributed more than a little to Greve's eventual ruin and near-complete erasure from German literary history.

Felix Greve's senior by eight years, the Austrian-born Dr. Franz Blei had already assumed a respected position in the literary circles of Vienna and Munich when Greve first embarked upon his literary career. Blei had contributed to Count Kessler's legendary magazine *Pan* (1897–1998), had afterwards spent time working and travelling in the United States (visiting Poe's grave) and was then called back to become an editor of the new magazine *Die Insel*. He worked under its manager, the poet Otto Julius Bierbaum (who published a damning review of *Wanderungen* in its pages), until the magazine folded in 1902. The publishing house of the same name continued to exist. Thanks to his wife's income and a small inheritance, Blei was financially independent. As a publicist he was a jack-of-all-trades, often witty, and of exquisite taste. There is no indication that in 1902 Blei was sufficiently interested in Wilde or Gide to publish translations of their works in book form. Greve, on the other hand, had translations of works by Wilde to show and had published a short excerpt from Wilde's aphorisms in *Die Insel* (Blei, then with *Die Insel*, "accidentally" omitted Greve's name).

It has been suggested that sometime during this period Greve attempted to win a contract for all the German Gide translations from Gide's publisher Alfred Vallette, which Gide is supposed to have signed in 1903 (Theis, *Blei* xv). New evidence proves otherwise. No contract between Greve and Gide was signed before 1909 and no contract was drawn up before December 1903. This is not insignificant, since the erroneous 1903 date was used to justify Blei's indefensible actions with regard to Greve, whose "enthusiasm," "egocentric behaviour" and "astonishing insensitivity," as has been suggested, was seen as a threat (xiv).

This line of reasoning should be dealt with in some detail, since the evaluation of Greve's role and his description of the Gide-Blei-Greve relationship is the only one by a respected Gide and Blei scholar in existence. By misreading his source, the critic cements the false image of Greve (and his antagonist) spread by Blei, thus falling into Blei's trap:

> It becomes clear, however, that [Blei] thought that he had to protect Gide from Greve. In spite of all antagonisms and professional envy this appears to have been all the more in order when we learn from unpublished documents in the Gide Archive that Greve had offered Gide the edition of all his works in German translation by him, Greve, by wrongly and boastfully misrepresenting his financial possibilities. Gide had already signed Greve's projected contract. We do not know why the contractual delivery of the German Gide (edition) into Greve's hands did not come about (Theis *Blei* xiv–xv).[34]

It is understandable that the critic would use the (nonexistent) contract of 1903 to explain Blei's later vehement intercessions in his letters to Gide against Greve, since this construct alone would provide sufficient initial (though indirect) cause for Blei's later behaviour. Nevertheless, even this premise would only appear valid if Greve was made out to be a monster of (largely unspecified) depravity, to whom the fictional contract would have delivered Gide whole (*vertragliche Auslieferung*), supposedly to be ruined for life. This narrative maneuvering in the introduction to the Gide-Blei correspondence eventually makes Blei into a St. George to Greve's dragon— again closely following Blei's own strategy. In this scenario, Blei's virtuous dealings could only be matched by Gide's selfless charity (explaining his otherwise incomprehensible continued trust in Felix):

> It is typical of Gide that he did not break off his relations with Greve after fending off the 1903 threat, but, on the contrary, was able to generate an amused admiration for that man's foolery and reckless amorality. After all, Gide's unhoped-for largesse at least for once forced Greve to question his nature when he called on Gide to explain himself after his release from debtor's prison (Theis, *Blei* xv).[35]

Apparently Theis was not aware of Gide's "brutal" (Gide's word) insistence that Greve *become* his translator (GG 66). The "explanation" mentioned was Greve's first meeting with Gide. This, however, was not an occasion for settling past differences of whatever sort, had there been any. What was wrong with Greve's "nature," in the critic's opinion, that it should, under Blei's influence, be called into question? The critic does not say. But why, in the first place, would Felix have to be made to resemble a monster by "nature?" Greve, for a time, had been something of an impostor, misguided and reckless. Naturally, there was disappointment and jealousy among former friends, and his erstwhile admirers in the George circle felt exposed. Now that Greve had fallen from grace, he was being cut, and ignominy could be heaped upon him with impunity. That he did not take his defeat lying down while still in prison may have been seen as part of his supposed perfidy. The trouble with him was, it seems, that he fought back and attempted to re-embark upon his once-promising literary career. Gide seemed to want to help him, and Blei, like an avenging angel, swooped down on him to prevent it. Apart from what appears to have been pure spite and jealousy, this was the reason for Blei's intervention. Blei's intuitive grasp of the threat Greve posed to Gide, as Blei's editor Theis sees it, and to "poor Blei" himself, who suppos-edly did not realize the "danger" he put himself in by his valiant resistance to Greve, cannot have been the reason: "Although Blei did not know about the fraudulent offer of a contract nor of the 'Conversation,' he grasped with astonishing accuracy Greve's threat to Gide, feeling himself helplessly exposed to Greve and therefore probably also underestimated Gide while misjudging—in spite of Nietzsche—Gide's playfully daring vitality" (Theis, *Blei* xv).[36] These statements precede the Blei-Gide letters in Theis's edition. When evaluated in the context of the evidence of the Gide-Greve correspon-dence, and without introductory caricature of Felix, the story reads differently.

When Greve first met André Gide on the morning of June 2, 1904, he must have appeared to Gide, as we have seen above, as the incarnation of his own "immoralist." Before meeting Greve, Gide had been informed about Greve's background by Vollmoeller, a mutual friend. As Blei would find out, there was no need for a warning. In fact, Michel, Gide's "immoralist" hero in the book of the same title, is as disappointed by the poets and novelists of his time as Greve had been by those of Stefan George's circle. To read and translate, as he did in Gide's book, that most writers "did not live but were satisfied with a semblance of life and almost regarded life as little more than a worrisome obstacle to writing" must have seemed a challenge to him. And in referring to the "solitude glacial" ("icy solitude") of his life, he seems to have been suggesting to Gide that such a life was not an easy one to lead. The insights he granted Gide into his personality were, considering Greve's usual secrecy and in spite of their twistedness, extraor-dinarily frank. In their correspondence, both Gide and Greve tease each other with patterns of advancement and withdrawal. Gide was very attracted to Greve at the beginning, in 1904 and 1905. He followed each of his trans-lator's schemes, including plans to found a political and literary journal and to publish a satire called *Der Zahnadel* (*The Nobility of Teeth*, GG 137–138).

Whatever Felix sent, Gide read "le plus attentivement du monde" ("in the most attentive manner in the world"). Clearly, he could not—nor did he want to—make up his mind whether what he read of Greve's could be—or even should have been—understood. Gide was in the same quandary as many of Grove's later readers: he did not know if what he read was fact or fiction, literature or literary autobiography. As a reader of Greve's productions, Gide resembles a reader of his own early writings that Felix translated. "S'agit-il ici d'une oeuvre littéraire? ou d'un document sur vous-même?" ("Is this a work of literature? Or is it a document about yourself?") the perplexed but intensely interested French author once felt compelled to ask his correspondent (139–40). For Gide, meeting Greve must have resembled one of his own works of art come to stirring life. Even two years later, after disappointments on both sides and when, from Greve's perspective, Gide had seemed to turn to Blei, Gide would both chide Greve and reaffirm his deep personal commitment: "Quand tout le monde vous tournait le dos je me suis rapproché de vous" ("When all the world turned its back on you I have approached you," 165–67). Gide continued two weeks later, after Greve had not reacted: "You interest me as much as you did on the first day, and it is, if I may express it like this, as much an interest of the heart as of the head; however, if it is not a matter of penetrating deeper into your life, I do not feel the need to see you again" (170–72).[37]

The pattern of attraction and rejection explains a great deal about similar movements in their professional dealings, especially since they involved a formidable rival such as Blei. On the personal level, one is struck by the lover-like pattern of hurt and aggression, attraction, rejection and the relief of final reconciliation. When he learns that Gide failed to meet him in Berlin, Greve writes as one whose affections have been trifled with: "I remain hurt to the quick." In the same letter, he nevertheless does not fail to affirm: "This doesn't take away from the interest I feel for you and which is wholly personal" (169–70).[38] Their mutual attraction was firmly supported by Gide's professional regard for his translator.

It should be noted that, in contrast to Blei, Felix Greve wrote to Gide in French. He did not always write fluently and not without the occasional howler. By using Gide's native language, however, he demonstrated his ability to identify with the language and the personality he was translating— an invaluable skill for a translator, and much more important than the schoolmasterly insistence on mere linguistic correctness. On the other hand, knowing that Gide could read and understand German reasonably well, Blei opted to write his letters to Gide in German, while Gide answered in French.

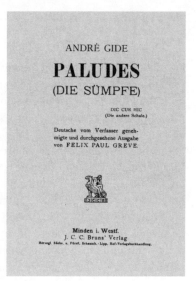

❋ *Title pages for André Gide's* Der Immoralist *(1905) and* Paludes *(1905)*

By choosing to write in French, Greve approached Gide on his own linguistic "turf," so to speak, taking the risk of being misunderstood, baring himself. Still, his French seems to have been good enough for Gide's latterday German editor to assume that Greve had become a Canadian writing in French (Theis, *Blei* 7n.).[39]

In August 1904, two months after FPG's meeting with Gide in Paris, Franz Blei sent a letter to Gide for the first time. He informed him that a translation of *L'immoraliste* by an unknown gentleman had been turned down by Insel, only to be accepted by another publisher. Blei felt it his duty to warn Gide of contracting with the new publisher because he wanted to see to it that "you should inhabit a decent house in Germany."[40] The translation in question was Greve's and the publisher with whom a contract had already been signed was, of course, J.C.C. Bruns of Minden. From the beginning, and not yet mentioning Greve by name, Blei did not hesitate to assume a high tone of moral authority, as if J.C.C. Bruns were somehow an "indecent" firm when, in reality, Insel was the upstart and Bruns the tried and proven company of high repute.

The point of Blei's "good advice" was to make it appear that Insel had turned down Gide not because of the quality of *L'immoraliste* ("Poellnitz found the book too 'involved'," Greve had written) but because of the purported moral deficiencies of the publisher and, by inference, the translator whom Bruns chose. Unhappily for Blei, his remarks misfired. Greve had been careful to ask Gide's opinion: "Would you be terrible unhappy if you were published by Monsieur Bruns, next to my edition of Wilde's works? (GG 69–70)"[41] Since he could not match Greve's achievements as a translator, Blei attempted to put himself between Gide and Greve on false moral and aesthetic grounds. He assumed an air of authority in an attempt to squash a rival translator and a publisher at the outset of their business relations with the French author. Gide, however, having just remembered himself to Greve in glowing terms as his "impassioned listener," showed no inclination to heed Blei's warnings or even to accept the proffered guidance.[42]

On the contrary, Gide now proceeded to make use of Blei's self-proclaimed stature and connoisseurship, asking him to help place Greve's fragmentary translation of *Les Nourritures terrestres*. To be saddled with the task of championing work of a despised rival must have been galling indeed. Unfortunately for Blei, performances of his translation of *Le Roi Candaule* were being postponed while Greve's translations of *L'immoraliste* and now also *Paludes* were published without delay by the not very "decent" publisher. Blei promptly wrote to Gide in sour terms: "Too bad that Bruns who has neither taste nor money is now going to serve up 'Paludes' in his forget-me-not-blue paper." A welcome occasion for additional moralizing arose when FPG complained about Blei's omitting his name in *Die Zukunft*.

For Blei, Greve's complaint presented a welcome occasion for writing about Greve's "deranged excitement." He called it a symptom of illness and he tells his correspondent that he was suing Greve. Blei simply could not grasp what all the fuss concerning translators' names was about. Then, no longer mincing his words, he openly went on the attack: "Under normal circumstances this man is incomprehensible to me; he presupposes such strange mores and customs in others that it causes me to think him either a crazy man or a dirty little journalist." Still, the one whom Blei now unabashedly called "a criminal" (December 23, 1905) continued to translate Gide, although Blei appeared to be catching up. The conflict culminated in January 1907.

Having finally received the translation rights for the entire text of *Le Prométhée mal enchaîné*, Blei attempted to get the director Max Reinhardt, then already famous, to stage Gide's *Saül* in his translation. To his chagrin, he learned that Greve was already in possession of the German rights. In an interesting reversal, now that Blei could not have the translation rights, he wrote to Gide that he had not wanted to translate the play: "Mr. Greve is a good translator, that's all that counts for you. You don't care that he is a bad writer and a lying individual. Since I now do not want to be considered the translator *next to* Greve—and since what I am otherwise does not seem to

enter into your consideration—I would rather not be the translator..."
(February 8, 1907).[43] Blei succeeded, however, in talking Max Reinhardt into
appointing him the director for *Saül* in Greve's translation. Writing to Gide
about this development, Blei seemed to have misgivings about Gide's
possible reaction to his machinations and thus added: "We shall not let
anybody or anything disturb the peace of our good friendship, dear Herr
Gide, will we?" (February 14, 1907).[44]

Obviously "Dear Herr Gide" thought otherwise for he kept Greve on as
his correspondent and valued translator. But he did have a crisis of
conscience, since he knew how well connected and influential Blei was.
Felix Greve, by contrast, was well known but shunned by many, now apparently not least because of Blei. But Gide intended to keep his promises even
though he might have a better chance of seeing his play staged by Blei, as he
wrote him on February 5, 1907: "Furthermore I very well know that I have a
better chance of being played with you than with Greve who does not have
all the friends you have—I am certainly acting against my interests, but I
prefer this to going against Greve and going back on the word I have given"
(Theis, *Blei* 75).[45]

Why was it impossible for Blei, in spite of his many efforts, to talk André
Gide out of keeping Greve on as translator? First, of course, Greve's talents
were excellent, as Gide could see for himself, and Gide did not hesitate to
recommend his translator to his closest friends such as the well-known writer
Henri de Régnier (April 22, 1905). To other writer friends, like Paul Claudel,
he praised Blei in such lukewarm terms that they were dissuaded from taking
him on as a translator (Gide to Paul Claudel, October 24, 1907). To Gide,
Franz Blei was a useful connection while Felix Paul Greve was one to admire
and even love, although from a distance. He was the difficult stuff of literature. The personal and literary ties to Greve were too strong to cut. On the
contrary, they had to be kept alive.

Felix Greve continued to translate Gide until his disappearance from
Germany. At Greve's repeated urgings, Gide finally consented to provide
him with an option for the exclusive translation rights for his past and future
works. This, it seems certain, was the contract Theis thought Greve had
"forced on" Gide in 1903. Now, on the eve of his disappearance, Greve wrote
out, and Gide apparently accepted, the comprehensive contract (although a
watered-down version) which Blei must have dreaded. The first book to be
translated was *La porte étroite*. One of the contract's stipulations, that the
new book be published first in Berlin before its publication in France, was
fulfilled. *La porte étroite* became Gide's biggest success thus far. Greve had
made good on the promises he had made to Gide.

What is most baffling is that after he "had his way" with Gide, at least contractually, he did not continue as the sole translator and editor of Gide's works, as Blei had feared, but departed from Europe. There is still no full explanation for this action. From 1910 on, however, Blei's name appeared side by side with Greve's on the title page of their formerly separate translations of Wilde's fairy tales. Blei also no longer objected to translating for J.C.C. Bruns whom he had earlier claimed to despise. He would only complete one more Gide translation, in 1914. In the 1920s and early 1930s, he made an attempt to become the editor of Deutsche Verlagsanstalt Publishers' comprehensive Gide edition. He failed, not least because he had laid himself open to the accusation of deriding Gide for his sexual preference (Theis, *Blei* 180–81). Now Gide knew what it was like to draw Blei's fire. Although a kind of reconciliation was achieved, their relationship was ended. Interestingly, Blei's modern editors make a point of celebrating him less as a writer than as a *Kulturvermittler*, a mediator of culture (Harth 1997). But if we compare their oeuvres as mediators of culture, Felix Paul Greve's easily dwarfs Blei's (and many others') comparatively few efforts. There can be little doubt that André Gide owed much of his early international reputation to Felix Paul Greve's work, and both knew it.

◆ MARGIN AND CENTRE

After June 1904, Felix began a period of restless travel and rapid changes of address. One of the reasons for this may have been other than the expected harassment by creditors or the pursuit of literary matters. Felix had not been required to fulfill a term of obligatory military service. Back in Hamburg he had been provided with the official testimony that he had a clean police record, which was necessary to exempt him from a lowly tour of duty as a private. The Johanneum final exam—or *Abitur*—enabled him to limit his commitment to only one year of voluntary service. The law would have forced him to begin his service in the fall of 1898, unless he had obtained a special permit allowing him to pursue his studies in Bonn first. His prison sentence effactually voided his formerly clean record and also his chances of serving as a volunteer. He must have dreaded not only the attachment of his earnings but also the mandatory three years of military service. This would have destroyed his chances of getting back on his feet again as a writer. He would also have had to pay a hefty fine of up to three thousand marks or serve another prison sentence of up to a year.[46] Surely this was reason enough to cover his tracks as quickly as possible by leaving the country. How he managed to elude the military until 1909 remains a

Hotel-Pension Bellevue, Wollerau (Switzerland), ca. 1900 (Collection Theo Kümin)

mystery, since he had to register with the police. A "change of birthdate" might have helped, as it did in Canada where he gave 1871–72 (instead of 1879) as the years of his birth, effectually forestalling a call to serve at the beginning of the Great War.

Greve met Gide in Paris and H.G. Wells in Sandgate immediately after his release from jail. Then he proceeded in Else's company via Bad Reichenhall in Bavaria to Wollerau, a small resort on Lake Zürich, where they found a temporary home for the rest of the year in the Hotel Bellevue, overlooking the lake. The Greves were in exile. Here, even malicious rumours could not touch them. On the other hand, Wollerau was located centrally enough for quick visits to Germany, France and England if the need arose. It is unlikely that the move had been motivated by the wanderings of Greve's former master, Stefan George. Like Felix, he had been in Cologne in early June 1904 (Seekamp et al., 157). Greve could have met him after his return from the meeting with Gustav Bruns in Wiesbaden. In July and August, when Felix and Else headed for Switzerland, George was on an extended tramp through the same region of Lake Zürich (158f.). He would have wanted to meet the master again. At any rate, he may already have been working on the (unpublished) send-up of the Munich circle, "a small book" called *Stephan* [sic] *George und die Blätter für die Kunst,* which was to be published in Berlin.[47]

Initially Felix had made fanciful plans to go elsewhere, as he had written to O.A.H. Schmitz on the eve of his release from prison:

Afterwards I am thinking of travelling to the North (to visit Iceland, Greenland, etc., perhaps). Possibly I might be sending you a postcard from some impossible place...Wouldn't you like to go to some god-forsaken, tiny seaside resort where one may swim and ride and—? (a few ladies could easily be provided).[48]

Else and Switzerland proved sufficient for this. He found the seaside resort soon enough. As for a multiplicity of persons to live with, Felix assumed multiple pseudonymous personae, making of himself a veritable palimpsest of the kind he would produce again in his Canadian autobiographical writings. In a most astonishing development, he decided to "multiply" in order to fulfill his obligations as a writer. He assumed a terrible workload under several names (necessitated, no doubt, by the danger of his fees being seized by his creditors), as he—not without a measure of ironic pride—announced to Gide from Wollerau:

And as to myself: I have to work in a very peculiar manner. I am not *one* person anymore; I am *three*; I am 1) Mr. Felix Paul Greve; 2) Mrs. Else Greve; 3) Mrs. Fanny Essler. The latter, whose poems I am soon going to send you and whose poems—still a secret—are addressed to me, is a lady poet already pretty well regarded in certain parts of Germany. She has published only poems so far. But I, F.P. Greve, her patron and introducer, am preparing the publication of two novels she wrote in the prison of Bonn on the Rhine (a prison which I, F.P. Greve, have come to call 'the villa'). All this, of course, in the strictest confidence, please. Nobody suspects this state of affairs. In addition, the translation of Flaubert's *Correspondence* is being published with Mrs. Else Greve's name on the title page. Unfortunately, however, Italian is the only [foreign] language Mrs. Greve knows; as a consequence, I, F.P. Greve, had to do the translation in the course of [several?] summer nights.[49]

Of Flaubert more below. "Fanny Essler," of course, would be the title of his first novel, constructed—as was his second novel—from "Mme Else Greve's" biographical recollections. Seven of "Fanny Essler's" poems were soon to appear in the magazine *Die Freistatt*. It might be said that the final dispersal of these personae also meant a separation from Else and her biography as both source and cover for Felix's writings. It became necessary to embark upon a new life as a fresh source for his writing, (cf. Spettigue 1992).

In June 1905 Felix and Else moved from Wollerau to a vacation spot on the French Channel coast. After some searching and consultation with Gide, they had found a little "chalet" in the seaside resort of Paris-Plage on the southern side of the inlet called "La Canche" that separates it from Étaples. It was conveniently located near the ferry to Folkestone and therefore just a few miles from Sandgate and H.G. Wells — "en face de vous," as Felix wrote to Wells on October 6, 1906. As late as 1933, Grove would recall conversations "with H.G. Wells as we were walking on the cliffs of Sandgate, overlooking the channel" ("Thoughts and Reflections" 318). He was also not far from Paris and André Gide in nearby Cuverville, situating himself between two of his most important sponsors of the day. Paris-Plage was then already a part of the municipality and elegant resort town of Le Touquet. Although frequented by tourists since the second half of the nineteenth century, Paris-Plage had become fashionable only in 1905 when it could comfortably be reached by the French railroad, the *Chemin de Fer du Nord*, via the Boulogne line and the station at Étaples, a four-hour train ride from Paris. The wide beach with its fine white sand was bordered by a boardwalk and ornamental pseudo-baroque gardens with many restaurant and hotel buildings opposite it. Felix and Else lived on one of the narrow streets that ran slightly uphill at right angles from the boardwalk. The building was a gabled wood and brick house — today's nos. 9 and 11, rue d'Étaples — with each address fronted by a small porch and containing three apartments. From the chalet "Odette," as it is still called, one had a view of the English Channel (leaning over the porch rail and craning one's neck to the right). The beach and the nearby pine forest were easily accessible for walking or horseback riding. (Greve recalls horseback riding in *Fanny Essler*, but in the Norman town of Coutances, situated on the south side of the next peninsula on the French coast between Calais and Brest, south of Le Touquet.) Paris-Plage was a place for the well-to-do from London and Paris. As in Palermo, Felix and Else, although not among the resort's monied clientele, must have made a striking pair in the bracing sea air, with the little dog they had with them on a leash.

This French "bain de mer" and Greve's little "ménage" after the French fashion in Paris-Plage — as he off-handedly called it in a letter to Wells[50] — would, in various disguises and with slight changes of address, be mentioned again in Grove's Canadian writings. They were places Phil Grove had known and where Phil Branden's fictional father had retired: "a little cottage between Boulogne and Étaples — a coast which he loved as I have always loved it" (SFA 9). It must have seemed like another propitious new beginning. Felix's translation of *L'immoraliste* had been published to some acclaim and he was working on the proofs for *Paludes* and considering a translation of another Gide work, the drama *Saül*. He had found a publisher for *Fanny Essler* and may already have been working on his second novel, *Maurermeister Ihles Haus*. It is also possible that he was working on a manuscript for an unpublished third novel. In July he could proudly send a copy of his translation of Flaubert's *La tentation de saint Antoine* to Gide. Their lodgings must have been comfortable enough to provide both rest and good working conditions, with mornings and afternoons spent writing on the porch. Felix and Else returned the next summer for another extended vacation and more work. A new Wilde translation of *The Sphinx*, and of Flaubert's *Reiseblätter*, featured introductory remarks dated "Paris-Plage."

For a writer who must have felt close to the breakthrough he had longed for, the summer residence seemed such a good choice that Felix and Else decided to stay until the end of the year. They were planning another excursion to England, including a visit to H.G. Wells for eight days in early September, but, due to overwork, cancelled at the last minute.[51]

In January 1906, they moved into an apartment in Berlin's Fasanenstrasse, a quarter near the lively Kurfürstendamm, filled with bookstores, galleries and the offices of agents and magazines. Felix probably went to oversee the printing of his second novel. He also needed to renew his contacts with Insel and to establish new connections with other publishers. Although he still needed new authors to translate to maintain a sufficient level of income, he seemed to be rapidly developing from an overworked translator into an accepted author. Filled with hope and enthusiasm, he wrote to Gide on March 16, 1906:

> I have a new novel being printed and a third [sic] *under my pen*. The first, Fanny Essler, has been published in a second edition, the second one [sic] is entitled: "Maurermeister Ihles Haus" and will soon appear (it is a study of a kind of Übermensch conscious of himself: the Mastermason is something like a wild animal turned bourgeois). The third, finally, is my *Sentimentalist*, the story of a young Berliner—but without the slightest resemblance to *L'Education* by Flaubert—the intention, to call it that, of my novel concerns a world different from Flaubert's novel. In the meantime I have to translate and translate: I need a successful author (of novels, if possible; they don't have to be *good*: quite the opposite!)—do you know of one?[52]

Due to the success of his work from the margins of the continent in Paris-Plage, he had moved to the centre, Berlin. It must have been a heady period for him to report to Gide—who was then very far from being a bestselling author—that his first novel was now in its second edition. Greve, however, needed the returns from each copy sold; Gide, an affluent heir, most certainly did not.

Soon "the Greves" moved again, this time to nearby Nachodstrasse, not far from the offices of the new, increasingly political magazine *Die Schaubühne*, a publication influential among theatre people and not far from the apartment of one of its major contributors and later editor, the young satirist Kurt Tucholsky.

◆ A PLAY LOST

A glance at Felix Paul Greve's development as a translator and writer shows his continuing attraction to the theatre. His little dialogic play for his intended bride, the somewhat precious *Helena und Damon*, had been his first attempt in the genre. Following this, he had had great expectations in 1902 for anticipated performances of his translations of Wilde's plays on stages throughout Germany. But his innocence in the intricacies of copyright conventions had prevented him from realizing his high hopes. When he finally succeeded in introducing two Wilde plays on an important Berlin stage, the event had to be restricted to an invited audience. In the meantime, his (former) friends and acquaintances Ernst Hardt, Karl Gustav Vollmoeller and several others had succeeded with their plays, earning laurels and considerable incomes. Although his two published novels are clearly constructed along theatrical principles, including much dialogue, they did not enjoy popular success. But Greve had continued writing for the stage. We gather from announcements in books he had translated that he had written "Three Grotesque Plays" entitled "Schiller, Pindar and Herr Märzenbach." In the field of translation, the only author he was then translating and who had also written plays was André Gide. Unfortunately, Gide had either given them to his competitor Blei, who had excellent contacts in the Berlin theatres, or—if Greve was the translator, as in the case of Gide's *Saül*—they were staged by somebody else.

In early 1907, however, when the battle between Blei and Greve for Gide's *Saül* and the support of Max Reinhardt was at its height, Felix seemed about to score a major success. He had continued trying for the stage. Unfortunately, there are no surviving lists of accepted or declined plays preserved in Berlin theatre archives. As in the case of other products from Greve's desk, we have to rely on his own announcements in other books authored, translated or edited by him. Thus we find another play of his announced in *Brümmer*, the leading literary dictionary of the time, solicited from Greve. In it he mentions among his own works a "comedy" entitled *Der heimliche Adel* (*Secret Nobility*), possibly a version of the "satire," *Der Zahnadel*, that he had previously announced. What happened to the play? Unfortunately, in Greve's case not a shred of his German papers appears to have survived.

Sometimes, however, an unexpected stroke of luck reveals a small piece of evidence, much like the debris that comes to the surface after a ship disap-

‡ *"Der heimliche Adel"*
(1907) in Die Schaubühne's
"Acceptances." Greve's
play is the eighth listed.

Ueberlieferung, gegen Schablone, Lüge und Bequemlichkeit auflehnt. Manch wahres Wort gibt zu denken, manche geben hat und immer weiter gibt, und sprechen der Sammlung ihr Lebensrecht zu. Felix Stössinger

Aus der Praxis

Annahmen

.: Die Halben, Tragikomödie. Hamburg, Thaliatheater.

.: Die Andere, Lustspiel. Wien, Raimundtheater.

Herbert von Berger: Irmingart, Drama. Berlin, Friedrich-Wilhelmstädtisches Schauspielhaus.

Albert Bernstein-Sawersky: Die steinerne Tafel. Breslau, Schauspielhaus.

Dora Duncker: Falsches Ziel, Schauspiel. Mainz, Stadttheater.

Frederik van Eeden: Ysbrand, Tragikomödie. Stuttgart, Hoftheater.

Ernst Gettke: Das glückliche Gesicht, Schwank. Wien, Raimundtheater.

Felix Paul Greve: Heimlicher Adel, Komödie. Berlin, Hebbeltheater.

Fritz Hartmann: Der Wunderliche von Berlin, Drama. Braunschweig, Hoftheater.

Melchior Lengyel: Die dankbare Nachwelt, Schauspiel. Wien, Raimundtheater.

Karl Freiherr von Levetzow: Der Bogen des Philoktet, Tragödie. Berlin, Berliner Theater.

Rudolf Lothar: Die Diebin (nach dem Englischen). Berlin, Friedrich-Wilhelmstädtisches Schauspielhaus.

Louis Parker: Der Kardinal, historisches Schauspiel. Wien, Raimundtheater.

Uraufführungen

1. von deutschen Dramen

13. 4. Ludwig Löfer: Herostrat von Ephesus, Tragödie. Braunschweig, Hoftheater.

15. 4. Herbert Eulenberg: Ulrich, Fürst von Waldeck, Schauspiel. Köln, Schauspielhaus.

Albert Bernstein-Sawersky und Arthur Lippschütz: Eine Hofkomödie. Stettin, Stadttheater.

16. 4. Ernst Soehngen: Nach Jena, Tragödie. Elberfeld, Stadttheater.

18. 4. Moritz Schlesinger: Der Allerweltsonkel, Schwank. Köln, Residenztheater.

22. 4. Frank Wedekind: Die junge Welt, Komödie. München, Schauspielhaus.

Paul Bliß: Der Goldsucher, Einaktiges Lustspiel. Wiesbaden, Residenztheater.

617

pears at sea. It turned out that Felix's new contacts to Berlin theatres, its directors and to the new magazine *Die Schaubühne* had not been without use. The *Schaubühne* featured a column (discontinued only a short time later) listing plays accepted and rejected by various theatres, apparently on the basis of information provided by the theatres themselves. In 1907 there is a listing for *"Felix Paul Greve: Heimlicher Adel, Kömödie. Berlin, Hebbel Theater"* (*Schaubühne* 1908, 617). But there is no further mention of the play at the brand new Hebbel Theatre or elsewhere in Germany. Something must have happened to convert Greve's success in seeing one of his works accepted into one of his many defeats. Once again, he had to endure another piece of bad luck; comedy, for him, had turned into small tragedy. As it happened, performances at the Hebbel Theatre were delayed until well into the 1908 season. Due to the delay, plays that had been accepted earlier were staged first. All this was the result of a catastrophe. The theatre's founder and director, the well-known Richard Vallentin, who must have accepted Greve's comedy, died suddenly in January. The theatre stayed open and the season began with performances of plays by Hebbel and Strindberg, followed by comedies by such young authors as Julius Bab. The season ended with the *Cyprienne* by Sardou and Narjac. Greve's play is not mentioned again. Had

Greve's play been forbidden by the official censor? This was not unusual, but no mention of Greve could be found. This is all that is known.

It remains to mention a curious little legend which was published under the silly pseudonym "Matta-Fatta" in a 1907 edition of the *Schaubühne*. It bears the curious title of "Bunbury," the title Greve first gave to *The Importance of Being Earnest* as Wilde's translator. In intentionally awful doggerel, this spoof details oddities about a Berlin playwright whose plays were constantly returned by the leading Berlin theatres:

A German poet wrote a play,
received it back and, by the way,
who knows if it was worth it
for nobody's ever read it.
This particular poet you read,
if you are really right in the head,
certainly not before he's dead.
'Tis not, however, true always,
For our poets don't starve in every case.
If they play him when alive, I wot,
then a poet he is truly not.

The doggerel goes on about theatre directors spending all their time in court and having no more time to read. "The reason: *Bunbury*." Everybody wanted it, even famous directors such as Victor Barnowsky and Max Reinhardt. The problem: Barnowsky had the rights and Reinhardt wanted to stage it. Although the play is "so much drivel," English is nevertheless "all the rage," and the spat is free advertising. Indeed. It appears that Greve's originally unauthorized 1902 translation of *Bunbury* had now been officially staged, duly licensed to Barnowsky by Reinhardt. The translator probably wanted a cut. English literature was indeed all the rage and Greve was one of its most prominent mediators. In 1907, he again seemed back in business, although no real breakthrough had occurred. It must have appeared to the public that if one of his works had not been published then another one was already being advertised. Second editions of his novels had appeared or were in preparation. New editions of his translations of Wilde's prose works were in the stores and *Der heimliche Adel* was to be staged soon. The translation of a large Balzac edition and—the crowning achievement—his Insel edition of the twelve volumes of the *Arabian Nights* had been credited to his name. Greve's name-recognition must have been high for Blei to react to his excellent relations with Gide as aggressively as he did.

In view of all of these achievements (and several failures), the time must have seemed ripe to secure a greater measure of independence from both his publishers and the print media. In his correspondence with Gide and Wells he had begun to think about editing a magazine of his own. He was impressed by the reputable *Mercure de France*, from which he and Max Bruns had taken hints regarding new authors to edit, translate and publish. He wrote to Wells: "I am founding a sort of German 'Mercure de France'—only on a somewhat larger scale—a revue in connexion with a large publishing firm" (Greve to H.G. Wells, October 6, 1905). In a similar vein he had already written to Gide, even naming the projected title of his magazine *Das Einundzwanzigste Jahrhundert* (*The Twenty-First Century. GG* 138). We do not know which publisher he may have had in mind. There is no further mention of the plan. He was also thinking about translating novels by George Gissing, the famous author of *New Grub Street*. One may surmise that Felix could easily identify with Edwin Reardon, Gissing's protagonist who, while attempting to preserve his integrity as a writer, was driven into poverty. If Greve had translated this novel it would have been another one of his pioneering translations. As it happened, another eighty years had to pass for it to be published in a German translation in the former G.D.R. (Gissing 1985). He now also felt that the Wells project might be profitably continued. When J.C.C. Bruns refused *Love and Mrs. Lewisham*, he offered *A Modern Utopia* and *Mr. Kipps*. To him, the Bruns firm seemed both too slow and too careful. He, on the other hand, was in a hurry. In fact, his production speed was breathtaking. After Bruns's refusal, he turned to a new publisher, the firm of Julius Hoffmann in Stuttgart, specializing in art books. In early 1907, however, Greve quarrelled with Hoffmann. Since he had made positive mention of Hoffmann to Wells, Hoffmann had quickly secured the rights to further books by the English author. Naturally, Hoffmann dropped Greve and a new translator was soon found, in spite of Greve's appeals to Wells. Both *Mr. Kipps* and the great novel to appear the same year in England, *Tono-Bungay*, might have done much for Greve's reputation. Too late. Again, as was soon also to happen in the cases of Meredith and Gide, Felix Greve initiated a groundbreaking venture but failed to play his hand with care and circumspection, losing everything he had worked hard to bring about. In 1909, shortly before quitting the country, Greve resumed contact with Wells in a renewed effort to secure the rights for *Mrs. Kipps* and *Love and Mrs. Lewisham*. If Wells were prepared to break with Hoffmann, he wrote, he, in his turn, would be ready to translate the English author's other "phantastic" novels (Greve to H.G. Wells, June 14, 1909). It is not known whether Wells would have been willing to work again with his pioneering German translator. If he had been, a positive answer would have come too late to reach Greve. If it had been negative, and Greve had received it, it may have contributed to the reasons that led to his departure. Yet another reason may have been the spectacular failure of one more ambitious enterprise.

◆ FLAUBERT

Felix Paul Greve and J.C.C. Bruns had been ahead of their time in championing and translating English and French authors who were coming into their own in Germany. This was as true of Flaubert and Gide as it would be of Wells.

The novels of Meredith and, on a much grander scale, Wells were high-class potboilers intended to make money for the publisher and translator— although much less for the latter. While these authors were being published in Germany, Bruns and Greve tackled a third project dear to the hearts of both. The plan was for a German edition of the works of the great French novelist Gustave Flaubert, first published in single volumes and afterwards in differently priced sets. It would undoubtedly be an expensive undertaking which, if it were to make money, could be expected to do so only as a long-range project. On the other hand—and here the publisher was not mistaken— it would help to increase the firm's already well-established reputation as a publisher of quality literature. Rarely had such a significant publishing venture been undertaken with higher hopes (and at higher costs) by all involved, and rarely was such a venture to end in greater disappointment.

While in jail, Felix Paul Greve was busily translating Meredith and Wilde, writing poetry and preparing for his own first novel, which would be his revenge on those who had forsaken him in his disgrace. Meanwhile, Max Bruns was thinking about a major edition of Flaubert's works, to succeed the firm's groundbreaking editions of Poe and Baudelaire. Greve would approve of the plan, and it would occasion a drastic stylistic departure from aestheticism to realistic and naturalistic modes of writing. Indeed, as early as May 1903 he had suggested a translation of Flaubert's *Contes* to the Bruns firm. Now Max and Felix, two authors and translators from the French, would come together in a joint enterprise of mutual interest.

Unfortunately Max considered the project his own and did not want to share. He had prepared for it. By May 1901, if we are to believe the diary of his reading, he had studied Flaubert's *Hérodiade*, *La légende de St.-Julien L'hospitalier*, *Un coeur simple*, *La danse des morts* and *Novembre* and was then about to read the major novels:

> What overwhelming riches! What wonders of beauty to introduce to the Germans!—My plan was: To create a German Flaubert Edition.

Now I see the announcement of two translations: The "Mad[ame]. Bovary" and the "Salammbô." And not the "Antoine?" And also not the "Contes?" I do not want to drop the plan; as soon as my selection from Baudelaire has been made I want to begin with Fl[aubert]. I also want to do something for [Joris-Karl] Huysmans and [Stéphane] Mallarmé.[53]

In December 1901 he read *La tentation de saint Antoine* very carefully, followed by Flaubert's *Souvenir intimes* (*Intimate Recollections*), a volume edited by the author's niece, Caroline Commanville, and the first volume of Flaubert's *Correspondance* (*Correspondence*). At the same time Max Bruns closely monitored other publishers' activities regarding Flaubert. Trouble was brewing in Munich, where Georg Müller Publishers had issued *Madame Bovary* in a translation by René Schickele (later a much-respected Expressionist author and editor), which was to serve as an introduction to a complete edition of Flaubert's works. Müller's edition, however, had not got off to a good start, prompting Bruns to fill the gaps in Müller's edition with his own. But it was clear to him that he would not be content with a number of volumes decided upon in this haphazard way. What's more, as with the Baudelaire edition, he would be his own editor and translator. By the end of 1902 he noted that Flaubert's letters were "a great hoard I am very desirous of translating into German; this would be done out of a great inner urge and with much joy." A few months later he wrote to Karl Röttger, then a well-known poet belonging to Otto zur Linde's "Charon" circle of poets (a rival of Stefan George's): "Flaubert's letters are the most meaningful artistic documents I know…You will comprehend why no translator of Fl[aubert]'s could be found. I shall probably soon edit them in German."[54] The sensible strategy decided upon by late 1903 would begin with the lesser-known works and conclude the series with the better-known ones, including those already published elsewhere, in new translations. It was a project not without financial risk. If Max Bruns had hoped to play a decisive role in it, he would be disappointed, for he soon realized that his father had asked others to edit and translate. Felix Paul Greve, already dominant in the publisher's English-language department, was now asked to assume a similar role in the French, usurping, as it must have seemed to Max, his own domain and intruding upon his own long-ripened plans. Although Max was to act as the publisher's reader, exerting an influence upon the texts and the order of their appearance, the edition he favoured had been ruined. At first, not Greve but an unknown woman from Berlin, Luise Wolf, had been asked to submit a sample translation of Flaubert's *L'éducation sentimentale*. She signed a contract with Bruns in February 1904, after being kept waiting for almost

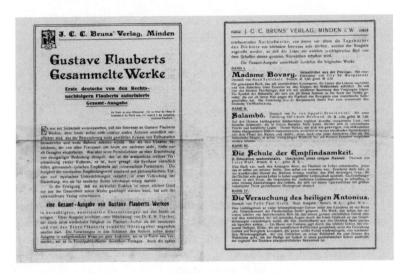

❉ *Advertisement for "Gustave Flaubert's Collected Works" pages one and two.*
Greve translated volumes IV, VII, VIII, and IX (J.C.C. Bruns Archiv, Minden)

❉ *Pages three and four*

three months. The Bruns firm had learned to be careful; it had asked Wolf to check whether she had the authorization for the book and was entitled to translate it. With the help of friends in Paris, Wolf succeeded in this. There was, however, a legal obstacle that Wolf, Bruns and Greve were unaware of. Flaubert's works were protected until thirty years after his death (1911); another law, though, stipulated that those works remained unprotected which had not been translated until ten years after their first publication (Ernst, "Kunst" 30). This major, then-undetected difficulty eventually spelled disaster for all involved in Bruns's Flaubert edition.

If Max Bruns had reserved the determining role in editing and translating Flaubert for himself, as he was doing with the Baudelaire, then Felix Greve must have envisioned the same as a result of his experience with the ongoing Meredith and Wells editions. At any rate, he was now asked to translate *La Tentation de saint Antoine* and three volumes containing Flaubert's correspondence. The correspondence, the publication of which Max had suggested, was now divided up and published under new titles: *Briefe über seine Werke* (*Letters about His Works*), *Reiseblätter* (*Letters from His Travels*) and *Briefe an Zeit- und Zunftgenossen* (*Letters to Contemporaries and Colleagues*). These three volumes represented two volumes in the original: *Correspondances* and *Par les champs et par les grèves*. The contract (which has not survived) probably contained a clause defining how work on the edition was to be divided between Max and Felix. That their cooperation entailed compromise is evident from the official titles for the "Letters From His Travels" or *Reiseblätter* (*Briefe aus dem Orient—Über Feld und Strand* [*Letters from the Orient—Over Field and Strand*]). In June 1905 Greve's work had progressed so far that Max, probably in a cold rage, must have thought it fit to set Felix to rights, as we deduce from Greve's reply:

> [I]t does <u>not</u> say in the contract that the "Volumes of correspondence by Flaubert should be produced according to your instructions," but: "the suggestions of Mister Max Bruns are to be taken into considerable account concerning *the order of appearance* of different volumes of Flaubert." You see, *that* I could sign…As for the rest, do not think that I am not capable of taking measures of the publishing house objectively. I always have and will continue to do so. In case I do not understand a measure of the publishing house I, if need be, attempt to undo them; in most cases I have succeeded. Other than that I recall that a publishing house is not an ideal machine but a business directed by human beings which as a corporation is superior to my judgement at one time and inferior at other times. Nevertheless, I maintain my unaltered respect for it, which its very extraordinary merits deserve.[55]

Considering his difficult financial situation and his continuing dependence on the publisher's goodwill regarding their financial arrangements, this was a courageous letter. The Flaubert correspondence had clearly been finished in a hurry, to be published—according to the arrangement with Gustav Bruns in Wiesbaden—under the pseudonym "E. Greve," with Felix appearing merely as "editor." Max Bruns's comments in the diary of his reading are bitter indeed:

> For years I have tried to suggest a German Flaubert edition to Bruns Publishers, finally with success. Since I myself was still too busy with my Baudelaire edition I had to leave to others the work for Flaubert and have limited myself to solicited and unsolicited advice...

Max's comments read like a self-justification now that things could not be changed by him. Apparently Felix (who now appeared as the one who had made the editorial decisions regarding the selection of letters and who was the author of the notes) had had much more of a hand in the edition than Max could stomach. In the privacy of his diary he criticized Greve's work:

> The volume Letters about his Works has been translated in a bleak and undignified manner; the outer appearance of Bruns's German Flaubert is certainly also not dignified: one hardly wishes to place the volumes in one's bookcase. For full measure, the Letters about his Works have been edited by an incapable person who was *afraid* to give the impression of tiring, crushing boredom—and tried to avoid it...Flaubert's being as an artist has finally succumbed to that ennui which had already corroded the mind of the youth.[56]

It was a difficult relationship, although Felix certainly had to act the more precarious part. It was true that the appearance and material of the first volumes of the Flaubert edition fell far behind subsequent editions by the same publisher. Still, Max's judgment was not quite fair. Some printings of the first four volumes were done in rough, yellow parchment-like cardboard covers with wine-red and gold print on the spine. Max's criticism seems to have been far in excess of what he actually found fault with, reflecting on much more grievous complaints directed at his father who had favoured Greve over himself. This explains his attack on the translator who was far from "incapable." No less an authority than the great Viennese poet and dramatist Hugo von Hofmannsthal would soon comment favourably on the translation. By late fall of 1905 three volumes of the edition had been published and advertised in anticipation of voluminous Christmas sales. Apart from the infighting between Max and Felix, everything seemed to be going very well indeed. It was exactly at this point that a new catastrophe occurred in the form of an unexpected letter to the publisher.

The writer was a certain Dr. E.W. Fischer who introduced himself as the only authorized agent of Madame Franklin-Grout, Gustave Flaubert's niece and heiress, then residing in Antibes. Fischer's letter forced Bruns and Greve's whole Flaubert enterprise to come to a halt. Years later, Berta Huber, an editorial assistant and translator later employed by the Bruns firm, explained what had happened to yet another lawyer involved in a lawsuit of Dickensian protraction that lasted, in effect, until the Minden publisher sold the literary arm of his firm:

> [As Bruns] was now getting ready to bring out the [translation] of the "St. Anthony," Dr. Fischer from Bielefeld came to the fore with the information that a rather little known translation of the ["St. Anthony"] had already been published, the book's copyright thus not having elapsed, and that he, as the sole and legitimate agent of the heirs, was in possession of the translation right for [the "St. Anthony"] and that the other, still protected works of the author were available from him.[57]

In short, it turned out that all the translations that the publisher had asked Greve to do were by no means his to commission—contrary to Luise Wolf's assurances and best knowledge. As in the disastrous affair with Wilde's plays, publisher and translator had again become entangled in the web of old and new copyright laws. Only this time it was the publisher's fault. Worse, Fischer could not merely prevent the sale of Bruns and Greve's Flaubert translations; he could now authorize a rival edition begun by the Munich publisher Georg Müller, distinguishing it from Bruns's failed attempts and leaving Greve and the Minden publisher hopelessly behind. In short, Fischer had Bruns and Greve by the throat and could dictate his conditions to them. He proceeded to do exactly that in a new contract, allotting a central position to himself: Greve's translation of the *St. Antoine* had to be taken out of the stores "until April 1907." J.C.C. Bruns would have to pay a stiff penalty in case of further sales (as, for instance, via the Swiss book market as had been done with a portion of the Wilde plays). One thousand marks would have to be paid to acquire the rights to this first volume only; thereafter, any remaining copies of *St. Antoine* could be sold. By this, Bruns had legally acquired the rights to the book—"with the exception of the translation which would be done by Herr Dr. Fischer himself." The whole procedure would have to be made public in the central bookseller's magazine, the *Börsenblatt für den deutschen Buchhandel*.

It could not have been worse. Once again Felix had to give up hope of introducing an internationally famous author to a German audience as a volume editor and translator. Fischer would now be the series and volume editor and would also have a hand in the translations and the choice of additional translators. The weapon Fischer wielded—the authorization—was too valuable an asset in the production and marketing of the edition. It also seemed impossible for J.C.C. Bruns to renounce the edition, since that would mean an insufferable loss of face. It also meant loss of face for both Max Bruns and Felix Greve. Max was replaced by an outsider and Felix would not continue as a translator after the *St. Antoine* (edited by Fischer) and the three volumes of correspondence.

After the penalty for the five volumes already published had been paid, the next step was to integrate these books and the forthcoming ones into a new, comprehensive Flaubert edition. The new beginning and the comprehensiveness of the edition were indicated on the left side of the two-page inside title. On the right-hand side the author's name and the book's title were repeated, followed by name of the translator in smaller type, succeeded by Fischer's name as the editor and the proud statement *Autorisierte Ausgabe* ("authorized edition").

Bruns and Greve's Flaubert edition had now become Fischer's. He quickly proved himself an insufferable pedant, meddling with the edition whenever he could, threatening the publisher with suspending the authorization or with beginning a rival edition when he felt the need. In some cases he felt that Bruns did not sufficiently advertise the edition or that the publisher's accounts were incorrect or, on another occasion, that the books were not attractively enough made. Fischer now did the translation of Flaubert's *Contes* which Greve had suggested to Bruns in 1903; he also translated *Bouvard et Pécuchet* which Max had thought his. Fischer wrote or solicited introductions, afterwords, translations and advertising copy. He also conducted the correspondence with other translators and published essays based on the edition. It is not hard to imagine the wrath and bitterness of those he had displaced. Finally, after Max Bruns had become owner and publisher of the Bruns firm in December 1908, his resistance to Fischer stiffened. An endless string of litigation followed, eventually resulting in new translations of all the Flaubert books in which Fischer had a hand (by Bruns's faithful editor Berta Huber). A volume of Flaubert's dramatic writings was added in the 1920s.

A look at the various Bruns editions of Flaubert in complete sets or single volumes reveals that, in spite of all the changes, those books for which Felix and "E. Greve" had been responsible remained in print. The Greve name remained the immutable core of the German Flaubert that Felix had helped to champion. A look at a passage from Greve's translation of *Par les champs et par les grèves* (a title Felix must have thought appealing, since "Grève" was Gide's way of spelling his name) makes it clear that even the hurried translation had resulted in a literary work of considerable quality in its own right:

> Saint-Malo, built upon the ocean and encircled by waves, appears upon arrival as a wreath of rocks placed upon the waves whose flowers are the moucharabies. The rollers pounce against the walls and, at ebb tide, break against their foot on the sand. Small rocks, covered by sea-wrack, rise a little from the sand, resembling black spots on the yellow expanse. Perpendicular and rising smoothly, the larger ones bear on their irregular peaks the foundations of the battlements, thus continuing the grey colour and extending its height.[58]

The Flaubert edition, now in Fischer's hands, meant the end of the business relations between J.C.C. Bruns and Greve. If there was a question the publisher had to ask Greve, it was Fischer who replied: "Herr Greve tells me that he is about to travel to England on business" (Fischer to Bruns, July 7, 1906). Little remained of the temporarily good relations between Bruns and Greve. Gustav, who had helped him to get back on his feet in 1904, was old, ill and reaching the end of his life by 1907. Out of necessity, Max was rapidly turning from a sensitive poet, editor and translator into the harrassed publisher and owner of the Bruns firm. Soon he would be obliged to think almost exclusively in financial terms, saddled with an enormous debt (not least due to his father's gambling in Wiesbaden). Both Max and Felix now lived on the brink. Only for Felix there was no safety net, no family, no inheritance, no reputation to sustain him.

In the spring of 1907, Greve sent his last Flaubert translation to Minden. At the same time Fischer was busy preparing contracts with other notable translators, including Friedrich von Oppeln-Bronikowski (noted as Maurice Maeterlinck's German "voice") and two outstanding figures in the approaching Expressionism, Max Brod and René Schickele. Brod, Franz Kafka's friend and literary executor, later declined. Schickele, soon to be the editor of the Expressionist magazine *Die Weissen Blätter*, and von Oppeln-Bronikowski signed on in December. The latter received 700 marks for his translation of Flaubert's *Salammbô* (1908), the second volume in Bruns and Fischer's new edition; this was more than Felix Greve had ever received from Bruns for a single volume (Martens, *Bruns* 108). The last scrap of paper Greve sent to Minden is dated April 7, 1907. Addressed to the bookkeeping department, it does not even contain the obligatory salutation:

> I gladly acknowledge receipt of 24.73 marks in payment of the remainder owed me for the 3rd volume of the Flaubert letters. This all the more

since you have so completely conceded my point regarding the number of pages and even found it necessary to pay a honorarium for the title of the book which did not originate with me.

FELIX P. GREVE

All in all, Greve did not have much luck with his German publishers. Grove would feel the same about his experiences with Canadian publishers. One suspects that his contentiousness, noticeable even in his German years, and his irrepressibly cutting irony would not have endeared him to his correspondents. J.C.C. Bruns did not profit greatly from the publishing ventures in which the firm was involved with the help of Greve. Neither did Greve ever earn enough income from Bruns to satisfy his creditors. But after a while it must have been evident to both parties that they had been literary pioneers in championing such authors as Wilde, Wells, Meredith, Gide and Flaubert in Germany.

Of Felix Greve's other publishers, only Insel was able to profit from Greve's literary talents. It was solidly, even lavishly financed and more ably run than J.C.C. Bruns, with a carefully orchestrated program directed at long-range successes. Greve's enormous capacity for concentrated work and his masterly command of the most different linguistic registers proved highly profitable to Anton Kippenberg, the able new Insel manager as of 1905. Several Greve projects went on to become long-selling money-makers: the excellent edition of the costly bound and printed twelve-volume edition of the *Arabian Nights*, translated from Richard Burton's English edition; the several shorter editions and spin-offs derived from it; his participation in Insel's large Balzac edition; and his edition and translation of Cervantes. Apparently he had even done a six-volume Dickens edition for Insel—or at least it had been completed to such a degree that Insel advertised it in the March 1909 *Börsenblatt*, inviting orders. It never appeared under Greve's name. Two months later he had left the country. Not only Insel, but Felix Greve too earned a sizeable income from this work. But, as he told Gide in his typical mixture of complaint and braggadocio, he had translated and edited no less than sixty-two books during the past two years and nine months, and he felt sick and utterly worn out. A heavy smoker, his lungs had suffered and he had to spend more than seven weeks in bed. He anticipated another ten years of health-impairing work before paying off his debts (GG 161–63). The pace at which he was working resembled a slow suicide, anticipating the one he would stage in 1909. In a letter to the "widow" Else, Anton Kippenberg describes the situation:

I have certainly always acknowledged that much of his work, and I can say most of it, was excellent and in accordance with his great talents.

Some of it, on the contrary, was not at all that way, and I am not the only one who pointed that out, but in many discussions and written remarks contained in letters to us this became obvious: Your husband almost always realized and candidly admitted this himself...[W]hen your husband as a matter of course revised and altered manuscripts or proof-sheets that I had returned to him with annotations, then this may be seen as proof that he himself admitted his inadequacy in these cases. The reason was not a lack of ability—nobody could have appreciated the talent of your husband more than I—but rather that he felt forced to take on more work than he could produce in good quality, in spite of his tremendous capacity for work. He needed the money to pay off an old debt, as he often told me.[59]

Kippenberg also mentions that Greve had apparently sold a manuscript twice. He must have been thinking of Greve's four-volume edition of the works of Jonathan Swift which was finally published by the firm of Erich Reiss. What could have prompted such rashness, a relapse into the old habits that had brought the prison term upon him? He could not have believed that his deception would remain undetected. He had already been trying to collect what funds he could lay his hands on in view of his imminent departure. Had he also attempted to beg for another four thousand marks from his erstwhile friend Kilian, as has been suspected elsewhere? It is very doubtful that his largest debtor would have lent him an additional sum (Kilian had cast him out once before, when Felix had contacted him after his release from prison). But he did have rich friends. André Gide was one of them. He had, after all, just succeeded in signing a new contract with him. Felix Greve, gambling his all, despairing of ever repairing his reputation, now decided to damage it even further. He concentrated on one more toss of the dice—in Canada.

He must have carefully prepared for this last step. He spent the summer of 1907 ceaselessly working on an idyllic island in the Baltic, Hiddensee, soon to be home to the dramatist Gerhart Hauptmann. In the village of Neuendorf he occupied yet another small vacation residence which he had come to prefer for his monk-like drudgery. No word about his Else, although her hometown of Swinemünde was not too far away to the east. Even closer were the old harbour town of Stralsund, once a Swedish possession, and the port of Rostock where ferries to Malmö and other Swedish destinations left daily. Felix's essay *Reise in Schweden* (*Travel in Sweden*), published in 1909, may have been written (or imagined, it is so general) on a journey to Sweden first conceived of in Neuendorf (GG 202–08). On both occasions, he may have explored ways of inconspicuously leaving the country for England and then Canada. In addition to the monetary reasons already discussed, there are others not to be discounted. A change was in the air. His lack of funds coincided with an imminent change in taste. Those, like Felix Greve and Max Bruns, who had belonged to the literary revolutionists of 1899, now had to make way, change direction or open their doors to another crop of literary revolutionaries, the Expressionists. Bruns did not have the money to support and develop the talents of these new authors. Although some of them, such as Paul Scheerbart, were not "new" at all and had made much of their reputation on Bruns's literature list, new publishers such as Kurt Wolff and Ernst Rowohlt published new authors such as Georg Heym and Franz Kafka. Others, Ernst Reiss for instance, whom Greve worked for until the day of his departure, managed to keep going for a while. The literary scene of which he had been a part—even as an occasional vilified outsider—was disintegrating. This made way for a new, socialistically oriented movement in which he, with his earlier aestheticist writings and aristocratic habits and tastes, had no part. Although not entirely in this vein, his novels had been rejected by both his past friends and the readers he had hoped to win. Ironically, his Canadian novels would contain themes similar to those of the Expressionists. It has been suggested that the domineering father figures Grove invented in *Our Daily Bread* and *Fruits of the Earth* showed the influence of Knut Hamsun. But father-son conflicts were common in Expressionist writings, from Franz Kafka's unfinished emigrant novel *Amerika* to his tellingly named story *Die Verwandlung (The Metamorphosis)* and such dramas as Reinhard Sorge's *Der Sohn (The Son)*.

◆ TRANSLATORS

By the time of his departure, Felix Greve's own German fiction was losing touch with the literary avant-garde. Fortunately, his translations, taken from several literary periods and styles, retained their validity as exemplars of literary mediation. In spite of occasional weaknesses, they would influence other authors for a long time to come. Wells's *The Island of Doctor Moreau* is still available in Greve's German translation, and so are his translations of Swift and Balzac. If Felix Paul Greve has remained literarily "alive" in Germany, it is as a mediator and translator of literature. Accounts of Wilde still show the important role Greve played in bringing him to German audiences. His monumental twelve-volume edition and translation of the *Arabian Nights* remains a sought-after literary rarity. His edition of the Brownings' correspondence, as well as his early Browning volumes for Insel, are not only bibliophile treasures but are still quoted.

The best example of the literary influence of his translations is in Hermann Hesse's recollection of Greve's important role in mediating André Gide:

> My earliest acquaintance with works by André Gide was owing to the translations by Felix Paul Greve which were published between 1900 and 1910 [sic] by Bruns in Minden. There was "Strait is the Gate" which, although in a more Huguenot stance, urgently reminded me of the pious atmosphere of my childhood [...] Then there was "The Immoralist" which spoke to me even more strongly [...] And in addition there was a thin booklet which, owing to the translator, had retained its French title: "Paludes," a very strange, single-minded, rough, youthfully precious little book which irritated and confused me, cast a spell on me, angered me and in the course of the following years, during which I drifted away from Gide and almost forgot him, subterraneously continued to work its effect on me (Hesse, *Gedenkblätter* 217).[60]

Hesse was an old man when he wrote this in 1951. He may confuse dates and publishers but he did not mistake Greve. He correctly remembered the lasting impression Gide made on him by way of Greve's work (a man said to have died over four decades before and then certainly dead to German literature), and he gratefully recorded its enduring inspirational power. The importance of Greve for Gide also remained clear to Gide's later translator and editor, Ernst Robert Curtius (also T.S. Eliot's German translator). In 1931, Gide permitted Curtius to translate Gide's account of his memorable first meeting with Greve into German (which Gide had previously published in French, omitting Greve's name), and to mention Greve in the essay's title, "Meeting with Felix Paul Greve" ("Treffen mit Felix Paul Greve")—the only memorial of Greve in Germany between the wars.

In this context, "Else Greve" must not be omitted. She was more than just another pseudonym of Felix, who, as we have seen, did not reject an androgynous appearance. She was also more than the creature he invented to fool his creditors, as he had done when he presented "her" to Bruns and Gide. Greve appropriated some events of Freytag-Loringhoven's early life for his fictional works. We may assume not without her consent. Later he used her name as a pseudonym on various occasions. However, she should be considered a translator in her own right, although at first in cooperation with her "husband." In this she followed the examples of Franziska zu Reventlow and Helene Klages, both of whom she must have known in Dachau, then "an artist colony near Munich" where she had been trying to "do art" prior to meeting her first husband, August Endell (BE 54).

As a translator, her name appears on the title pages of volumes seven and eight of Bruns's new Flaubert edition, *Briefe über seine Werke* and *Reiseblätter (Briefe aus dem Orient, Über Feld und Strand)*. But are we correct in assuming that only her name was used? It appears that she participated in various attempts to produce acceptable German versions of Keats's works before the Great War. We know that Felix and Else (according to the diary of Richard Schmitz) spent time in Vienna in early 1907 when Felix was proofreading an essay on Oscar Wilde that had been accepted for inclusion in a Wilde edition by Wiener Verlag. In addition, Schmitz mentions in his journal that Greve was corresponding with a Viennese woman by the name of Kraus. Whoever she was—and she was no relation of the critic Karl Kraus—"the Greves" had Viennese connections. During the 1907 visit, "Else Greve" must have met Hugo von Hofmannsthal, because at the same time Hofmannsthal asked his publisher Piper to consider a manuscript of German translations of Keats's letters from the hand of "a lady translator who is a friend of mine" and who had already made a name for herself:

> The letters of John Keats are among the most beautiful poets' letters I know and the translation I have seen is far above the level of what passes in Germany for a good translation. The lady translator has recently published an extraordinarily beautiful selection of the writings of Flaubert, unfortunately, however, in a clumsily chosen publishing house under whose flag a cultivated product of this kind was lost, so to speak.[61]

Hofmannsthal enclosed a letter by the translator (which seems to have been lost). There is little doubt that Felix Greve and Hofmannsthal had met in Munich during the busy year of 1902 (which also involved, we recall, a spat between George and Hofmannsthal). Since both Felix and Freytag-Loringhoven had moved in the Wolfskehl and George circles, they may have met the Austrian poet independently of each other. The idea of a translation of Keats's letters may have occurred to Felix and Else after their translation of the Elizabeth Barrett-Browning/Robert Browning correspondence for S. Fischer Publishers in 1905. Around this time, Rudolf Kassner, whom we remember as Gide's first German translator, wrote an essay on Keats which Gide helped to translate into French (Bohnenkamp/Foucart, "Kassner-Gide" 92). As an *homme de lettre*, as Schmitz described Felix in this phase, a new Keats vogue would not have escaped him. Hofmannsthal's artistic judgement and recommendation were not to be taken lightly, especially in light of his rival Stefan George's 1905 publication of two volumes of translations of poetry. A translation of Keats by Felix, Else or both, with a laudatory note by Hofmannsthal, would have greatly enhanced Greve's reputation (and could be seen as part of the ineffectual vendetta against his former friends in the George circle, begun with *Fanny Essler*). A Keats translation touted by Hofmannsthal would have counted even more in light of the Keats translations that were finally published in 1920 by Gisela Etzel (also a noted translator of Poe). They bore the Insel signet and were expensively bound and printed. However, Alexander Bernus, later also a Keats translator himself and the editor of the influential magazine *Freistatt*, in which Greve had published several pieces, referred to Etzel's enterprise as something "not to be surpassed in its awfulness" (Bernus 99).

Felix and Else's Keats project was never published. If "E. Greve" was indeed not just a foil for Felix, then Else was slowly beginning to emerge from his shadow as a literary artist in her own right; she ceased to be a puppet for her companion to move about at will. She had, as she claims in her recollections to Djuna Barnes, already written rather sexually explicit poems of her own while waiting in Palermo and elsewhere for Felix to be released from prison (BE 107). Greve's boast to Gide in 1904 that he had become "three persons" now begins to sound less convincing, provided that "Mme. Essler" and "Mme. Else Greve" had never been mere ciphers on paper. This may be concluded from a scene described by O.A.H. Schmitz, who had been on a visit to "the Greves'" apartment in 1906:

> Tea at the Greves'. He all literature, theatre, publishing. She is aging but well made-up, still the splendid, elegant figure. They work together, while she holds fast to her standpoint of a courtesan to view everything as entertainment. She particularly enjoys it when he translates the very erotic 1001 Night Tales with her while she sews and may remain under the impression that he is reading to her.[62]

This is an ambiguous statement. *He* works on the text while *she* appears aroused by the text which he translates aloud. That is, *if* she was listening. The ambience of the scene suggests that she may have done more than her sewing. She is sure to have commented and sought out translation solutions for problems posed by the English text (Richard Burton's). Her optimism and ironic, clear-eyed enjoyment of life would not have kept her in the role of the demure seamstress in awe of her learned husbandly master. Did she copy his manuscripts for him? Hardly. Even though American and Canadian publishers turned down Grove's first handwritten manuscripts, Greve, by then a professional, had begun in 1906 to use a typewriter "in order to cope

✼ *Else Lasker-Schüler,*
1909
(Schiller Nationalmuseum/
Deutsches Literaturarchiv,
Marbach)

with my work load."[63] The absence of a typewriter during many of his
Canadian years may be explained by poverty far in excess of that comparatively "genteel" version of it familiar to him in 1906. The homely tableau at
the Greve's apartment may tend to obscure the situation as it really was. An
older Freytag-Loringhoven, with her well-developed dramatic qualities and
her insight into men, would have played an important role recollecting and
detailing scenes for Greve in contexts other than the composition of *Fanny
Essler,* helping to visualize whatever they then verbalized together. Else had
clearly won an integral place in Greve's *ménage.*

In fact, Freytag-Loringhoven appears to have been much more "liberated"
than her male companion(s), then or later, at ease with herself, able to shrug
off stuffy conventions. She was amusing but also amused at the men she had
met, those aspiring young men full of pretensions such as the members of

the George circle she had come to know intimately. They seem to be exemplified in the figure of her would-be drawing master at Dachau who knew nothing about the art he would teach and kept prattling about "the golden cut" (golden rule), unwittingly speaking the truth since all that counted was the money to be made. To the lesser lights of his circle, Stefan George's much-touted *Tempelkunst* ("art of the temple") ultimately meant the money to be made outside of it. Although not high born like Franziska zu Reventlow or initially well-to-do as that other contemporary "dame-de-lettre," the wonderful poet and dramatist Else Lasker-Schüler (1869–1945), she shared an ironic view of the cerebral men surrounding her with them. If Reventlow slaved at her translation work to provide for herself and her child, remaining fiercely proud and independent and fighting to establish herself as a writer in her own right, Else had learned to forestall utter poverty by attracting artistic men to support her. She did not hesitate to escape from such dependencies if she found a worthwhile mate. As much as she initially must have relied on Felix to carry her away from her sad and barren marriage to Endell, she stayed with him through his prison term in Bonn, sometimes using other men to support her. Afterwards, she actively worked with him in spite of their continued poverty. Initially it must have seemed to her as if she had escaped Endell only to be trapped in another, literary cage. In this she resembles Lasker-Schüler, that other Else, who had escaped from her dismal marriage to the physician Lasker, supporting herself through periods of dire poverty before becoming the spouse (1903–1911) of Herwarth Walden, from 1910 the editor of the leading Expressionist magazine *Der Sturm*. Walden had achieved what Felix had longed for. For Felix, we remember, had planned on founding and editing just such a magazine (although patterned on the *Mercure de France*) throughout the period after his release from prison. His Else would have made an excellent partner for the *homme de lettre* Felix had hoped to become—not content with sewing unless her sewing involved binding layered sheaves of paper filled with her own writing. In 1906 and 1907 Felix and Else were "working together" on the edition of the *Arabian Nights*, soon to be followed by the partial translation of a four-volume spin-off edition of the *Arabian Days*. In the same period, Else Lasker-Schüler (who kept the pen-name "Tino of Bagdad" given to her by the poet Peter Hille, and later called herself "Yussuf, Prince of Thebes") published a volume of poetry in 1907 she called *Die Nächte Tino von Bagdads* (*The Nights of Tino of Bagdad*). They all profited from the strong oriental vogue in Berlin which had grown since the 1896 Berlin Colonial Exposition with its large-scale reproductions of Cairo and the pyramids (even the Treptow waterworks, which have survived to this day, were built in the shape of a mosque). Before that, the successful female novelist Helene Böhlau (a J.C.C.

Bruns author) had married a Turkish gentleman, and from 1887 on signed herself with delight as "Madame Al-Rashid Bey" and appeared in public in the correspondingly appropriate costumes (Martens, *Bruns* 54–55). For her part, Else Lasker-Schüler then flamboyantly appeared in public in flowing, colourful "oriental" robes of her own invention, living her art and incorporating it, becoming herself the work of art she had made. Twelve years later, Greve's Else, by then Else von Freytag-Loringhoven, acted similarly when she turned herself into a Dadaist work of art of her own invention, tailoring herself to her situation, making an artistic display of her state of utter poverty and dereliction. Back in conservative Berlin, she had been the flashing *demimonde*, laughing with Felix at bourgeois standards of morality. In New York, her nakedness and crass self-ornamentation—once famously with a coal shovel on her shaved head and postage stamps glued to her face—introduced a gesture of *épater les bourgeois* into the still somewhat dour American art and literature scene. It both roused and turned away her lovers (notably William Carlos Williams), as well as, in the end, what audience she had found (Naumann). Freytag-Loringhoven's literary art but also her *art vécu* in New York was another development of the "oriental" scene in which she had moved in Berlin.

◆ WRITER

Else Lasker-Schüler's second book of poems, *Tino von Bagdad*, was published by the Danish-born Axel Juncker, a revisionary publisher of socialist leanings and owner of a much-frequented Berlin bookstore. He had published the notorious anarchist Gustav Landauer's translations of three tracts by Oscar Wilde before accepting the first novel by that notorious translator of Wilde, Felix Paul Greve. In his persistent search for what seemed classy, Greve had ignored these three Wilde pieces. Still, the prose he began writing in prison, based on Else Endell's recollections, now explored decidedly unglamorous aspects of life in Berlin and Munich and even touched upon the issue of female sexuality. With such themes Greve transcended his somewhat silly youthful outpourings in *Wanderungen* and *Helena und Damon*. The rhapsodies contained in these slim volumes (and in his *Randarabesken zu Oskar Wilde*) now made way for a new, realistic, even naturalistic style of writing. This style was not meant for a small and carefully selected elite audience, but for the same mass of ordinary readers addressed by Arno Holz and the socialist and naturalist Johannes Schlaf, as well as their famous ephebe, the dramatist Gerhart Hauptmann. Where there had formerly been chastity and noble feelings, there were now the strong pull of sexuality and the fight for women's rights. Where an idyllic and fairy tale-like quiet had dominated his

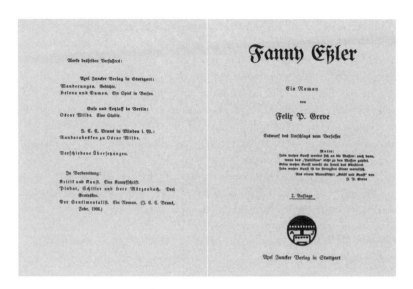

✖ *Felix Paul Greve,* Fanny Essler *(1905), title page left and right*

writings, Felix Greve now inserted the wrangling and greedy egotism of people fighting for survival against a backdrop of seedy stores and suburbs. It is no surprise, then, that he would turn to the house of Axel Juncker to be published in the company of Johannes Schlaf and, most importantly, Else Lasker-Schüler.

If *Helena und Damon* was meant to be merely ludic, a precious entertainment for those in the know about his erstwhile adoration of Helene Klages, then *Fanny Essler* was a book of revenge aimed at Felix's former idols and a public celebration of his raw passion for Else Endell. The action of the novel takes place roughly "from 1892 until 1903." In short, it leads up to the year of the author's "elopement" with Else and his imprisonment. Since the last four of the novel's five chapters deal with Munich and Berlin, they were likely written first in jail while the memory of Felix's own rise and fall was still fresh. This was underlined by the unusual tone—reminiscent of ballad and broadside—already evident in the titles of the book's first part: "The Heroine is Introduced" and "The Novel's First Part: Berlin," and of the subheadings that are reminiscent of the waystations on a somewhat comic pilgrimage: "Theatre," "Love," "Marriage," "Death."[64] The parodic element is pervasive and has many examples in the text, beginning with the novel's first sentence: "On an early May morning of the year 1892, before the sun destined for the Pomeranian flatland had yet ascended over the horizon, the figure of a young girl flitted over the still night-forsaken streets of the little seaside town on the Baltic."[65] The author artfully dodges clichés without completely obscuring them: "In the month of May," "the little town," "the young girl," and, as if to compensate for such near lapses into the ordinary, introduces variations as in "the sun destined for" the Pomeranian flatland and the newly coined adjective "night-forsaken." It seems as if he is indicating his intention to proclaim the extraordinary in the midst of the ordinary (including, for good measure, a nod to Gerhart Hauptmann and his epoch-making drama *Vor Sonnenaufgang (Before Sunrise)*.

The development of the novel, as indicated by the subheadings, is not unlike that of a melodrama, proceeding in episodes. The long narrative is made up of a succession of scenic pictures, illustrated and structured much like a sequence of dioramic images shown at a fair. In each of these scenes, "Fanny" figures with a succession of lovers. This is particularly true of the first three chapters. Herbert Koch may have been right when he suggested to Reventlow that Else must have "stunningly reenacted" crucial scenes with her former lovers for Felix.[66] As a once professional actress (at the municipal theatre of Cottbus), Else would have had no difficulty reproducing the specific tones of Ernst Hardt, Marcus Behmer and August Endell. Here, too, lies the peculiar attraction of *Fanny Essler*: in the unmistakable rendering of each character's language in expressing their greed, vanity and repression. The "passion" of Fanny, the central figure (though not the dominating one), logically comes to a natural, if sudden end, announced—as by a barker at a fair declaiming from a broadside—by the narrator: "Thus a quiet death saved Fanny Essler from the biggest disappointment of her life."[67] Else, of course, would not be spared what must have been *her* greatest disappointment: to be left behind by Felix in the United States. Fanny Essler, Else Endell—they become recognizable as lesser avatars of W.M. Thackeray's Becky Sharp, boldly fighting their ways up on the vanity fairs of Munich and Berlin.[68] In fact, in Greve's first novel the often playful tone of the narrator seems to consciously echo that of Thackeray's "Manager of the Performance" introducing his fair and the puppets playing on its stage, "not a moral place, certainly; nor a merry one, though very noisy." Much more importantly, like Becky, Fanny and Else are—in fiction and in real life—the real and quite heroic actresses of their lives led in Berlin in the years before the Great War. They stand independent, ironically smiling above the real and would-be literati of which their authors (and companions) remained inextricably part.

During the fall and early winter of 1904, after Felix and Else had finished *Fanny Essler* in their rooms in the Hotel Bellevue in Wollerau, they must have discussed possible publishers. Naturally they would have contacted J.C.C. Bruns and Insel. No correspondence touching on the new novel has been found, however. As to the book's actual publisher, Axel Juncker, near to nothing has survived, although letters from Juncker's other authors such as Maximilian Dauthendey and Johannes Schlaf have been preserved in Copenhagen. But no trace of Felix Greve. This is baffling since Juncker was not a prolific publisher and other correspondence relating to the period in question has survived. It is quite possible that whatever contacts existed between publisher and author may have been only of a "technical" nature, touching solely upon matters of cost for production and distribution. This would indicate that Felix followed the same course he had entered upon when he published his first two books. *Wanderungen* and *Helena und Damon* had been job-printed by Otto von Holten and distributed (on commission) by Littauer, but they never figured in the lists of a trade publisher. These small volumes were carefully made, with every step of the production process supervised by the author.

With *Fanny Essler* there is a similar preoccupation of the author with the appearance of his first novel. The cover was "designed by the author." The prominently placed "motto" on the title page derives from an unpublished "manuscript 'Kritik und Kunst' by F.P. Greve." In addition, there is an extensive list of Greve's writings. The book of poetry and the play are now listed as about to be (re-)published by "Axel Juncker Verlag in Stuttgart," apparently the intended sale of unsold copies in the possession of the author since no second editions were indicated. "Several translations" are mentioned but not identified, as well as his two Wilde booklets published in 1903 by Bruns and Gose & Tetzlaff. In addition to his *Drei Grotesken* (*Three Grotesques*), a new novel was announced as forthcoming: "Der Sentimentalist. Ein Roman (J.C.C. Bruns, Febr. 1906)." This is generous advertising space for a new novelist—more, probably, than would have been the case if, as may be assumed, Felix had not again shouldered most of the production costs in order to have Juncker distribute the book under his imprint.

That Felix did much of the work and had to contribute to the costs of the book seems even more likely if we compare the only account we have of Juncker's business practices. Else Lasker-Schüler published her first books with Juncker—the poems in *Styx* (1902), her edition of the works of Peter Hille (1906) and *The Nights of Tino of Bagdad* (1907). Her account of her dealings with him is as bitter as it is hilarious. When she submitted the manuscript of *Styx* he courteously wrote:

Most highly esteemed poetess. It has been a great honour for my publishing house to receive your beautiful poems for examination. They are as interesting as they are original and are exactly because of this—caviar for the masses. Which attests to their worth but constitutes a risk for the publisher. I will try anyway. Please come in sometime when you happen to be passing by my bookstore.[69]

Risks, of course, were to be avoided by the publisher. Lasker-Schüler does not say if she received a honorarium for her first book from "Hex-Axel" Juncker, as she called him. Probably not. Of her 1907 book she said bitterly that "it again fell prey to Juncker." She did not receive anything for it but gave him the book anyway, since he indicated that the new book would "pull" the other two with them, eventually making money for *her* (which it did not). In hindsight, Lasker-Schüler says, she did not then know she had "entrusted her books to somebody who was not quite spotless." All in all, she reports, she received for her first three books a grand total of 100 marks, paid for the Hille edition. Juncker refused to allow her a single free copy after she had received the presentation copies contractually agreed upon, and, when asked, suddenly could not speak German anymore, only Danish. The poor "poetess" then began stealing an occasional copy of her book from Juncker's bookstore counter; the Dane had his clerk chase after her. She escaped each time by jumping on the platform of a passing tram, sticking out her tongue at him (Lasker-Schüler, *Werke* II 524–25).[70]

In short, *Fanny Essler* was quite likely published at the author's own cost, much like many European dissertations. Again, like many dissertations, it bears a dedication: "To my parents." It is a surprising dedication in a book of somewhat risky fiction, all the more so since Greve's mother had died in 1898 and he had had no further contact with his father since his parents' separation. One thing, though, becomes almost painfully clear: to Felix Paul Greve, his first novel ranks equally with the dissertations in archaeology, ancient philology, Germanic languages and other academic disciplines by his former friends and acquaintances—Delbrueck, Vollmoeller, Koch, but also Kilian. With this novel of mine, the author clearly says, I too have arrived, and without a wealthy family's support. He produced the book himself, from the text to the cover; it is possible that he had done even more. He reports to H.G. Wells, in the context of making plans for a visit to Sandgate: "It depends on my publisher, as I am printing a modern novel of my own, the typesetting of which must be complete before I can think of removal" (April 4, 1905). In the ordinary course of things, his presence would have been required for proof-reading but not for the typesetting unless he was actively involved in it. There can be little doubt that Felix had had a hand in every step of making his book, if only to lower his costs. At any rate, his first novel was a piece of work all his own, serving to publicly rehabilitate the author as son and author.

In light of Freytag-Loringhoven's remarks about her former lovers' two German novels, however, the story reads less proudly solipsistic: "He had written *two novels*. They were each dictated by me as far as *material* was concerned—it was my *life* and persons out of my life—he did the executive part of the business—giving the thing a conventional shape and dress" (BE 65). We have seen that *Fanny Essler* was not really as conventional as that, neither was the shape Greve gave it. Freytag-Loringhoven's words ought, therefore, to be understood literally, for conventional shapes and dresses had not been Else's *métier* in Berlin (or later in New York), as Schmitz gathered from his 1906 visit to the Greves. No, there was elegance and good makeup, but it was Felix who was "all literature." The other Else, Lasker-Schüler, combined both outlandish elegance and literary activity. Possibly Freytag-Loringhoven had learned from Lasker-Schüler the unconventionalities in literary and personal style she was to push to extremes in New York, while back in Berlin Lasker-Schüler was the outstanding example of the self-made literary woman. Lasker-Schüler and "the Greves" had a stake in literary orientalism and they shared publishers (Juncker and Oesterheld). They may have known of each other, after all, since both had worked as illustrators. Lasker-Schüler's example helped, directly or indirectly, to tailor Else von Freytag-Loringhoven as person and author. As an author she may have profited from the linguistic liberties Lasker-Schüler had always taken, occasionally assuming an *Ursprache* ("Ur-language") she claimed to have rediscovered and which, she says, had been "spoken in the time of King Saul, the Royal Wild Jew:"

Elbanaff:

Min salihihi wali kinahu
Rahi hatiman
fi is bahi lahu fassun—
Min hagas assama anadir
Wakan liachad abtal
Latina almu lijádina binassre…(Lasker-Schüler II, 520-21)

This heady linguistic concoction of pseudo-Latin and pseudo-Arabic (although prefigured by texts written by Kurt Schwitters and other Dadaists of the 1920s) parallels Freytag-Loringhoven's own near-English, near-German and purely invented language in many of her poems. Consider, for instance, Freytag-Loringhoven's 1918 poem, published in *The Little Review*, entitled "Mefk Maru Mustir Dass," a linguistic fabrication along similar lines, involving German and English. *Saül*, Gide's little play translated by Felix, was published in 1909, although it contained not a shred of this Ur-language. Lasker-Schüler and Freytag-Loringhoven had moved in overlapping circles of the Berlin literati and followed the same trends. They were subject to similar influences and had emancipated themselves to follow independent careers as women writers—just as Helene Böhlau (and also Ricarda Huch [1864–1947], the most famous of these women authors) had done. Each woman was very successfully following the example set by such famous fighters for emancipation as Helene Lange and Helene Stöcker (Peterfy 44–45). Among other European women writers published in the circles in which Felix and Else moved, Marguerite Vallette (1860–1953), the wife of Gide's publisher Alfred Vallette, who wrote under the pen-name Rachilde and previously and characteristically had been known as "Mlle. Baudelaire," was another model—prolific, eccentric and self-confident (Martens, *Bruns* 109–11). These women writers were no less unconventional in their private lives, leaving their parents' houses early and declining to follow lives laid out for them by others, entering into relationships or marrying men of their own choice and divorcing them when they felt that the independence they praised and had fought for was threatened.

The extent of "Else Greve's" active role in publications officially designated as Felix's between 1904 and 1909 probably has been underestimated by some and overestimated by others. On the other hand, we cannot form a definite judgement of the part she took in Greve's many literary productions for lack of textual or external evidence. Of course we must not discount the evidence of the entry *Schriftsteller* ("author") for both Else and Felix in the 1910 Berlin Register. Perhaps Freytag-Loringhoven's unwritten memoirs (intended for Djuna Barnes) would have matched Franziska zu Reventlow's sarcastic and funny observations in her autobiographical *Von Paul zu Pedro* (*From Paul to Pedro*, 1912) and *Herrn Dames Aufzeichnungen* (*Mister Lady's Notes*, 1912) as well as Else Lasker-Schüler's *Ich räume auf* (*Sorting It Out*, 1925) from which I have quoted above.

If *Fanny Essler* did not contain a printer's identification, Felix Greve's second novel was printed in the widely known and well-respected printing facility of Spamer in Leipzig. The publisher is again the partnership of Axel Juncker and Karl Schnabel in Berlin and Stuttgart. Since Juncker owned a bookstore, known for its good selection of foreign-language books, Greve (like Moeller-Bruck, the editor of J.C.C. Bruns's Poe edition) may have first become acquainted with the publisher when looking for French and English books to translate. This may also mean that Juncker confined himself to selling the majority of the books he published through his store (as Lasker-Schüler was aware), not really going to much of an effort to distribute them. Greve's colleague O.A.H. Schmitz was not impressed by Juncker's business sense. He noted in 1906: "At Axel Juncker's whom I get to see for the first time. Endearing sleepy-head. Pretty much reduced establishment. I don't

felix Paul Greve
Maurermeifter
Ihles Haus
Roman

Vom Verfaffer erfchienen bisher:

Wanderungen, Gedichte.
Helena und Damon, Ein Spiel in Verfen.
Oscar Wilde, Eine Studie.
Randarabesken zu Oscar Wilde.
fanny Effler, Ein Berliner Roman.

In Vorbereitung find:

Das Blutbad im bayrischen Nationalmuseum und andere
fowohl grauenha..e wie ergötzliche Geschichten
von Leuten, die . . .
Der Sentimentalift, Ein Roman.

1906
Berlin
Karl Schnabel

*Felix Paul Greve*, Maurermeister Ihles Haus (1906), *title page left and right*

understand how anybody could recommend him to me."[71] Juncker's surviving correspondence with his authors shows that he had very small financial resources and was excessively stingy, if we are to believe Lasker-Schüler. It comes as no surprise that Greve at first tried to find another publisher for his second novel.

There is no record of *Maurermeister Ihles Haus* in the Bruns archive, although the publisher might have been shown the manuscript. The only surviving record of his submission to another publisher is a letter to Alfred Janssen in Hamburg. He, we recall, was the socialist publisher who had turned down Greve's *Wanderungen* in 1902. The letter was sent from Berlin's Fasanenstrasse where Felix and Else stayed after leaving Wollerau and before moving into nearby Nachodstrasse. It contains a carefully written proposal:

Having published my first novel ("Fanny Essler" — a Novel of Berlin) a few months ago with Axel Juncker in Stuttgart, today I want to see to a second book which was finished this winter. It is a kind of a novel from the region of *Hither Pomerania* which must by all means appear in a northern German publishing house. The form is very new to the extent that the narrative itself is being very much relegated to the back-stage vis à vis the scenes dramatically worked up and strung together. The "scenes" take place in the house of a well-to-do citizen, a self-made man par excellence. The title is "Master Mason Ihle's House;" the whole thing is short (20 sheets at the most) and—apart from Book the First ("Daughters of the Elite:" Milieu of the children in the house of the "grim Master Mason" and in the Girls' Public School)—the action takes place with almost catastrophic speed. Its harshness is only mitigated by the comicality of many details. The whole thing is the tragedy of a family.[72]

Although somewhat extended, here again is the stage-directed dramatic orientation of the first novel. Greve clearly foregrounds the scenic, theatrical construction of his tale—a structural design again quite in keeping with the actual career of his companion Else, a former actress, whose recollections of her youth form the nucleus of the novel. In spite of Freytag-Loringhoven's later contention that Flaubert had been Felix's model, Greve again foregoes the "well-constructed realistic novel" in favour of a melodramatic and dioramic sequence of "scenes." By means of "humour" the narrator distances himself from the actual melodrama depicted, showing a trait that the supposedly "dour" Canadian author rarely showed (unless we consider his "boy's novel," *The Adventures of Leonard Broadus*). Although Greve wishes to emphasize the "catastrophic speed" of his book—the sheer inevitability of the deterministic action—thus pointing to a specific trait of naturalistic German drama of the Hauptmann school, the overall impression of well-made and ironically viewed colportage remains. Another remark in the letter to Janssen, however, makes a far greater claim to success than the appeal to the dramatic writings of Hauptmann.

"The Tragedy of a Family," the projected subtitle Greve mentions to Janssen, is evidently meant to remind the publisher of one of the greatest publishing successes of the period: Thomas Mann's novel *Buddenbrooks* (1901), subtitled "The Decay of a Family." Felix Greve must have seen a certain amount of justice in almost duplicating the well-known subtitle of Mann's famous novel. The parallels between his own and Mann's protagonists' wanderings between Bavaria and the German North, between Munich and Hamburg and Luebeck, cannot have escaped him. Mutual acquaintances such as the brothers Friedrich and Roderich Huch formed a link between Thomas Mann and Felix Greve. In addition, they had shared the same address at Munich's "Pension for Young Men" at 15 Giselastrasse. This had been the period between Greve's return (with Helene Klages) from Lake Garda and the Mann brothers' preparations for their removal to Riva, also on Lake Garda. Thomas Mann had moved into Felix's "Pension Gisela" on September 8, 1902 and moved out again on October 2, 1902, shortly before Felix moved to Berlin.[73] These six weeks had been some of the most exciting and promising weeks of their lives. Mann had landed a major success with *Buddenbrooks* and Greve anticipated making the big time with his translations of Wilde's plays. Greve had then also still hoped to publish his poetry in George's *Blätter für die Kunst*. Both Stefan George and a friend, the Dutch poet Albert Verwey, had also lived at the pension during Greve's sojourn there, possibly even staying in his rooms. August and September 1902 were the period of Greve's much-criticized "opulent dinner" for his friends and the time when he exclaimed that he would "astonish the world." Mann, of course, succeeded in astonishing the world; Greve did not.

What was the reason for George's and Vervey's and later Thomas Mann's stay at Greve's rooming house? One cannot help thinking of the secret preference the young novelist from Luebeck shared with some of the members of George's circle as well as with Greve and Kilian and several other Rhenus sportsmen. One of Mann's biographers finds apt words to help us understand some of the emotional tensions that may have been "in the air" in the Pension Gisela:

> The blond and blue-eyed youngsters lured him again and again with irresistible power, but in those early days in Munich he would hardly have forgotten for a moment that the love for one's own sex—although it existed a thousand-fold—also in stodgy Munich and not just as a remotely felt magic—was surrounded by dangers: dangers for one's own soul, one's bourgeois reputation—yes, even for the security and freedom of one's existence for it was up to state attorneys and police beadles to ruin the life of everyone of "a deviant" and "degenerate nature" on the strength of the ominous paragraph 175 of the Book of Criminal Law (Harpprecht 127).[74]

Even if the two merely passed each other on the stairs, Mann could not have failed to notice in Greve the ideal type of his preference, while Greve must have been impressed by a writer whose career was so different and much less endangered than his own. More than a quarter of a century later, after Greve had become an established writer in Canada and the Nobel Prize-winner and world-famous Thomas Mann was in exile in Princeton, there was a small exchange of letters we know about, although only Mann's letters seem to have survived. Not Felix Paul Greve but Frederick Philip Grove wrote to his famous contemporary in early 1939 offering to send him a "luxury edition" of one of his novels, as we gather from Mann's reply. To someone familiar with Greve's life in Munich, the offer of such a "luxury edition" could have been a clear signal, reminiscent of those earlier luxury editions on costly paper that Greve had commissioned and distributed to his friends in

Munich, Paris and Berlin. When Grove sent Mann a signed copy of his 1939 novel *Two Generations* and Thomas Mann, in response, praised Grove's "true Anglo-Saxon humour," it seemed as if the Canadian had now successfully established that his incognito would remain unlifted. Grove then announced to Mann a package with a copy of his *A Search for America* while he was, at the same time, working hard on variations of his real European past, eventually to be published as *In Search of Myself.* This gesture showed Grove's typical ambivalence that he, while continuing to hide his German identity, clearly wished to tip Mann off in at least a roundabout way. He must, after all, have written in perfect German. Mann understood differently and expressed friendly parallels between them. He thanked the *Sehr geehrter Herr Grove* ("esteemed Mr. Grove") for his help in building bridges between his own lost Europe and America:

> I have been living in this country for almost a year now; however, the work brought from the other side serves as an insulation; in addition, at my age, one does not so easily surrender to new impressions. Thus I am very grateful for any help in building bridges, and your novel means that to me. The dissociation of the doubting "spirit" from "ground," "nature," in short: "life"—this central theme of my own oeuvre is, if I am not mistaken, also yours in your book. The synthesis between the telluric and the intellectual forces that I am bent upon, is with you a very appealing, subdued, typical Anglo-Saxon humour which does not die in being understood. I will be much delighted to read "A Search for America" on the return from my summer trip to Europe.[75]

What might have turned into a promising and more extensive correspondence ended right there. For his part, it appears, Mann never sent a dedication copy to Grove in Simcoe. Maybe Grove had been disappointed. On the other hand, Grove may have felt that he had already gone too far. His desire to keep his disguise may have won out over his longing for recognition from a famous colleague who had played a role in his early life. It seems no surprise that the short period of contact between the two writers occurred at the same time when mention of an André Gide biography roused the Canadian to reflect on *their* former relationship and the very different lives they were to lead.

Felix Paul Greve's letter to the publisher Alfred Janssen alludes not only to Thomas Mann's major novel but also to current drama. One might think of plays by Henrik Ibsen or even of *Die Familie Selicke* (1890) by Arno Holz and Johannes Schlaf. Much like Greve's dramatically structured novels, this play by the most prominent exponents of the movement of "consequent Naturalism," as it was called, works with only loosely connected dialogue sketches. In Greve's time, this technique had come to be identified as "a true-to-nature, loose assemblage." Both the play and the novels, in true Naturalist fashion, make use of North German dialect variants.[76] There is still another parallel. Greve adds to the second edition of *Fanny Essler* a new subtitle, calling it *Ein Berliner Roman* (*A Berlin Novel*). Here, again, is an implied reference to the naturalistic works of Holz and Schlaf whose subtitle for their drama *Die papierne Passion* (*The Paper Passion*) was *Eine Berliner Studie* (*A Study of Berlin*). These interactions between a somewhat belated Naturalism and plays of the leading Naturalist authors of more than a decade before make it clear that Greve wanted not only to demonstrate his departure from the reigning aestheticism but also, paradoxically, to turn toward Berlin as subject and centre of realistic, then Expressionist writing. This was the same direction taken by Johannes Schlaf, who had become an Axel Juncker author—motivation enough for Greve to do the same with *Fanny Essler* and then *Maurermeister Ihles Haus*.

At first, however, what would turn into an attempt to become "all Berlin" was shaped to fit the Hamburg mould of Alfred Janssen's literature list. Greve let the publisher know that he was pressed for time and wanted to have his second novel published as quickly as possible, and also excused himself for the hurried and cramped handwriting of the manuscript. He then reminded Janssen that the author himself was from Hamburg and that one reads his writings there:

> As to the distribution, it remains to be said that after my long years as a writer I am by no means still an unknown; and especially in Hamburg my publications of English authors have been from the beginning reviewed positively and vividly laudatory. To you, personally, I may not be entirely unknown, since a few years ago you—quite rightly—turned down a volume of my poems.[77]

The favourable reviews Greve mentioned had been those of his Wells translations which had appeared in the respected *Hamburger Fremdenblatt*. J.C.C. Bruns would use these reviews for advertisements for years to come both in books and magazines.

In spite of Greve's efforts, Alfred Janssen turned the book down. However, after several more months Greve was able to report to his colleague O.A.H. Schmitz:

> My novel will appear—if the printing can be finished by mid-October (I am hurrying it through the press)—still before Christmas, otherwise

by the end of January. Again one has been begun too late. Of course I have renounced Juncker. You probably are not any more in need of this. Your books are beginning to move by themselves. You lucky man![78]

He was back where he had begun. Greve again did most of the work of producing and distributing his novel himself, possibly also paying for the printing and binding, merely using the Juncker imprint. Since the book was not published in early 1907, as he had feared, it did not become one of the "Christmas books" that usually sold relatively well. Greve would never belong to those whose books sold well. *Fanny Essler* alone had its small *succès de scandale*. Fittingly enough, Greve's last communication with Juncker concerned that novel. The terse words say more than a long letter would have about the success of the author's works in Germany and about what he could reasonably expect to gain as a writer:

> Since I have been again kept waiting for weeks for the account and payment [*handwritten addition in the left-hand margin*: of the honorarium for "Fanny Essler"], I inform you by this that if both will not be done within three days from this, i.e. until the 26th of the month, noon, I shall consider our contract dissolved.
>
> Sincerely,
> FELIX P. GREVE
> By registered letter[79]

Since Juncker's account books have not survived, we do not know whether the publisher paid up or whether the copyright was returned to the author. If it was, he did not use it again. The monetary value of both would have been low in either case. What becomes obvious is that in February 1909 Greve was busy collecting all monies due him (and whatever he could borrow) to put aside for his imminent departure. A new departure had become overdue. In spite of "the Greves'" desperate attempts to keep up appearances in the literary circles in which they moved—Schmitz wrote that he found them impressive as they managed to keep up "such an intensive elegance during their strenuous fight for survival"—the necessary expenditure no longer served a useful purpose.[80] Felix Greve's own writings did not sell and they were going quickly out of fashion. The J.C.C. Bruns firm had almost stopped adding new authors to its list. Insel Publishers still provided him with translation work but the competition was intense. The political situation also seemed to point toward a change. At the last minute he must have collected outstanding fees from Juncker, Insel, Reiss, Oesterheld—even for such quickly translated potboilers as Dumas's *The Count of Monte Cristo*. Furthermore, he must have arranged that fees be paid after his "suicide" to an account which he had arranged somewhere under a different name — "Fritz Thurow," say, the name attached to Reiss Publishers' 1916 Swift edition. The last new book of note that bore his name was his long-fought-for translation of André Gide's *La porte étroite*. The last sentence of the book, in Greve's German version, reads: *Ich möchte jetzt sterben, schnell, ehe ich von neuem begriffen habe, dass ich allein bin* ("I want to die now, quickly, before I am made to understand again that I am alone"). It was through a narrow gate, a *porte étroite*, that he managed to slip from Europe and his past life of debt, overwork and obloquy to become a new man.

7

A·TRAVELLING
AUTHOR

BETWEEN FELIX PAUL GREVE'S EUROPEAN CAREER and his comparatively well-documented time in Canada, there remains a short but crucial period about which little is known and which he fictionalized above all in *A Search for America*. It covers approximately three years from Greve's staged suicide in Berlin, early in the summer of 1909, to the appearance of "Fred Grove" in Winnipeg in December 1912.

There has been no dearth of speculation about the interim. We now know how he made his way to the New World after Else had informed the publisher Anton Kippenberg about his supposed suicide (Letters 548). But we do not know much about his motivation, apart from his pressing financial problems. Did he take a ferry from Rostock or Stralsund to a Scandinavian port and then another boat to England in June or early July 1909? Easily reached from Berlin, Rostock was and is a major point of debarkation for destinations in Scandinavia, most notably Trelleborg and Malmö near Lund (where Grove later claimed to have resided with his parents). It now seems that Grove quite faithfully recorded his trip from Europe to Canada in *A Search for America* (SFA 10–11), albeit shifting the year of his departure from 1909 back to 1892:

> What I resolved to do was this. I intended to step in at Cook's tourist office in London—on the Strand, if I remember right—and to ask for the next boat which I stood any chance of catching, either at Liverpool or at Southampton…As it happened, when, a day or two later, I carried

❀ *The* Megantic *(Ulster Folk and Transport Museum)*

this idea out, a White-Star liner was to weigh anchor next day, going
from Liverpool to Montreal. The boat train was to leave Euston
Station the same night at ten o'clock. I bought my passage—second
cabin—received a third-class railway ticket free of charge and—had
burnt my bridges. Thus I became an immigrant into the western hemi-
sphere (SFA 11).

He followed this course exactly, travelling by train from London to Liverpool
after booking a passage to Canada aboard the brand new White Star liner
Megantic. This liner was one of White Star's faster medium-sized ships then
plying the North Atlantic; it carried immigrants, Americans, returning
Canadians and tourists (in spite of its name, however, it was by no means the
size of the *Titanic*). According to Canadian arrival records, the *Megantic* left
Liverpool on July 22 and arrived in Québec on July 29, 1909 with the thirty-
year-old Greve among its passengers. Greve now styled himself "Grove" but
apparently still retained his first name and his middle initial, "P" (as far as
can be made out from the purser's handwriting in the ship's register). He had
not yet decided whether to stay in Canada or to return to Europe, for he
listed his occupation as "travelling author," stating his intention to proceed
west on the Canadian Pacific Railroad. Did he really first travel west,
spending the money he carried with him until it dried up?[1] (One of the

names nearest to his on the passenger list was that of another prospective C.P.R. passenger, a blacksmith from Winnipeg.)

According to *A Search for America*, Phil Branden then went on to Montreal, worked in a restaurant in Toronto, continued on to New York and Philadelphia hawking books with a dubious outfit, and then, in a self-liberating move, entirely freed himself from his past and the conventions of "good society" by striking out on his own. Not unlike an older and latter-day Huck Finn, he proceeded down the Ohio River toward Indiana on a raft, working as a factory hand in small towns and as a farm worker and clerk during the wheat harvest in the Dakotas before making his way to Winnipeg.[2] But this is Phil Branden's story, not Grove's autobiographical record, although the two share more biographical facts than has been hitherto assumed. Towards the end of his life, Grove would again make reference to his travels in the Midwest (ISM 205–40).

Not until the publication of "Baroness Elsa's" memoirs in 1992 was anything known about an unspecified period (about a year) which Else and FPG spent "in the midst of the county [sic] of Kentucky in the small farm country." As Baroness von Freytag-Loringhoven added, "That is how I came to America in the first place" (BE 66). Finally, a timeline on "Schalk," one of Grove's German poems—"Sparta, Kentucky, am Eagle Creek"—brought us closer to solving the riddle of Grove's whereabouts between Germany and Canada (Divay 1993, lxxvii).

On the basis of previous research and advice offered by Grove's son, A. Leonard Grove, further investigation of the "American episode" in Grove's life seemed necessary. A research trip in October 1997 led to promising finds in a number of archives in Cincinnati and across the river in Kentucky in Covington, Frankfort, Owenton, Warsaw and elsewhere. There, along with the odds and ends of new material, I found helpful new informants, among them descendants of those who lived in the Sparta area when Grove may have farmed and taught in the "small farm country of Kentucky."

Two sources make it clear that Grove was aware of German theories of education and also of their practice at the grade-school level: the books Grove mentioned to and ordered from his young Winkler, Manitoba, colleague Isaac Warkentin, who had gone to Leipzig for study (Letters 4 n.1); and Grove's and his wife Catherine's teaching in their own school in Ontario (Stobie, *Grove* 31). In fact, after his first year in Canada he published a paper about Jean-Jacques Rousseau in *Der Nordwesten* in Chicago (Grove 1914).[3] In Manitoba, he quickly secured full certification as a teacher. Stobie even claimed that "whatever else Grove may have been, he was a professional and professionally trained elementary school teacher before he arrived in Manitoba" (Stobie, *Grove* 31).

So had he really been a teacher in Kentucky? In light of Grove's successful teaching record in small-town Manitoba and what had appeared as his utter lack of such experience in Germany, there might be something to this suspicion. Adding to the mystery, Stobie wrote of Grove's first appearance on Canadian soil, emphasizing that "here was a mature man, obviously intelligent, with evident teaching experience," of use in several bilingual schools in the Mennonite community (Stobie, *Grove* 25). Stobie did not explain how Grove's teaching experience manifested itself as "evident." Intelligence may quickly become obvious, but would teaching experience have been apparent during Grove's first interview with the Manitoba Deputy Minister of Education? During the months before his departure from Berlin, did Grove (as Greve) pick up some of the necessary skills? His last Berlin address, an apartment at 42 Münchner Strasse, was only a few hundred yards away from a training centre for teachers grounded in the principles developed by Froebel. A look at a contemporary map of Berlin shows that the Greve residence was virtually surrounded by such institutions. He could not have spent the last half year of his life in Berlin in an area more proximate to educational resources. Within easy walking distance were several high schools and lesser schools, as well as the *Bibliothek und Auskunftsstelle für das Höhere Schulwesen* (Library and Information Centre for Advanced Schooling), the important *Pestalozzi-Fröbel Haus* and even the *Amerikanisches Vereinsbüro* at Nollendorfplatz—in short, all the educational resources necessary for a teacher in North America. No wonder Grove received a temporary teaching permit in Winnipeg in the summer of 1913. If his teaching experience had been "evident," however, why did he have nothing to show for it?[4]

Even if he had a previous certificate, would he have shown it to the Manitoban authorities? A difficult question. If he had one, there would have been no reason not to show it—provided, of course, it had been in his new name, Fred Grove, with which he introduced himself in Canada. Had it been one issued in Berlin under a different name (Felix Paul Greve, for instance), he would not have shown it, especially if he had something to hide in connection with his former name and his desertion of Else whom he may not have wanted to find him.

Grove may have made other attempts to begin a farming career or even a new life. One is reminded of Freytag-Loringhoven's remark that Greve had wanted to become "a potato king" in Kentucky (BE 65), although Kentucky is not particularly well known as a potato-growing state. Or had he planned on becoming a tomato king? There is, after all, an anecdote in which Grove attempts to drive "a load of tomatoes a hundred miles" to Cincinnati (*FPG* 174). But even if such an anecdote were true, a hundred miles south of

Cincinnati is about thirty miles south of Lexington or Louisville—horse country, not tomato or potato country. And why, in that case, go to Cincinnati from Louisville when other centres and markets were much closer? All of this is a bit confusing and almost certainly meant to be misleading.

There is yet another conundrum bound up in Grove's American doings and whereabouts. On the basis of a note by Djuna Barnes, it has been suggested that Freytag-Loringhoven, having been left behind by Grove in Kentucky, had "started posing as a dancer in Cincinnati" (Divay, "Fanny Essler's" 189 n. 13). Unfortunately, intensive search in Cincinnati failed to uncover any indication that she spent time as a dancer before appearing in New York and achieving notoriety there as a Dada queen.[5] Further investigation in the archives of the Cincinnati Historical Society provided nothing more than a scrap of paper from a Mrs. Lula Dohrmann addressed to one "Belle Greve." The piece of paper, however, bears the date of May 22, 1915, at least two years after Freytag-Loringhoven's arrival in New York, invalidating the note as evidence. Furthermore, the little note makes clear that the dancing was of an amateur nature, evidently part of a respectable dancing class for society ladies. Fortunately, other Cincinnati and Sparta records did reveal some items that had previously escaped notice.

Records in Cincinnati and its sister city Covington in Kentucky mention several Greves. This is no surprise, since the German name "Greve" was not rare in Cincinnati, a city traditionally favoured by great numbers of German immigrants. It was easily reached by railroad from Baltimore and Philadelphia or via Ohio riverboats from Pittsburgh and Wheeling. Two Greves in the Cincinnati city directory for the years in question are of special interest. The first is a "manufacturer's agent" called "F.C. Greve," who first appears in June 1910 as the occupant of a one-room office. Five years later, more than two years after Grove's appearance in Canada, he was missing from the records. One is reminded of Grove's claim that his hero Branden had worked elsewhere as a book agent. Grove's early short-term absence from his teaching in Manitoba also comes to mind. He claimed: "At Christmas I went down to Arkansas—into the hospital!! And when I came out I did not know my world any longer! I was so changed" (Letters 13). Had he, during a return to the Cincinnati area, actively changed "his world"" there by liquidating it and a former life? The initials "F.C." recall Felix Greve's initials in the pseudonym "F.C. Gerden," which he used in his dealings with Insel. The second noteworthy person in the directory to share Grove's former name was "Fred Greve Jr.," a "conductor" living on Cincinnati's Spring Grove Avenue during the period in question. Was he related to Greve's father, the tram conductor in Hamburg? "Fred Greve" sounds like the missing link in

Greve's transition from Felix Paul Greve to Felix P. Grove to Fred Grove and eventually Frederick Philip Grove. There is no record of anybody else resembling Grove among the more than 175 Germans then teaching in Cincinnati. The city was the home of several more or less prominent German-American writers and literary mediators, among them Karl Knortz, a teacher and later an influential literary historian and translator of Walt Whitman.[6]

◆ SPARTA

Did Grove spend one or two years in Kentucky, just across the Ohio River from Cincinnati? If he did, as seems very likely, then many questions remain: why did he stay for only a short time, hardly enough to engage in any business venture of the kind he had in mind? Of course, a family quarrel with Else may have provided reason enough to leave. The two may have quarrelled over the failure of their long-range plans. Nevertheless, the initial choice of place does not indicate accident but rather careful premeditation. Sparta, in the northwest corner of Kentucky, a mere thirty-six miles southwest of Cincinnati, must have seemed a good choice for more reasons than poetry and potatoes. Stobie details what type of farming Grove may really have attempted there. She mentions a story told by some of his pupils that "when he was a tobacco farmer in Kentucky he sewed on the ear of his wife that had been bitten off by one of their favorite Percherons" (Stobie, *Grove* 34).[7] Never a dull moment with teacher Grove. But apart from the sensationalism Grove occasionally liked to indulge in, there may be some substance to the story of tobacco farming, if not to the bitten-off ear and to a likely stint of teaching and farming. Indeed, Grove has his fictional alter ego Branden enter the "tobacco belt," expertly mentioning "hands" and "braids" of tobacco (SFA 256).

But why did Grove go to Sparta of all places and not to any of the neighbouring towns—Carrollton, Owenton or Warsaw, so much more attractive even today? Apart from the surrounding hilly landscape, present-day Sparta is not a particularly stirring place.[8] There is a tiny business district with an abandoned depot, two stores, two pool halls, a liquor store, a gas station and a post office, in addition to a number of residences along side roads and a few scattered farms along Eagle Creek. In Greve's day, however, the town was quite different. Classically named after a grist-mill on Eagle Creek, a tributary of the Kentucky River, Sparta was then a major railhead and stopping place—three times a day—for the Cincinnati and Nashville Railroad. A stagecoach line boasting horse-drawn cabs connected Sparta's busy train depot to Owenton and Warsaw, towns in nearby Owen and Gallatin coun-

❈ *Rural school once occupied by the Groves in Falmouth, Manitoba.*
(Collection Klaus Martens)

ties. Farmers, businessmen and travelling salesmen for miles around had to go to Sparta to pick up and deliver products and passengers. Tobacco growers' associations and the tomato cannery in the local town of Sanders also used the Sparta depot.[9]

In 1905, somebody invested considerable sums of money in the new and well-appointed Sparta Exchange Hotel on Highway 35 between the depot and the post office. From then on, people not only passed through but were induced to stay in the company of travelling salesmen and farmers who carried bundles of cash from the sale and shipment of their crops. Among those who stayed during the period 1907–11 was somebody resembling Buffalo Bill, a man called "Colorado Grant" who had his own travelling Wild West show. He eventually made his home in Sparta and the town became, for a short time, famous.[10] This was also the age of new health centres. Towns in the Midwest and the South were discovering their appeal for moneyed questers after health and entertainment. A sojourn in Sparta was not really spartan anymore, because the place became something resembling a spa. To be sure, it was much less so than the neighbouring town of Sanders (in Carroll County), then a noted resort with artesian springs in the hilly and well-wooded countryside crossed by streams under overhanging trees and along the fields of tobacco (mostly Burley). In short, Sparta was a good choice for an immigrant recently arrived from Europe. It offered diverse business opportunities, a touch of society and some entertainment, as well as small occasions for displaying one's learning and education. Even before going to Sparta, Grove had excelled in smaller, more rural places such as Wollerau, Paris-Plage or Neuendorf on the island of Hiddensee. The small towns in Canada where he would later teach—Kronsfeld, Winkler, Virden, Gladstone, Falmouth, Leifur, Eden, Ashfield, Rapid City and Simcoe—were no less rural.

At the time of Grove's likely arrival in Sparta, there was already a large and prosperous tree nursery. It had been founded as recently as 1908–09 and was owned by one J.A. Donalson, an Englishman.[11] In light of Grove's stories about the parental Swedish estate where trees were raised and sold throughout the Baltic (ISM 20), Branden's decision to hire himself out as an expert on pruning, grafting and transplanting trees on his Ohio River tramp is interesting. Nowhere else in his real life did Grove have a chance to learn anything about such a trade. "I had grown up in a tree-nursery," says Phil Branden. "I had never done any of the work myself; but I had looked on so often, and I had so often heard the directions given to 'new hands' by a trained superintendent or foreman that I knew the underlying principles thoroughly" (SFA 320). Branden makes a success of the job and continues working for a while as a "peripatetic tree-pruner" who was not a "tree-butcher" (SFA 320). It is the author's insistence on such facts that may make them more than naturalistic detail. Several such situations in Grove's *roman vécu* (Stobie, *Grove* 63) seem to indicate that the author had lived them. Many of these are centered around Branden's going to and from the Ohio River, so many, it seems, that the prudent author must have gathered them in one fictional place recognizably patterned on the real one.

Finally, of course, Sparta was far enough removed from Cincinnati to promise a certain degree of voluntary invisibility. As an incidental boon, Sparta also offered an unique opportunity to escape the law at the local level. The covered wooden bridge across Eagle Creek connected two parts of the same town and divided two counties. Thus, in a local historian's own words, "if you got in truble with the law, and the Sheriff, all you had to do was walk out on the bridge a peace, and you was in Owen County, and the Gallatin County Sheriff couldn't tutch you." Grove might have thought this useful.

If Grove had in fact taught in the Sparta area, where did he do so? In the fall of 1909, at the time of Greve's disappearance from Germany, Sparta opened a new schoolhouse (its third). It was an imposing two-storey brick building topped by a small bell-tower under a gabled roof. Called an "Independent Graded and High School," or "Class B school," it granted its first diplomas in 1914 when it became a four-year high school. Things were looking up in Sparta, even though the school district was not yet as well

✽ *(left) Sparta School, ca. 1910.* (Collection C.N. Varble) *(right) Detail showing F.P. Grove (?)* (Collection C.N. Varble)

✽ *Frederick Philip Grove with students, Rapid City, Manitoba, 1923*
(Collection A. Leonard Grove/Elizabeth Dafoe Library, University of Manitoba)

organized or run as in Cincinnati. First, teachers had to be found and a curriculum organized. Teaching jobs were probably advertised in Cincinnati, a major stopping point for immigrants, although some were recruited from the local population. In the beginning, the school must have seemed an ideal place for newcomers without professional experience.

Extensive research in Sparta has led to the discovery of two indistinct and badly yellowed amateur photographs from 1910–11. The first shows the new schoolhouse. The second offers a glimpse into a schoolyard scene with a view of part of the school's front. This picture is tantalizing both for what it shows and what it conceals. Of course it is not the brawny young man in the foreground or the homely chickens pecking in the dirt which deserve scrutiny. Rather, attention should centre on the half-concealed figure in the school window in the building's upper right-hand corner. A formally clad man is in the act of withdrawing, as if not wanting to have his picture taken. The outlines of his face and long torso closely resemble Grove's distinctive features. These are more clearly discernible at the back of the well-known group picture from 1922 in Rapid City.

To be sure, no teacher in Sparta named Greve or Grove or any of the other names he is known to have used is on record. Yet this absence need not be telling. Until early 1912, no certification of teachers from normal schools or universities was required. Accordingly, no formal records of teachers working in Sparta during the period in question have survived.[12] Even the school building has disappeared. It burned down in 1927—a fateful year which not only saw the diminution of Sparta's importance as a railhead but also the death of Freytag-Loringhoven (in Paris) and the publication of *A Search for America*. The disappearance of the school unfortunately means that no school attendance records in the teachers' handwriting remain. By contrast, such records in Grove's hand with his name on them have survived, testifying to his career as a teacher in Canada. Grove could have taught in Sparta's brick schoolhouse until it became imperative to show proof of his education and identity in the spring of 1912. This would have been one reason for his leaving. Such a failure, if it actually occurred, should probably be seen in the context of Grove's suspected farming venture. A teaching job may have served to supplement an income, the way it later did for the Grove family in Simcoe, where the Groves again supported their initially large farm by teaching. Grove may have remembered something from his time in Kentucky. He did after all have a tendency for repetition.

"How Ye Gonna Keep 'em Down On the Farm (After They've Seen Paree)?" is the title of a once-famous World War I ditty. In 1910, of course, before the Great War and when he had already seen "Paree" and much else, Grove would have welcomed the farm, at least for a while. If he had indeed farmed in the Sparta area then, it would have been a tobacco farm, tobacco being the staple crop, although there was also a tomato cannery nearby, the only one for many miles around, possibly forming the basis for the anecdote mentioned above.[13] Grove could not have owned even a small farm under any of the aliases we know, since his name is not in the tax records. Neither is Else's. But they may have held a short-term lease or rented part of a farm. In fact, between 1910 and 1912, according to the Gallatin County mortgage records, there was a man, tantalizingly called Abe Groves, who owned a 3 1/2 acre tobacco farm on the Gallatin County side of Sparta, "adjoining the land of one Pat Riley" not far from the school. This Abe Groves worked the farm with his sons and additional help. Did he have help from—or lease part of his land to—a recent arrival who later used variations of the name in reality and in his fictions? There were others by the name of Groves in Gallatin County and nearby regions, called Conrad and Edward Groves. Of these, Conrad Groves had a tract of land he farmed in Sparta. If Grove did farm, under whatever name, while doing some part-time teaching, he could not have started at a more unfortunate time. Prices for tobacco were at a low of nine cents a pound, sometimes less, and the crop of 1911 was of unusually bad quality because of severe flooding along Eagle Creek. Many farmers had to take out large loans or mortgages to recover their losses or give up farming altogether.

Grove may have left the Sparta area and the last link to his former life for a number of reasons: losing a farm on account of inclement weather; crop failure and resulting low prices; losing the money he had brought with him; the end of teaching possibilities for someone without a certificate or academic credentials. It also meant leaving Else behind. According to her own account, their relationship failed because of her diminishing attraction for him and his longing for respectability. She became hostile because he had rejected her, and Grove left her "helpless in this strange country," abandoning her because he felt left alone "in the hardest struggle of my life," as Freytag-Loringhoven later reported (BE 92).

But why did Grove turn to Canada? Why not strike out to other lands of Goshen, to Texas or even California? In A Search for America, Branden accidentally became a hobo and imagined travelling to California, but at the first opportunity he left his boxcar and backtracked east (SFA 314). In real life, there were easier ways of heading north. In the summer of 1911 and the spring of 1912, agents from the Canadian railroads, aware of the plight of those working farms in Kentucky, placed regular notices in the local papers: "50,000 Men Wanted in Western Canada. 200 Million Bushels Wheat to be Harvested. Harvest Help in Great Demand. Manitoba, Saskatchewan, and Alberta. Low rates will be given on all Canadian Roads" (Owenton Herald-

Gazette, August 3, 1911). Another reads "Splendid Canadian Crops" (October 10, 1911). These advertisements were repeated for months and well into 1912. They may have prompted Greve to strike out north for the Dakotas and Manitoba, finally to spend a season working as Branden did—as a "store boss" and "driving boss" on one of the huge "bonanza farms" owned by the Mackenzie family west of Fargo, North Dakota (SFA 339, 344f, 355).

But there is an alternative reading to the Sparta sojourn. Branden's tramp in *A Search for America* leads him down the Ohio past Wheeling towards "Cincinnata" (SFA 263) which the narrator makes a point of avoiding, going instead in the direction of Indiana. Having proceeded on the Ohio past the town of Vevay (SFA 307) and since it was getting cold, he spent time working in a "mill town." Vevay, named after the Swiss town of Vevey on Lake Geneva, lies in a region called "Little Switzerland" directly across from Gallatin County and a mere seventeen miles or so from Sanders and Sparta. Thus Phil Grove's Branden, instead of landing in Cincinnati and then going southwest to Sparta, may have gone there in a roundabout way, first making a feint, so to speak, by appearing to avoid Cincinnati and then heading west into Indiana. From the "mill town" near Vevay, Branden goes on for an unspecified distance until he falls ill with a fever. Asking for help, he is first lead to a place he cannot accept as a refuge: "We came to the barn. It was of that half-open type that marks the tobacco barn, boards and open spaces alternating in the walls" (SFA 284). But there are few or no tobacco fields in eastern Indiana or in southwestern Kentucky. Branden was still in the tobacco-growing regions of Gallatin and Owen counties.

It has been shown with essentially circumstantial evidence that the several towns Branden visits during his tramps between Books Three and Five of *A Search for America* all centre on the Ohio River region. It seems not unlikely that the "Mill Town" was actually Sparta with its grist mill, tree nursery, school, small tobacco farms and some of the amenities later described in the fictional town of "Minor" in *Settlers of the Marsh*. ("Minor," incidentally, was also the name of the teamster and railroad agent in actual Sparta.)

These details add to the little we know about Grove's arrival in Canada and the period he spent in the United States; they also contribute to the background of his writing. The following may serve as a convenient example. Abe Groves and his family in Sparta may have been models for the composite figure of the patriarch Abe Spalding in *Fruits of the Earth*. It is of Spalding that Grove writes, "throughout that summer of 1912 [he] never ceased worrying about his crop" (FOE 113). The timeframe of the novel might indicate that the rains which destroyed the wheat crops of Abe's fictional neighbours were the rains that in actuality destroyed the tobacco crops of the small Kentucky farms of the time. Some of his Manitoban pupils later

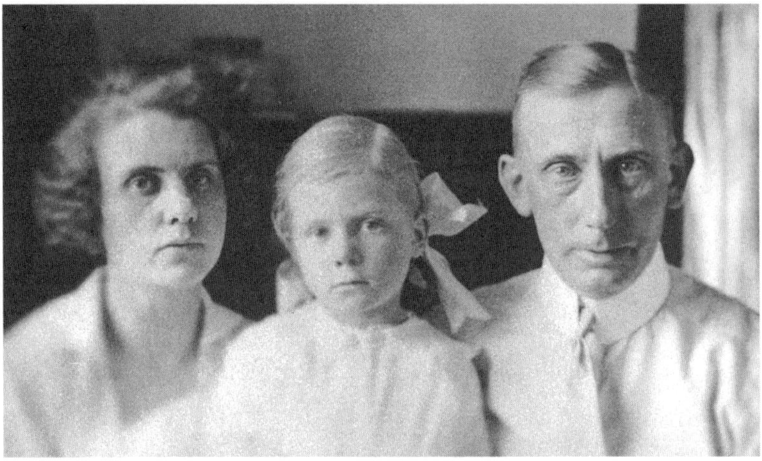

⌘ *Catherine, Phyllis May and F.P. Grove, ca. 1920*
(Collection A. Leonard Grove/Elizabeth Dafoe Library, University of Manitoba)

recalled that Grove mentioned a family—a wife and sons back in the States. Perhaps they were not his own, but the sons of Abe Groves, with whom he may have been growing Burley tobacco and pruning trees while gathering experience as a teacher.

◆ MANITOBA MARSHES

"Seven Drives over Manitoba Trails / By a Manitoba Teacher" is the title of the handwritten manuscript bearing the dedication: "These pages were written for / My Wife / and / My Little Daughter / to read by the evening fireside / when I am gone." The text of the undated copybook manuscript, enclosed between wine-coloured cardboard covers and bound in red, was published in 1922 as Grove's first Canadian book.[14] (Clearly it was a copy especially written out for the family.) The work includes a series of seven interlinked essays in celebration of nature, the introspective self and the tension between the solitary existence of a man and the need for human attachment. By then Grove had taught for several years in various communities, met Catherine Wiens and settled down with her and their much-beloved daughter, Phyllis May (b. 1915). But his first English-language book is not yet the fruit of a life come to rest, a soul at peace, a wanderer come home. Although the narrator often seemed lost in the contemplation of nature and

✹ *Frederick Philip Grove,* Over Prairie Trails *(1922),* title page left and right

celebrated a studied pragmatism of living, like his hero Henry David Thoreau, smooth continuities provided him with no contentment. On the contrary, the fits and starts of the beginnings and endings of the essays, the upheavals on brush- or snow-covered trails, the hair-breadth escapes, the dangers surmounted, the safe haven attained and the ever-recurring leave-takings—these are at the heart of the book Grove called *Over Prairie Trails.* "At six o'clock I was on the road again," begins the book's characteristic last sentence. But as the handwritten manuscript testifies, he had not yet shaken off his past. "In *Over Prairie Trails* he is always the man to arrive, the man who is always on the road, the traveller, the one who is not really at home anywhere, just someone on the way" (Lane, "Afterword" 163). The unusual manuscript contains a few stray German words, some crossed out again, others accidentally left in, which must have made strange reading for his wife. It may be assumed that she proofread the English text much as Freytag-Loringhoven may have done with Greve's German texts in the past. One of these German words has remained unchanged in the text throughout all successive editions. When, at the end of the third chapter, the narrator returns to the cottage where his wife and child are waiting for him, the child "shrilled out" to him in a charming girlish lisp that secretly reveals, in the inadvertent use of the German personal pronoun, the author's linguistic origin: "Oh, Daddy, Daddy, did *du* see Santa Claus?" (OPT 101; my italics).

The romance and rhythm of departure and arrival, a lusting after adventure and risk-taking, the archetypical image of single man, the creator and protector, the lowly and unassuming teacher as the Canadian version of the Franklinesque "philosopher in homespun" (to borrow Herman Melville's words in *Israel Potter*)—all of this was as different as possible from the roles Grove had played in Europe. Still, it probably would have been too much to ask of a man in his forties, who had moved among the learned, the extravagant and the monied in France and Germany, to remain content with the artful unpretentiousness celebrated in his "Seven Drives over Manitoba Trails." A coy awareness of the literariness of idyllic nature crept into Grove's subsequent book, *The Turn of the Year*. Grove, however, managed a reversal back to the earlier style in his third Canadian book (and his first novel in English), published in 1925 after he had stopped teaching in Rapid City for reasons of health. The strong, somewhat obtuse and grimly determined hero of *Settlers of the Marsh*, Niels Lindstedt, emerges out of the very snowstorms and barely discernible trails west of Lake Manitoba that had led the narrator of Grove's first volume to the light shining in the window of his home. Much like Grove in Kentucky, Niels at first fails to find this home in spite of an incredible amount of drudgery and sacrifice—reminiscent of the author's backbreaking work tilling his literary fields in Munich, Berlin, Paris-Plage and other places. The astonishing story of Mrs. Clara Vogel—the sexually jaded woman whom Niels naïvely marries, thereby ruining his prospects of a home and station in rural society—has correctly been traced to two sources. The first, autobiographical, seems based on the nearly ten years Felix Greve spent in the company of Else in Berlin and elsewhere, flaunting their "immorality." In Clara Vogel, Grove may be recalling both Freytag-Loringhoven's liberated and matter-of-fact sexuality and Stefan George's terrible remark about those former members of his circle who preferred "to produce literature and to spend their lives with whores" (Landmann, *George* 183). The second source, as has often been claimed, may be Flaubert's Emma Bovary. To be sure, Clara gives Niels *Madame Bovary* to read, although it fails to enlighten him (SOM 207). There is, in fact, another parallel between Clara and Emma: their liveliness and *joie de vivre* contrasts with the unimaginative inexperience of their husbands and the stifling boredom of the lives they are forced to lead. It was Freytag-Loringhoven who, in her recollections of Felix, first drew our attention to Flaubert as one of Felix's models—a recollection which warranted increased attention since Greve had translated Flaubert. But *Madame Bovary* is not among the works

Greve translated and the resemblances are far too superficial to be telling.[15] In *Settlers of the Marsh*, Clara is afforded none of the carefully worked-up bourgeois societal background which leads Emma to desert her husband. More importantly, before marrying Bovary Emma was unencumbered by any of the infamy that was already attached to Clara Vogel. Niels is the improbable innocent, a kind of unbelievable working-class Parzival (or Felix Greve in his naïve pursuit of Helene Klages), completely ignorant of the darker strains in Clara's character. His only distinguishing features are his boundless energy and his ability for sustained work. The woman he hopes to win and carry away, like a prize to display in his house, resembles the former Else Endell much more than she does Emma. There is something in Greve, as remembered by Freytag-Loringhoven, that makes us think of Niels's limitations:

> He had his trouble with me—trying to make me behave conventional. He bore it with staunch conviction and pride—yet also like a hidden yoke—for his infatuation with me enslaved him more than he dared to confess—even to himself—for again, in the last truth—he was no womanlover—he was no lover at all—he was a man who liked to love only himself—who after the vainglory of youth has vanished is too unbendingly rigid—too conceitedly intelligent—too much wanting in imagination—too immodest—in short—too limited masculine—to feel himself in need of a medium for emotional expression. He becomes a mere outward driving force by restless neurasthenic ambition—infertile within himself (BE 109).

Grove, of course, was never really "infertile within himself," but he may not have been a "womanlover" in Freytag-Loringhoven's sense. He did not, for instance, subordinate his own aims and ambitions to hers and he may have lacked the sort of empathy she desired. He was also limited by his conventional masculinity. But that same masculinity made him, to his credit, a good husband to Catherine and an adoring father to May. His homecomings in *Over Prairie Trails*, the contented "we" of "John and Ellen" and their children in *The Turn of the Year*, Niels's wistful looks at his friend Nelson's children in *Settlers of the Marsh*—the pioneer family, in short, appears to be at the core of Grove's Canadian writings. Perhaps it even served as the final destination of Phil Branden, who came from Europe to the rootless society of the restaurant crowd in Toronto to a band of unscrupulous booksellers, wandering alone throughout *A Search for America*. Having reached forsaken and desperate depths, he slowly re-developed into a social animal, picking up a companion here and there, finding community among the children he taught in Manitoba. He would finally marry another young teacher and ultimately turn the lonely "teacherages" in the marshes into homes for his own family. Grove grew in a way Freytag-Loringhoven could never have known, compensating in the end for the broken background he had emerged from in Hamburg. "Life," Arthur L. Phelps wrote in the foreword to *The Turn of the Year*, "has wrung a cry from Mr. Grove, and the cry is in all his speech." Felix Paul Greve had come alive again in a creative rebirth unshared by Freytag-Loringhoven in her lonely and unusual situation in Greenwich Village. "We can but become what we are," muses John Elliot in Grove's 1928 *Our Daily Bread*, a novel written at the peak of his powers and at the height of his reputation. Grove, it seems, had developed his talents to the utmost of his capacity. But he had also matured as a man. True to what the author had become, *Our Daily Bread* culminates in the long homecoming of the last chapter, a homecoming to a house long deserted and a wife long dead. It is as if in writing that final, fictional return Grove was referring to his own former deserted "house" and his now-dead former "wife." Only in their wake could another new beginning be made. He could leave the hideouts in the half-deserted landscapes and villages of the marshes since "nothing would suddenly come up," forcing him to leave like a thief in the night, as he once intimated to his wife Catherine (Makow, "Rebirth").

He had already left indelible traces. Phyllis May, the Groves' cherished daughter, had become emblematic to many local settlers of the marsh, as Stobie reports. Grove had turned areas such as Amaranth, Odensee and Leifur into literature, much as Margaret Laurence would do with the Neepawa area. A post office was named after May (kept by a Swedish couple named Branden from whom Grove borrowed the name of the hero of *A Search for America*), and her name appeared on milk trucks cruising the region (Stobie, *Grove* 51–52). The inhabitants of the Big Grassy Marsh kept the name of May Grove alive long after the Groves moved to Rapid City and long after May's tragic death of a ruptured appendix in 1927. Grove had to leave his prairie home and another of his selves died. He only returned twenty years later to Rapid City, to be buried next to the first fruit of his new beginning, May, the emblem of his long Canadian phase of "Retrospection and Anticipation," as he named the spring chapter of his second book. "Early spring is the season of youth…":

What takes hold of us when we see the first sign of the seasons is something akin to tenderness; it partakes of compassion, of commiseration almost: there is still so much time to reflect…And we do reflect: as if we foresaw at the birth of a child a career of great endeavour and great achievement; but bought at what cost! A future cost of suffering and disappointment, a cost of anger, strife, and tears (Grove, TOY 19).

After his daughter's death he composed a cycle of poems, written in English over a period of five years, and dedicated it to her, "In Memoriam Phyllis May Grove." One of them contains lines addressed "To C.G.," his wife:

> Then knew we, nought on earth had changed but we
> Who stood alone, we two, and grasped at last
> What blow had wrenched the present from the past:
> That there were two who had but now been three.

◆ ONTARIO'S SHORE

As of October 14, 1930, the Groves were three again. Their son Arthur Leonard was born. One year later, to the day, they moved into a white ten-room farmhouse—a "white range line house" (Stobie, *Grove* 157) like the one that first figured in *Over Prairie Trails*. It also resembled the house in the title of one of Grove's long, unwieldy manuscripts from which *Settlers of the Marsh* was fashioned. The only house the Groves ever owned still stands two miles north of the Ontario town of Simcoe, where the author had first come as a guest speaker in 1929 (Letters 239). The period between the death of May on August 15, the departure from Rapid City on September 1, 1928 and the move to Simcoe was Grove's most successful as a writer and sought-after public figure. *A Search for America* had been published by two different publishers in Canada and the United States; *Our Daily Bread* (1928) had found another publisher; Grove's collection of literary essays, *It Needs to Be Said* (1929), had been issued; and *The Yoke of Life* (1930) was published in the same month that the Groves settled in Ontario. If name recognition was what Grove had always desired, he had finally attained it. Three extensive speaking tours from coast to coast—from February to April 1928, from September to November 1928 and from January to March 1929, all sponsored by the Association of Canadian Clubs—had made him well known from British Columbia to Nova Scotia. In 1929, he was so well known in Ottawa that he coyly contemplated refusing an invitation to tea with Canada's wartime Prime Minister, Robert Borden (Letters 232). He felt that the universal praise would make his head swell, had it not been swollen long ago (Letters 248).

In many ways, the period between resembled the heady times in 1902 when his translations of Wilde's plays seemed about to make a hit with German theatres, and, again, between 1906 and 1908 when, for a time, he had begun making serious money as a translator and had become known as an author in his own right. But there is yet another parallel. If he had earlier entertained hopes of becoming a publisher and an editor in Germany, this prospect was finally held out to him in Canada. He eagerly accepted.

From February to June 1929 he acted as an associate editor of *The Canadian Nation* (Letters 236–37). In December 1929, Grove was invited to become a reader for Graphic Press in Ottawa, then the manager of Ariston, one of Graphic's subsidiaries. Unfortunately, he found that he had gained none of the independence he had hoped for but remained an employee of the owners who held the purse strings (Letters 278f.). Moreover, he learned that the prominence he had gained as a speaker had evaporated. As yesterday's celebrity, he was now being ignored. His disappointment was great. He even considered pulling up stakes again and leaving Canada:

> I have not only failed to secure a university berth...but anything whatever which would provide bread and butter or even bread without the butter. I am simply one of 500,000 unemployed; and I am only sorry that I did not leave the country in the fall of 1929 when my situation was similar though not quite so urgent and desperate.

> I, too, sold my car last night, to convert it into tickets for Europe...We shall sail within a month or so; and I think this is final; I do not expect to see Canada again (Letters 296).

Grove's impulse to withdraw and move to a distant place, so much a part of his earlier identity, would not be repeated in Canada. In fact, a return to Europe, especially to Germany where things were no better than in Canada, would have ruined him as it had ruined Else von Freytag-Loringhoven. Grove's business sense kept him from making any rash moves and prevented him from going down with the firm when Graphic Press (and Ariston with it) went bankrupt in 1932. He pulled out in time and seemed to have done so in such a way that he escaped not only financial loss but managed to earn three thousand dollars for himself, enabling him to become both a gentleman-farmer and a literary man in Ontario. The Groves were "probably quite glad," their son surmised, "to wipe the Manitoba gumbo and snow off their boots."

Writing, tending his new purebred Jersey cows, working his team of Percherons, trying to farm, overseeing the redecoration of his house, becoming a respected and admired member of Simcoe society—Frederick Philip Grove appears to have sought the rustic ideal of Meliboeus, the farmer-poet of Virgil's "First Eclogue," a text familiar to him since his Hamburg days. Grove even got himself involved in politics as a candidate for the left-of-centre CCF in the provincial elections of 1943. Although he lost (as he had been promised) with a respectable number of votes to another candidate, his actions resembled those of the farmer-citizen he relentlessly praised, particularly in the novels from his first decade in Ontario, *Fruits of the Earth* (1933) and *Two Generations* (1939). Honours were coming his way, beginning with the Lorne Pierce Medal of the Royal Society of Canada in 1934. Sales of his books, however, were dropping off dramatically. For the first time since his Berlin days, Grove suffered the indignity of again having to publish a novel privately. He sold less than half of the five hundred numbered copies of *Two Generations* "as a manuscript" before offering the remaining copes to Macmillan in 1940 (Letters 379). A shift had occurred in the 1930s, not only in readers' spending power but also in taste; Grove's brand of ponderously treated agricultural thematics no longer attracted much interest. Daily economic hardships were better met with optimism and the jocularity of those such as the poet Don Marquis, whose famous phrase "toujours gai" helped set the tone for the survivors of the terrible period. It was the second time since 1909 that Grove had become the victim of such a change.

Still, the role of the literary country squire suited him well. He gave talks on the "appreciation of literature" ("Thoughts and Reflections" 313) and on the subject of "The True Farmer." He founded an "English Club" that met first at his house and then elsewhere in Simcoe. He went on tramps among the cedars and white pines of the neighbourhood, and he seems to have enjoyed, for the first time since leaving the fraternal society of the Bonn boathouse, a sense of quiet "companionship" with neighbours (Stobie, *Grove* 158–59). Local luminaries belonged to Grove's circle: Monroe Landon, the wealthy farmer (even by today's standards); the lawyer Archie Grass and his family; Dr. Felix Redlich (a Jewish emigré from Austria, arrived after 1938, with whom Grove enjoyed conversing in German); and another lawyer and admired raconteur, Perry MacKay. If Dr. Redlich became a "cultural soulmate" to F.P. Grove, Landon, an "accomplished naturalist and botanist," helped the Groves to settle in.[16] Their neighbour also possessed woodworking skills, making "a beautiful cedar lined walnut chest" for Mrs. Grove and "several items of playground equipment" for her school when it opened again. Grove himself had little interest in "handyman activities." He was, however, interested in flowers and gardening. His son remembers:

At one side of the vegetable garden he planted several rows of bulbs, each row being twenty or twenty-five feet long, containing about fifty bulbs each. The flowers were glorious! When in bloom, there were always vases of gladiolus in the house and in his study. When the

flowering was over, there was the task of digging up the bulbs, drying
them and wrapping each bulb in newspaper for storage until the next
year. He was also fond of a flower called lupin, a beautiful blue colour
that also grew from bulbs. These were planted in front of the house,
on both sides of the front porch. Along the entire length of the drive
leading to the garage was a thick, dense lilac hedge, about twenty feet
high. When it was in bloom in the late spring, one could smell the
fragrance everywhere, both inside the house and outside.

Unfortunately, after a brief period of squiring, the teaching life the Groves
had left behind in Rapid City resumed in Simcoe. The Groves' house now
provided teachers and pupils with a standard of comfort wholly different from
the cramped and sometimes icy quarters in the tiny schools of the Grassy
Marsh. A sense of futility, however, of an inescapable rhythm of repetition,
must have overcome the writer. He had often seemed on the verge of lasting
success, and yet his hopes often amounted to nothing. First, a kindergarten
of the Froebel type, so well known to him, was established. This was soon

¤ *Frederick Philip Grove,* The Turn of the Year *(1922), title page left and right*

followed by a boarding school, run by Catherine Grove and assisted by her niece, which brought in most of the income needed for the upkeep of the family. Much as May had sat near the teacher's desk or among the pupils in Falmouth, Ferguson, Eden and elsewhere, little Leonard now slipped into that role.

Arthur Leonard Grove was named after one of Grove's earliest and strongest supporters, his godfather Arthur Leonard Phelps, a professor of English at Winnipeg's Wesley College (now the University of Winnipeg), when the author and his wife were still teaching and writing in Rapid City. Phelps was a tireless critic, reader and promoter of Grove's works, and Grove owed much of his start in Canadian literature to him and his circle of friends (Stobie, *Grove* 15). Naming his only son after Phelps, then, may be seen in part as the creation of a living icon to accompany his Canadian rebirth as a writer. Phyllis May sealed Grove's union with Catherine and marked his turn away from his old life. If, for some in the Big Grassy Marsh, Grove was an emblem of everything that was attractive about the new teachers among the settlers, then, in a talismanic move, naming his son after his most influential mentor memorialized his successful public inauguration as a Canadian writer. And if, in a similar gesture of continuity and development, *Over Prairie Trails* and *The Turn of the Year* were modestly written "to read by the evening fireside after I am gone" in remembrance of the Groves' hard times together, then

In Search of Myself and Grove's "boy's book," *The Adventures of Leonard Broadus*, were a public celebration of personal growth and a claim to his and his family's Canadianness.

◆ ADVENTURES OF FATHER AND SON

One of the more striking features of Frederick Philip Grove's almost obsessive accounts of his life are the curious father-and-son relationships. Overpowering, dominating fathers figure both in the novels of the Big Grassy Marsh and in the books set in Ontario, from *Settlers of the Marsh* to *The Master of the Mill*. In his autobiographical writings, Grove pits the cultured, suffering mother against the powerful father. Only in *Over Prairie Trails*, *The Turn of the Year* and *The Adventures of Leonard Broadus* are both parents lovingly and sympathetically drawn and their children depicted as cherished by them. It also comes as no surprise that the Ontario novel published immediately before *Leonard Broadus*—*Two Generations*—is the one in which the father figure, Ralph Patterson, apologizes to his son in the closing scene of the book for the ill treatment which he subjected him to.

Near the end of his writing career, there was a loosening of Grove's strict and stern persona as a teacher and writer in his new nation. The reason may be that these books were most closely patterned on the very early life of Felix Paul Greve and the settled and comparatively happy later life of Frederick Philip Grove and his family. Moreover, these books exhibit less of the author's overt and almost strenuous commitment to produce "serious art," of which the overly complicated and laboriously "modern" work *The Master of the Mill* (1944), the second Ontario novel, is an example. Of Grove's works only the first third or so of *Over Prairie Trails* has the appearance of being wholly uncontrived, and only the seemingly simple *Leonard Broadus*, masterfully told as it is, lays no claim to being anything but a boy's entertainment. Nevertheless, thirteen years after *A Search for America*, while he was writing what would become the final version of *In Search of Myself*, Grove clearly included major elements of his own life story into the little book ostensibly written in celebration of his son and their Canadian family.

In her commentary on *Leonard Broadus*, Mary Rubio, whom we have to thank for the rediscovery of the story, first pointed to the strikingly similar "passages by water" in *A Search for America* and *In Search of Myself*. There is, in particular, the well-known "boat-stealing episode" in *In Search of Myself* (SOM 33–52) in which young "Phil" takes a boat from the beach near the family estate of Thurow out into the dangerous waters of the Skagerrak narrows between Sweden and Denmark (Rubio, "Afterword" 133). It is hard to overlook the analogy between this and young Leonard's raft, drifting

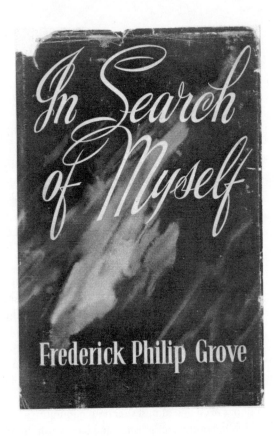

Frederick Philip Grove, In Search of Myself (1946), *dust jacket*

during a flood from the creek in back of the Broadus's (and the Groves') house out into the dangerous waters of Lake Erie. There is more. Although ostensibly shaped after the mansion-like house of Grove's friend Monroe Landon, the imposing manor of Leonard's fictive uncle Bill Broadus, called "the Squire" (and also patterned after Grove himself and his fictive father in his autobiographical writings), is clearly an early version of the mythical "Castle Thurow" of *In Search of Myself*. Of course there are several references and intertextual links in *Leonard Broadus* to other adventure stories. It might even be called a proto-postmodern *assemblage* of several famous adventures, romances and novels. Not only does Grove mention *Robinson Crusoe* (57), but also the romances of Cooper and "Stevenson's complete works" (30). The region of the Great Lakes is, of course, "Cooper country." On the other hand, Leonard's rafting links him to Mark Twain's youthful heroes. On Lake Erie's shore and at the house of his uncle Bill, Leonard meets another boy, the ragged Tom Matthews, who is a kind of Huckleberry Finn to Leonard's own Tom Sawyer (77). *Leonard Broadus* reads like a lighter and compacted version of the "childhood" chapters of *In Search of Myself* and of Phil Branden's epic journey on a raft down the Ohio River in *A Search for America*. There are vivid echoes of the extended boat trips Grove himself took as a young man from Bonn on picturesque rivers in Germany. Furthermore, the cameo appearance in *Leonard Broadus* of somebody named "Vanderelst"—here a Belgian farmer—points to a relative of the mysterious Uncle Jacobsen's equally obscure "cousin Van der Elst, a settler on the island of Java, not far from Batavia" (ISM 154), who would also appear in a slightly more elaborate version in *In Search of Myself*. Elsewhere in the 1927 autobiographical novel we recall that the narrator refers to a "von Els" as one of the "parasitic young men of Europe" he had met (SFA 29). Was Grove playing with Else's name and alluding to those young men, including his former self, she had consorted with? If nothing else, then this playing with a name also points both to the close "family relationships" between *Leonard Broadus* and Grove's own boyhood narrative which he was also writing in 1939–40, then simply called "My Life." Clearly he was writing for his boy of himself as a boy, to a degree fusing the two. Grove's "impenetrable disguise" of his family and youth began to be lifted.[17]

But it was not all faint echo or distant recollection. There had been a real raft Grove built for his son that provided the factual basis of this element of the story, as Leonard Grove recalls. For him, the story also began with the "creek flowing through the meadow just a couple of hundred metres from the house":

> It has since been dredged and straightened to alleviate flooding in the spring but then it was as nature had made it. It was hip deep with reedy banks which were home to muskrats. It had fish and crawfish and a couple of deep holes for swimming. Huge blue herons nested nearby and fished in the stream. The meadow was full of groundhog burrows. It was heaven for a young boy.

> Well, my father decided to build me a raft to sail on the creek. He acquired two large cedar logs (fence posts) and a number of smaller logs and with fence wire, nails and decking boards constructed a raft. It had a wooden box nailed to the deck to sit on. A mast of sorts carried a bed sheet sail. The raft was built in the back yard, some 200 meters from the creek. To launch it we had to harness a horse to drag it to the water. Of course, the journey destroyed the raft. However he (we) rebuilt it at the creek's edge and successfully launched it. I spent endless days poling up and down the creek on it until the next spring it was washed away and lost in the flood.

This was the flood of 1939 that, in the story, carried the raft out onto the lake and got the story on its way. The March flood (in the story it is May, a month better suited for a boy's adventures in the open) actually broke up the real raft. The fictional May flood also allowed the author to connect it with the visit of the King and Queen of England. In a letter to Lorne Pierce, Grove averred that he had to wait until after the departure of the royal couple before he could go on with the story's last chapter (Rubio, "Afterword" 150–52; Letters 355–56). Leonard Grove recalls:

> We did not go to Toronto to see the King and Queen in 1939. Instead we went to St. Catharines which is closer to Simcoe. As I remember, I saw the Queen's hat (blue) and damn all else. My father was quite tall, so he may have seen more. The King and Queen were in a motorcade and went past us so quickly that there was time for only a glance.

There is, in the story, another unification of elements that had come apart in Grove's two lives (like the real raft). The Broadus family consists of four members: Mr. Stephen Broadus ("tall and spare"), Mrs. Broadus ("a plump, good-looking, but delicate woman of forty"), Leonard ("singularly good-looking") and his sister Mary ("patient"). In addition, there are Alice, the maid, and Stubbing, the "senior hired man"—the kind and number of personnel employed by the Groves (cf. Rubio, "Afterword" 146). Leonard Broadus's age, thirteen, corresponds to the number of years passed since Phyllis May Grove's death, and approximates May's age when she died (twelve), while the real Leonard Grove was almost ten when the story was written. Mary, Leonard Broadus's sister, is only seven. She remains a shadowy presence, not fully realized as a character (it is, after all, a boy's book). But it is noteworthy that Frederick Philip Grove did include a sister, however palely drawn she remains, making a point of her inclusion. In the context of his own youth, of course, there had also been a sister, Henny, who had left when Felix was about the age of his Leonard Broadus. She too remains somewhat pale in his recollections. In *The Adventures of Leonard Broadus*, Grove reconstructed both the German family he came from and his Canadian family in a fictive reunion that celebrated continuities via signs of manifest Canadianness and monetary success. This financial success in turn symbolized the recognition accorded Leonard and his family by the King and Queen of England and Leonard's gift of his $500 to his father, money he had received as a reward for helping to catch some thieves who had broken into their house.

In real life, Felix Paul Greve never had very much to offer to his parents—unless one counts the money he claimed (to André Gide) to have made tutoring up to eighty hours per week, helping to support his mother and contributing to the costs of his own excellent education. (Leonard Broadus's father, incidentally, wants him to apply the reward to exactly that end.) After a period in the Groves' own home-school, Leonard Grove's parents decided to send him to a boarding school, St. Andrews. Although he was "two and often three years younger" than his peers, Leonard thought "that it was a credit to [his parents] that I could enter High School" at an early age. He also points to another unavoidable parallel: "My parents, probably mostly my father, wanted to see me off to an education that was as similar to his own as was possible in Canada. This was grade 10 that I was entering at St. Andrews. I was enrolled in French, Latin, Greek and German as well as the usual grade 10 subjects." Life, for young Leonard, only became tolerable again after he entered Simcoe High School, "a year older and a hundred years wiser." Life for the Groves in the early 1940s continued much as it had been after their move to Simcoe. They had a dog (as Felix and Else had as part of their *ménage* in Paris-Plage), "first a Cocker Spaniel named Captain," later "a magnificent Doberman named Quito…He was shot by a farmer" (unidentified). Although he managed to crawl home, he had to be put down. An earlier venture into the pet field involved a goat. In August 1939, they visited Richard Crouch for four days "at his cottage on Lake Erie south of London in Rondeau Park" (Letters 361):

> The cottage was loaned to my father for a week (two weeks?) one summer and my father and I spent this time there as a holiday. My mother did not come with us. I do not know why. I remember very little of that vacation except that there was a small sailboat, a dingy, with the cottage. We sailed it a bit but I do not remember doing so often.

Grove still knew how to sail. Was it a passion, a talent that he may have felt connected him so closely to his past that he wanted to show it to his son without allowing his wife to see how experienced he was at it? That it *had* been a passion we know from his own recollections, his time in Bonn and from the metaphors he would unfailingly choose from his boating experiences.

Grove's everyday workload was heavy. It included teaching and domestic chores. In his 1933 autobiographical piece "Thoughts and Reflections," published by Hjartarson in 1986, he mentions that it was his turn to teach in the afternoon, after preparing dinner for his wife who taught in the morning. It was a heavy load: "From 1 o'clock on it is my turn to teach: 1st 4 elementary classes; 2nd a grown-up class in French literature; 3rd a subnormal boy of 19 years whom I am trying to teach 4 yrs. Latin and French in a single year"

ᛆ *A. Leonard Grove, 1974*
(Collection A. Leonard Grove)

(317). What was Grove's writing life like in his declining years? Leonard recalls his father's morning routine:

In order to avoid the busy early morning hassle of breakfast, etc. my father would not come downstairs until about 9:00 am and would then breakfast alone in the kitchen. By this time, school would be in progress and he would be undisturbed. In warm weather he would often go outside to smoke a cigarette and walk around for a while. By the time I am speaking of [before 1944] he had sold the farmland and had no farm business to attend to. He might work in the vegetable garden, mow the lawn or do similar chores outside for a while and, by 10:00 o'clock or so, he would go upstairs to his study to work.

My father's work had priority over all domestic considerations. He was not to be disturbed. I was not to make a noise. The school was conducted in the rooms furthest from his study. School recess was pretty well confined to the front lawn or to an area fairly far from his window so that the noise would not bother him. It sounds strict and cold, and perhaps it was, but it was accepted by all and it worked. There was no resentment that I can remember.

There is another unforeseen and unfortunate parallel between Grove's recollections of his own youth and his son's. If help for his ailing mother had been the real-life destiny of Felix Greve, it soon fell to Leonard to care for his ailing father. On April 14, 1944, Frederick Philip Grove suffered the first of two strokes, paralyzing his right side and impairing his speech. Luckily, "his speech came back rapidly," he began walking with a cane and he even began typing again with one finger of his left hand (Stobie, *Grove* 183). The improvements did not last, however, no matter how hard he worked on himself: "In the early days of his illness, he would walk slowly and in some danger of falling up and down the cement walk in front of the house carrying a weight in his paralyzed hand. The weight was usually one or two horseshoes which might have weighed two or two and a half kilos" (Leonard Grove). Another stroke, in May 1946, rendered his speech unintelligible and left him largely immobile. Leonard Grove remembers the last years:

Now he could no longer work or, indeed, do much of anything on his own. He could not even dress himself, could not go up or down stairs alone, could not move about the house and, although not a complete invalid, required care and assistance in most matters of daily life. I would take his breakfast to him in his bed upstairs in the morning before I left for school. After school, I would hurry home to do whatever needed to be done for him. I would shave him, help him back upstairs to bed (my mother would have helped him down during the day), take up his supper and help him to bed. Then I would do whatever schoolwork I had been assigned. It was a long day.

From 1944 till his death in 1948 things went on much the same year round except that he became less and less able to do anything at all for himself. His speech deteriorated to the point that only my mother could understand him. He tried to read but found handling a book and turning pages very difficult. He smoked quite heavily and found that this, too, presented problems. He always used a cigarette holder and it was hard, often impossible for him to place the cigarette in the holder and also difficult to strike a match. Matches and cigarette lighters presented a constant danger of fire because he was quite likely to drop the lighter which was not self-extinguishing.

Before the second stroke, Grove, strong willed and clear of mind as ever, had witnessed the publication of *In Search of Myself* and changed part of the introduction to his last published work of fiction, the utopian fable *Consider Her Ways*, begun in 1925 as his frequently discussed "Ant Book" and substantially rewritten in 1933. In an autobiographical vein, "F.P.G." figures as the "human editor" of an exploratory march of an army of giant ants from Venezuela to New York and the return of a few survivors. The fable makes oblique reference to the Greek historian Xenophon's account of the march of his 10,000-strong Greek army to Persia and its long return home in ever-diminishing numbers. The ants' expedition becomes the occasion for observations on human nature, an attack on a former Grove critic and a long and critical look at the uses of learning and culture. Grove, too, had lived among Americans and had returned to the land of his arrival in the New World. Reports on the findings of the ant expedition were sent home by the leading sage of the army, the learned Wawa-quee, to be preserved by her on "scent-trees," the ants' archives or Alexandrian Library. This mode of preserving self and experience is analogous to the one immortalized by Robert Frost in the title of his book *A Witness Tree*, published five years before *Consider Her Ways* and poetically expounded in "Beech," the book's opening poem, in lines that have a curious applicability to Frederick Philip Grove's searches for himself in Europe, Manitoba and Ontario:

Where my imaginary line
bends square in woods, an iron spine
And pile of real rocks have been founded.
And off this corner in the wild,
Where these are driven in and piled,
One tree, by being deeply wounded,
Has been impressed as Witness Tree
And made commit to memory
My proof of being not unbounded.
(Frost, *Poems* 331)

Grove, gnarled and wounded, was not unbounded. He died in the early morning of August 19, 1948 and was buried in Rapid City next to his daughter May. Mary Grove (Mrs. A. Leonard Grove) reports Catherine Grove confiding to her later that in his final moments he cried out the name of the companion he had deserted in Kentucky: "Else, Else!"

That Catherine burned Grove's manuscript book "Felix Powell's Career" — a book said to have been strongly autobiographical and much praised by those few who read it at the time — may have been her attempt to keep the

⌘ *Frederick Philip Grove's tombstone in Rapid City, Manitoba, 1996*
(Collection Klaus Martens)

boundaries of her life with the author intact. The unbinding of Frederick Philip Grove, as far as knowledge of his identity was concerned, did not occur during his lifetime. It may be argued, however, that gradual discoveries about his formerly hidden lives may help to reinstate him into the cultural memory of the country of his origin and to maintain him in Canadian literary memory as a central twentieth-century writer.

AFTERWORD
FPG Posthumous

FPG'S FOOTLOOSE LIFE HAD COME TO A REST. His past had made him a wanderer, constantly changing addresses, "teacherages" and hotels, never committing himself to a single place for long. He resembled his former mentor Stefan George, who had said of himself that he was "everywhere like a visitor." Much as in his own first published volume of poems, Felix Greve's real or imagined wanderings continued as one of the major themes of his early Canadian writings and his autobiographical novels. The ageing and ailing Grove used the German word to identify his chronic urge for wandering, much as one would point to a recurrent illness: "In such seasons I am to this day subject to violent attacks of Wanderlust" (ISM 184). It is clear from this sentence, published two years before his death, that he had retained a sense of himself as a young man, filled with the desire for a different kind of life, hoping to move among colourful people in exciting parts of the world, becoming one of them, easily assimilating new impressions and experiences. His penchant for role-playing remained, for embarking again and again on his "Munchausen-like behaviour," as Karl Wolfskehl called Felix's bouts of self-inventive storytelling (alluding to the famous Baron Munchausen's "lies"), often getting ahead of himself in his abilities and means. From early on, in Bonn, Rome and Munich, Felix Greve had become one of those endangered artist-characters living on the brink of sudden descent into an artistic or criminal abyss—a member of a "Bohème." In Munich, he became the repressed dark double of those chosen few

moving in the orbit of their only sun, the master Stefan George, who ultimately rejected him. But as Grove, in a Nietzschean mood, would recall in
the role of his Zarathustra-like character "St. Nishivara," "I have done only as
others do; but being myself and not they, I did it more fearlessly and without
restraint." There is a sense here of the extraordinary life led, an awareness of
the boldness of the paths taken in his youth, a pride in having foregone the
pettiness which often accompanies the recollection of youthful trespasses,
sexual or otherwise. To others he had remained "that Greve," the man whose
life was the meat of excited conversation and, no doubt, fiction-making.

It does not take a very large leap of the imagination to realize that Felix
Greve himself became (or made himself) the stuff of literature, posing as the
model not only of his own literary alter ego in *Fanny Essler*, F.K. Reelen, but
also of others' memorable fictional confidence-men from the first decade of
the twentieth century. One such character to unavoidably come to mind,
already mentioned previously in a different context, is the hero of O.J.
Bierbaum's novel *Prinz Kuckuck* (*Prince Cuckoo*) of 1905, called "Felix Henry
Hauart." Another novel famously built around a similar character and
conceived at about the same time as Bierbaum's was published is Thomas
Mann's *Felix Krull*. It was published as a fragment as late as 1954, towards the
end of its author's life and six years after the death of F.P. Grove in Canada.
Both authors' novels, different as they are, centre around their youthful heroes'
talent for role-playing and masquerade and the occasional desire to perform as
impostors.

The central figure of Bierbaum's novel is clearly patterned on Arthur Walter
Heymel, the millionaire and financier of Bierbaum's former employer, Insel
Publishers. Bierbaum was having his revenge on his former employer who had
come into enormous amounts of money as an adopted child—a cuckoo's egg
placed in somebody else's well-feathered nest. Bierbaum, however, called his
hero by the first name of somebody whom, like Heymel, he had known well
enough to write a bad review of—Greve and his only book of poems,
Wanderungen. Considering Bierbaum's and Greve's long association with
Insel, Bierbaum may have followed Felix's subsequent sensational career
closely. He must have remembered Greve's affinity to all things English and
Greve's friend of Scottish ancestry, Kilian. This may explain Bierbaum's choice
of the name "Felix Henry Hauart" (a last name which is near enough to a
phonetically correct version of "Howard"). The stages of both Heymel/Hauart's
and Felix Greve's youthful development are strikingly analogous: periods of
study in Bonn ("to choose a course of study and to be on the lookout for the
most famous professors"), fraternity life, aspirations for a career as a diplomat,
interrupted university education, a small, infinitely precious volume of poetry
in a limited edition ("the thickest, real hand-drawn paper of the famous make

of Herr van Geldern"), the fraternity house room decorated with exotic weapons on the walls.[1] In depicting his hero as a rich heir and a writer of precious poetry, Bierbaum had clearly not described Heymel alone. He appears to have delineated a contemporaneous type which Greve also was aware of and emulated. It is the type characterized by Franziska zu Reventlow in her reminiscences of the bohemian circles she had moved in and which she depicted in her little novel *Von Paul zu Pedro*. Reventlow called her hero not "Felix Henry Hauart," like Bierbaum, or "Felix Paul," but simply "Paul:" "One chances to meet him in watering places, in hotels and while travelling. A fixed place of residence—no, I hardly think so, only when he lives there temporarily. Paul is always seen near a suitcase and a barman, in some ephemeral place, full of longing for distant shores" (Reventlow 1976, 17).

Just as Bierbaum's Felix and Reventlow's Paul should be seen as typical of restless sojourners in Swiss and Italian hotels frequented by well-to-do guests, Thomas Mann likewise turned to this type who, in perfect mimicry, adjusts to a monied and well-educated society, supplying what's lacking in wealth with an abundance of wit, natural grace and good manners. Felix Greve and Felix Krull share an inborn restlessness, a knack for perfect role-playing and a certain proximity to those who serve others, like Phil Branden in *A Search for America*. Not unlike Heymel/Hauart and Felix Greve, Felix Krull springs from a most ordinary, even somewhat dubious family. Because Thomas Mann was careful to create his hero from many different sources, tracing particular literary origins and influences to one definite source is impossible. Nonetheless, there are striking analogies which are suggestive and deserve discussion.

In close parallel to Stefan George, whose family owned vineyards near Bingen, Felix Krull is made to hail from a family owning a distillery in a town on the Rhine, not far from Mainz—like Bingen. It appears, however, that Mann intended less a nod in the direction of George himself than some of the young men of his circle, none of whom Krull is made to resemble more than Greve. Felix Krull is said to accord his first name a "secret meaning." The child Krull sometimes dreams that "he were the Emperor." We recall that young Felix Greve, who must have, not so secretly, thought himself happy indeed, presided over a banquet in honour of the Emperor. He may have used this event in his Munich conversations, according himself a stature similar to that of Count Kessler who had indeed been close to Emperor Wilhelm I. Like Greve's, Krull's family disintegrates when he is still a boy. The mothers of both open boarding houses, Greve's in Hamburg, Krull's in Frankfurt. Neither Felix nor Krull had to join the army. (Whether Greve put on a spectacular show similar to that of Krull before the military medical examiner one would indeed like to know.) Reading about Krull's career as a liftboy and waiter at the famous Hotel St. James and Albany in Paris, we are not only reminded of Phil Branden working as a waiter at "Johnson's Café" in Toronto (SFA 31), but also of Greve's stay at the famous Paris hotel as a guest with Kilian in 1902 and his announcement to Gide that he was planning to stay there for their meeting in early June 1904 (GG 68). Young Felix Greve would not have kept hidden from his acquaintance his knowledge of the interior of that opulent hotel. Had Thomas Mann seen through Greve's braggadocio when, for a few weeks in the early fall of 1902, they both occupied rented rooms in the Munich Pension Gisela?

There are further parallels and coincidental details between Mann's impostor-hero and Greve's fraudulent behaviour during the period. There is, for instance, Greve's slipping into Kilian's part-Scots identity and fortune. This strikingly corresponds to Krull's assumption of the identity of his rich acquaintance, the Marquis de Venosta, in Mann's picaresque novel. Enough. The question remains whether Greve's Canadian alias had been lifted when he approached Mann, a German exile in Princeton in 1939. Had Thomas Mann finally read Grove's "Prologue" to *In Search of Myself*, which was then still an article bearing the title of the purportedly autobiographical novel? Grove's reminiscences, then called "My Life," were being written out in longhand while he was corresponding with Mann. No wonder, then, that he recalled the man who had also stayed at the Pension Gisela. By means of Felix Krull's reminiscences, which Mann calls "memoirs," the author styles the recollections of a gifted climber who, as the narrator, writes down the events of his life in his own idiosyncratic way:

I pay no attention to suspense and proportion and leave such niceties to authors who have recourse to their imagination in order to bring forth beautiful and regular works of art from invented matter, while I am simply putting forth my own, singular life, and do with it as I please (293).

Frederick Philip Grove, in the most successful of his books, resorts to a comparable convention:

Only what moves us deeply do we remember across the gulf of time. Above all, the chronology of events is confused. Many impressions refuse to fall back into their proper places. The only help I can get is from associations of locality. Where an impression or an event is indissolubly linked up with the scenery in which it arose or took place, I can fit it back by putting it into the proper point of my itinerary (SFA 225).

In his first-person narration in *A Search for America*, Phil Branden claims to reassemble the puzzle of his travels from memory, making it appear artless and coincidental. In this, the Canadian's narrative anticipates the studied simplicity of Mann's fictional first-person narrator, Krull. Both Mann and Grove, even before *Felix Krull* and *In Search of Myself*, had been writing the stories of young men. Greve's *Fanny Essler*, the story of a young woman, had also been the story of the young and arrogant F.K. Reelen. Oscar Wilde's *Dorian Gray* and André Gide's *L'immoraliste* and *Paludes* had similarly been the stories of young men and the conflicts peculiar to their time and age. Felix Hauart, Felix Krull and F.K. Reelen were, as to type, representative of the vast turn-of-the-century interest in young men's development. One thinks of Joris-Karl Huysmans's *A Rebours*, Jens Peter Jacobsen's tale *Mogens*, part of August Strindberg's earlier *Röda Rummet* (*The Red Room*)—particularly as regards the development of young Arved Falk—Friedrich Huch's *Peter Michel*, Robert Musil's *Törless* and Thomas Mann's Christian and Hanno Buddenbrook, brother and son to the staid Thomas Buddenbrook in the novel bearing their last name. Rainer Maria Rilke's eponymous hero *Malte Laurids Brigge* and numerous other works used similar conventions of the Goethean *Bildungsroman* to portray the lives of young men of sensibility. Outside of German and Scandinavian literary circles, James Joyce's *A Portrait of the Artist as a Young Man* stands out as possibly the most famous example of the genre.

The novel missing here, of course, is Greve's—a novel at the centre of which would not have been the adventurous young woman, as in *Fanny Essler*, but a novelistic variation and development of that novel's male hero, F.K. Reelen. Stefan George, once the adored master of his own Munich circle of young men, curiously did not allude to any of the authors and titles just mentioned in his conversations with Edith Landmann. In 1919 he recalled Felix Paul Greve alone, not to censure him, as he had done previously, but to remember that Greve had wanted to write "the novel of the young man," as if nobody else had attempted anything similar in the meantime (Landmann 86).[2] Since there is no conclusive evidence that George met Greve after 1905, it is not unreasonable to conclude that the plan for a novel that George remembered must have been an early plan for the novel first mentioned in print in 1905, Greve's unpublished *Der Sentimentalist*. It is also reasonable to assume that the manuscript of Grove's unpublished novel *Felix Powell's Career*, said to have been "the story of a young cad," may have been based on the original plan for a "novel of the young man" (Letters xxiv–v, n. 5). This "college story with a multiple sexual theme," as Grove described it to Lorne Pierce, sounds tantalizingly similar to Felix Greve's own sexual adventures in Bonn, Rome, Munich, Palermo and elsewhere—or, at least, those he had witnessed or heard about from Else (Letters 386). After circulating among publishers, the unpublished Canadian manuscript was stowed away in the Groves' attic until Mrs. Grove burned it in 1969. Grove called the book "the most powerful thing I have written" (Letters 462). Stefan George's rumination makes it clear that Greve's book about the "education" of a young man would have been particularly appropriate, since Greve's own youth was ideally suited to the task. It is also possible that George may have considered Greve the very type immortalized by Thomas Mann and others. In a 1931 essay, Grove arrived at a similar insight: "Indeed, it sometimes seems to me that I am the typical man of a period of transition" ("Rebels All" 69). Since, it may be argued, there is rarely a time that is not somehow a period of transition, it may be more fitting to see Grove (as he saw himself) as the type of man both of and out of his time—unzeitgemäss ("unseasonable"), to use the German (and Nietzschean) term he would have known.[3]

This may be one of the reasons why Canadian and, more recently, German readers and critics have maintained a firm interest in his person and his (auto) biographical books: FPG's intercultural career, as he himself never failed to point out, remains inextricably linked with a number of international decadent and aestheticist authors. He translated these writers and belonged among them as an author before violently rejecting them in his two German novels. He had been exactly that kind of sexually and morally adventurous young man that others had only written about. Using his own experience, Grove might have written the most informed account of all.

Finally, far too much has been made of Felix Greve's supposedly innate propensity for lying, used not only by Franz Blei but later by other Grove critics whenever it seemed convenient to question his character. Grove's intentions in creating fiction should not be subject to easy moral indignation; we are, after all, dealing with lying in the context of literature, not life. To later readers, Greve's confession to Gide about his lying may, at first sight, appear to bear out Blei's assumption that there was a flaw in his nature. But Greve's *claim* to Gide about his lying (and he did, in fact, falsify the account of his life he gave the French writer) should first and foremost be read as his claim to membership in the visionary company of writers to which Aubrey Beardsley, Ernest Dowson, André Gide, members of Stefan George's circle and Oscar Wilde belonged. It was a company into which he attempted to force himself—although somewhat belatedly—by dint of his efforts as a translator. Indeed, we hardly need to remind ourselves that "lying"—exalted by Wilde in "The Decay of Lying" in *Intentions*—was a distinguishing feature of their turn-of-the-century art and thought. Friedrich Nietzsche had been the tutelary deity of Greve and many of the writers he emulated and translated.[4] In his essay *Über Wahrheit und Lüge im aussermoralischen Sinn* ("On Truth and Falsehood in an Extra-moral Sense"), Nietzsche was the first to write about "lying" in an entirely new and scarcely moral context. The source of Greve's "lying" is the same as that of his claim, made to Gide, that "I am terribly strong," which

❋ *Frederick Philip Grove,* A Search for America *(1927),* Carrier edition, *dust jacket*

echoes Nietzsche's exaltation of the will (and which Grove would reiterate later through the person of his St. Nishivara, calling himself more fearless and less restrained than others). Rainer Maria Rilke's famous postulate, *Du musst dein Leben ändern* ("You must change your life"), may also be read as FPG's maxim in this context. To "change one's life," to slough off the old skin, to leave a dead past and enter into the present, to rewrite the past to suit the present, to make oneself over *in literature*—this may be seen as the necessity for "lying" as FPG saw it.

As has been observed elsewhere, Grove's tenure as a teacher in small Manitoba communities was no doubt helped by the outbreak of the Great War and the ensuing shortage of teachers. Canada's contribution to the Allied victory helped to raise the nation's consciousness of itself as an independent nation and sparked increased self-awareness of its cultural heritage and promise. Ironically, the xenophobia caused by the war years and their aftermath helped Grove's career as a writer in the mid-1920s because of his insistent praise of pioneer values and his call for literary and cultural progress and independence. The same circumstances that brought the Group of Seven to the attention of a larger public helped Grove's career as a writer and, for a short time, a famous public speaker (Hjartarson, "Staking a Claim" 22). It must be emphasized again that Grove found "America" in Canada in *A Search for America*. A footnote on page 436 of the first Canadian edition comments on the narrator's conclusion that "America is an ideal and as such has to be striven for": "I have since come to the conclusion that the ideal as I saw and still see it has been abandoned by the U.S.A. That is why I became and remained a Canadian." Canada, of course, held out the promise of contributing to a new "Canadian literature worthy to exalt our name among the nations" (NS 131), and possibly of becoming its major spokesman. For Grove, his many readers and his audiences on nationwide tours, it may have appeared that such a goal was within reach in the late 1920s. Unfortunately, although critical interest in Grove grew at a steady pace, he became somewhat old-fashioned as the second half of the twentieth century progressed. To be sure, the continued presence of at least four of his books in McClelland & Stewart's "New Canadian Library" series assured small but steady sales and kept his name alive (Lecker 154f.). Spettigue's discovery of his German origin caused a flurry of renewed readerly interest in his works. Ironically, however, only the discovery of the papers of Baroness Else, his erstwhile companion, awakened renewed interest in FPG as a figure worthy of study in larger artistic and literary contexts. Today, other and more recent Canadian writers of international fame seem to have a much larger claim to readers' attention. They certainly have been more in the public eye than even Grove in his heyday.

Still, Grove clearly continues to exert an influence on major Canadian writers. Although he did not pioneer Canadian naturalism (he came too late for that), he helped to place pioneer life in the Canadian prairie provinces on the literary map. The lives he depicted were often those of immigrants, but of immigrants less articulate than himself. To an extent, he became their spokesman. Members of the Group of Seven ventured into the wild Ontario woods and studied the less-than-picturesque aspects of Canadian industrial civilization. For his part, Grove lived among Ukrainian, Scandinavian and German settlers and used the first-hand knowledge of their harsh and primitive lives to eke out a meagre living against sometimes impossible odds. It is this part of Grove's writings that lives in the celebrated work of Robert Kroetsch and Rudy Wiebe—both, incidentally, of German ancestry. That Grove had hit upon a prairie world ready for literary treatment became evident, outside of his own Canadian essays and novels, in Margaret Laurence's "Manawaka" series of five novels. Her fictional town of Manawaka is of course the northern Manitoba town of Neepawa, approximately halfway between two places where the Groves taught—Eden to the north and Rapid City to the south. The town is only an hour's drive southwest of the marshes that became the setting for Grove's early work. Although Grove ignored the indigenous Métis and Cree population in the 1920s, he did not repudiate other immigrants, being one himself. In this, too, he was truly a pioneer. To integrate his western vision into aboriginal history—to historicize his literary worldview—would have been beyond the writer who, thrown into this rugged land, had to survive using his European wits.

NOTES

♦ INTRODUCTION

1   In addition to recent articles in leading magazines and newspapers in Germany, FPG has received belated recognition in a review essay in the magazine of the Stefan George Society, the first official mention since 1903 when he was cast from the group of George's followers (von Bock).

2   I owe some of these insights to joint research with Armin Paul Frank under the auspices of the Göttingen *Sonderforschungsbereich* 309 ("Special Research Center on Literary Translation"). Cf. Frank xii–xvii and Martens, "Institutional Transmission" 1991.

3   There is a sizeable collection of Axel Juncker's correspondence in the National Library in Copenhagen, Denmark. It contains letters from Johannes Schlaf, Max Dauthendey and others, but nothing to or from Greve.

1 ♦ A PRIZE STUDENT IN HAMBURG

1   Certificate from the "Transport Shareholders Society" (formerly J. Hevecke) in Hamburg, July 31, 1890. Carl Eduard Greve and his family were accepted with a deed into the Hamburg City Association on October 28, 1890.

2   "I saw the 'Director' of my school...Within a few weeks I began to have pupils, mostly young boys attending the gymnasia of the city...in addition to keeping myself at school. I was able to pay for my mother's stay at the hospital, keep myself in pocket money..." (ISM 108–09).

3   Following the publication of *A Search for America*, Grove travelled through Ontario on the invitation of the Organization of Canadian Clubs. He allowed

himself expensive hotels and bought new clothing, despite considerable poverty and sparse earnings. Thus he wrote to Mrs. Grove on March 2, 1928: "As far as travel goes, this is the way. Room with a bath. Give orders. Taxi when I go out. Call in the stenographer when I write to other people, etc. Shall send my underwear for cleaning tomorrow morning—by the bell-boy." (Letters 87). For the reading list and the previously unpublished papers from the Johanneum regarding Greve, I am grateful for the attention of Dr. Fritz Kasten.

4   For his second-year exams at the University of Manitoba in April 1916, Grove received only 74 and 68 (out of a possible 100) for his knowledge of Latin grammar and Latin authors (Stobie, *Grove* 43).

5   Schultess was the director of the Hamburg Johanneum from 1888 until his death in 1919.

6   Grove continued: "I flushed with gratification. I had always adored the man: to this very day his life seems to me the embodiment of the highest there is in mankind; his estimation of my gifts and powers still whispers with subtle flattery. But have I justified it?" (Grove, "Rebels" 67–68).

7   "Der Oberprimaner *Felix* Paul Berthold Friedrich Greve, Neuburg 16, ist vor [*ausgestrichen: allen*] anderen geeignet, auf Ihre sehr gütige Anfrage für das nächste Mündensche Stipendium empfohlen zu werden. Er ist begabt und fleißig und tüchtig, was sich schon daraus ergibt, daß er den ungewöhnlichen Weg durch die Realschule zum Realgymnasium und dann zur Gelehrtenschule erfolgreich und ohne Zeitverlust zurückgelegt hat, indem er sich [*ausgestrichen: die ihm fehlenden*] ganz die Lateinische, darauf die griechische Sprache angeeignet."

8   In his memoirs, Count Kessler describes the Literary Society founded at the Johanneum in 1817 and claims that it was there that he was acquainted with the leading German authors (Kessler, *Gesichter* 160–62).

9   Schultess's note for a response to a letter of September 13, 1900 from Dr. Hagedorn.

10 Staats archiv Hamburg.

11 Spettigue (*FPG* 46) suggests that Greve may have filled out the application form himself and thus offered it as the first example of Greve's handwriting. The normal practice of civil servants and comparison with Greve's handwriting from school documents contradicts this supposition.

2 ◆ A STUDENT IN BONN

1   This and other information regarding Felix Greve's period as a student in Bonn between April 20, 1898 and October 24, 1901 have been taken from the "Registry" (No. 384 of the University Albums) in the archives of the Rheinische Friedrich-Wilhelms University in Bonn.

2   This monogram shows more than passing similarity to the one which F.P. Grove designed, commented upon and sent to Lorne Pierce on 4, 11 and 15 February 1939. Since every Rhenus club member was to include his initials upon transcribing the monogram, the technique would have been less than difficult for

Grove. Indeed, it is not at all difficult to discover similarities between the Rhenus monogram and the one Grove used to sign his early letters to Warkentin. The "F" and "T" appear almost identical. Numerous early examples remain of Greve's signature with and without the Rhenus monogram. See Letters 350 and the accompanying "Appendix B" for a facsimile of a letter to Warkentin. For more on monograms, cf. Spettigue, *FPG* 236 n.15.

3 For another assessment of Kilian, cf. Spettigue, *FPG* 99.

4 "Er war wie benommen von diesen Farben, zu denen noch ein paar andere Mützen mitkneipender Korpsburschen befreundeter Korps, sowie die bunten Fahnen und Wappen an den Wänden kamen, alles in dem gelben Lichte zahlreicher, auf alten, messingnen Leuchtern stehender Kerzen, aber bereits schummrig umnebelt von Tabakswolken aus langen und kurzen Pfeifen. Dazu viel blitzendes Metall von strahlenförmig zusammengruppierten Schlägern, Säbeln und Spießen, und das mattere Blenden der wie in einer einzigen großen Glasfläche wirkenden, dicht nebeneinandergehängten Photographien und Silhouetten früherer Korpsangehöriger."

5 "Semester Report" 1 (October 19–November 30). *Club News* 1.2 (December 1898).

6 Frederick Philip Grove's story "The Boat" treats an episode in similar terrain with analogous plot and protagonists (Grove, *Tales* 234–48).

7 "Der 'Dramatische Verein' zu Bonn, in dessen vorstande ich mich befinde, beabsichtigt, sich im laufe des nächsten monates in eine freie literarische gesellschaft zu verwandeln, und zwar soll die publikation durch eine vorlesung vor geladenem publikum erfolgen, in der junge wiener dichter zu worte kommen sollen."

8 "Der Apparat, den der Minstrel befohlen hatte, verdunkelter Saal und Kerzenschein, verstimmte und entrüstete, die menschliche Erscheinung, deren jugendliche Anmut durch affektierte Vornehmspielerei und die prätentiöse Halbeleganz des Berliner Ausnahmeliteraten nicht gehoben sondern verdächtig gemacht wurde, die celebrierende Vortragsweise, so wirksam bei halber Stimme vor dem einzigen Hörer, so falschklingend vor hunderten im nüchternen Saale—dies und mehr, was ich verschweige ärgerte, ergrimmte/enttäuschte. Usener, den prachtvollen silbersträhnigen Kopf zurückgeworfen harrte mit unlesbarer Miene aus…das Publikum lachte/murrte und drohte laut zu werden, und als [Professor] Justis Riesenleib langsam aus den verschatteten Sitzreihen sich hebend ins Stehen und Gehen kam, und seine schwere Hand sich begütigend auf meine Schulter legte—die Worte 'Lassen Sie mich gehen, ich halte das Opium nicht länger aus', von Umsitzenden vernommen sich von Mund zu Mund fortpflanzten, brach der halbe Saal stühlescharrend auf und sprengte die künstliche Nacht."

9 See the letters from Botho Graef to Ernst Hardt, February 2, 1901, March 1, 1901 and August 24, 1901. Usener dedicated his poems to Botho Graef, Ernst and Polyxena Hardt and to Sabine Lepsius (Usener, "Erste Verse" 1906).

10 "Der George-Abend in Bonn war eindrucksvoll—etwa 100 geladene Gäste—die mit einem über alles Erwarten starken Eindruck davongingen—Ich hatte das

Licht, während ich las, ausdrehen lassen, so daß die zwei Kerzen zu Seiten meines Kopfes die einzigen Lichtquellen in dem recht großen Saale waren— Die Heiligkeit der Verse türmte sich in der Dunkelheit, daß die Menschen sich sehr wohl vor einem Altar empfanden—die [atem-?]lose Stille, die auch geraume Zeit den Schluß überdauerte—gehört zum Schönsten, was ich in meinem Leben empfand." Letter to Karl Wolfskehl, Berlin, no date ("after an absence of 8 days").

11 "Semester Report II: November 12, 1899–January 1, 1900." *Club News* 11:2 (January 1900).

12 "My mother…prophesied nothing but evil from the reign of Wilhelm II" (ISM 72–73).

13 All page numbers for *A Search for America* (SFA) refer to the American edition published by Louis Carrier (1928).

14 The *Club History* of both 1955 (16) and 1990 (12) makes reference to this tour. My paraphrases and citations are based on Thiel's report in the 1906 *Festschrift*, 176–95.

15 The Latin inscription, which survives only in fragments, begins with the words "INTER TOUTONES." The obscure portions had to be reconstructed from the presumed function of the column as a border marker (Röder, *passim* and *Archäologischer Anzeiger* 1901: 89). For discussion of Loeschke's role in the reconstruction of the boundary of the Roman Empire and Greve's possible interest in the matter, see Chapter Three.

16 Along with parallels to *Huckleberry Finn* are clear echoes of *Robinson Crusoe*. See Stobie, "Grove in Simcoe" 163.

17 Maximilian Dauthendey (1867–1918) achieved fame with his volume of poetry *Ultra-Violett* (1893). The poems from *Des grossen Krieges Not* (1915) were first published in Medan. For discussion of the relationship between George and Dauthendey, see Kluncker, *Blätter* (who also mentions Greve). Scarce additional information on Dauthendey is in Geibig, *Max Dauthendey*. The poet died on August 29, 1918, and is interred in Malang, Java.

18 "Der gestrige Kaiser-Commers in der Beethovenhalle gestaltete sich…zu einer großartigen Kundgebung der vaterländischen Gesinnung in unserer Studentenschaft. Die Halle bot ein farbenprächtiges, lebensvolles Bild. Ihre äußeren Umrisse verschwanden fast unter Laubgewinden, Fahnen und Wappenschildern. Der Hintergrund des Saales mit seiner Orgel war durch ein gewaltiges Riesengemälde verhüllt, das den Kaiser zu Pferde mit seinem Gefolge darstellt. Zu beiden Seiten prangten in stolzem Verein die stattlichen Banner der studentischen Körperschaften. Während im Saale Tisch an Tisch eng umlagert war, zeigten die Ehrentafeln auf dem Podium allerdings gar manche Lücke. Die Zahl der zum Fest erschienenen Professoren war verhältnismäßig gering. Unter den Ehrengästen befanden sich außer dem Rector und dem Universitätsrichter die Generale Bartholomäus und Krummacher, der Oberberghauptmann a.D. Excellenz von Huyssen und der Erste Staatsanwalt Müller. Zu ihnen gesellte sich später noch der Oberst Frhr. V. Gayl. Den Vorsitz führte stud. Greve vom Akademischen Ruderclub Rhenus."

19 "Unser Erstchargierter Greve wurde seiner ebenso arbeitsreichen wie ehren-
vollen Aufgabe als Leiter des ganzen Kommerses in jeder Hinsicht gerecht,
wofür ihm auch von den verschiedensten Seiten Anerkennung nicht versagt
wurde." Semester Report III. *Club News* II.4 (March 1900).

20 This is perhaps the actual source of a remark from Frederick Philip Grove's
article "Rebels All: Of the Interpretation of Individual Life:" "I have, in my
youth, associated with royalty" (Grove, Rebels 69). According to Henry Makow,
the article was presumably written in 1919. In *Prinz Kuckuck*, Bierbaum also
mentions Bonn's Borussia fraternity and its illustrious members: "According to
[Felix Hauart's] rather arrogant and indifferent facial expression and the perfectly
fitting though perhaps too new English suits, one could presume that the goal of
his journey was not the rather inelegant and entirely unaristocratic Jena, but
rather Bonn — Bonn the superb, the city which could claim the merit of being
home to the Club Borussia " (*Club History*, 300).

21 "Wie war er in die Fluthen geraten? Als seine Freunde beschlossen, wegen des
dichten Nebels draußen zu übernachten, hat er sich da allein auf den Heimweg
gemacht, um der wartenden Mutter keine Sorgen zu bereiten? Hat er in dem
dichten Nebel sich verirrt? Ist er unversehens an den steilen Uferrand gerathen
und hinabgestürzt? Ist er von dem Sturze betäubt worden? Hat in dem kalten
Wasser ein Herzschlag seinem Leben ein Ende gemacht? Oder hat er als rüstiger
Schwimmer mit den Fluthen gekämpft, bis die Kraft erlahmte? Hat er um Hülfe
gerufen, und Niemand hat in der stillen Nacht seine Stimme gehört? Niemand
ist da, der diese Fragen beantworten kann; darum stehen wir vor einem Räthsel."

22 "Unser inaktives Mitglied Kilian mussten wir wegen gänzlicher Interesselosigkeit
und unwürdigen Benehmens–er war weder bei der Überführung der Leiche
Lombergs, noch bei dem Begräbnis erschienen, hatte kein Wort der
Entschuldigung geschrieben und überhaupt sehr wenig Notiz von dem ganzen
Unglücksfall genommen–ausschliessen."

23 Besides Kilian, Karl Gustav Vollmoeller could also be intended. Vollmoeller was
long considered a promising talent in the George circle.

24 "Unserem früheren Mitglied Greve ist sein Austrittsgesuch gewährt worden."

3 ◆ ARCHAEOLOGY AND LITERATURE

1 Greve to Karl Wolfskehl, April 22, 1902. The letter was written on paper from the
Hotel de Rome in Berlin. Greve also mentions this hotel in *Fanny Essler*, 502,
519.

2 There are two extant letters from Thomas Mann to Frederick Philip Grove.
Grove had presented Mann with *Two Generations* which had just then appeared
in print. During the same period, Grove mentions a conversation he had with
Gide in June 1904 quite openly: "My whole individualistic leanings…sprang up
within me in a conversation with Gide, over an excellent dinner at Paris, when
we were talking of Wilde who had recently been released from prison" (Grove,
"Thoughts and Reflections" 318). It was Greve, not Wilde, who had just been
released from prison.

3   "I felt confident that, henceforth, I could even undertake to lead 'personally conducted tours' of Europe...but invariably some university professor who knew nothing of Europe got the job while I went without" (ISM 202).

4   Else and Polyxena were the daughters of the Bavarian envoy in Athens, Dr. Konstantin von Hoesslin. The picture of Else in the library of the DAI is in Rieche, *150 Jahre* 97.

5   I gratefully acknowledge two conversations with Mrs. Rose String, Herbert Koch's daughter, for this information. Mrs. String generously allowed me access to the documents and correspondence between Koch and the Delbrueck family.

6   The relevant documentation is in Karl Wolfskehl and Ernst Hardt's correspondence in the Deutsches Literaturarchiv, Marbach.

7   Ludwig Curtius (1874–1954) provides a description of the contemporary situation in archaeology among the leading archaeologists (Curtius, *Deutsche* 116–127; *Archäologenbildnisse* 186–87). Like Greve, Curtius was also close to the George circle for a period of time.

8   Richard Delbrueck (1875–1957) studied law, classical archaeology and philology in Neuchatel, Munich, Berlin and Bonn. Under Loeschke's supervision, he wrote a dissertation entitled "Linienperspektive in der griechischen Kunst" ("Linear Perspective in Greek Art"). From 1909 on, he was commissioned with the direction of the DAI in Rome; he served as the director from 1911–15. In 1922 he became a professor in Giessen and in 1928 accepted Loeschke's chair in Bonn (*Archäologenbildnisse*, 188–99).

9   Their experiences in Greece were summed up in a joint article, "Das Quellhaus des Theagenes in Megara" (*Mitteilungen Athen*, 1900).

10 University Registry, Bonn.

11 "We know that Felix was in Italy about the end of 1900 or beginning 1901 until the fall of 1901; we know he was not enrolled at the Archaeological Institute" (*FPG* 60).

12 The chronology and topics for the meetings from this period are taken from the *Mitteilungen*, Vol. XIV, 94–95; and *Jahrbuch*, Vol. XV, 223.

13 "Ich sitze wieder auf dem Monte Tarpeo, melancholischerweise sogar in Delbruecks altem Zimmer. Es ließ sich nicht vermeiden und ich finde es etwas komisch wie das meiste Menschliche. Die dürre Hausfrau erzählt mir eben von Greve, der eines Abends bleich und schlotternd vor ihrer Thüre stand und sie ihn gratis beherbergt und ihm einen extra Morgenkaffee gekocht. Das war damals als er nach Bonn fuhr. Er behauptete noch, schlecht geschlafen zu haben, weil er seinen Koffer auf der Bahn nicht zugeschlossen hatte. Und darin waren doch seine Brillianten. (Entre nous: ER hat mir bei der Entlassung einen komischen und sehr bösen Brief geschrieben, den ich aufbewahre)." Vollmoeller to Hardt, November 1, 1904.

14 Vollmoeller to Ernst Hardt in an undated letter (presumably in late 1903 or early 1904): "D[ear]. H[ardt]. Here are your Gerden cards."

15 "Dich lockten meerbewegte Inselwelten / Und ferner Sagen liedumwobne Küsten, / Der Sonne Land mit seinen weißen Zelten / Die schon in deine frühsten Träume grüssten..."

16 "Der Verfasser des mit gleicher Post an Sie abgehenden Manuscriptes, in Hamburg beheimatet, steht dem Münchener Kreise der 'Blätter für die Kunst' nahe. Er hat lange Zeit im Süden verbracht, und eine Frucht dieser Reisen, die frühste, ist eben das kleine Buch, das er Ihnen nunmehr zum Verlage anbietet. Das Thema der Gedichtsammlung, die als Ganzes gedacht ist, ist die Entwicklung aus lebenfliehendem Pessimismus zu einer zwar einseitigen aber starken Zukunftsbejahung. Das Ziel des Verfassers ist eine Kunst, die das Leben mit sich zur Höhe trägt." Greve to Alfred Janssen, December 5, 1901.

17 The comment on Greve's style is taken from an evaluation by Greve's Johanneum German teacher in assessment of his graduating assignment.

18 "Ein wenig lieber sah ich die Leute meines Standes wieder, Archäologen und Philologen, aber mit ihnen zu Plaudern machte mir kaum mehr Vergnügen, gab mir nicht mehr Anregung, als wenn ich in guten historischen Handbüchern blätterte. Ganz im Anfang konnte ich hoffen, bei ein paar Romanciers und Dichtern ein etwas direkteres Erfassen des Lebens zu finden; aber wenn sie dieses Erfassen hatten, so muß man gestehen, zeigten sie es kaum; mir schien, die meisten lebten nicht, begnügten sich mit dem Schein des Lebens und hätten das Leben um ein geringeres als ein ärgerliches Hindernis des Schreibens angesehen" (FPG's German translation from Gide's French).

4 ◆ A POET AND TRANSLATOR IN MUNICH AND BERLIN

1 Felix Greve later wrote: "At times conducted hurriedly, at times calmly, my studies took me to Bonn, Paris, London, Rome, Naples, Greece and finally to Munich." Greve to Franz Brümmer, March 6, 1907. Staatsbibliothek Preussischer Kulturbesitz, Berlin. See Letters 538–39.

2 Greve to Friedrich Schultess, November 5, 1901.

3 In his novel *Fanny Essler*, Greve savagely caricaturized the *Jour* at the Wolfskehls' home. In a racist turn of phrase, he called Wolfskehl "Katzwedel," along with other members of the Munich circle.

4 Greve to Wolfskehl, letters from December 2, 10 and 24, 1901.

5 "Gleichzeitig gestatte ich mir, Ihnen neun beliebig herausgegriffene Sonette meiner Dante-Übertragung zu überreichen. Fast schäme ich mich, es zu thun, da sie mir beim Abschreiben alle schlecht und matt erschienen. Die einzige Entschuldigung ist, dass sie eben vor 3 Jahren entstanden sind. An einer Stelle, die mir völlig verfehlt schien, habe ich sogar während der Abschrift ein Plagiat an Ihnen begangen. (3. Sonett)." Greve to Karl Wolfskehl, undated.

6 Cf. Spettigue's commentary on Greve's Dante translations: "That Dante reference interests me because many years ago the German scholar Robert Boehringer wrote me from Switzerland that he had found in possession of the Wolfskehl family a translation of Dante's *Vita nuova* that included parts by Greve. When I asked for more details, he replied cautiously that the family members he was dealing with were simple people, and apparently nervous, so that retrieving the book would be difficult. The book never did appear, but now it seems certain that Boehringer was correct, though I no longer have that corre-

spondence, and I have not been able to identify which Dante edition he was referring to" (Spettigue, "Felix , Elsa" 15).

7   "Ein Wort aber muß ich Ihnen noch sagen und ich bitte Sie sehr aufzumerken und klug zu sein: Es scheint, dass unsres gemeinsamen bekannten F[elix] P[aul] G[reve] Münchhausiaden sehr bedenkliche Grade erreichen und dass es erlaubt sein muss Freunden zu sagen wie wenig weit man irgendwelche Pfade des Zutrauens zu ihm wandeln darf. Hier scheint er vieles verwirrt zu haben und es haben die Besten nicht in Frieden leben können vor ihm. Ob er krank ist?"

8   This translation has yet to be located.

9   Greve to Karl Wolfskehl, both letters approximately January 1902. "Knight Errant" and "Herakles Farnese" appeared in Greve's collection of poetry *Wanderungen*.

10   Undated letter from Herbert Koch from Capua to Countess Franziska zu Reventlow.

11   Koch to Reventlow, undated letter ("Thursday," ca. early 1904).

12   "Aber dort oben am Odeonsplatz...drängen sich die Leute um die breiten Fenster und Schaukästen des großen Kunstmagazins, des weitläufigen Schönheitsgeschäftes von M. Blüthenzweig...Prachtbände, Triumphe der neuen Ausstattungskunst, Werke modischer Lyriker, gehüllt in einen dekorativen und vornehmen Prunk...Er sah die Nachbildungen von Meisterwerken aus allen Galerien der Erde, die kostbaren Rahmen in ihrer simplen Bizarrerie, die Renaissanceplastik, die Bronzeleiber und Ziergläser, die schillernden Vasen, den Buchschmuck und die Porträts der Künstler, Musiker, Philosophen, Schauspieler, Dichter. [E]ine Fülle von Farbe, Linie und Form, von Stil, Witz, Wohlgeschmack und Schönheit."

13   "Traum von einer schmalen Lorbeerkrone"

Und irrend schweift mein Geist in alle Runde,
Und schwankend fass' ich jede starke Hand
Ich bin ein kindischer—schwacher Fant,

Und dennoch regt die Hoffnung sich im Grunde,
Daß etwas, was ich dachte und empfand,
Mit Ruhm einst gehen wird von Mund to Munde.

Schon klingt mein Name leise in das Land,
Schon nennt ihn mancher in des Beifalls Tone:
Und Leute sind's von Urteil und Verstand.

14   For Friedrich Huch's role in the Mann family and in the Schwabing Bohème see Mann, *Fünf* 103–09.

15   Ludwig Klages, "Friedrich Huchs *Peter Michel*." *Der Lotse*, 2.7 (16 November 1902): 206–13. During the twenty-one months of its existence, *Der Lotse* published articles on Stefan George (no. 11, 1901) and August Endell (no. 23, 1902), while Ernst Hardt contributed an article on Reinhold Lepsius (no. 10, 1901).

16 Undated letter from Friedrich Huch in Munich to his mother in Dresden.

17 "Am Abend sagte ich zu Franziska Reventlow, der einzigen Frau, für die [Klages]
je entbrannte: 'Heute habe ich Ludwig Klages vorgemimt, wie man Gänschen
verführt. Er fand mich 'kolossal'." Und sie seufzte: "Mich findet er auch
'kolossal'. Wenn im Tanze meine Haare flattern, dann steht er hinter der Säule
und verachtet. Er verachtet Hentschel und verachtet Wedekind und verachtet
Felix Greve und verachtet Ohaha Schmitz. Kurz alle verachtet er, die mich
nehmen und küssen. Denn ich soll mich läutern und mit ihm fliegen. Und ich
will ja auch fliegen. Aber man kann nicht lange oben fliegen. Und weil er der
einzige ist, mit dem ich fliegen kann, so muß ich doch mit den andern mich
küssen" (Lessing, *Einmal* 334).

18 I gratefully acknowledge the assistance of Dr. Margit Peterfy in researching the
Klages information.

19 Dülberg to Klages, April 22, 1902.

20 "I sent back to him [Ludwig Klages] all of the hundreds of letters which could,
knowing they were in my hands, cause him discomfort and did not insist that he
return mine" (Lessing, *Einmal* 383). Little remains of Ludwig Klages's correspondence, either. Klages's biographer, Hans Eggert Schröder, failed in his
hagiographic account to provide any source references. The Klages papers in the
Marbach Archives contain extensive documents, although many references have
been rendered illegible or were scissored out.

21 Lessing describes the Klages family home in Hanover and the enclosed atmosphere of the middle-class world in which brother and sister were raised (Lessing,
Einmal 178–80). Schröder reports that Countess Reventlow visited the Klages's in
their shared Munich apartment for the first time on September 23, 1901, which is
approximately when Greve moved to Munich.

22 "In my childhood, it was a neat and tidy, if also sober little city full of bourgeois
efficiency" (Lessing, *Einmal* 20).

23 Klages Estate.

24 "Was die Übersetzung betrifft, das wäre doppelte Arbeit lieber Freund, denn ich
bin darauf doch durch meine lange Praxis so geübt, daß ich es nur vom
Französischen abschreibe, besonders wenn dieses sehr leicht ist. Wissen Sie, es
schreibt jeder einen so ganz anderen Stil, ich habe das schon öfters mit
Bekannten versucht, die sogar auch Übung in solchen Sachen hatten und habe
jedes Mal gefunden, daß die Arbeit aus anderen umzumodeln weit größer ist,
wie dies gewohnheitsmäßige Heruntersudeln. Nur darf Helene das nicht mißver-
stehen, als ob ich ihr nicht zutraute, daß sie es könnte" (Reventlow, *Briefe* 358).

25 Spettigue is of another opinion and writes of Helene Klages: "Helene Klages was
a writer; was she going to look over Greve's translations for him?" (Spettigue,
"Felix, Elsa" 16). The evidence suggest that Greve was the teacher and Klages
the novice.

26 In the table of contents in the first edition of the translation of *Intentions*, the
reference to the essay "The Decay of Lying" with "German by H.F.C.K." was
removed from the "second re-edited edition" of 1905. Also missing is the short
foreword by the translator and the listing of his earlier publications. Instead, a

new "Note" before the text, along with the reference "Paris-Plage, November 1905," reflects the accepted changes: "This new edition of my translations of *Intentions* differs from the first in that, firstly, an entire range of mistakes and oversights have been removed and, secondly, all omissions have been avoided. This translation is based on the text of the Heinemann edition of 1891."

27 Greve to Karl Wolfskehl, dated "Saturday, 1 a.m."

28 "Haben Sie den Roman vom F.P. Greve gelesen? Wir und Helene Klages kommen noch nicht drin vor–aber ich habe besonders bei der Hochstapler-Atmosphäre des letzten Teils viel an die alten Zeiten denken müssen. Else Ploetz muss ihm übrigens die betreffenden Leute (Lechter, Endell und besonders Ernst Hardt geradezu glaenzend vorgespielt haben). Im übrigen arg talentlos und etwas gemein." Herbert Koch to Franziska Reventlow from Capua, undated.

29 J.C.C. Bruns archives in Minden.

30 See Freytag-Loringhoven's remark about Kilian: "I felt an instinctive distrust—dislike—first founded merely upon the sound of his name: 'Kilian.' Why—I cannot explain" (BE 101). Else may have been influenced by the figure of Kilian in Carl Maria von Weber's opera *Der Freischütz*.

31 For similar reasons, F.P. Grove suggested the pseudonym "Andrew Rutherford" to his Canadian publisher McClelland & Stewart during the production of *Over Prairie Trails*. Grove's publisher agreed: "The pen-name Andrew Rutherford would be quite a good one, and shall we consider this adopted" (McClelland & Stewart to Grove January 29, 1920). Grove Collection, University of Manitoba.

32 Greve to Wolfskehl, March 17, 1902.

33 In my discussions of the publishing house J.C.C. Bruns, I differentiate between the publisher Gustav Bruns; the publisher's son Max Bruns, a poet and occasional reader; and Heinrich Stiller, the business manager. There is no justification for speaking of the "publisher Max Bruns" before 1908 on the basis of incomplete or unreliable sources (cf. Sarkowski, "Bruns").

34 I have in mind Arthur Moeller-Bruck, Alfred Mombert, Wilhelm Spohr and Paul Scheerbart, among others. See Martens, *Bruns* passim.

35 Postcards from Greve and Kilian to George, May 5, 1902 and to Wolfskehl, May 17 and 21, 1902.

36 Bierbaum's novel has been read as an attack upon the wealthy Alfred Walter Heymel, who not only acted as Bierbaum's sponsor—until refusing to do so anymore—but who also wrote poetry himself. In my opinion, Bierbaum's novel is not to be restricted to Heymel, just as Thomas Mann's *Felix Krull* ought not to be reduced to one single con-man as the sole character source. See my Afterword.

37 Greve's succinct and elegant translation: "Der Archäolog liefert den Stoff, der Künstler die Form" (*Fingerzeige* 254). It comes as little surprise that Greve changed the suggested German title *Ziele von Oskar Wilde* (*Intentions by Oscar Wilde*) and replaced it with one he claimed in a letter to Bruns he had "Mr. Stefan George to thank for:" *Fingerzeige von Oscar Wilde* (*Signs of/from Oscar Wilde*). Greve responded to these signs himself.

38 "Sie müssen nämlich wissen, daß ich die Romane sehr willkürlich behandle, kürze, wo mir etwas zu lang scheint (den letzten...habe ich von 600 Seiten auf 450 gekürzt) etc."

39 Max Bruns to Gustav Bruns, June 2, 1900.

40 "Ein *homme grave*, fraglos. Wilde meint es ernst mit seinen Paradoxen; er hat keine Leichtigkeit, sich über sich selbst zu erheben. Was er aber doziert, ist wirklich ein Evangelium, das sich hören läßt: Überführung des Künstlerischen in das kritische Schaffen."

41 I take Max Bruns's comments on the writings of Baudelaire, Wilde and Greve from entries in his handwritten and chronologically arranged notes, *Meine Lektüre (My Reading)*.

42 In contrast to the preferences of Max Bruns and Felix Greve, the volume translated by Lachmann and Landauer presented a different Oscar Wilde. Their collection contained an essay treating the desperate situation of children in prisons; "The Soul of Man Under Socialism;" Wilde's introduction to Rennell Rodd's poems, which Rodd had named *Rose Leaf and Apple Leaf* (1882) in accordance with Wilde's advice, "L'Envoi," and the poem "Sonnet to Freedom" (1881). Through their choice of texts, literary mediators shape translations and their readers' impressions of an author.

43 Greve to Bruns, March 19, 1902.

44 Greve to Wolfskehl, letters from April 21 and 22, 1902.

45 George interessiere "noch heute nichts so sehr wie Übersetzen," denn er lerne von der Sprache: "er habe eigentlich nie neue Worte geprägt, sondern alte wieder herausgeholt."

46 Greve to Wolfskehl, postcard from May 10, 1902.

47 Greve to George, May 29, 1902. Reference here is to the Daisy Broicher translation, not published until 1910 (Seekamp et al., *Stefan George* 125).

48 Greve to George, June 19, 1902.

49 Greve to George, June 19, 1902.

50 Greve to Wolfskehl, June 21 and July 14, 1902. An abridged segment from Vollmoeller's *Catharina* appeared in *Blätter für die Kunst*, instalment V (1901).

51 Greve to Wolfskehl, October 7, 1902.

52 Greve to J.C.C. Bruns, July 17, 1902. Greve was referring to George's translations of Dowson in *Blätter für die Kunst* (IV: 4), which also contained translations of Dowson by Borchardt. George's poem "Juli-Schwermut" in the first bookstore edition of his volume *Der Teppich des Lebens und Lieder von Traum und Tod* (1901) was inspired by Dowson's early death and dedicated to him. Bondi Publishers produced George's other translations, including the Dowson text, in a collected volume of 1905 which contained George's translations of Rossetti, Swinburne, Jacobsen, Kloos, Verwey, Verhaeren, Verlaine, Rimbaud, de Régnier and D'Annunzio.

53 Greve to Wolfskehl, August 18, 1902.

54 Max Bruns would publish several of his numerous translations of poetry alongside his own poems in his collection *Die Gedichte 1893–1908* (1909). The favourable critical response is in Soergel, *Dichtung 1928*.

55 Greve to Bruns, July 18, 1902.

56 Greve to von Poellnitz, August 12, 1902.

57 Greve to Wolfskehl, August 3, 1902.

58 Greve to Bruns, August 2 and 4, 1902.

59 Greve to Wolfskehl, July 15, 1902. Parts of the letters to Wolfskehl which deal with events in Gardone were first discussed in Spettigue 1992.

60 "Ich möchte nun eine grosse Bitte an Sie richten. Durch beträchtliche Einbussen an meinem kleinen Vermögen bin ich in die Lage gekommen, bis zum 15. September eine grössere Summe zu benötigen. Im Falle der Annahme aller Manuscripte wollte ich Sie bitten, den Vertrag über diese fünf Bände (ca 70–80 Bogen) dahin zu ändern, dass Sie mir bis zum 15. September 1800 M. zahlen, den Rest aber erst bei Erscheinen des letzten dieser fünf Bände. Wenn Ihnen das möglich wäre, so würden Sie mich zu grossem Dank verpflichten und zugleich in Stand setzen, meine Arbeit an meiner Wilde–Übertragung in Ruhe fortzusetzen." Greve to Bruns, August 2, 1902.

61 Greve to Wolfskehl, August 13, 1902.

62 The correspondence between S. Fischer, D'Annunzio, Vollmoeller and Insel, part of which is privately owned, is included in an appendix to Vignazia's book. The earliest letter from D'Annunzio to Vollmoeller it offers is dated November 19, 1902; it is friendly enough to suggest great familiarity and trust. An earlier friendship between D'Annunzio and Vollmoeller, who married the dancer Maria Carmi in Florence in 1902, cannot be ruled out (Vignazia, D'Annunzio 25, 298).

63 "Ich möchte Sie fragen, wann ich wohl an Herrn George Manuscr. schicken muss, wenn ich Aussicht haben will, dass das eine oder andere Verslein von mir in die Bl[ätter für die Kunst]. kommt. Mir würde sehr daran liegen. Aber ich habe den Kopf so voll, dass ich es so lange als möglich hinausschiebe." Greve to Wolfskehl, August 18, 1902. Cf. Spettigue 1992. Felix had the upcoming sixth volume of Blätter in mind. It appeared in book form in May 1903.

64 Greve to Wolfskehl, August 8 and 18, 1902.

65 A copy of Hofmannsthal's Der Tod des Tizian sold for 1 mark in 1903; a limited first edition of his Kleines Welttheater oder die Glücklichen, printed in two colours and bound in vellum cost eight marks. His "dramatic play" Der Kaiser und die Hexe in a "limited luxury edition on Dutch van Geldern paper with rich multi-coloured title page illustrations, initials and end-paper by Heinrich Vogeler, Worpswede" cost 30 marks (Insel Verlag, Neues vollständiges Verzeichnis, 1903, 18).

66 The review of Greve's Wanderungen by Otto Julius Bierbaum exemplifies the importance of appearance over the substance of the text: "Yet the book was printed by van Holten on von Geldern's hand-made paper and in such a limited number of copies that its exclusivity will conquer all doubts" (Bierbaum, "Wanderungen" 196).

67 Grove had his Phil Branden comment on the same situation: "My criticism probed into the lives and careers of all the young men I had known over yonder…Those who apparently had been the most independent, had been so because they had inherited money" (SFA 28).

68 Greve to Bruns, September 20, 1902.

69 "Ich werde diesen Winter die Welt in Erstaunen setzen, hoffe aber noch nach Darmstadt kommen zu können."

70 "Lieber Herr Doctor!

Ich vergass ganz, Ihnen für diesen Winter noch mehr Ereignisse in Aussicht zu stellen; seit einigen Tagen belagert mich noch ein halbes Dutzend Theater wegen Wilde Ich möchte wissen, wer sie auf meine Spur gehetzt hat. Alle reden von mir als dem 'bekannten' Übersetzer, und dem 'genauesten Kenner' (wörtlich aus Berlin!) des Dichters. *Io non capisco. Lei?*" Greve to Wolfskehl, undated.

71 In Greve's first novel, Fanny (Else) asks her husband Barrel (Endell) in the autumn of 1902: "When is your drama going to finally appear?" He answers, "In January...And for that I have only Mr. Reelen [i.e., Greve] to thank" (FE 489).

72 Greve to Bruns, August 19, 1902.

73 "Die Theater wollen jedes ein anderes Stück aufführen und wollen von mir Übersetzungen...woher soll ich sie nehmen?" Leider scheinen die Leute "so unglaublich unvernünftig," daß sie "meinen, ich könne ein vieracktiges Drama in einem Nachmittag übersetzen."

74 Greve to Wolfskehl, August 23, 1902. Friederich Gundolf's *Habilitationsschrift*: *Shakespeare und der deutsche Geist* was dedicated to his friend Arthur Salz (b. 1881) who had also completed his *Habilitation* at Heidelberg and who had inspired him to further scholarly work. "At the beginning of 1902, Salz went...to Wolfskehl's." Besides George, whom he adored, there were "many other interesting people" (Helbing, et al., *Stefan George* 216–17). It may be assumed that Greve was among these others.

75 Greve to Bruns, August 19, 1902.

76 On the inner title page we find the following: "Of this book, apart from the regular edition, 20 copies on Dutch hand-made paper (Van Geldern Zonen) have been prepared which may be purchased at the price of twelve marks from the translator only: Felix Paul Greve, Munich, 15 Giselastrasse."

77 Greve to Bruns, August 24, 1902.

78 Greve to Bruns, August 23, 1902.

79 Greve to Bruns, September 15, 1902.

80 "Von den beiden Komödien gefiel mir nur der 'Ideale Ehemann' in manchen Teilen (in manchen nicht)—'Bunbury' ist für die Galerie gemacht...Welch leere Mache in seinen Dramen—und gerade da im 'idealen Ehemann,' wo Töne des Herzens herausklingen sollten, versagt er fatal!...Wilde wird wohl nicht anders gesprochen haben als sein Gilbert. Aber welch ein Unterschied freilich, ob man das liest, ob in bewegter Art gesprochen hört!" Max Bruns, "My Reading" (October 1902), 39.

81 "Kuno Zwymann" was the pseudonym of Heinrich Goesch and Hermann Kantorowicz. On August 19, 1902, George himself noticed "the aberration of an extreme form of scholarship" in the book (Seekamp et al., *George* 128). Given that Greve wrote jokingly in the same letter of a "two-man book," he must have

known that it was written under a pseudonym: "For when one reads it, two have to hold on to him." Greve to Karl Wolfskehl, September 14, 1902.

82 "Aber ich muß offen gestehen, daß mir in Klages' Schrift über Sie an unendlich wichtigen Stellen der Ausdruck, also die Kraft das Innerlichgeschaute zu verleiblichen, peinlich zurückzubleiben schien. Es fanden sich da Metaphern, die ich zu vergessen trachte. Fast möchte ich so weit gehen, eine fast monomanisch starre Methode, die ein Herr Zwymann auf Ihr Werk anwendet, anständiger und nützlicher zu finden."

83 Greve to Wolfskehl, September 14, 1902. Greve to von Poellnitz, September 19, 1902.

84 "Vielleicht erwartet man an dieser Stelle eine Rechtfertigung dieser deutschen Neuausgabe des Wildeschen Hauptwerkes. Ich habe sie in meiner Besprechung der Gaulkeschen Übersetzung in der Beilage zur Allgemeinen Zeitung, München, Juli 1902, gegeben. Hier sei nur wiederholt, dass bei Herrn Gaulke die Vorrede und sechs Kapitel ganz, im einzelnen viele Stellen fehlen, und dass sein Text von absoluter Unkenntnis des Englischen und geringer Beherrschung des Deutschen zeugt."

85 "Etwas eingehender muß ich mich mit dem Uebersetzer Felix Paul Greve beschäftigen. Die Erbitterung hat ihm die Feder in die Hand gedrückt, der gerechte Zorn über Herrn Johannes Gaulke, der mit seiner Verschimpfierung des 'Dorian Gray' einen Rekord in der Unkenntnis des Englischen und der Misshandlung des Deutschen aufgestellt hat. Also entschloss sich Greve zu einer neuen, pietätvolleren Uebertragung des Romans 'Das Bildnis des Dorian Gray'. Wäre lediglich der deutsche Stil für die Beurteilung eines Uebersetzers maßgebend—dieser Ansicht huldigen leider viele mit dem Wort rasch fertige Kritiker, so brauchte man Greve nicht gerade zu tadeln…Fühlt man Greves englischen Kenntnissen auf den Zahn, so erlebt man teilweise eine sehr böse Enttäuschung."

86 "Wenn Herrn Gaulkes Übersetzung günstig rezensiert worden ist, so kann es nur daran liegen, dass die sehr seltenen und kostbaren Originalausgaben in Deutschland so gut wie unbekannt sind (außer den Intentions). Vor Herrn G. hatte ich schon, längst ehe ich daran dachte, Wilde zu übertragen, gewarnt…Das schlimmste aber ist, dass bei Herrn G. Dinge stehen, die bei Wilde *nicht* stehen. Z.B. Bemerkungen, die sich in der Richtung auf Betonung des Homosexuellen bewegen, wofür ich leicht Beispiele anführen könnte…Herrn Gaulkes Dorian Gray-Übertragung, die ausdrücklich für den Homosexuellen Verlag zugeschnitten zu sein scheint, war für mich der erste Anlass, selbst zu übersetzen." Greve to Bruns, October 6, 1902.

87 Greve to Bruns, November 25 and December 12, 1902. Von Poellnitz was not informed of the circumstances around the Wilde dramas by Greve but by Langen. Greve to Insel Publishers, December 3, 1902.

88 "Ihr gefl. Schreiben vom 9. de[s]. M[onats]. über die Dramenfrage erfüllt mich erklärlicherweise mit tiefem Bedauern, denn ein großes Stück Arbeit ist vergeblich gewesen. Ich vermisse in ihrem Schreiben aber jedwede Anhabe oder Andeutung, in welcher Weise nun die Angelegenheit zwischen uns geordnet

werden soll, denn ich habe in das Unternehmen doch sowohl
Honorarzahlungen als auch die nicht unerheblichen Druckkosten gesteckt, und
mit Ihrer einfachen Mittheilung, daß die 'Deutsche Bühne' nun abschlägig
geantwort habe, kann es doch nicht einfach gut sein." Stiller to Greve,
December 12, 1902.

89 "I have now a library of nearly nine hundred volumes, over seven hundred of
which I wrote myself." Henry David Thoreau, *Journals* (October 28, 1853).

90 "Am Freitag oder Samstag kommender Woche findet Nachmittags 3 Uhr im
Kleinen Theater (Unter den Linden 44) die Premiere von Oscar Wildes
Einakter: Salome und der Komödie Bunbury vor geladenem Publikum statt.

"Wollen Sie und Herr George mir das Vergnügen machen, dazu zu
erscheinen? Da ich die Liste meiner Gäste der Polizei einzureichen habe
(wegen des Zensurverbots), so bitte ich um freundliche Antwort. Den genauen
Tag der Premiere werde ich an einem der ersten Tage der Woche mittheilen."
Greve to Lechter, November 6, 1902.

91 "Im 'Kleinen Theater,' das augenblicklich von allen Berliner Bühnen die
größten litterarischen Ambitionen ins Treffen führt, wurden…zwei Stücke des
englischen Dichters vor gesichtetem Publikum, sozusagen hinter verschlossenen
Thüren, gespielt: die geniale 'Salome,' ein Akt von unerhörter Verdichtung, und
die tiefsinnig-blödsinnige Komödie 'The Importance of being Earnest,' der ich
ruhig ihren behäbig-stelzenhaften Titel: 'Wie wichtig ist es, Ernst zu sein,'
gelassen hätte (der Uebersetzer drückte sich ein wenig daran vorbei, indem er
'Bunbury,' den Namen des unsichtbaren Helden und Strohmanns der Helden,
supponierte).

"So lächerlich es klingen mag: an diesem Nachmittag wurde Oscar Wilde in
der Hauptstadt des deutschen Reiches entdeckt."

5 ◆ OFF TO AFRICA AND INTO THE DESERT

1 Lieber Herr Doktor!
Ich bin im Begriff, Ihnen einige Worte zu schreiben, *nach deren Gründen ich
Sie herzlichst bitte, nicht zu fragen.* Sie werden mich in München nicht mehr
vorfinden. Ich gehe fort. Wohin, weiss ich noch nicht. Vielleicht zunächst nach
Berlin, bis ich alles vorbereitet habe, um Europa zu verlassen.

Nun möchte ich Ihnen und Ihrer Frau Gemahlin gern so recht viel
Herzliches sagen. Was man mündlich nicht zu sagen brauchte–denn dann
genügte ein Händedruck. Nur so viel: das letzte Jahr war das glücklichste meines
Lebens. Und vieles, sehr vieles davon verdanke ich Ihnen. Lassen Sie mich alles
mit dem einen Worte sagen: Ich danke Ihnen und Ihrer Frau Gemahlin. Dass
dieses Jahr zugleich das Jahr meiner grössten Hoffnung war, und dass diese
Hoffnung nun zerbrochen ist, daran werde ich vielleicht zu Grunde gehen. Ich
bitte Sie nochmals, nicht weiter zu fragen. Ich will Ihnen statt alles anderen ein
paar schlechte Verse hersetzen.

Das Leben ist die bitterste Satire
Auf allen Bühnen buntgeflickten Staat:
Man heizt den Ofen, dass man nicht mehr friere,
Mit seiner Brust ins Kraut geschossen Saat.
Ich verkaufe meine Sachen. So wie ich damit fertig bin, reise ich ab." Greve
to Karl Wolfskehl, October 7, 1902.

2 "Nun habe ich noch eine grosse, etwas seltsame Bitte. Mir wurde dieser Tage
eine Kollektion sehr seltener englischer Dekadenzwerke zu relativ geringerem
Preise angeboten. Da ich aber mein kleines Vermögen, das mir meine
Unabhängigkeit sichern soll, nicht angreifen darf, wollte ich Sie fragen, ob es
Ihnen im Fall der Annahme des Marius möglich wäre, mich durch einen
Vorschuss auf die drei Bände, die dann in ihren Händen sind, in Höhe von ca
800 M. zu dieser Erwerbung, die für meine Studien sehr wichtig ist, in Stand zu
setzen. Ich würde Sie in dem Fall bitten, mir umgehend zu antworten, da ich
das Recht an die [sic] Sachen nur bis Sonntag früh reserviert habe. Sonst gehen
sie in andere Hände." Greve to von Poellnitz, October 9, 1902. See also Letters
520–21.

3 "Ich schreibe Ihnen schon heute aus fremder Wohnung. Bei mir sind alle Zelte
abgebrochen. Am Sonntag fahre ich nach Berlin, um meine letzten Sachen zu
ordnen. In Kurzem gehe ich in Hamburg an Bord eines Deutsch-
Ostafrikadampfers. Ich habe Billet für eine halbjährige Fahrt um Afrika. So kann
ich bleiben, wo es mir zusagt…Ich bin in einem Zustande, dass ich jeden
Augenblick definitiv zusammenzubrechen fürchte. Ich werde an Ihr Haus in
München stets als an eines der ganz wenigen denken, in denen ich Stunden
vollkommener Ruhe, freien Glücks und heiteren Geniessens verlebte. Einen
weniger komplizierten Menschen würde vielleicht Ihr Haus trotz allem in
München zu halten vermögen. Meine Wanderjahre sind noch nicht vorüber
und ich muss wieder fort. Glauben Sie mir, dass es mir vorkommt, als schnitte
man mir meine Wurzeln ab. München war seit langer, langer Zeit der erste Ort,
in dem ich es ein Jahr lang aushielt. Ich fühle mich ein wenig damit
verwachsen, und jetzt liegt eine grosse Leere vor mir. Wenn ich körperlich
arbeiten müsste, so wäre das vielleicht gut." Greve to Karl Wolfskehl, October 10,
1902.

4 Spettigue observed that the title to Greve's novel may refer to Franziska zu
Reventlow's self-designated nickname "Fanny" or to the well-known nineteenth-
century Viennese dancer Fanny Elssler (1810–74). See *FPG* 237.

5 The page numbers in FE refer to the first German edition on which our translation of excerpts is based.

6 Greve to von Poellnitz, October 19, 1902.

7 Endell also designed some of the furniture in the sanatorium, including
wardrobes, tables and chairs—all modestly ornamented but expensively
produced (*August Endell*: Exhibition numbers 4, 5, 7, 8, 9).

8 Von Poellnitz to Greve, November 4, 1902.

9 Greve to von Poellnitz, November 8, 1902.

10 "Als wir uns zum ersten Mal in Leipzig persönlich sahen, erklärte ich Ihnen, dass ich Ihren Vorschlägen sehr sympathisch gegenüber stehe, dass ich jedoch zur Zeit nicht in der Lage sei, mich mit den Manuskripten zu befassen. Dowson und Wilde wollte ich im Frühjahr bringen, Pater später. Sie sagten mir, dass Sie durchaus keine Eile hätten, und verlangten einige Wochen später auf eben diese Ms. einen Vorschuss von mir. Ungefähr gleichzeitig mit Ihren Briefen schrieben resp. sagten mir einige Münchner und Berliner Bekannte Wunderdinge über ein unglaublich opulentes Diner, zu dem Sie eingeladen haben sollten. Es wurde ferner hinzugefügt, dass der Insel-Verlag eine grosse Anzahl Ihrer Bücher bringen würde. Alle diese Notizen sollten von Ihnen persönlich stammen und wenn ich Ihnen auch die nötigen Uebertreibungen abzog, so bleibt schliesslich ein Rest übrig, der mir nicht besonders behaglich war." Von Poellnitz to Greve, November 12, 1902.

11 Greve to von Poellnitz, November 19, 1902 (first reproduced in Letters 523–24).

12 Roderich to Ricarda Huch from Berlin, November 28, 1901. Huch continued that he could "no longer feel as content and secure as I used to in Munich and I always feel that some day they will say 'Now we've pampered you enough.' For it is only my youth that they love. And for that reason I would like to leave and if I am able occasionally to come to you, apart from the few unerotic friends I will always have, then that will be enough for me…You wouldn't be able to believe how much I am looking forward to being able to behave in an unerotic way; it's as if I had been fed sweet rich liquors and cakes for years and now they make me nauseous."

13 Two letters from Greve to Stefan George, both from Berlin, December 8, 1902. Greve excused himself, citing his "poor state of health" which he had attempted to improve with "an excursion."

14 "Aber ich soll auch über andere Bekannte von mir, deren Namen zu erwähnen mir nie beifiel, die tollsten Gerüchte ausgestreut haben, und, wie mir mein Freund August Endell erzählt, gehen auch über mich die unmöglichsten Gerüchte um. Man behauptet, mich allabendlich in einem verrufenen Hôtel zu sehen, wo ich dem 'jeu' obliege u.d.m. Ich erzähle Ihnen das alles, um Ihnen die von Ihnen vernommenen Gerüchte begreiflicher erscheinen zu lassen." Greve to von Poellnitz, October 19, 1902 (see the complete text in Letters 523–24).

15 "…war ein hochgewachsener, dünner Mensch mit grüblerisch-schlenkerndem Gang und leicht gebeugter Haltung…Auf dem Kopf trug er einen großen Schlapphut. [Sie sah] hinter einer goldgefaßten Brille auffallend große, runde, dunkle Augen, und unter dem breiten Hutrand ziemlich langes, aschblondes Haar. [Sie sah] in seinem Kopf eine sonderbare Ähnlichkeit mit einem Vogelkopf; vielleicht lag es an der Blässe seines Gesichtes." Greve called the thin and bird-like Endell "Barrel" in the novel, ironically alluding to the English word "barrel."

16 "Nur eine neue Erscheinung bemerkte sie, einen auffallend großen und schlanken, auffallend blonden, auffallend eleganten jungen Mann von etwa dreißig Jahren [W]enn er…angesprochen wurde, so antwortete er mit einer so

verbindlichen Höflichkeit, das [sic] jedermann in diesem Kreise in Verlegenheit geriet. Auch schien es, als wagten nur wenige mit ihm zu reden: seine äußerliche Akkuratesse in Anzug und Formen schien alle abzuschrecken. Dabei blickte er, einerlei ob er schwieg oder liebenswürdig lächelte, stets mit denselben, beinahe blöden, hellblauen Augen ins Leere. Sein Mund war unter einem nach englischer Art herabhängenden rotblonden Schnurrbart verborgen. Seine große Nase lief ohne Einsenkung in die schräge Stirn hinüber und war leicht nach außen geschwungen, ohne Stumpfnase zu sein. Sein sorgfältig gescheiteltes Haar, die zwei mittelstarken Brauen waren so lichtblond, daß sein ganzer Kopf durch die Helle ausdruckslos erschien. Dabei überragte er selbst Eduard um Kopfeslänge."

17 Greve to J.C.C. Bruns, December 9, 1902.

18 Else Endell to Marcus Behmer, postcard, December 27, 1902.

19 This is reminiscent of Greve's stay in Dresden during his friendship with Kilian, which was apparently necessitated by health problems. Like Kilian's grandfather, one of Gmelin's forefathers, Johann Georg Gmelin, had connections to Russia and Siberia (*Reichshandbuch* 554–55).

20 See the fictional treatment of such symptoms of ill-health and their treatment in T. Coraghessan Boyle's novel *The Road to Wellville* 341–42.

21 Endell to Kurt Breysig, dated "End of Jan. 1903" by someone else, perhaps Breysig.

22 "Ich hatte jedes Zutrauen verloren. In München wäre das unmöglich gewesen, dort hätte ich stets Hilfe gehabt, und es wäre nicht so weit gekommen. In Berlin hatte ich niemand als diesen Halbverrückten, der mich verriet und mich noch tiefer in die Verzweiflung jagte, indem er mit seiner Kraft und seiner Leistungsfähigkeit prahlte, indem er durch tausend Kniffe mich immer mehr meine Schwäche [und] meine Unfähigkeit fühlen ließ, alles unter dem Deckmantel des Helfenwollens – bis ich schließlich mir als das elendeste [und] wertloseste Geschöpf vorkam und alles mit mir machen ließ, ohne Wissen und ohne zu wehren. Ich *war* dem Wahnsinn nahe. Und mit der Zeit immer meine Erregungen. Der Mann ein gemeiner Schwindler, die Frau, die ich mehr liebte, als irgend etwas – und sie war doch mehr als du denkst – im Elend. Ich ohne Kraft und Hoffnung, ohne Möglichkeit etwas zu tun. Die Situation *ist* ernst, sehr ernst." Endell to Kurt Breysig, July 6, 1903.

23 From a two-page advertising brochure dated "Berlin, August 1904." Another advertising brochure from "September 1906" contained a breakdown of the course of study and stated: "The goal is to provide students with the ability to make designs for studios and factories specializing in the production of artistic products." The subsequent development by Endell, who would become prominent in the "Werkbund/Studio Alliance," is evident here.

24 "Das Kopieren fremder Arbeiten alter und neuer Zeit ist grundsätzlich ausgeschlossen: Freies Erfinden in Farbe und Form ist das Ziel." *Die Zukunft* no. 1 (October 7, 1905) [Verso]. The address provided, 43 Fasanenstrasse, was across the street from 42 Fasanenstrasse, which was Greve and Else's address at

the end of 1905 and for part of 1906. Endell and the Greves apparently made no attempt to avoid each other.

25 "Ich nehme [Greve] dann mit mir in die Stadt, um mir den Fall Endell aufklären zu lassen, werde aber nicht klug daraus. Schwer gravierendes für ihn kann ich nicht finden, aber ebensowenig für Endell. Die Erpressungsgeschichte klärt sich so, daß Endell ihm circa 3000 M. schuldig war, ihm zunächst 1500 zurück gab, um die Trauung in England zu ermöglichen, die Endell im Inland dadurch unmöglich gemacht haben soll, dass er den Ehebruch seiner Frau aus Rache als Scheidungsgrund benützt habe. Greve soll deshalb eine Revision des Prozesses angedroht haben, um beiderseitige Schuld der Gatten zu erzielen, damit das Ehehindernis wegfällt, das betrachte die Gegenseite als Erpressung. Klar ist die Sache jedenfalls nicht. Endell sagte mir vor zwei Jahren in München, gerade er habe vermeiden wollen, den Ehebruch als Scheidungsgrund zu nehmen, aber sei damit an Manövern der Gegenpartei gescheitert. Endell muss jedenfalls sehr neurasthenisch gewesen sein, soll Greve weinend und drohend überall hin bis nach Neapel verfolgt haben, weil er nicht allein sein konnte usw." Oscar A.H. Schmitz, diary (November 25, 1906), 395–96. Deutsches Literaturarchiv, Marbach.

26 Greve stayed with Wells at Sandgate twice: on June 23, 1904 and with Else from July 17–20, 1906. On June 28, 1908, Greve wrote to Wells from Berlin that "Mrs Greve would accompany him on a short trip along the English Dutch border."

27 Greve to Oscar A.H. Schmitz, December 14, 1906.

28 Greve to J.C.C. Bruns, January 28, 1903.

29 " Herr Reelen…ja, der war Sportsmann, das sah man ihm an. Er ritt und focht und schwamm und spielte Tennis. Der war kein Künstler!…Wie sie die Künstler verachtete. Die Halbmänner, die sich für die Krone der Schöpfung hielten!…Die Götter der Träume: Götter im Traum, weil sie untüchtig sind für das wirkliche Leben!"

30 Greve to J.C.C. Bruns, January 28, 1903.

31 Telegram and letter, Hôtel de l'Europe, front desk to J.C.C. Bruns, January 29 and February 3, 1903. See Else von Freytag-Loringhoven: "In Naples we went to a swell hotel" (BE 88).

32 "Berta Franzos" to J.C.C. Bruns, February 5, 1903. In 1920, "Franzos" would become the German translator of Lafcadio Hearn. "Berta Franzos" is a pseudonym of Franz Blei (see Chapter Six). I am grateful to Raimund Theis on this point.

33 Greve to J.C.C. Bruns, March 6, 1903.

34 Thomas Grah in the *Bonner Zeitung*, May 31, 1903. Compare this account with an unsigned report in the Bonn newspaper *Deutsche Reichs-Zeitung* of May 30, 1903, which Spettigue (*FPG* 95–96) used as the basis for his discussion of the affair. This depiction is less reliable, shorter and more sensational than Grah's.

35 Richard Cavell has little doubt about Greve's homosexual orientation and makes an interesting case for it against the background of the social and political climate in Berlin. Cavell, "Felix Paul Greve."

36 Greve to von Poellnitz, telegram dated March 25, 1903.

37 Greve to von Poellnitz, May 6 and 12, 1903. The catalogue of Insel publications until the end of 1903 includes a text based on Greve's keywords. Obviously it avoids personal reference to the imprisoned Insel translator, then working under a pseudonym. "Dowson was a member of the Wilde circle. In England his books are out of print and difficult to obtain. // As a writer, his distinctive personal style was lightly influenced by Verlaine. The limited number of his works—he died young of consumption—are diaphanous and delicate, startling when dealing with large issues. A marked tendency to describe the endings of lives is apparent in his novellas. His psychology is of the subtlest kind and finds its most concentrated expression in his style, which is fascinatingly limpid and clear" (*Neues vollständiges Verzeichnis* 10).

38 The two first volumes cost three marks in sewn binding and fours marks 50 bound in leather. Five hundred copies of each were published with titles and illustrations by Walter Tiemann on thick, feather-light, hand-made English paper in two-colour print. The *Paracelsus* translation cost four and five marks depending on the binding. All three were announced in Insel's *Verzeichnis* as translated by "C.F. Gerden." The copies which I have examined indicate the correct translator's pseudonym—"F.C. Gerden"—and contain a dedication "To Mr. J.C.C. Bruns [sic] from the translator."

39 "Wie Sie wissen, habe ich nicht nur für mich allein zu sorgen, und infolgedessen stehen jetzt die pekuniären Fragen bei mir im Vordergrunde des Interesses. Ich wäre ohne weiteres bereit, jede Arbeit, die ich leisten kann, zu übernehmen, um dadurch Geld zu verdienen, selbst, wenn sie mir nicht so nahe liegen sollte, wie die Dinge, die ich bisher getrieben habe. Ich beherrsche außer dem Deutschen drei Sprachen vollständig: Englisch, Französisch und Italienisch.…Daß die gelieferte Arbeit an Sorgfalt und Genauigkeit nichts zu wünschen lassen würde, brauche ich nicht erst zu versichern. Auch aus den alten Sprachen würde ich als studierter Altphilologe natürlich mit Vergnügen übersetzen." Greve to von Poellnitz, May 12, 1903 (see *Letters*, 525–26). Most of Greve's letters to von Poellnitz and Kippenberg, the Insel managers, may be checked against Pacey's edition of Grove's letters. No additional German originals of these are included here.

40 Greve to von Poellnitz, May 14, 1903.

41 "Der Angeklagte habe nicht glauben können, daß er in absehbarer Zeit das Geld werde erstatten können. Er habe das Geld in leichtsinniger Weise mit einer Frauensperson in Palermo durchgebracht. Daß er dorthin gegangen sei, um ehrlich zu arbeiten, sei nicht nachgewiesen. In schmählicher Weise habe er das Vertrauen seines freigebigen Freundes mißbraucht. Als mildernd sei einzunehmen, daß er mehr aus Leichtsinn als aus verbrecherischer Absicht gehandelt habe."

42 See the entry above in Oscar A.H. Schmitz's diary (November 25, 1906), 395–96 and BE 86.

43 "Eine erschütternde Lektüre! Welch grauenhaftes Land ist diese Heimat der Puritaner! Das Land der Nüchterlinge und Spekulanten. Entsetzlich hat der arme Wilde leiden müssen – ein deutscher Kritiker, so las ich kürzlich, gönnte

es ihm, daß er gründlich geduckt ist, weil er so arrogant war, als sei er wunder was besonderes…Wilde's Mängel sind zum Teil die Korrelate seiner Vorzüge, seines glänzenden Stils und seines gewandten Intellekts; diese Mängel – oder sage ich: sein Mangel ist vor allem eine flüchtige Rhetorik an den Stellen seiner Werke, wo herztiefe Leidenschaft hervorbrechen sollte." Max Bruns "My Reading," (May 1903) 28, 154.

44 Greve to von Poellnitz, June 20, 1903.

45 Freytag-Loringhoven recalls somewhat tersely that Felix "made contracts with his editor—bought himself the right to do his own work in jail—bribed the keepers cleverly—and came out after a year a man well started in his career with a highly promising future" (BE 108).

46 Greve to Wells, October 6, 1905. Spettigue assumed that Greve completed the translation (FPG 129).

47 Peuker's signature is on a contract for a translation of a novel by Amelia E. Barr for J.C.C. Bruns. I have compared it with Greve's and am confident that Greve and Peuker were not the same person.

48 Greve to von Poellnitz, August 15, 1903.

49 Greve to von Poellnitz, August 3, 1903.

50 Greve may have seen parallels between Wilde's time at Berneval following his discharge and his own situation. Wilde received Dowson (who was also translated by Greve) at the seaside resort, and he developed a fruitful correspondence with Gide in Paris. It was a continuation of their contact from 1895 in Algiers. Gide later visited Wilde in the Hôtel de la Plage (Ellmann, *Wilde* 507–09).

51 Vollmoeller to Hardt, November 1, 1904. See also Chapter Three.

52 Poem by Frederick Philip Grove from c. 1930. Manuscript, Grove Collection, University of Manitoba Libraries. See Divay 1993: 52.

53 See the announcement made on the endpaper of Greve's *Maurermeister Ihles Haus*.

6 ◆ FELIX PAUL GREVE, LITTERATUS

1 "Er hat mir nie verziehen, dass ich, wie übrigens die meisten seiner Jünger, eines Tages 'vom Tempel auf die Gasse gegangen bin,' will sagen für Zeitschriften und Zeitungen ohne sakrale Weihe schrieb und mich mit vielerlei profanen Dingen befasste."

2 Greve to J.C.C. Bruns, July 25, 1903.

3 "Ich übersetze neben der Arbeit an Browning [für den Insel Verlag] einige Werke des noch lebenden Engländers *H.G. Wells*, von dem ich mir gerade buchhändlerischen Erfolg verspreche. Vielleicht sind Sie geneigt, gelegentlich ein MS. zu lesen. Wegen der Autorisation trete ich mit dem Autor selbst in Unterhandlung. Doch müsste man mehrere Bände bringen, etwa drei, da sie unter sich zusammenhängen.

Ferner möchte ich eine Reihe der bedeutendsten englischen Romane des letzten Vierteljahrhunderts herausgeben. Auch von dieser Serie könnte ich

Ihnen das erste Werk: *George Meredith, The Ordeal of Richard Feverel* im Laufe des nächsten Monats vorlegen." Greve to Bruns, August 17, 1903.

4   *Festschrift J.C.C. Bruns* 1914, 79–80. We do not know if FPG had already translated this book, but he seems to have attached some importance to it since Grove mentions it again in 1940 (see Letters xx).

5   "Zu dieser kleinen Schrift, die Wilde in Deutschland einzuführen dienen soll, hatte der geschmackvolle [*crossed out:* Herr] Verfasser zunächst den Titel 'A propos d'Oscar Wilde' sich erkiest. Ich konnte verhindern, daß dieser Widersinn nicht durchging. Die Schrift selbst? Geschwafel. Lange Rede mit kurzem Sinn. Der Stil kaum genießbar. Affektationen eines völlig affektlosen Menschen. Die Schrift verdiente eine Abfertigung von Seiten der Kritik (die sie aber vielleicht ignoriert?). Max Bruns, "My Reading," November 1903, 212.

6   "Nun möchte ich Sie ferner um Gehör für eine Auseinandersetzung über weitere Publikationen bitten. Ihnen liegt je ein Band Browning & Meredith im Manuskript vor. Für beide thue ich schon jetzt mein Möglichstes. Für Browning ist ein lebhaftes Interesse vorhanden: Ellen Key hat bei Fischer ein Buch über ihn und seine Frau erscheinen lassen. Ich werde vermutlich Studien über ihn publizieren. Einige Kleinigkeiten, die ich in meinen grösseren Bänden nicht unterbringen konnte, erscheinen im Insel Verlage (ich werde Ihnen nächstens Exemplare überreichen). Seine Korrespondenz gebe ich bei Fischer heraus. Auch von Meredith ist seit fünf Jahren in Deutschland fortwährend die Rede. Man weiss, er gilt in England als Prosa-Shakespeare. Man redet überall von Ihm mit geheimnisvoller Ehrfurcht: und niemand kennt ihn…Von Meredith wird man zwar nicht alles deutsch bringen brauchen (obgleich die Originale wegen ihrer immensen Sprachschwierigkeiten, über die Wilde ja in den Intentions spricht, in Deutschland kaum als Konkurrenz in Frage kommen. Dasselbe ist bei Browning der Fall), aber doch noch zwei bis drei Bände, von denen schon einer bei mir vorliegt." Greve to J.C.C. Bruns, November 9, 1903.

7   Surprisingly, translation is not an issue in any of the available accounts of Wells's life or the collections of his letters. Recent interest in Wells (and FPG) and a flurry of new publications have not yielded a single reference to his pioneering German translator.

8   This sentence, underlined in pencil, is probably by Bruns.

9   "Aber da komme ich zu meinem Punkt. Ich werde im nächsten Sommer, etwa im Juni[,] grössere Summen nötig haben, und dafür muss ich jetzt sorgen. Im Fall einer Annahme auch des Verga z.B. wäre ich, falls bis zum Sommer nichts erschienen wäre, gezwungen, damit zu rechnen, dass Sie mir um die genannte Zeit vorstreckten (ich werde einige tausend Mark—sagen wir 3000 nötig haben. Natürlich würde sich dieser Vorschuß <u>unter</u> dem für die Bücher in Aussicht stehenden Betrage halten müssen, da ich nicht wünsche, wie Sie sich denken können, von neuem in die unangenehme Lage eines Minus auf meinem Konto zu kommen. Ich sage Ihnen das alles im Voraus, damit Sie absolut klar sehen: auch den Grund will ich Ihnen mitteilen: ich habe die Absicht, mich zu verheiraten. Ich bitte Sie also, falls Ihnen meine Offerten nicht zu viel werden, oder falls Sie nicht geneigt, oder nicht in der Lage wären, mir eventuell in der

dargestellten Weise zu helfen (bis zum Sommer dagegen werde ich, abgesehen vielleicht von ein paar Kleinigkeiten, auch im Fall eines grösseren Plus auf meinem Konto, voraussichtlich nichts abheben brauchen)—mir das freundlichst schreiben zu wollen, da mir ja neuerdings eine Reihe anderer Verlage offen stehen. Ich hoffe, Sie werden meinen Brief nicht missverstehen und mir verzeihen, dass ich Ihnen mit meinen Privatangelegenheiten lästig falle. Es ist für mich eine Lebensfrage, mehr als je, mir meine Finanzen so einzurichten, dass ich eine genügend lange Zeit vorher mit festen Summen rechnen kann." Greve to J.C.C. Bruns, November 9, 1903.

10 It remains unclear which of Giovanni Verga's (1840–1922) novels Greve had offered to J.C.C. Bruns (and to Insel).

11 "Und bei dieser Gelegenheit möchten wir Ihnen die Bitte ans Herz legen, für gute Lesbarkeit der Manuskripte doch thunlichst Sorge tragen zu wollen: die Schrift Ihrer "Richard Feverel" Übersetzung ist so klein und schnörkelig, daß wir Ihnen vor Ablauf weiterer drei Wochen kaum unsere definitive Entscheidung mitteilen können. Abgesehen davon, daß die Lektüre also sowohl Sie wie uns viel Zeit kostet, fällt es auch für den Lesenden schwer, die Ermüdung, die ihn stets wieder beim Lesen befällt, nicht auf sein Urteil über das Gelesene einwirken zu lassen." Max Bruns to Greve, December 2, 1903. Only a a draft copy in Max's handwriting has survived. In his perpetual haste, it appears that Greve had already developed Grove's "infinitesimally small hand of the original versions of his novels, short stories, and poems (Saunders, "Grove Papers" 7–8).

12 Meredith's *Harry Richmond* was also published in two volumes. Printed on the flyleaf is a note that "Meredith's outstanding novels are to be published in a German edition. Prospectus available on request."

13 I wonder whether Else contributed to this translation as she would to the volume of Flaubert's correspondence.

14 "[E]ine wirkliche, genaue Übertragung des 'klippenreiches Originals' mit 'seiner verwegenen Diktion, seinen kühnen Neuschöpfungen, seinem Bilderüberfluss, seinen sprachlichen Vergewaltigungen' (Max Meyerfeld in der 'Zeit') [muß] von vornherein als Unmöglichkeit erscheinen…dazu bedürfte es eines Jean Paul als Übersetzers. Jede Übersetzung ist ein Kompromiss. Der Literaturbeflissene greift zum Original. Der Leser weiterer Kreise will eine Vermittlung zwischen sich und einem der Nationalität nach fremden Geist. – So hat also der Herausgeber, der früher glaubte, den Kompromiss, so sehr es in seinen Kräften stand, einschränken zu müssen, im vorliegenden Werke an einer Reihe besonders schwieriger oder dunkler Stellen die Paraphrasierung des Sinns an die Stelle wortgenauer Übertragung gesetzt. Immerhin hat er trotzdem versucht, sich möglichst selbst im sprachlichen Ausdruck in die Komplikationen des Originals hineinzuschmiegen. Inwieweit ihm dieser Kompromiss gelungen ist, darüber zu urteilen steht ihm nicht zu. Nur eine Forderung möchte er von vornherein als unberechtigt abweisen: die eines eleganten, leichtflüssigen Stils" (*Diana* ix, xiv–xv).

15 Bruns, "My Reading," March 1904, 306.

16 "Lieber Vater – ich habe nun bis auf einen kleinen Rest 'Moreaus Insel' gelesen. Es ist eine grandiose Parodie auf das Schöpfertum, das Menschentum, das Dasein…Wenn auch Wells ein nervöser Vielschreiber ist, so ist er doch Künstler genug in der traumhaften Art seines Schauens…wenngleich die feineren Geister weniger den manchmal etwas groben äußeren Apparat als vielmehr das 'geistige Band', das diesen Spuk durchwebt, aufsuchen werden. Und so scheint mir denn ein sehr, sehr großer Leserkreis bei Wells vollauf seine Rechnung finden zu können: Ich halte für sehr möglich, daß wir, wenn ein anderer Verleger die Wells'schen Bücher auf den Markt würfe, mit neidischem Bedauern von seinen Auflageziffern Kenntnis erhalten könnten. Es läßt sich mit solchen Büchern etwas machen; das ist mir gar keine Frage. Wells ist viel phantasiebegabter als Scheerbart…er ist ein vergroberter Poe mit allen Allüren eines flotten Erzählers (und für die Masse wird er *nichts* sein als das)." Max to Gustav Bruns, February 3, 1904 (handwritten draft).

17 Letter to Gustav Bruns, February 3, 1904.

18 Sydney Pawling (for W.H. Heinemann) to H.G. Wells, January 4, 1904.

19 Greve to H.G. Wells, June 23, 1904.

20 The original of this letter is in the archive of Zsolnay Publishers, Vienna.

21 Contracts ("Vereinbarungen") for *The Time Machine* and *The Island of Dr. Moreau* are dated February 24, 1904, at a time when Greve was still in prison. The next agreement for *The First Men in the Moon* and *The Food of the Gods* bears the date July 2, 1904. H.G. Wells's letters to Bruns are dated July 5, 1904 and March 3, 1905 (the latter extending Bruns's option until July 1, 1906). Copies of surviving correspondence and some helpful commentary were kindly provided by Ms. Alma Zsolnay and Ms. Olga Kaindl of Paul Zsolnay Publishers, Vienna.

22 Max Bruns to Piller (typewritten copy).

23 "Sache greve so nicht gangbar, die schenkung ist anfechtbar nach paragraph drei anfechtungsges[etz]. anfechtbar waere auch verkauf durch haende der braut an uns, weil uns absicht greves, auf diese weise das vermoegen seinen glaeubigern zu entziehen und sie zu benachteiligen nicht verborgen ist, umsomehr wenn zahlung an braut erfolgt. gangbar erscheint der weg, von greve direkt zu kaufen, greve muss dann aber dafuer sorgen, dass er ueber das geld moeglichst schnell verfuegt, damit ihm desselbe nicht bei zusammentreffen unguenstiger umstaende durch gerichtsvollzieher abgenommen wird. schenkung an braut nicht zulaessig. direkter kauf von greve durch uns moeglich, weil der vorliegende pfaendungsbescheid auf neue geschaefte keine wirkung hat" (Telegram. Stiller to Gustav Bruns, June 6, 1904).

24 Freytag-Loringhoven's rueful desciption of Felix's figure and hair (BE 110) and Gide's diary recollection of Greve's pallor from their meeting two days previously (GG 30, 221).

25 Greve to Gide, June 22, 1908; enclosed in a letter from Pacey to A. Leonard Grove, March 22, 1973. J.C. Mahanti later provided a translation. After Pacey's death in 1974, Mahanti apparently kept up his interest in the FPG-Gide relationship. He sent additional copies of Greve's letters to Gide to A. Leonard Grove on February 23, 1978 but did not publish them. Catherine Gide authorized Mahanti

to use letters he had received for a biography of FPG in 1988 (but not to publish them separately). The biography never appeared. In a long 1992 magazine article, Spettigue finally published an account containing English translations, paraphrases and summaries taken from parts of the correspondence. I was given to understand that Professor Spettigue later donated or sold what he had of the correspondence to the Manitoba Grove Archive. The correspondence which I have constitutes a larger portion of the extant letters than had been seen before by other Grove researchers. I was authorized to use and publish it by Gide's daughter, Catherine Gide, and by A. Leonard Grove, the son of Frederick Philip Grove. I also thank A. Leonard Grove for permission to use his correspondence with Pacey and Mahanti regarding Gide. All of these materials form the basis of my remarks here. Jutta Ernst and I edited and published this authorized edition of the correspondence in 1999.

26 "Non, dis-je enfin...l'action ne m'intéresse point tant par la sensation qu'elle me donne, que par ses suites, son retentissement. Voilà pourquoi, pour passionnément qu'elle m'intéresse, elle m'intéresse davantage encore commise par un autre. J'ai peur—comprenez-moi—j'ai peur de m'y compromettre; je veux dire de limiter, par ce que je fais, ce que je pourrais faire. Penser que, parce que j'ai fait *ceci*, je ne pourrai plus faire *cela*, voilà qui me devient intolérable. J'aime mieux *faire agir* que d'agir" (GG 224–25).

27 "Non, cette phrase ne m'a pas «échappé». Qu'on songe à qui je la disais, à celui que j'étais aux yeux de Grève, aux circonstances, etc. Ce serait à recommencer, je ne pourrais rien dire d'autre; tout au plus expliquerais-je un peu mieux? L'étonnant, c'est que Grève, en me répondant, ne faisait que réciter l'enseignement de mes *Nourritures*. En s'emparant de mon rôle, il me précipitait à droite. Somme toute, je me défilais.

«Si tant est que mon enseignement mène au crime, je préfère que le crime, ce soit vous qui le commettiez.» Voici ce que ma phrase voulait dire. Grève jouait devant moi le rôle d'ilote. Par amour-propre, je tâchais de sauver la face; mais je sentais son avantage, et qu'il avait raison de moi. J'étais vaincu par mon «disciple», et désavouais mon éthique si c'était là qu'elle devait mener. Le conflit de sentiments était ici trop complexe pour qu'on puisse tirer argument de ma phrase, me semble-t-il. Voir une affirmation, une profession de foi, la déclaration d'une éthique, dans cette battue en retraite est pour le moins hasardeux. Mais le critique reste libre de voir dans ma déclaration un «aveu involontaire» (*Journal* II, 338–39).

28 A côté d'eux, derrière un flacon d'alcool de menthe, une photographie ne l'inquiéta moins: sur une plage de sable, une femme, non plus très jeune, mais étrangement belle, penchée au bras d'un homme de type anglais très accusé, élégant et svelte, en costume de sport; à leurs pieds, assis sur une périssoire renversée, un robuste enfant d'une quinzaine d'années, aux épais cheveux clairs en désordre, l'air effronté, rieur, et complètement nu (Gide, *Romans* 1957, 715).

29 Ne sentez-vous pas que j'ai besoin qu'un mot de vous m'apprenne que ma dernière lettre vous a guéri de la si mauvaise opinion que vous preniez de moi? Faut-il insister encore, vous certifier que non seulement je ne cherche pas à me

détacher de vous, mais que, si vous vous écartiez à présent ou me forciez à prendre un ton peu amical avec vous, ce serait un des chagrins de ma vie (GG 168–69).

30 De toutes les figures que j'ai rencontrées, vous êtes une de celles qui m'a le plus intéressé (J'ai transcrit, une fois rentré à la campagne, tout au long, la conversation que nous avons eue à Paris)—mais quand je vous ai revu à Paris nous n'avons plus rien su nous dire. Vous m'intéressez autant que le premier jour et c'est là, si je puis ainsi dire, un intérêt du coeur autant que de la tête, mais, à moins que ce ne soit pour pénétrer un peu plus avant dans votre vie, je n'éprouve pas le besoin de vous revoir. Et pourtant, quand je retournerai à Berlin, il est certain que je vous tendrai la main avec plaisir—si je sais que vous me tendez la vôtre volontiers. Mais vous imaginez difficilement la difficulté que j'éprouve à *causes*; j'y deviens de mois au mois plus inhabile et cela devient une réelle fatigue pour moi (GG 170–72).

31 "Aber die Pose wurde ihm [Wilde] Wirklichkeit, und die Wirklichkeit verblasste danebem, und wo sie nicht blass war, da verwechselte er den Traum und die Dinge, und dafür rächte das Leben sich" (Greve, *Randarabesken* 36).

32 "Si je fais quelque chose, ce sera de la ... révolution." "J'ai fait bataille pour vous." For the full text of these and other extant letters between Gide and Greve, see GG 64–191.

33 Kassner's (1873–1959) translation of Gide's text was published in 1904. An Austrian, like Blei, he achieved prominence as the author of *Die Mystik, die Künstler und das Leben. Über englische Dichter und Maler des 19. Jahrhunderts*, an influential book about English poets and painters. In 1901 he published the first German-language essay on Gide (Bohnenkamp/Foucart 87).

34 "Jedenfalls wird verständlich, daß [Blei] glaubte, Gide vor Greve schützen zu müssen. Trotz aller Ressentiments und allem Kollegenneid erscheint dies umso berechtigter, wenn wir durch unveröffentlichte Dokumente aus Gides Archiv erfahren, daß Greve unter falscher, prahlerischer Darlegung seiner finanziellen Möglichkeiten Gide die Herausgabe aller seiner Werke in deutscher Übersetzung durch ihn, Greve, vertraglich angeboten hatte. Gide hatte Greves Vertragsentwurf bereits unterschrieben. Wir wissen nicht, warum die vertragliche Auslieferung des deutschen Gide an Greve nicht zustande kam." Theis apparently takes the insight into Greve's "wrong and boastful representation of his financial possibilities" from a letter to Gide in late 1908. However, the sums were quite correctly based on FPG's considerable translation earnings for the Insel edition of the *1001 Nights* and other works.

35 "Es ist bezeichnend für Gide, daß er nach Abwehr dieser Bedrohung aus dem Jahre 1903 nicht die Beziehung zu Greve abbrach, sondern im Gegenteil dessen auftrumpfende Duperie und rücksichtslose Amoralität amüsiert zu bewundern vermochte. Immerhin nötigte diese unverhoffte Großzügigkeit Gides Greve wenigstens einmal zu einer Infragestellung seiner Natur, als er nach der Entlassung aus dem Schuldengefängnis 1904 Gide zu einer Aussprache aufsuchte."

36 "Obgleich Blei von beidem, vom betrügerischen Verlagsangebot wie von der 'Conversation' nichts wußte, erfaßte er erstaunlich sicher Gides Bedrohung durch Greve, empfand sich aber selbst kopflos Greve ausgeliefert und unterschätzte wohl daher auch Gide, wobei er—trotz Nietzsche–Gides spielerisch wagende Vitalität verkannte."

37 "Vous m'intéressez autant que le premier jour et c'est là, si je puis ainsi dire, un intérêt du coeur autant que de la tête, mais, à moins que ce ne soit pour pénétrer un peu plus avant dans votre vie, je n'éprouve pas le besoin de vous revoir."

38 "...je reste vivement blessé." "Ça n'amoindrira pas l'intérêt, que je porte à vous et qui est tout à fait personnel."

39 Such a misreading may validate my point about critical resistance to Greve's life and biography, since recent Canadian and German research on Greve/Grove (or at least his oeuvre) had not been consulted.

40 "Ich möchte doch sehr dafür sorgen, dass Sie in Deutschland ein anständiges Haus bewohnen" (Theis, *Blei* 6).

41 "Poellnitz trouvait le livre trop 'pénible'." "Est-ce que vous seriez très malheureux de paraître chez M. Bruns, à côté de mon édition des oeuvres de Wilde?"

42 Only a few of Gide's original letters to Greve have survived.

43 "Herr Greve ist ein guter Übersetzer, das allein kommt für Sie in Betracht. Dass er ein schlechter Schriftsteller und ein lügenhafter Mensch ist, ist Ihnen gleichgültig. Da ich nun nicht in Ihren Gedanken der Übersetzer *neben* Herrn Greve sein will—weil auch das, was *ich* sonst bin, für Sie nicht in Betracht kommt zu kommen scheint—so möchte ich doch lieber nicht der Übersetzer sein..." (Theis, 76–77).

44 "Nicht wahr, lieber Herr Gide, wir wollen uns die Ruhe unserer guten Freundschaft durch nichts und niemanden stören lassen?" (Theis 82).

45 "De plus je sais fort bien que j'ai plus de chances d'être joué avec vous qu'avec Grève, qui n'a pas tous les amis que vous avez; je vais donc contre mes intérêts; mais je préfère cela que d'aller contre Grève et de revenir sur ma parole donnée."

46 I am grateful to Dr. Karl-Otto Tröger for expert information on these points.

47 He mentions this plan in a letter to O.A.H. Schmitz (May 28, 1904). He also indicates that he plans to write an essay to be entitled "George Meredith and the English Romantic Tradition."

48 "Nachher gedenke ich im Norden zur See zu reisen (vielleicht Island, Grönland etc. zu besuchen). Ev[entuell]. schicke ich Ihnen einmal aus irgend einer unmöglichen Gegend eine Karte....Haben Sie nicht Lust, sich in irgend ein gottverlassenes, ganz kleines Seebad zu setzen, wo man schwimmen und reiten und–kann? (denn für ein paar Damen liesse sich ja sorgen)." Greve to O.A.H. Schmitz, May 28, 1904.

49 "Et de moi-même: Il me faut travailler d'une façon bien singulière. Je ne suis plus *une* personne; j'en *sommes trois*: je suis 1) M. Felix Paul Greve; 2) Mme Else Greve; 3) Mme Fanny Essler. La dernière, dont je vous enverrai prochainement les poèmes, et dont les poèmes—encore un secret—sont addressés à moi, est un

poète déjà assez consideré dans certains parties de l'Allemagne. Jusqu'à présent elle n'a publié que de vers. Mais moi, F.P. Greve, son patron et introducteur, prépare la publication de deux romans, qu'elle a écrits dans la prison de Bonn sur Rhin (une prison que moi, F.P. Greve, j'ai pris l'habitude d'appeler 'la villa'). Tout cela, bien entendu, sous le sceau de la confession, s'il vous plaît. Personne ne se doute de cet état des choses. En outre la traduction de la *Correspondance* de Flaubert paraît avec le nom de Mme. Else Greve figurant sur la frontispice, mais malheureusement la seule langue que Mme. Greve connaisse, c'est l'italien, par conséquent moi, F.P. Greve, j'ai dû faire sa traduction pendant les nuits d'été" (GG 74–75). First discussed by Spettigue (1992).

50 "…I am glad to pass some months very calmly here 'au bain de mer,' where I have established my little 'ménage' in the French manner." Greve to H.G. Wells, July 8, 1905.

51 Greve to H.G. Wells, October 6, 1905. Felix and Else announced another visit for July 17, 1906 (Greve to Mrs. Wells, July 6, 1906).

52 "J'ai un nouveau roman sous presse et un troisieme [sic] *sous plume*. Le premier, Fanny Essler, a paru en 2me édition, le deuxieme [sic] a pour titre: "Maurermeister Ihles Haus" et paraîtra prochainement (c'est l'étude d'une sorte de Übermensch inconscient: le Maurermeister est quelquechose [sic] comme une bete [sic] fauve devenue bourgeois). Le troisième, c'est enfin mon *Sentimentalist*, l'histoire d'un jeune homme Berlinois—mais sans la moindre ressemblance à *L'Education* de Flaubert—l'intention, pour ainsi dire, de mon roman est d'un autre monde que celle du roman de Flaubert. En moyen temps il faut traduire et traduire: j'aurais besoin d'un auteur de succès (romans, s'il est possible; il ne faudrait pas du tout, qu'ils fussent *bons*: tout au contraire!)—est-ce-que vous en connaissez un?" (GG 16, 148–50).

53 "Welch erdrückender Reichtum! Welche Wunder von Schönheit, die den Deutschen hier zu erschließen sind! Mein Plan war: Eine deutsche Flaubert-Ausgabe zu schaffen. Nun sehe ich die Ankündigung zweier Verdeutschungen: Die 'Mad[ame]. Bovary' und die 'Salammbô.' Also der 'Antoine' nicht? Und die 'Contes' auch nicht? Ich will den Plan nicht fallen lassen; sobald meine Baudelaire-Auswahl hergestellt ist, will ich mit Fl[aubert]. beginnen. Auch für Huysmans und Mallarmé will ich dann noch etwas thun." Max Bruns, "My Reading" (1901).

54 "Sie sind 'ein großer Schatz und ich habe sehr den Wunsch, *sie* zu verdeutschen; es würde ganz aus innerstem Bedürfnis geschehen und mit viel Freudigkeit'." Max Bruns, "My Reading" (December 1902). "Flauberts Briefe sind die bedeutsamsten künstlerischen Dokumente, die ich kenne…Sie werden einsehen, dass sich für Fl[auberts]. Briefe bislang kein Übersetzer finden konnte. Ich selber gebe sie später wohl deutsch heraus." Max Bruns to Karl Röttger, January 24, 1903.

55 "[Es] steht in meinem Vertrage *nicht*, die 'Flaubertbände sollten nach Ihren Angaben fertiggestellt werden,' sondern: '*Für die Reihenfolge des Erscheinens* verschiedener Flaubertbände sollen die Vorschläge von Herrn Max Bruns massgebende Berücksichtigung finden.' Sie sehen, *das* konnte ich

unterschreiben....Im übrigen glauben Sie ja nicht, dass <u>ich</u> es nicht verstände, Massnahmen des Verlages objektiv zu nehmen. Ich habe es von je gethan und werde es weiter thun. Wenn ich eine Massnahme des Verlages nicht verstehe, so suche ich unter Umständen, sie rückgängig zu machen; meist ist es mir bislang gelungen. Sonst aber erinnere ich mich daran, dass ein Verlag keine Ideale Maschine, sondern ein von menschlichen Wesen geleitetes Geschäft ist, das als Gesellschaft meinem Urteil diesmal überlegen, ein anderes Mal unterlegen ist. Ich bewahre eben deshalb doch unverändert diejenige Hochachtung, die seinen ganz ausserordentlichen Verdiensten gebührt." Greve to Max Bruns, June 26, 1905.

56 "Ich habe seit Jahren den Bruns'schen Verlag zu einer deutschen Flaubertausgabe anzuregen versucht, endlich mit Erfolg. Selbst noch zu sehr mit meiner Baudelaire-Ausgabe beschäftigt, habe ich die Arbeit für Flaubert anderen überlassen müssen und mich auf erbetene und unerbetene Ratschläge beschränkt..." "Der Band Briefe über seine Werke ist trostlos unwürdig übersetzt; auch die Ausstattung des Bruns'schen deutschen Flaubert ist durchaus nicht würdig; man mag die Bände kaum in seinen Schrank stellen. Die Briefe über seine Werke sind zu allem Überfluß auch noch von einem unfähigen Menschen redigiert, der den Eindruck ermüdender, bleischwerer, zermalmender Langeweile – *fürchtete!* und zu vermeiden suchte...Flauberts Künstlerschaft ist zuletzt vielleicht am meisten, vielleicht einzig dem ennui erlegen, der schon das Gemüt des Jünglings durchfressen hatte." Max Bruns, "My Reading" (October 1905). Cf. Martens, *Bruns* 105.

57 "[Als Bruns] nun die [Übersetzung] des 'Antonius' bringen wollte, meldete sich Herr Dr. Fischer aus Bielefeld mit der Mitteilung, es sei bereits eine ziemlich unbekannt gebliebene Übersetzung des Antonius erschienen, dieser sei somit nicht frei und er als alleiniger und bestellter Vertreter der Erben in Deutschland habe das Übersetzungsrecht für Antonius und die übrigen, jetzt unter das ausgedehnte Schutzgesetz fallenden Werke des Dichters zu vergeben." Berta Huber to Breuer (a lawyer), December 14, 1922. See also Martens, *Bruns* 95–96.

58 "Saint-Malo, aufs Meer gebaut und von Wellen umschlossen, scheint, wenn man ankommt, ein Kranz aus auf die Wellen gelegten Steinen, deren Blumen Pechnasen sind. Die Wogen schlagen gegen die Mauern und brechen sich bei Ebbe zu ihrem Fuß auf dem Sande. Kleine, seetangbedeckte Felsen steigen niedrig aus dem Strand auf und gleichen schwarzen Flecken auf der gelben Fläche. Die größeren tragen, senkrecht und ganz glatt aufsteigend, auf ihren ungleichmäßigen Gipfeln die Fundamente der Befestigungen und verlängern so die graue Farbe und verstärken ihre Höhe" (Flaubert, *Reiseblätter* 1906, 267).

59 "Ich habe stets durchaus anerkannt, dass viele seiner Leistungen, und ich kann sagen die meisten, vortrefflich waren und seiner hohen Begabung entsprachen. Andere dagegen waren es durchaus nicht, und ich bin nicht der einzige, der darauf hingewiesen hat, sondern in vielen, an sich ganz uninteressierten Besprechungen und brieflichen Äußerungen an uns ist das zum Ausdruck gekommen: Ihr Gatte hat das fast immer selbst eingesehen, oft auch unumwunden zugegeben. Wenn...Ihr Gatte Manuskripte oder Revisionsbogen,

die ich ihm mit Bemerkungen zurücksandte, durchaus änderte, so liegt darin
wohl der Beweis, daß er selbst fühlte, in diesen Fällen nicht genügt zu haben.
Das lag nicht an einem Mangel an Können—die Begabung Ihres Gatten hat
niemand höher geschätzt als ich—sondern daran, daß Geldmangel und die
Notwendigkeit, eine alte Schuld—wie er mir óft sagte—abtragen zu müssen, ihn
zwangen, viel mehr Arbeiten zu übernehmen, als er trotz enormer Arbeitskraft in
guter Qualität auszuführen fähig war. Dies liegt so klar auf der Hand, daß ich
mich auch da auf die einfachste Feststellung beschränken kann: gerade heute
noch habe ich gehört, wieviel Arbeiten er in letzter Zeit auch für andere
Verleger gleichzeitig in Angriff genommen hatte." Kippenberg to Else Greve,
September 21, 1909. Cf. Letters 548–50. I have taken the liberty of slightly
altering the translation in Pacey's edition of the *Letters* on the basis of my own
copy of the original letter.

60 "Meine früheste Bekanntschaft mit Schriften von André Gide fand statt dank der
Übersetzungen von Felix Paul Greve, die zwischen 1900 und 1910 im Verlag
Bruns in Minden erschienen. Da war die 'Enge Pforte,' die mich, freilich in
mehr hugenottischer Haltung, dringend an die fromme Atmosphäre meiner
Kindheit erinnerte...Dann war da der 'Immoralist,' der mich noch stärker
ansprach...Und außerdem gab es da ein ganz dünnes Bändchen, dem der Übersetzer seinen französischen Titel gelassen hatte: 'Paludes,' ein sehr wunderliches,
eigensinniges, widerborstiges, jugendlich preziöses Büchlein, das mich verwirrte
und nasführte, bald bezauberte, bald ärgerte, und in den folgenden Jahren, in
denen ich Gide wieder fernrückte und ihn beinahe vergaß, unterirdisch in mir
nachwirkte."

61 "Die Briefe von John Keats gehören zu den schönsten Dichterbriefen die ich
kenne und die Übersetzung, in die ich Einblick hatte, ist weit über dem Niveau
dessen, was in Deutschland als gute Übersetzung passiert. Die Übersetzerin hat
vor Kurzem eine ausserordentlich schöne Auswahl aus den Schriften von
Flaubert publiziert, leider in einem ungeschickt gewählten Verlage, unter dessen
Flagge ein cultiviertes Product dieser Art so zu sagen verloren gieng" (Piper,
Briefwechsel 102, 532).

62 "Zum Tee bei Greves. Er ganz Litteratur, Theater, Verlag. Sie altert, macht sich
aber gut zurecht, immer noch die prachtvolle, elegante Figur. Sie arbeiten
zusammen, wobei sie ihren Courtisanenstandpunkt festhält, Alles vom
Standpunkt des Vergnügens aus zu betrachten. Besonderen Spass macht ihr,
wenn er die sehr erotischen Tausend-und-eine-Nacht-Erzählungen mit ihr übersetzt, wobei sie näht und das Gefühl hat, er liest ihr vor" (O.A.H. Schmitz, diary
entry, November 25, 1906).

63 "Um meine Arbeitslast bewältigen zu können, habe ich mit der
Schreibmaschine zu schreiben begonnen." Letter to O.A.H. Schmitz,
September 6, 1906. Compare Grove's remark in *In Search of Myself*: "'No
wonder,' he said, 'that you've never been able to interest a publisher. Your books
have never been read. Don't you know that these days manuscripts must be typewritten and on one side of the page only?'" (ISM 339). See also Spettigue, *FPG*
159. It was Grove's habit to write his manuscripts out in minuscule longhand.

When he had reached the end of the copybook he preferred using, he turned the book around and continued writing, creating something resembling a true palimpsest.

64 Cf. the English translations of Greve's German novels in 1976 (*The Mastermason's House*) and 1984 (*Fanny Essler*). These interesting translations attempt to reproduce the "German" atmosphere of their originals to the point of imitating versions of "German script" on the dustcovers. They did not, however, preserve the artificially "old-fashioned" tone of the headings and subheadings.

65 Regarding the centrality of women's roles in *Fanny Essler*, cf. Gammel, *Sexualizing Power* 9. Blodgett, *Alias* first dealt with the parodic and picaresque elements of this novel. "An einem frühen Maimorgen des Jahres 1892, ehe noch die Sonne für das pommersche Flachland über den Horizont gestiegen war, huschte die Gestalt eines jungen Mädchens durch die noch nachtöden Straßen einer kleinen Seestadt an der Ostsee" (Greve, *FE* 3). The English translation in the 1984 Canadian edition (by Christine Helmers, A.W. Riley and D.O. Spettigue) renders this passage as follows: "Early one morning, in May of the year 1892, before the sun had yet risen above the horizon of the Pomerian [sic] plains, the figure of a young girl hurried through the dark, deserted streets of a small Baltic seaside town" (Greve, *FE*, vol. 1, 17).

66 Herbert Koch to Franziska zu Reventlow, undated postcard from Capua.

67 "So rettete ein ruhiger Tod Fanny Eßler vor der größten Enttäuschung ihres Lebens" (Greve, *FE* 563).

68 German translations of *Vanity Fair* were published in 1898 and 1909 as parts of larger editions. Thus Thackeray was read and discussed during Greve's life in Germany.

69 "Hochverehrte Dichterin. Es gereicht meinem Verlage zur grossen Ehre, Ihre schönen Gedichte zur Durchsicht empfangen zu haben. Dieselben sind so interessant wie originell und aus diesem Grunde eben—Kaviar für's Volk. Was für ihren Wert zeugt, aber ein Risiko für den Verlag bedeutet. Ich will es dennoch versuchen. Sprechen Sie einmal bei Gelegenheit vor, wenn Sie an meiner Buchhandlung vorbeikommen" (Lasker-Schüler, *Werke* II 522).

70 Lasker-Schüler's next publisher, Oesterheld, confessed his impecuniousness during their first interview. Oesterheld also published Gide's *Saül* in Felix Greve's translation.

71 "Bei Axel Juncker, den ich zum ersten Male zu sehen bekomme. Liebenswürdige Schlafmütze. Ziemlich reduzierte Einrichtung. Ich begreife nicht, wie man ihn mir empfehlen konnte" (O.A.H. Schmitz, Diary, November 11, 1906).

72 "Nachdem ich vor einigen Monaten meinen ersten Roman ('Fanny Essler'— einen Berliner Roman) bei Axel Juncker, Stuttgart, veröffentlicht habe, möchte ich heute für ein zweites Buch sorgen, das in diesem Winter beendet wurde. Es handelt sich um eine Art Roman aus dem *Vorpommerschen*, das unbedingt in einem norddeutschen Verlag erscheinen muss. Die Form ist in sofern sehr neu, als die eigentliche Erzählung gegenüber dramatisch ausgearbeiteten und aneinandergereihten Szenen stark zurücktritt. Die 'Szenen' spielen im Hause

eines wohlhabenden Bürgers, eines self made man par excellence; der Titel
lautet 'Maurermeister Ihles Haus;' das ganze ist kurz (höchstens 20 Bogen); und
die Geschehnisse spielen sich, abgesehen vom ersten Buch ('Höhere Töchter:'
Milieu der Kinder im Hause des 'grimmigen Maurermeisters' und in der
Höheren Töchterschule), mit fast katastrophaler Geschwindigkeit ab, deren
Härte nur durch die Komik vieler Einzelheiten gemildert wird. Das Ganze ist
die Tragödie einer Familie." Greve to Alfred Janssen, February 21, 1906.

73 Information from the "Meldeblatt des Quartiergebers." The "Pension Gisela,"
Giselastrasse 15, third floor, was owned and run by a Mrs. Rusbeck. Cf. the
facsimile of Thomas Mann's registration (Heisserer, *Schwabinger Bohème* 103).

74 "Die blonden und blauäugigen Jünglinge lockten ihn immer wieder mit
betörender Macht, aber in jenen frühen Münchner Tagen vergaß er wohl kaum
einen Augenblick, daß die Liebe zum eigenen Geschlecht – obwohl es sie
tausendfach gab – auch im biederen München, und nicht nur als ferner Zauber
– von Gefahren umstellt war: Gefahren für die eigene Seele, seine bürgerliche
Reputation, ja für die Sicherheit und Freiheit seiner Existenz, denn es stand im
Belieben der Staatsanwälte und Polizeibüttel, das Leben jedes 'Andersartigen'
und 'Abartigen' unter Berufung auf den ominösen Paragraphen 175 des
Strafgesetzbuches zu ruinieren."

75 "Ich lebe nun fast ein Jahr in diesem Lande, aber die von drüben mitgebrachte
Arbeit übt ihre abdichtende Wirkung aus; auch ergibt man sich in meinen
Jahren nicht mehr so rasch neuen Eindrücken. So bin ich denn für jede brück-
enschlagende Hilfe dankbar, und Ihr Roman bedeutet mir eine solche. Die
Ablösung des zweifelnden 'Geistes' von 'Boden,' 'Natur,' kurz dem 'Leben,'
dieses Zentralmotiv meines eigenen Werkes ist, wenn ich nicht irre, auch das
Ihre in diesem Buche; die Synthese zwischen den tellurischen und den intellek-
tuellen Kräften, um die ich mich mühe, ist bei Ihnen ein sehr liebenswerter
verhaltener, echt angelsächsischer Humor, der am Begreifen nicht stirbt. Ich
werde mich sehr freuen, 'A Search for America' zu lesen, wenn ich von meiner
Sommerreise nach Europa wiederkomme." Thomas Mann to Frederick Philip
Grove, April 19 and June 5, 1939. Mann did not go to Europe. The outbreak of
World War II apparently prevented further communication between the two
writers. One may assume that Grove was not intent on running the risk of having
his identity revealed at such a critical time.

76 In their discussion of *Maurermeister Ihles Haus* (translated by Paul P. Gubbins),
A.W. Riley and D.O. Spettigue comment on German Naturalism and the use of
dialect. Greve, *Master Mason* 7–9.

77 "Für den Vertrieb käme wohl noch in Frage, dass ich nach meiner langjährigen
Publizistentätigkeit keineswegs mehr ein Unbekannter bin, und gerade in
Hamburg hat man gerade meine Publikationen englischer Autoren von jeher
wohlwollend und lebhaft anerkennend besprochen.

Ihnen persönlich bin ich insofern nicht ganz unbekannt, als Sie vor einer
Reihe von Jahren einmal – sehr mit Recht – einen Gedichtband von mir
ablehnten." Greve to Alfred Janssen, February 21, 1906.

78 "Mein Roman wird, wenn der Druck sich bis Mitte Oktober beenden lässt (ich jage ihn durch die Presse), noch vor Weihnachten, sonst Ende Januar erscheinen. Es ist wieder einmal zu spät begonnen worden. Natürlich habe ich auf Juncker verzichtet. Sie haben es vielleicht nicht mehr nötig. Ihre Bücher beginnen von selbst zu gehen. Sie Glücklicher!" Greve to O.A.H. Schmitz (September 6, 1906).

79 "Da ich jetzt wiederum seit Wochen Abrechnung und Zahlung* [hand-schriftlicher Zusatz am linken Rand: *der Tantiemen für 'Fanny Essler'] vermisse, so teile ich Ihnen hierdurch mit, dass ich, falls beides nicht innerhalb von 3 Tagen erfolgt, d.h. bis zum 26. d[es]. M[ona]ts., mittags 12 Uhr, den zwischen uns bestehenden Vertrag als gelöst betrachte.

Hochachtend

Felix P. Greve

Einschreiben"

Greve to Axel Juncker, February 23, 1909.

80 Schmitz writes: "Die Greves imponieren mir, wie sie bei ihrem angestrengten Kampf ums Dasein eine so solide, aber intensive Eleganz aufrecht erhalten." O.A.H. Schmitz, Diary, November 29 and December 11, 1906; 398, 405.

7 ◆ A TRAVELLING AUTHOR

1 Information from the arrival records in the Canadian National Archives in Ottawa. I first published new data about Grove's passage and arrival as an Internet publication in July 1999, albeit in a slightly different version. It was also included in my *Pioneering* 43–45.

2 The reference to Mark Twain's youthful hero was first made by Stobie, *Grove* 63. Grove's impersonation of a literary hero was probably the realization of a child-hood dream. It resembles Archibald Belaney's impersonation of an Ontario native who called himself "Grey Owl."

3 *Der Nordwesten* also dealt with literary and political matters, catering to a large German reading audience in the Midwest. Articles published in it did not go unnoticed in Germany. In fact, one of its correspondents, the much-respected Amelia von Ende, worked for it and became a major cultural mediator between the United States and Germany. Felix Paul Greve may have read her contribu-tions in German magazines while still in Berlin.

4 "Not that he necessarily would have had a degree [in the United States], but most institutions of any pretensions would have required a degree; at least state-operated would. It therefore is another matter for speculation whether Grove had had a degree but could not claim it because it had been earned under another name" (*FPG* 22).

5 For an early but neglected account of Else's Dada career and her relations with Margaret Anderson, Jane Heap, Ezra Pound, William Carlos Williams and others, see Cary Nelson, *Repression* 71–72, 79, 230. It includes a useful biblio-graphy of Else's publications (267–268n63, n64). Irene Gammel's excellent work from 1993 on significantly deepens earlier research on von Freytag-Loringhoven

as a central figure of early intercultural Modernism long repressed by American literary historians.

6 For Karl Knortz and his roles as a translator and teacher see Martens, *Longfellow* 165–68.

7 In Grove's works, the only percherons are Nils Lindstedt's in *Settlers of the Marsh* (SOM 190) and the ones Branden encounters on his tramp from the shores of the Ohio to Indianapolis (SFA 309). In Ontario, the Groves owned a pair of these horses (A. Leonard Grove).

8 According to Kathleen Gibson, Sparta is about to come to life again, since it may become the site for an automobile racetrack.

9 Cf. Forsee, 241–42. Forsee was the County Clerk of Owen County and was on the County Board of Education in the 1930s.

10 Source: two undated (c. 1979) newspaper clippings among C.N. Varble's papers, signed "J.L. Samuel of Sparta" and "Jack Hicks," respectively. "Colorado Grant" was killed in Taylorsville, Kentucky. He was shot after a performance by a drunk whom he had removed from the audience. He is buried in the Owenton cemetery. Unless otherwise noted, I have taken all details about Sparta from C.N. Varble's handwritten accounts.

11 Varble writes that Donalson was born in London in 1875. Apparently, he came to Sparta in search of Indian relics, bought fifty acres bordering on Eagle Creek and made a great success of the tree nursery. The nursery was sold in 1925. From 1910 on, Donalson employed various people for planting and grafting, including a boy from Holland. He made a fortune sending up to two carloads of young trees per week. He may have been another model for Grove's (and Branden's) fictive "father."

12 C.N. Varble remembered quite a few names of teachers at the three Sparta schools from the 1870s to the 1970s, almost all of them from families he knew. However, Varble himself did not come to Sparta before 1916 and may not have heard about somebody serving a short term as a teacher.

13 Following Else's remark about "the small farmcountry" in Kentucky, one wonders what made a farm "small" or "large." According to the U.S. Agricultural Census of 1935, "All tracts of land containing three or more acres are classed as farm." Forsee writes that "small farms consist of about 50 acres" and may be obtained on the basis of "crop rent," which is a lease arrangement paid from income from crop sales. As to Grove's driving a wagonload of tomatoes, he could have done this as a driver for the hauling business of Leslie Minor, who was an operator and agent for the railroad.

14 I thank A. Leonard and Mary Grove for permission to examine this manuscript book.

15 Felix Paul Greve had, of course, translated *The Temptation of St. Anthony*. In a manuscript version of *Settlers of the Marsh*, Clara Vogel reads this book (presumably in English, not in German translation). Stobie notices quotation and praphrase from Flaubert's work in Clara's denunciation of Niels in Grove's novel (Stobie, *Grove* 80).

16 For this and the following information I am much obliged to A. Leonard Grove, who was kind enough to share it with me in a memoir written for use in this book.

17 Cf. Grove's comment to Barker Fairley on autobiographical elements in his novel *Two Generations* (Letters 367).

◆ AFTERWORD

1 See Bierbaum, *Prinz Kuckuck* 296, 304f., 296, 294, 663.

2 I owe the reference to George's recollection of Greve, included in Landmann's conversations with the poet, to a review of the German edition of this book by Claus Victor Bock (87).

3 Others arrived at related conclusions in different ways, notably Paul Hjartarson in *A Stranger to My Time*.

4 Cf. Blodgett, "Ersatz Feminism" for glimpses of Nietzsche's *Zarathustra* and *Metamorphoses* in Greve's *Fanny Essler*. Also see Knönagel.

BIBLIOGRAPHY

Note: Most of the books published by J.C.C. Bruns were not dated so they could be issued in rapid succession, or often simultaneously, in different bindings using the same book block. Presumed dates of Bruns books and others appear in square brackets and are based on information taken from letters, contracts and other documents from various archives (cf. Martens, *Bruns* 171–205).

♦ FELIX PAUL GREVE

Works Published

"Nachgelassene Werke von Friedrich Nietzsche, Vol. XI, XII. Hg. Ernst and August Horneffer." *Beilage zur Allgemeinen Zeitung* 235 (1901): 6–7. Repr. in Ernst/Martens, *Greve-Gide.*

"Lucien Leuwen. Ein neues Werk von Stendhal (Henri Beyle)." *Beilage zur Allgemeinen Zeitung* 224 (30 Sept. 1901): 1–2. Repr. in Ernst/Martens, *Greve-Gide.*

Wanderungen. Munich: J[acob]. Littauer, [1902].

"Wanderungen." [Review of his own book ("Selbstanzeige").] *Die Zukunft* 39 (1902): 164–65.

Helena und Damon. Ein Spiel in Versen. Munich: J[acob]. Littauer, 1902.

"Fingerzeige. Von Oscar Wilde." [Review of his own translation ("Selbstanzeige").] *Die Zukunft* 41 (1902): 466–67.

Randarabesken zu Oskar Wilde. Minden: J.C.C. Bruns, [1903]. [Same as introduction to Oscar Wilde, *Das Bildnis des Mr. W.H., Lord Arthur Saviles Verbrechen.* Trans. Felix Paul Greve.]

"Das Bildnis Dorian Grays. Von Oscar Wilde." [Review of his own translation ("Selbstanzeige").] *Die Zukunft* 44 (1903): 208.

Oscar Wilde. Berlin: Gose & Tetzlaff, 1903.

"Die Hexe." *Die Freistatt* 6 (25 June 1904): 519.

"George Meredith." *Die Freistatt* 6 (1904): 721–23. Repr. in Ernst/Martens, *Greve-Gide*.

"Gustave Flauberts Theorien über das Künstlertum." *Rheinisch-Westfälische Zeitung* 1065 (16 Nov. 1904): 3. Repr. in Ernst/Martens, *Greve-Gide*.

"Vorrede" to *Diana vom Kreuzweg* by George Meredith. 2 vols. in 1. Minden: J.C.C. Bruns, 1905.

George Meredith und sein Stil: Eine Entgegnung. Minden: J.C.C. Bruns, 1905.

"H.G. Wells: *Die Zeitmaschine — Dr. Moreaus Insel — Die Riesen kommen!'* [Review of his own translations of H.G. Wells's novels ("Selbstanzeige").] *Die Zukunft* 50 (1 Jan. 1905): 266–67.

"Der Immoralist." *Die Zukunft* 52 (1905): 305–06. Repr. in *Bulletin des amis d'André Gide* 41 (1979): 81–82.

"Ausblicke auf die Folgen des technischen und wissenschaftlichen Fortschrittes für Leben und Denken der Menschen." [Review of his own translation of H.G. Wells's novel ("Selbstanzeige").] *Die Zukunft* 53 (30 Dec. 1905): 483.

Fanny Essler. Ein Berliner Roman. Berlin: Axel Juncker, 1905.

"'In einer Gondel' von Robert Browning." *Insel-Almanach auf das Jahr 1906.* Leipzig: Insel, 1907.

Maurermeister Ihles Haus. Berlin: Karl Schnabel, 1906; Dresden: C. Reißner, 1909.

"Die Übersetzungen von Tausend und Eine Nacht." *Zeitschrift für Bücherfreunde* 11.1 (Apr. 1907): 45–47.

"Erster Sturm." *Die Schaubühne* 6 (7 Feb. 1907): 154.

"Die Stadt am Strande." *Die Schaubühne* 23 (6 June 1907): 570.

"Saül von André Gide." *Die Schaubühne* 32 (8 Aug. 1907): 105–10.

"Francines Muff." [Excerpt from Henri Murger's *Bohème.*] *Insel-Almanach auf das Jahr 1907.* Leipzig: Insel, [1906].

"Oscar Wilde und das Drama." Introduction to *Oscar Wildes sämtliche Werke in deutscher Sprache.* Vol. 7. Vienna and Leipzig: Wiener Verlag, 1908.

"Reise in Schweden." *Neue Revue und Morgen* 22/23 (29 May 1909): 760–66. Repr. in Ernst/Martens, *Greve-Gide*.

"Der Luftkrieg." *Neue Revue und Morgen* 27/28 (8 July 1909): 954–55.

"Oskar Wilde." *Porträts.* Ed. Adalbert Luntowski. Berlin: Verlag Neues Leben-W. Borngräber, 1911.

Letters and Manuscripts

Letters and notes to or about F.P. Greve, letters to Friedrich Schultess [1901]. Hauptbibliothek des Johanneums, Hamburg.

Letters from F.P. Greve to Melchior Lechter, Ernst Hardt, Stefan George and others [1902–04]. J.P. Getty Museum, Los Angeles.

Letters to Alfred Janssen [1901, 1906]. Staats- und Universitätsbibiliothek Hamburg.

Letters and postcards to Karl Wolfskehl (1901–02). Schiller-Nationalmuseum/Deutsches Literaturarchiv, Marbach.

Vollmoeller, Karl Gustav. Letters to Karl Wolfskehl. Schiller-Nationalmuseum/Deutsches Literaturarchiv, Marbach.

Letters to Stefan George (1902). Stefan George-Archiv/Württembergische Landesbibliothek, Stuttgart.

Letters to Friedrich Gundolf [1902]. Friedrich Gundolf-Archiv, London.

Letters to Rudolf von Poellnitz (1902–03). Stiftung Weimarer Klassik/Goethe- und Schiller-Archiv, Weimar.

Letters to H.G. and Mrs. Wells (1903–09). Rare Book and Special Collections Library, University of Illinois, Urbana-Champaign.

Letters by H.G. Wells or his agents to J.C.C. Bruns and Felix Paul Greve (1904–06). J.C.C. Bruns-Archiv, Minden.

Letters to Oscar A.H. Schmitz (1904–06). Schiller-Nationalmuseum/Deutsches Literaturarchiv, Marbach.

Letter to Franz Blei (1905). Schiller-Nationalmuseum/Deutsches Literaturarchiv, Marbach.

Letters to Franz Brümmer (1907). Staatsbibliothek zu Berlin, Preußischer Kulturbesitz.

Letters, postcards, cables, etc. to J.C.C. Bruns or by Bruns et. al. to Greve (1902–07). J.C.C. Bruns Archiv, Minden.

Letter to Anton Kippenberg (1908). Stiftung Weimarer Klassik/Goethe- und Schiller-Archiv, Weimar.

Letter to Axel Juncker Verlag, Berlin (1909). Staatsbibliothek Preußischer Kulturbesitz, Berlin.

Anton Kippenberg to Else Greve (1909). Stiftung Weimarer Klassik/Goethe- und Schiller-Archiv, Weimar.

Thomas Mann to Frederick Philip Grove (1939). Thomas Mann-Archiv, ETH Zürich.

"Je vous écris en hâte et fiévreusement:" Felix Paul Greve-André Gide. Korrespondenz und Dokumentation. Ed. Jutta Ernst and Klaus Martens. Schriften der Saarländischen Universitäts- und Landesbibliothek. Vol 5. St. Ingbert: Röhrig Universitätsverlag, 1999.

Works by Greve in English Translation

The Master Mason's House. Trans. Paul P. Gubbins. Intro. A.W. Riley and D.O. Spettigue. Montreal: Oberon Press, 1976.

Oscar Wilde. Trans. and intro. Barry Asker. Vancouver: William Hoffer, 1984.

Fanny Essler. Ed. A.W. Riley and D. O. Spettigue. Trans. Christine Helmer, A.W. Riley and D. O. Spettigue. 2 vols. Ottawa: Oberon Press, 1984.

Works Unpublished or Not Seen in Print

Pater, Walter. "A Prince of Court Painters." Translation mentioned to Wolfskehl (1901–02).

Wilde, Oscar. "Salome." Translation mentioned in letter to J.C.C. Bruns, 2 August 1902.

"Stefan George und die Blätter für die Kunst." Berlin: Bard, Marquardt & Co. [Same as *Kunst und Künstler.*] Mentioned in letter to O.A.H. Schmitz, 28 May 1904.

"George Meredith und die Englische Romantische Tradition." Berlin: Bard, Marquardt & Co. Mentioned in letter to O.A.H. Schmitz, 28 May 1904.

"Kunst und Künstler." [Same as *Stefan George und die Blätter für die Kunst.*] Mentioned in letter to O.A.H. Schmitz, 28 May 1904 and in letter to André Gide, 17 October 1904.

"Der Sentimentalist. Ein Roman." Scheduled for publication by J.C.C. Bruns for 1906. Mentioned in *Fanny Essler* and *Maurermeister Ihles Haus.*

"Das Blutbad im Bayrischen Nationalmuseum und andere grauenhafte und ergötzliche Geschichten von Leuten, die..." Mentioned in *Maurermeister Ihles Haus.*

"Der heimliche Adel." Mentioned in letter to Franz Brümmer, 6 March 1907. Existence of manuscript proven by entry under *Annahmen* ["accepted for performance"] by the Hebbel Theater, Berlin. *Schaubühne* 4.23/24 (11 June 1907): 617.

"Kritik und Kunst. Eine Kampfschrift." Mentioned in *Fanny Essler.*

"Pindar, Schiller und Herr Märzenbach. Drei Grotesken." Mentioned in *Fanny Essler.*

◆ FREDERICK PHILIP GROVE

Works Published

Over Prairie Trails. Toronto: McClelland & Stewart, 1922.

The Turn of the Year. Toronto: McClelland & Stewart, 1923.

Settlers of the Marsh. Toronto: Ryerson Press, 1925.

"*Monsieur Ripois* and *Nemesis* by Louis Hémon." *Canadian Bookman* 7 (1925): 99.

"*Power* by Arthur Stringer." *Canadian Bookman* 7 (1925): 99.

"*Glorious Apollo* by E. Barrington." *Canadian Bookman* 7 (1925): 147.

Rev. of *Captain Salvation* by Frederick Wallace. *Canadian Bookman* 7 (1925): 148.

"Mr. Grove Protests." [Letter to the editor.] *Canadian Bookman* 7 (1925): 188.

"The Gypsy Trail." *Winnipeg Tribune Magazine* (9 Oct. 1926): 8.

"Camping in Manitoba." *Winnipeg Tribune Magazine* (20 Nov. 1926): 12.

"North of Fifty-Three. Part 1." *Winnipeg Tribune Magazine* (27 Nov. 1926): 12.

"Captain Harper's Last Voyage." [Part 2 of "North of Fifty-Three."] *Winnipeg Tribune Magazine* (4 Dec. 1926): 12.

"Lost." *Winnipeg Tribune Magazine* (11 Dec. 1926): 12.

"A Christmas in the Canadian Bush." *Winnipeg Tribune Magazine* (18 Dec. 1926): 12.

"The Boat." *Winnipeg Tribune Magazine* (24 Dec. 1926): 12.

"That Reminds Me." *Winnipeg Tribune Magazine* (31 Dec. 1926): 12.

"The Agent." *Winnipeg Tribune Magazine* (22 Jan. 1927): 12.

"The Sale." *Winnipeg Tribune Magazine* (29 Jan. 1927): 12.

"The Flood." *Winnipeg Tribune Magazine* (19 Feb. 1927): 12.

"A First Night on Canadian Soil." [Excerpt from *A Search for America.*] *Winnipeg Tribune Magazine* (5 Mar. 1927): 12.

"Beating it in." [Excerpt from *A Search for* America.] *Winnipeg Tribune Magazine* (12 Mar. 1927): 12.

"Water." *Winnipeg Tribune Magazine* (16 Mar. 1927): 12.

"Hobos." [Excerpt from *A Search for America.*] *Winnipeg Tribune Magazine* (19 Mar. 1927): 12.

"Lazybones." *Winnipeg Tribune Magazine* (2 Apr. 1927): 12. [Repr. in *Queen's Quarterly* 51 (1944): 162–73.]

"The Dead-Beat." *Winnipeg Tribune Magazine* (9 Apr. 1927): 12.

"Bachelors All." *Winnipeg Tribune Magazine* (16 Apr. 1927): 12.

"Relief." *Winnipeg Tribune Magazine* (23 Apr. 1927): 13.

"A Hero of the Flu." *Winnipeg Tribune Magazine* (5 Nov. 1927): 7.

"Prairie Character Studies: The Immigrant." *Winnipeg Tribune Magazine* (5 Feb. 1927): 12.

"Dave Chisholm Entertains." *Winnipeg Tribune Magazine* (12 Feb. 1927): 12.

"Dave Chisholm, 'The Goat.'" *Winnipeg Tribune Magazine* (26 Feb. 1927): 12.

A Search for America: The Odyssey of an Immigrant. Ottawa: Graphic, 1927; New York-London-Montreal: Louis Carrier, 1928.

"Mr. Grove on Nationhood." [Excerpt from a lecture delivered at the Canadian Club.] *Canadian Bookman* 10 (1928): 284.

Our Daily Bread. Toronto: Macmillan, 1928.

It Needs to Be Said. Toronto: Macmillan, 1929.

"The National Consciousness Idea." [Letter to the editor.] *Canadian Bookman* 11 (1929): 160.

"Indian Summer." *Canadian Forum* 10 (1929): 56.

"Science." *Canadian Forum* 9 (1929): 206.

The Yoke of Life. Toronto and New York: Macmillan, 1930.

"The Palinode." *Canadian Forum* 10 (1930): 444.

"From *The Dirge.*" *Canadian Forum* 10 (1930): 444; 12 (1932): 257–61.

"The Flat Prairie." *Dalhousie Review* 11 (1931/32): 213–16.

"Apologia pro vita et opere suo." *Canadian Forum* 11 (1931): 420–22.

"A Writer's Classification of Writers and their Work." *University of Toronto Quarterly* 1 (1932): 236–53.

"Thomas Hardy: A Critical Examination of a Typical Novel and his Shorter Poems." *University of Toronto Quarterly* 1 (1932): 490–507.

"Snow." *Queen's Quarterly* 39 (1932): 99–110. Rpt. in *Canadian Short Stories.* Ed. Robert Weaver. Toronto: Oxford University Press, 1960. Rpt. in *A Book of Canadian Stories.* Ed. Desmond Pacey. Toronto: Ryerson Press, 1962.

Fruits of the Earth. [1933.] Afterword by Rudy Wiebe. Toronto: McClelland & Stewart, 1992.

"Riders." *Canadian Forum* 14 (1934): 177–80.

"The Plight of Canadian Fiction? A Reply." *University of Toronto Quarterly* 7 (1938): 451–67.

Two Generations: A Story of Present-Day Ontario. Toronto: Ryerson Press, 1939.

"The Platinum Watch." *Canadian Bookman* 21 (1939): 5–12.

"In Search of Myself." *University of Toronto Quarterly* 10 (1940): 60–67.

"The Adventure of Leonard Broadus." *The Canadian Boy,* 1940: 14–25. Rpt. in *Grove Special Double Issue.* Ed. Mary Rubio. *Canadian Children's Literature* 27/28 (1982): 5–126.

The Master of the Mill. Toronto: Macmillan, 1940.

"Nationhood." [Excerpt from *It Needs to be Said*.] In *Recent Prose*. Ed. C.L. Bennet. Toronto and Halifax: Ryerson Press, 1941.

"The Desert." *Queen's Quarterly* 48 (1941): 219–32.

"Postscript to *A Search for America*." *Queen's Quarterly* 49 (Fall 1942): 197–213.

"Just a word..." [Preface to *Friendship* by H. Symons.] Toronto: Macmillan, 1943.

"Democracy and Education." *University of Toronto Quarterly* 12 (1943): 389–402.

"Peasant Poetry and Fiction from Hesiod to Hémon." *Royal Society of Canada Transactions* 2 (1944): 89–98.

"Morality in the Forsyte Saga." *University of Toronto Quarterly* 15 (1945): 54–64.

In Search of Myself. Toronto: Macmillan, 1946; Toronto: McClelland & Stewart-New Canadian Library, 1974.

Consider Her Ways. Toronto: Macmillan, 1947.

A Search for America. [1927.] School ed., abridged by J.F. Swayze. Toronto: Ryerson Press, 1947.

Tales from the Margin: The Selected Short Stories of Frederick Philip Grove. Ed. Desmond Pacey. Toronto: Ryerson Press, 1971.

The Letters of Frederick Philip Grove. Ed. Desmond Pacey and J.C. Mahanti. Intro. Desmond Pacey. Toronto: University of Toronto Press, 1976.

"An Edition of Selected Unpublished Essays and Lectures by Frederick Philip Grove and his Theory of Art." Ed. Henry Makow. Dissertation, University of Toronto, 1982.

"Rebels All: Of the Interpretation of Real Life." In *A Stranger to My Time: Essays by and about Frederick Philip Grove*. Ed. Paul Hjartarson. Edmonton: NeWest Press, 1986.

"Of Nishivara, the Saint. Chapter 1." In *A Stranger to My Time: Essays by and about Frederick Philip Grove*. Ed. Paul Hjartarson. Edmonton: NeWest Press, 1986.

"Thoughts and Reflections." In *A Stranger to My Time: Essays by and about Frederick Philip Grove*. Ed. Paul Hjartarson. Edmonton: NeWest Press, 1986.

Works by Grove in German

"Jean Jacques Rousseau als Erzieher." *Der Nordwesten* 25 (1914): 14.

"Schnee." In *Die weite Reise: Kanadische Erzählungen und Kurzgeschichten*. Ed. Ernst Bartsch. Trans. Karl Heinrich. Berlin: Verlag Volk und Welt, 1974.

Works in Manuscript

Note: The following list, with addenda, is based on the Register of *The Frederick Philip Grove Collection* compiled by Deborah Raths, Winnipeg. Department of Archives, Manuscripts and Rare Books, The University of Manitoba Libraries, 1979.

"Jane Atkinson."

"Democracy or Peasant Revolt or Town and Country."

"Heart's Desire; or, Two Lives." [Alternative titles: *Mortgages; Is it Business?*]

"The Hillside."

"The House of Stene."

"The Lean Kine."
"My Life." [Handwritten draft manuscript.]
"Murder in the Quarry."
"Seven Drives Over Manitoba Trails. By a Manitoba Teacher." [Handwritten manu-
    script version of *Over Prairie Trails*, for private use]
"The Poet's Dream; or, The Canyon." [Alternative title: *The Canyon: A Romance and
    its Sequel.*]
"Felix Powell's Career." [Manuscript, said to have been destroyed.]
"The Seasons." [469–page manuscript, incomplete.]
"The Weatherhead Fortunes." [Manuscript.]
"The Weatherhead Fortunes. A Story of the Small Town."
"The White Range Line House." [Typewritten manuscript, 1923.]

◆ GROVE AS TRANSLATOR AND EDITOR

Gustav Amann
The Legacy of Sun Yatsen. A History of the Chinese Revolution. New York and
    Montreal: Carrier, 1929.

◆ GREVE AS TRANSLATOR AND EDITOR

Anon.
Die Erzählungen aus den tausendundein Nächten. [First complete German edition.
    Trans. Felix Paul Greve, based on Burton's English edition. Intro. Hugo von
    Hofmannsthal. With an essay on the work's emergence and history by Karl
    Dyroff.] Leipzig: Insel, 1907.
*Tausend und eine Nacht. Selected from Felix Paul Greve's translation and edited by
    Paul Ernst.* 4 vols. Leipzig: Insel, 1909.
"Wie Sumurrud sich an dem Kadi rächte, der ihr Haus beleidigt hatte." [To be
    published as part of the collection *Tausend und ein Tag* by Insel.] *Morgen* 20 (13
    May 1909): 697–703.
Tausend und ein Tag. Selected and intro. Paul Ernst. Trans. Felix Paul Greve and
    Paul Hansmann. 4 vols. Leipzig: Insel, 1909–10.
"Die Geschichte vom Kalifen Omar Bin Al-Khattab und dem jungen Badawi."
    [Excerpt from *Die Erzählungen aus den tausendundein Nächten.*] In *Insel
    Almanach auf das Jahr 1909.* Leipzig: Insel, 1908.
"Die Geschichte Maliks und der Prinzessin Schirin." [Greve not mentioned as trans-
    lator.] *Insel-Almanach auf das Jahr 1910.* Leipzig: Insel, 1908.
"Geschichte des ersten Bettelmönches." [Excerpt from *Tausend und eine Nacht.*]
    Prisma 11 (1947): 5–7.

Honoré de Balzac
Die Menschliche Komödie. 16 vols. Leipzig: Insel, 1908–11. Trans. F.P. Greve: Vol. 1:
    Ein Junggesellenheim; Vol. 2: *Erzählungen aus der napoleonischen Sphäre*; Vol.

6: *Glanz und Elend der Kurtisanen*, Part 1; Vol. 7: *Glanz und Elend der Kurtisanen*, Part 2; *Die Geheimnisse der Fürstin von Cadignan*; Vol. 11: *Das unbekannte Meisterwerk*.

Robert Browning

Auf einem Balkon/In einer Gondel. Trans. F.C. Gerden. Leipzig: Insel, 1903.
Die Tragödie einer Seele. Trans. F.C. Gerden. Leipzig: Insel, 1903.
Paracelsus. Leipzig: Insel, 1904.
"Kleon." *Freistatt* 6 (1904): 556–59.

Robert Browning and Elizabeth Barrett-Browning

Briefe von Robert Browning und Elizabeth Barrett-Browning. Berlin: S. Fischer, 1905.

Miguel de Cervantes

Die Novellen des Cervantes. 2 vols. [Complete German editon based on older translations, revised and corrected by Konrad Thorer. Intro. Felix Poppenberg.]
Leipzig: Insel, 1907.
Der scharfsinnige Ritter Don Quixote von der Mancha. [Complete German pocket edition in 3 vols. Trans. Konrad Thorer using the anonymous 1837 edition. Intro. Felix Poppenberg.] Leipzig: Insel, 1908.

Charles Dickens

Charles Dickens' Romane. 6 Vols. Leipzig: Insel, 1909. [Advertisement in *Börsenblatt des Deutschen Buchhandels*, 1909.]

Ernest Dowson

Dilemmas. Leipzig: Insel, 1903.

Alexandre Dumas

Der Graf von Monte Christo. Berlin: Erich Reiß, 1909.

Gustave Flaubert

Die Versuchung des heiligen Antonius. Minden: J.C.C. Bruns, [1905].
Briefe über seine Werke. Minden: J.C.C. Bruns, [1906].
Reiseblätter. Selected by F.P. Greve. Trans. E. Greve. Minden: J.C.C. Bruns, [1906].
Briefe an Zeit- und Zunftgenossen. Minden: J.C.C. Bruns, [1907].

André Gide

Paludes (Die Sümpfe). Minden: J.C.C. Bruns, [1905].
Der Immoralist. Minden: J.C.C. Bruns, [1905].
Ein Liebesversuch und andere Novellen. Berlin: Oesterheld, 1907.
Saül. Berlin: Erich Reiß, 1909.
Die Enge Pforte. Berlin: Erich Reiß, 1909.
"Menalkas." [Excerpt from *Les nourritures terrestres*.] *Die Zukunft* 51 (1905): 294–98.
[Translator not mentioned.] Mentioned in letter to Franz Blei, 21 March 1905.

Christian Hofman von Hofmanswaldau
Auserlesene Gedichte des Herrn Christian Hofman von Hofmanswaldau. Ed. and
   intro. Felix Paul Greve. Leipzig: Insel, 1907.

Junius
Die Briefe des Junius. Leipzig: Insel, 1909.

George Meredith
Richard Feverels Prüfung. 3 vols. Minden: J.C.C. Bruns, [1904].
Harry Richmonds Abenteuer. 2 vols. Minden: J.C.C. Bruns, [1904].
Diana vom Kreuzweg. Minden: J.C.C. Bruns, [1905].

Henri Murger
Die Bohème. Szenen aus dem Pariser Künstlerleben. Leipzig: Insel, 1906.

Walter Pater
Marius der Epikureer. 2 vols. Leipzig: Insel, 1908.

A.R. Le Sage
Die Geschichte des Gil Blas von Santillana. Trans. Konrad Thorer. 2 vols. Leipzig:
   Insel, 1908.

Jonathan Swift
Prosaschriften. Ed., intro. and commentary by Felix Paul Greve. 4 vols. Berlin:
   Oesterheld & Co., 1909–10.

Algernon Swinburne
"Phaedra." [Fragment.] *Freistatt* 7, 18 February (1905): 105–07.

H.G. Wells
Dr. Moreaus Insel. Minden: J.C.C. Bruns, [1904].
Die Zeitmaschine. Minden: J.C.C. Bruns, [1904].
Die Riesen kommen! Minden: J.C.C. Bruns, [1905].
Die ersten Menschen im Mond. Minden: J.C.C. Bruns, [1905].
Wenn der Schläfer erwacht. Minden: J.C.C. Bruns, [1906].
Ausblicke (Anticipations). Minden: J.C.C. Bruns, [1906].
"Der Schatz im Walde." *Morgen* 7 (11 February 1909): 230–36.

James McNeil Whistler
"Ten O'Clock." *Neue Deutsche Rundschau* 14 (1904): 315–25. [Greve not identified as
   translator.] Mentioned in letter to Rudolf von Poellnitz, 11 July 1903.

Oscar Wilde
Fingerzeige (Intentions). Minden: J.C.C. Bruns, [1902]. Rev. ed. 1905.

Dramen. 2 vols. Minden: J.C.C. Bruns, 1902. [Not distributed, but "Eine Frau ohne
    Bedeutung" and "Bunbury" later appeared as part of vols. 9 and 10 of the Wiener
    Verlag's edition "Oscar Wildes Werke in deutscher Sprache."]
Dramen. Teil 1. Lady Windermeres Fächer; Eine Frau ohne Bedeutung. Minden:
    J.C.C. Bruns, [1902].
Dramen. Teil 2. Der ideale Ehemann; Bunbury. Minden: J.C.C. Bruns, [1902].
Lady Windermeres Fächer. Minden: J.C.C. Bruns, [1902].
Eine Frau ohne Bedeutung. Minden: J.C.C. Bruns, [1902].
Der ideale Ehemann. Minden: J.C.C. Bruns, [1902].
Bunbury (The Importance of Being Earnest): Eine Komödie. Minden: J.C.C. Bruns,
    [1902].
Salomé. Minden: J.C.C. Bruns, [1902]. [Possibly unprinted stage manuscript.]
Dorian Grays Bildnis. Minden: J.C.C. Bruns, [1903].
Apologia pro Oscar Wilde. Minden: J.C.C. Bruns, 1903.
Das Bildnis des Mr. W.H.; Lord Arthur Saviles Verbrechen. Minden: J.C.C. Bruns,
    [1904].
Die Sphinx. Minden: J.C.C. Bruns, [1911]. [Rpt. in J.C.C. Bruns's series *Auf silbernen
    Saiten* together with Wilde's "Die Ballade vom Zuchthaus zu Reading." Trans.
    Eduard Thorn (1910).]
Das Granatapfelhaus. Leipzig: Insel, 1904.

◆ PUBLICATIONS ON GREVE AND GROVE

Anon. rev. of *Over Prairie Trails. Canadian Forum* 3 (1923): 248–50.
Anon. rev. of *The Turn of the Year. Canadian Forum* 4 (1924): 152, 154.
Anon. "Realism." [Report on a lecture by Grove.] *The Author's Bulletin* 8 (1925):
    30–31.
Anon. "Only on the Threshold: Says F.P. Grove." *Canadian Bookman* 8 (1926): 223.
Anon. rev. of *A Search for America. Saturday Review* 148 (31 Aug. 1929): 252.
Anon. rev. of *Our Daily Bread. Queen's Quarterly* 36 (1929): 181–83.
Anon. rev. of *Our Daily Bread. Canadian Forum* 9 (1929): 238.
Anon. Rev. of *Two Generations. Queen's Quarterly* 46 (1939): 380–81.
Anon. "The Passing of Greatness." *Canadian Author and Bookman* 24 (1948): 46–47.
Anon. "Canadian Dreiser." *Canadian Forum* 18 (1948): 121–22.
Adeney, Marcus. "*It Needs to be Said* by Frederick Philip Grove." *Canadian
    Bookman* 12 (1930): 37–38.
Arnason, David. "The Development of Prairie Realism: Robert J.C. Stead, Douglas
    Durkin, Martha Ostenso and Frederick Philip Grove." Dissertation, University
    of New Brunswick, 1980.
Ayre, Robert. "Canadian Writers of Today: Frederick Philip Grove." *Canadian Forum*
    12 (Apr. 1932): 255–57.
———. Rev. of *Fruits of the Earth. Canadian Forum* 13 (1933): 271.
Bader, Rudolf. "Frederick Philip Grove and Naturalism Reconsidered." In *Gaining
    Ground: European Critics on Canadian Literature.* Ed. Robert Kroetsch and
    Reingard M. Nischik. Edmonton: NeWest Press, 1985.

Bailey, Nancy I. "F.P.G. and the Empty House." *Journal of Canadian Fiction* 31/32 (1981): 177–93.

B[ie], O[skar]. "Die Aesthetik der Lüge." *Neue Deutsche Rundschau (Freie Bühne)* 14 (1903): 670–72.

Bierbaum, Otto J. "Wanderungen von Felix Paul Greve." *Die Insel* 3 (1901/02): 195–96.

Birbalsingh, Frank. "Grove and Existentialism." *Canadian Literature* 43 (Winter 1970): 67–76. Rpt. in *Writers of the Prairie*. Ed. Donald G. Stephens. Vancouver: University of British Columbia Press, 1973.

Blodgett, E.D. "Alias Grove: Variations in Disguise." In *Configurations: Essays on the Canadian Literatures*. Downsview: ECW Press, 1982.

Bock, Claus Victor. "Gravamina über Felix Paul Greve?" [Review article.] *Castrum Peregrini* 237–38 (1999): 87–90.

Böckel, Fritz. "*Maurermeister Ihles Haus* von Felix P. Greve." *Das litterarische Echo* 10 (1907–08): 210.

Boeschenstein, Hermann. "Frederick Philip Grove: Lehrer, Dichter und Pionier. 1871–1946." In *Festgabe für Eduard Berend*. Ed. Hans Werner Seiffert and Bernhard Zeller. Weimar: Hermann Böhlaus Nachfolger, 1959.

Bonheim, Helmut. "F.P. Grove's 'Snow' and Sinclair Ross's 'The Painted Door' — The Rhetoric of the Prairie." In *Encounters and Explorations: Canadian Writers and European Critics*. Ed. Franz K. Stanzel and Waldemar Zacharasiewicz. Würzburg: Königshausen & Neuman, 1986.

Brown, E.K. "The Immediate Present in Canadian Literature." *Sewanee Review* 41 (1933): 430–42.

Cavell, Richard. "Felix Paul Greve, the Eulenburg Scandal, and Frederick Philip Grove." *Essays on Canadian Writing* 62 (1977): 12–45.

Clarke, G. H. "A Canadian Novelist and his Critic." *Queen's Quarterly* 53 (Aug. 1946): 362–68.

——. Rev. of *The Master of the Mill*. *Queen's Quarterly* 52 (1945): 254–55.

Cohn-Sfetcu, Ofelia. "At the Mercy of Winds and Waves? *Over Prairie Trails* by F.P. Grove." *University of Windsor Review* 11 (1976): 49–56.

Collin, W.E. "La Tragique Ironie de Frederick Philip Grove." *Gants du Ciel* 4 (1946): 15–20.

Collins, Alexandra. "An Audience in Mind when I Speak: Grove's *In Search of Myself*." *Studies in Canadian Literature* 8.2 (1983): 181–93.

Craig, Terrence L. "Frederick Philip Grove's 'Poems.'" *Canadian Poetry* 10 (1982): 58–90.

——. "Frederick Philip Grove's *Dirge*." *Canadian Poetry* 16 (1985): 55–73.

——. "F.P. Grove and the 'Alien' Immigrant in the West." *Journal of Canadian Studies/Revue d'études canadiennes* 20.2 (1985): 92–100.

——. "Frederick Philip Grove und der 'fremde' Einwanderer im kanadischen Westen." *German Canadian Yearboook/Deutsch-kanadisches Jahrbuch* 9 (1986): 141–51.

Dahlie, Halvard. *Isolation and Commitment: Frederick Philip Grove's Settlers of the Marsh*. Toronto: ECW, 1993.

Daniel, Roy. "An Important Canadian Writer Is Frederick Philip Grove." *Winnipeg Free Press* (24 Oct. 1945): 17.

Darling, Michael. "A Mask for All Occasions: The Identity of FPG." *Essays on Canadian Writing* 1 (1974): 50–53.

Deacon, William Arthur. "The Yoke of Life." *The Ottawa Citizen*, 11 Oct. 1930: 15.

——. "The Canadian Novel Turns the Corner." *Canadian Magazine* 86 (Oct. 1936): 16.

Dewar, Kenneth C. "Technology and the Pastoral Idea in Frederick Philip Grove." *Journal of Canadian Studies/Revue d'études canadiennes* 8 (1973): 19–28.

Dietz, Carl. "Oscar Wilde." *Literarisches Zentralblatt für Deutschland* 6 (1905): 117–20.

Divay, Gaby, ed. *Poems/Gedichte by/von Frederick Philip Grove/Felix Paul Greve and Fanny Essler*. Winnipeg: Wolf Verlag, 1993.

——. "Fanny Essler's Poems: Felix Paul Greve's or Else von Freytag-Loringhoven's?" *Arachne* 1.2 (1994): 165–97.

Eggleston, Wilfrid. "Frederick Philip Grove." In *Our Living Tradition*. Ed. Claude Bissell. Toronto: University of Toronto Press, 1957.

——. *The Frontier and Canadian Letters*. Toronto: Ryerson Press, 1957.

——. "F.P. Grove's Origins Finally Disclosed." *The Ottawa Journal*, 27 May 1972: 33.

——. "F.P.G.: The Ottawa Interlude." *Inscape* 11 (Spring 1974): 101–10.

Ettlinger, Josef. "Der Fall Hofmanswaldau." *Das litterarische Echo* 10 (1907): 19–23.

Fairley, Barker. Rev. of *Our Daily Bread*. *Canadian Forum* 9 (1928): 66.

——. "Philip Grove." Rev. of *Two Generations*. *Canadian Forum* 19 (1939): 225.

Fenwick, Mac. "Niels's Saga: Colonial Narrative and Nordic Naturalism in *Settlers of the Marsh*." *English Studies in Canada* 23.3 (September 1997): 297–314.

Ferguson, Mildred. "A Study of the Tragic Element in the Novels of Frederick Philip Grove." M.A. Thesis, University of Manitoba, 1947.

Frye, Northrop. "Canadian Dreiser." In *Frederick Philip Grove*. Ed. Desmond Pacey. Toronto: Ryerson Press, 1970.

Gammel, Irene. "The City's Eye of Power. Panopticism and Specular Prostitution in Dreiser's New York and Grove's Berlin." *Canadian Review of American Studies/Revue canadienne d'étudęs américaines* 22.2 (1991): 211–27.

——. "Two Odysseys of 'Americanization': Dreiser's *An American Tragedy* and Grove's *A Search for America*." *Studies in American Literature/Études en littérature canadiennes* 17.2 (1992): 129–47.

——. "'I'll be my own Master'. Domestic Conflicts and Discursive Resistance in *Maurermeister Ihles Haus* and *Our Daily Bread*." *Canadian Literature* 135 (1992): 15–31.

——. "Victim's of their Writing. Grove's *In Search of Myself* and Dreiser's *The Genius*." *Ariel* 23.3 (July 1992): 49–70.

——. "'No Woman Lover:' Baroness Elsa's Intimate Biography." *Ariel* 23.3 (1992): 49–70; *Canadian Review of Comparative Literature* 20.3 (Winter 1993): 451–67.

——. *Sexualizing Power in Naturalism: Theodore Dreiser and Frederick Philip Grove*. Calgary: University of Calgary Press, 1994.

———. "Breaking the Bonds of Discretion: Baroness Elsa and the Female Sexual Confession." *Tulsa Studies in Women's Literature* 14.1 (Spring 1995): 149–66.

———. "My Secret Garden: Dis/Pleasure in L.M. Montgomery and F.P. Grove." *English Studies in Canada* 25 (1999): 39–66.

———. "Klaus Martens: Felix Paul Greves Karriere: Frederick Philip Grove in Deutschland." Review article. *Zeitschrift für Amerikanistik und Anglistik* 47.1 (1999): 87–88.

———. "Baroness Else and the Politics of Aggressive Body Talk." In *American Modernism*. Ed. Jay Bochner and Justin Edwards. New York: Peter Lang, 1999.

———. "German Extravagance Confronts American Modernism: The Poetics of Baroness Else." In *Pioneering North America: Mediators of European Literature and Culture*. Ed. Klaus Martens. Würzburg: Königshausen & Neumann, 2000.

Gide, André. "Rencontre avec Félix-Paul Grève." [Gide's diary entry of June 2, 1904.] *Bulletin des amis d'André Gide* 32 (1976): 25–41. See also *"Je vous écris en hâte et fiévreusement:" André Gide und Felix Paul Greve. Korrespondenz und Dokumentation*. Ed. Jutta Ernst and Klaus Martens. Schriften der Saarländischen Universitäts- und Landesbibliothek. Vol 5. St. Ingbert: Röhrig Universitätsverlag, 1999.

———. "Conversation avec un Allemand quelques années avant la guerre." *Nouvelle revue francaise* 71 (Aug. 1919): 415–23. Rpt. in *Incidences* (1924): 135–45. Rpt. in *Oeuvres complets*. Ed. L. Martin Chauffer. Paris: Nouvelle revue francaise, 1935. 133–143. Translated by Ernst Robert Curtius as "Gespräch mit Felix Paul Greve." *Europäische Betrachtungen*. Stuttgart: Deutsche Verlagsanstalt, 1931. Translated by Blanche A. Price as "Conversations with a German Several Years Before the War." In *Pretexts: Reflections on Literature and Morality by André Gide*. Ed. Justin O'Brien. New York: Meridian Books, 1959.

Giltrow, Janet. "Grove in Search of an Audience." *Canadian Literature* 90 (1981): 92–107.

Grah, Th[eodor]. [Report about the lawsuit against Felix Paul Greve.] *Bonner Zeitung*, 31 May 1903. Galley proofs corrected by hand. J.C.C. Bruns-Archiv, Minden.

Groth, Max. "Fanny Eßler. Roman von Felix Paul Greve." *Der Kunstwart* 19 (1905/06): 549–50.

Grove, A. Leonard. "Memoir." [1999.] Unpublished typescript for use in the present book. Martens Archive.

Hamilton, Louis. "Letter to the Editor." [Rev. of *Our Daily Bread*.] *Canadian Forum* 9 (1929): 326.

Harris, John. "Canadian Bureauclassics: *Master of the Mill* and *Wind without Rain*." *The English Quarterly* 13 (1980): 47–58.

Harrison, Dick. "Rölvaag, Grove, and Pioneering on the American and Canadian Plains." *Great Plains Quarterly* 1 (1981): 252–62.

Healy, J. J. "Grove and the Matter of Germany: The Warkentin Letters and the Art of Liminal Disengagement." *Studies in Canadian Literature* 2 (1981): 170–87.

Hefling, Helen, and Jessie W. Dyde. *Index to Contemporary Biography and Criticism*. Boston: F.W. Faxon, 1934.

Heidenreich, Rosmarin. "The Search for FPG." *Canadian Literature* 80 (1979): 63–70.

Hesse, Hermann. *Gedenkblätter: Erinnerungen an Zeitgenossen.* Ed. Volker Michels. Frankfurt: Suhrkamp, 1984.

Hind-Smith, Joan. *Three Voices: The Lives of Margaret Laurence, Gabrielle Roy, Frederick Philip Grove.* Toronto and Vancouver: Clarke Irwin, 1975.

Hjartarson, Paul Ivar. "Design and Truth in *In Search of Myself.*" *Canadian Literature* 90 (1981): 73–90.

——. "Frederick Philip Grove at Work: A Study of the Drafts of *The Master of the Mill.*" Dissertation, Queen's University, 1981.

——. ed. *A Stranger to my Time. Essays by and about Frederick Philip Grove.* Edmonton: NeWest Press, 1986.

——. "Of Greve, Grove, and Other Strangers: The Autobiographies of the Baroness Elsa von Freytag-Loringhoven." In *A Stranger to my Time.* Ed. Paul I. Hjartarson. Edmonton: NeWest Press, 1986.

——. "On the Textual Transmission of F.P. Grove's *A Search for America.*" *Papers of the Bibliographical Society of Canada* 25 (1986): 59–81.

——. "The Self, its Discourse, and the Other: The Autobiographies of Frederick Philip Grove and the Baroness Elsa von Freytag-Loringhoven." In *Reflections: Autobiography and Canadian Literature.* Ed. Klaus P. Stich. Ottawa: University of Ottawa Press, 1988.

—— and Douglas O. Spettigue, eds. *Baroness Elsa.* Toronto: Oberon Press, 1992.

——. "Staking a Claim: Settler Culture and the Canonization of 'Frederick Philip Grove' as a 'Canadian' Writer." In *Pioneering North America: Mediators of European Literature and Culture.* Ed. Klaus Martens. Würzburg: Königshausen & Neumann, 2000.

Holliday, W.B. "Frederick Philip Grove: An Impression." *Canadian Literature* 3 (1960): 17–22. Rpt. in *Writers of the Prairies.* Ed. Donald G. Stephens. Vancouver: University of British Columbia Press, 1973.

Immel, Horst. *Literarische Gestaltungsvarianten des Einwandererromans in der amerikanischen und anglokanadischen Literatur: Grove, Cahan, Rölvaag, Henry Roth.* Frankfurt: Lang, 1987.

Jahn, K. "Allgemeines des 18./19. Jh.: Die deutsche Literatur und das Ausland." [Rev. of *Oscar Wildes sämtliche Werke in deutscher Sprache.* Vol. 7. Intro. Felix Paul Greve.] In *Jahresberichte für Neuere Deutsche Literaturgeschichte* 14 (1903). Berlin: B. Behrs Verlag, 1906.

K[irkconnell], [Watson]. "Frederick Philip Grove." *Canadian Bookman* 7 (1926): 110.

Keith, W. J. "Grove's *Over Prairie Trails*: A Re-examination." *The Literary Half Yearly* 13 (1972): 76–85.

——. "F.P. Grove's 'Difficult' Novel: *The Master of the Mill.*" *Ariel* 2 (1973): 34–48.

——. "The Art of Frederick Philip Grove. *Settlers of the Marsh* as an Example." *Journal of Canadian Studies/Revue d'études canadiennes* 9 (1974): 26–36.

——. "Grove's Search for America." *Canadian Literature* 59 (1974): 57–66.

——. "Grove's 'Magnificent Failure': *The Yoke of Life* Reconsidered." *Canadian Literature* 89 (1981): 104–17.

———. "Frederick Philip Grove (1879–1948)." In *ECW's Biographical Guide to Canadian Novelists*. Ed. Robert Lecker, Jack David and Ellen Quigley. Toronto: ECW, 1993.

Kingstone, Basil D. "L'étrange allemand de 1904." *Bulletin des amis d'André Gide* 3 (1975): 53–55.

Knister, Raymond. "Frederick Philip Grove." *Ontario Library Review* 13 (1928): 60–62.

Knönagel, Axel. *Nietzschean Philosophy in the Works of Frederick Philip Grove*. Frankfurt: Peter Lang, 1990.

"The Search for F.P. Greve/Grove: From First Doubts to a Greve Biography." *Connotations* 7.2 (1997–98): 246–53.

Kroetsch, Robert. "The Grammar of Silence: Narrative Patterns in Ethnic Writing." *Canadian Literature* 106 (1985): 65–74.

La Bossiere, Camille R. "Of Words and Understanding in Grove's *Settlers of the Marsh*." *University of Toronto Quarterly* 54 (1984/85): 148–62

Lane, Patrick. Afterword to *Over Prairie Trails*. Toronto: McClelland & Stewart, 1991.

Makow, Henry. "Grove's Treatment of Sex: Platonic Love in *The Yoke of Life*." *Dalhousie Review* 58 (1978): 524–40.

———. "Letters from Eden: Grove's Creative Rebirth." *University of Toronto Quarterly* 49 (1979): 48–64.

———. "Grove's *The Canyon*." *Canadian Literature* 82 (1979): 141–48.

———. "Frederick Philip Grove." In *Profiles in Canadian Literature*. Ed. Jeffrey M. Heath. Toronto: Dundurn Press, 1980.

———. "Grove's Garbled Extract. The Bibliographical Origins of *Settlers of the Marsh*." In *Modern Times: A Critical Anthology*. Ed. John Moss. Vol. 3. *The Canadian Novel*. Toronto: NC Press, 1982.

———. "*Ellen Lindstedt*: The Unpublished Sequel to Grove's *Settlers of the Marsh*." *Studies in Canadian Literature* 8.2 (1983): 270–76.

———. "An Edition of Selected Unpublished Essays and Lectures by Frederick Philip Grove Bearing on his Theory and Art." Dissertation, University of Toronto, 1982.

Martens, Klaus. "Ansichten und Kontexte des Literaturverlags J.C.C. Bruns. Zur Interaktion von Autoren, Übersetzern und Verlegern." In *Literaturvermittler um die Jahrhundertwende: J.C.C. Bruns' Verlag, seine Autoren und Übersetzer*. Ed. Klaus Martens. Schriften der Saarländischen Universitäts- und Landesbibliothek. Vol. 1. St. Ingbert: Röhrig Universitätsverlag, 1996.

———. "Felix Paul Greve." In *Literaturvermittler um die Jahrhundertwende: J.C.C. Bruns' Verlag, seine Autoren und Übersetzer*. Ed. Klaus Martens. Schriften der Saarländischen Universitäts- und Landesbibliothek. Vol. 1. St. Ingbert: Röhrig Universitätsverlag, 1996.

———. "Nixe on the River: Felix Paul Greve in Bonn (1898–1901)." *Canadian Literature* 151 (1996): 10–43.

———. *Felix Paul Greves Karriere: Frederick Philip Grove in Deutschland*. Schriften der Saarländischen Universitäts- und Landesbibliothek. Vol. 3. St. Ingbert: Röhrig Universitätsverlag, 1997.

———. "Felix Paul Greve. Ein Forschungsbericht." *Magazin Forschung* 1 (April 1997): 54–60.

——— and Jutta Ernst, eds. *"Je vous écris en hâte et fiévreusement:" André Gide und Felix Paul Greve. Korrespondenz und Dokumentation.* Schriften der Saarländischen Universitäts- und Landesbibliothek. Vol 5. St. Ingbert: Röhrig Universitätsverlag, 1999.

———. "Fieberhaftes Schreiben, leidenschaftliches Zuhören." In *"Je vous écris en hâte et fiévreusement:" André Gide und Felix Paul Greve. Korrespondenz und Dokumentation.* Ed. Jutta Ernst and Klaus Martens. Schriften der Saarländischen Universitäts- und Landesbibliothek, vol. 5. St. Ingbert: Röhrig Universitätsverlag, 1999.

———. "'Blei et Grève se canardent:' On the Making and Unmaking of Reputations." In *"Je vous écris en hâte et fiévreusement:" André Gide und Felix Paul Greve. Korrespondenz und Dokumentation.* Ed. Jutta Ernst and Klaus Martens. Schriften der Saarländischen Universitäts- und Landesbibliothek, vol. 5. St. Ingbert: Röhrig Universitätsverlag, 1999.

———. "Frederick Philip Grove in Kentucky: Spartanic Preparations — An Exploration." Internet Publication: (July 6, 1999). Also in *Pioneering North America: Mediators of European Literature and Culture.* Ed. Klaus Martens. Würzburg: Königshausen & Neumann, 2000.

———. "Battles for Recognition: Gide, Greve, also Blei." *Canadian Review of Comparative Literature* 25, 3–4 (2000): 328–48.

———. "Felix Greve and Else on the Channel Coast." Internet Publication: (April 4, 2000).

———. "A Reviewer Reviewed." Internet Publication: (September 22, 2000).

———. "Frederick Philip Grove (Felix Paul Greve)." In *Dictionary of Literary Biography. Canadian Science Fiction and Fantasy Writers.* Ed. Douglas Ivison. Forthcoming.

———. "Science Fiction and Autobiography: Frederick Philip Grove's *Consider Her Ways.*" In *foundation: the international review of science fiction* 30, 81 (Spring 2001): 90–96. Ed. Jennifer Burwell and Nancy Johnson. Forthcoming.

Martyn, Howe. "Great Ontario Novel." [Rev. of *Two Generations.*] *Canadian Bookman* 21 (1939): 43–45.

Mathews, Robin. "F.P. Grove: An Important Version of *The Master of the Mill* Discovered." *Studies in Canadian Literature* 7.2 (1982): 241–57.

Matthews, S. Leigh. "Grove's Last Laugh: The Gender of Self-representation in Frederick Philip Grove's *In Search of Myself.*" *Canadian Literature* 159 (Winter 1998): 114–37.

McCormack, Robert. "Recent Paperbacks." *Tamarack Review* 6 (1958): 97–101.

McCourt, Edward A. "Spokesman of a Race?" *The Canadian West in Fiction.* Toronto: Ryerson Press, 1949: 55–70.

McDonald, R.D. "The Power of F.P. Grove's *The Master of the Mill.*" *Mosaic* 7 (1974): 89–100.

McGillivray, J. R. "Letters in Canada: 1939 (Fiction)." *University of Toronto Quarterly* 9 (1940): 291–92.

——. "Letters in Canada: 1944 (Fiction)." *University of Toronto Quarterly* 14 (1945): 271–72.

McKenna, Isobel. "As They Really Were: Women in the Novels of Grove." *English Studies in Canada* 2 (1976): 109–16.

McKenzie, Ruth. "Life in a New Land: Notes on the Immigrant Theme in Canadian Fiction." *Canadian Literature* 3 (1961): 24–33.

McMullen, Lorraine. "Women in Grove's Novels." *Inscape* 11 (Spring 1974): 67–76.

McMullin, Stanley E. "Grove and the Promised Land." *Canadian Literature* 49 (1971): 10–19. Rpt. in *Writers of the Prairies*. Ed. Donald G. Stephens. Vancouver: University of British Columbia Press, 1973.

——. "Margaret Stobie's *Frederick Philip Grove*." *Canadian Literature* 60 (1974): 107.

——. "Evolution versus Revolution: Grove's Perception of History." *Inscape* 11 (1974): 77–88.

Meyerfeld, Max. "Von und über Oscar Wilde." *Das litterarische Echo* 6.8 (15 Jan. 1904): 541–44.

——. "Wilde, Wilde, Wilde." *Das litterarische Echo* 7.14 (15 Apr. 1905): 985–90.

Michael, Friedrich. "Verschollene der frühen Insel." *Börsenblatt für den Deutschen Buchhandel* 17 (29 Feb. 1969): A79–A82. Rpt. in *Der Leser als Entdecker: Betrachtungen, Aufsätze und Erinnerungen eines Verlegers*. Sigmaringen: Jan Thorbecke Verlag, 1983.

Michels, Volker, ed. *Die Welt im Buch: Leseerfahrungen 1. Rezensionen und Aufsätze aus den Jahren 1900–1910*. Frankfurt: Surhkamp, 1988. Containing reviews of translations by Felix Paul Greve:

Balzac, Honoré de. *Menschliche Komödie*. 313–14, 454.

Cervantes de Saavedra, Miguel. *Die Novellen*. Trans. K. Thorer. 266, 319.

Die Erzählungen aus den tausendundein Nächten. 259, 413–18.

Gide, André. *Der Immoralist*. 212–14.

Murger, Henri. *La Bohème*. 227.

Swift, Jonathan. *Werke*. 393, 506.

Tausend und ein Tag. 388–89, 413–18, 454.

Wells, H.G. *Dr. Moreaus Insel, Die Riesen kommen, Die Zeitmaschine*. 158–59, 360.

Middlebro, Tom. "Animals, Darwin, and Science Fiction: Some Thoughts on Grove's *Consider Her Ways*." *Canadian Fiction Magazine* 7 (1972): 55–57.

Ming-Chen, John Z. "Re-reading Grove: The Influence of Socialist Ideology on the Writer and *The Master of the Mill*." *Canadian Literature* 147 (1995): 25–44.

Mitchell, Beverley S.A. "The 'Message' and the 'Inevitable Form' in *The Master of the Mill*." *Journal of Canadian Fiction* 3 (1974): 74–79.

Morley, Patricia. "Over Prairie Trails: A Poem Woven of Impressions." *The Humanities Association Review* 25 (1974): 225–31.

Müller, Marianne. "Grove, Frederick Philip." In *BI — Schriftstellerlexikon*. Leipzig: Bibliographisches Institut, 1988.

Nause, John, ed. *The Grove Symposium*. Ottawa: University of Ottawa Press, 1974.

Nesbitt, Bruce H. "*The Seasons*: Grove's Unfinished Novel." *Canadian Literature* 18 (1963): 47–51.

Noel-Bentley, Peter. "The Position of the Unpublished *Jane Atkinson* and *The Weatherhead Fortunes*." *Inscape* 11 (Spring 1974): 13–33.

Pacey, Desmond. "Frederick Philip Grove." *Manitoba Arts Review* 3 (Spring 1943): 28–41.

——. *Frederick Philip Grove*. Toronto: Ryerson Press, 1945.

——. Rev. of *In Search of Myself*. *Canadian Forum* 26 (1946): 212–13.

——. Rev. of *Consider Her Ways*. *Canadian Forum* 26 (1947): 283–84.

——. *Creative Writing in Canada*. Toronto: Ryerson Press, [1952].

——. "Frederick Philip Grove: A Group of Letters." *Canadian Literature* 11 (1962): 28–38.

——. "Frederick Philip Grove." In *Essays in Canadian Criticism 1938–1968*. Ed. Desmond Pacey. Toronto: Ryerson Press, 1969.

——, ed. *Frederick Philip Grove*. Toronto: Ryerson Press, 1970.

——. "Grove's Tragic Vision." In *Frederick Philip Grove*. Ed. Desmond Pacey. Toronto: Ryerson Press, 1970.

——. "Introduction" to *Tales from the Margin* by F.P. Grove. Ed. D. Pacey. Toronto: Ryerson Press, 1971.

——. "In Search of Grove in Sweden." *Journal of Canadian Fiction* 1 (Winter 1972): 69–73.

—— and J.C. Mahanti. "Frederick Philip Grove: An International Novelist." *International Fiction Review* 1 (1974): 17–26. [German translation, slightly altered and illustrated: "Felix Paul Greve/Frederick Philip Grove: Ein internationaler Romanschriftsteller." Trans. Gerhard Kutzsch. *Der Bär von Berlin: Jahrbuch des Vereins für die Geschichte Berlins* Vol. 27. Ed. Gerhard Kutzsch und Claus P. Mader. Berlin und Bonn: Westkreuzdruckerei (in Kommission), 1978. 127–137.].

Pache, Walter. "On Editing the Letters of Frederick Philip Grove." In *Editing Canadian Texts: Papers Given at the Conference on Editorial Problems, University of Toronto, Nov. 1972*. Ed. Frances G. Halpenny. Toronto: A.M. Hakkert, 1975.

——. "Der Fall Greve — Vorleben und Nachleben des Schriftstellers Felix Paul Greve." *Deutschkanadisches Jahrbuch* 5 (1979): 121–36.

——. "The Dilettante in Exile: Grove at the Centenary of his Birth." *Canadian Literature* 90 (1981): 187–91.

——. "Comparative Aspects of German-Canadian Studies: The Case of Frederick Philip Grove." In *Annals/Annalen 4. German-Canadian Studies in the 1980s*. CAUTG Publications 9. Vancouver: CAUTG, 1983.

——. "Felix Paul Greve's Loneliness: Comparative Perspectives." *World Literature Written in English* 1 (1985): 104–11.

——. "Frederick Philip Grove (Felix Paul Greve) (1879–1948)." In *Canadian Writers, 1890–1920*. Ed. W.H. New. *Dictionary of Literary Biography*. Vol. 92. Detroit: Gale, 1990.

Parker, M.G. Introduction to *Fruits of the Earth* by F.P.Grove. [1933.] Toronto: McClelland and Stewart, 1965.

Padolsky, Enoch. "Grove's 'Nationhood' and the European Immigrant." *Journal of Canadian Studies/Revue d'études canadiennes* 22.1 (1987): 32–50.

Pajevic, Alexander. "Lebensentwurf. Detektivisch: Klaus Martens enttarnt Felix Paul Greve." *Frankfurter Allgemeine Zeitung* no. 217 (18 Sept. 1997): 38.

Perry, Anne Anderson. "Who's Who in Canadian Literature: Frederick Philip Grove." *Canadian Bookman* 12 (1930): 51–53.

Phelps, Arthur. "Frederick Philip Grove." In his *Canadian Writers*. Toronto: McClelland and Stewart, 1951.

Pierce, Lorne Albert. "Frederick Philip Grove." In his *An Outline of Canadian Literature: French and English*. Toronto: Ryerson Press, 1927.

———. "Frederick Philip Grove (1871–1948). *Royal Society of Canada: Proceedings and Transactions* 43 (1949): 113–19.

Potvin, Elisabeth. "'The Eternal Feminine' and the Clothing Motif in Grove's Fiction." *Studies in Canadian Literature/Revue d'études canadiennes* 12.2 (1987): 222–38.

Pratt, A.M. "By the Way." *Manitoba School Journal* 16 (1954): 12–17.

Preisberg, Ursula. "Literaturgeschichtliche Kostbarkeiten." *Campus* 1 (1996): 11.

Proietti, Salvatore. "Frederick Philip Grove's Version of Pastoral Utopianism." *Science Fiction Studies* 19.2 (1992): 361–77.

Raudsepp, Enn. "Frederick Philip Grove and the Great Tradition." *Dissertation Abstracts International* 38 (1978): 6147A.

———. "Grove and the Wellspring of Fantasy." *Canadian Literature* 84 (1980): 131–37.

Ranna, H.D. "Notable Canadian Author." *The Bookman* 80 (1931): 9.

Reichenbächer, Helmut. "Klaus Martens: *Felix Paul Greves Karriere: Frederick Philip Grove in Deutschland*." *University of Toronto Quarterly* 68.1 (Winter 1998–99): 511–13.

Rhodenizer, V.B. *Handbook of Canadian Literature*. Ottawa: Graphic Publishers, 1930.

———. Rev. of *Consider Her Ways*. *Dalhousie Review* 27 (1947): 116–17.

Riley, Anthony W. "The German Novels of Frederick Philip Grove." In *The Grove Symposium*. Ed. John Nause. Ottawa: The University of Ottawa Press, 1974.

———. "The Case of Greve/Grove: The European Roots of A Canadian Writer." In *The Old World and the New: Literary Perspectives of German-Speaking Canadians*. Ed. Walter E. Riedel. Toronto: University of Toronto Press, 1984.

Rimmer, Thomas D. "Soul of an Immigrant." [Rev. of *A Search for America*.] *Canadian Bookman* 10 (1928): 17–18.

Robins, J.D. Rev. of *It Needs to Be Said*. *Canadian Forum* 9 (1929): 388–90.

———. Rev. of *The Yoke of Life*. *Canadian Forum* 11 (1931): 185–86.

Roehl, Marita. "Frederick Philip Grove. Angloamerikanischer Autor der 20er und 30er Jahre des 20. Jahrhunderts." In *Literatur- und Gesellschaftsentwicklung der USA im Spannungsfeld der Epochenproblematik des 20. Jahrhunderts*. Ed. Horst Hohne and Heinz Wustenhagen. Potsdam: Wissenschaftlich-Technisches Zentrum der Pädagogischen Hochschule "Karl Liebknecht," 1988.

Rowe, Kay Moreland. "Here He Lies Where He Longed." *Manitoba Arts Review* 6 (1949): 62–64.

Rubio, Mary Henley. "Grove's Children's Novel: Its Text and Larger Context." *Dissertation Abstracts International*. 43.9 (1983): 2996A.

——. ed. "The Grove Special Double Issue." *Canadian Children's Literature: A Journal of Criticism and Review* 27/28 (1982).

——. "Afterword: Genesis of a Boy's Book." *Canadian Children's Literature: A Journal of Criticism and Review* 27/28 (1982): 127–69.

Saltzwedel, Johannes. "Ein Mann, fünf Leben." *Der Spiegel* 45 (1997): 236–40.

Sandwell, B.K. "Frederick Philip Grove and the Culture of Contemporary Canada." *Saturday Night* 61 (24 Nov. 1945): 18. Rpt. in B.K. Sandwell. *Frederick Philip Grove*. 1970: 56–59.

——. "Ants as Seen by Ants." *Saturday Night* 26 Apr. 1947: 12.

——. "Grove's Autobiography." *University of Toronto Quarterly* 16 (1947): 202–06.

Sarkowski, Hans. "Felix Paul Greve als Übersetzer für den Insel-Verlag." *Buchhandelsgeschichte* 1 (2000): B27–B34.

Saunders, Thomas. "The Grove Papers: Beginning of a Definitive Collection." *Winnipeg Free Press* 19 Sept. 1962: 15.

——. "The Grove Papers." *Queen's Quarterly* 70 (Spring 1963): 22–29.

——. "A Novelist as Poet: Frederick Philip Grove." *Dalhousie Review* 43 (Summer 1963): 235–41.

——. "*Settlers of the Marsh*: Realistic Canadian Novel by Frederick Philip Grove." *CBC Times* 6 (1965): 10–11.

Sirois, Antoine. "Grove et Ringuet: Témoins d'une Epoque." *Canadian Literature* 49 (1971): 20–27.

Skelton, Isabel. "Frederick Philip Grove." *Dalhousie Review* 19 (1939): 147–63.

Spettigue, Douglas O. "Frederick Philip Grove." *Dalhousie Review* 25 (1946): 433–41.

——. *Frederick Philip Grove*. Toronto: Copp Clark, 1969.

——. "Frederick Philip Grove in Manitoba." *Mosaic* 3 (Spring 1970): 19–33.

——. "Frederick Philip Grove: A Report from Europe." *Queen's Quarterly* 78.1 (1971): 614–15.

——. "Forschungen über den Schriftsteller Felix Paul Greve." *Der Archivar* 24 (1971): 240.

——. "The Grove Enigma Resolved." *Queen's Quarterly* 79 (Spring 1972): 1–2.

—— with A.W. Riley. "Felix Paul Greve *redivivus*: Zum früheren Leben des kanadischen Schriftstellers Frederick Philip Grove." *Seminar* 9.2 (1973): 148–55.

——. *FPG: The European Years*. Ottawa: Oberon, 1973.

——. "Fanny Essler and the Master." *A Stranger to My Time*. Ed. Paul Hjartarson. Edmonton: NeWest, 1986.

——. "Felix, Elsa, André Gide and Others: Some Unpublished Letters of F.P. Greve." *Canadian Literature* 134 (1992): 9–38.

Sproxton, Birk. "Grove's Unpublished *Man* and its Relation to *The Master of the Mill*." *Inscape* 11 (1974): 35–54.

Stanley, Carlton. Rev. of *Two Generations*. *Dalhousie Review* 19 (1939–40): 129–30.

——. "Voices in the Wilderness." *Dalhousie Review* 25 (July 1945): 173–81.

——. "Frederick Philip Grove." [Review of Pacey's 1945 article "FPG."] *Dalhousie Review* 25 (Jan. 1946): 433–41.

Stenberg, Peter A. "Translating the Translatable: A Note on the Practical Problems with F.P. Grove's *Wanderungen*." *Canadian Review of Comparative Literature/Revue canadienne de literature comparée* 7 (1980): 206–12.

Stevenson, Lionel. *Appraisals of Canadian Literature*. Toronto: Macmillan, 1926.

Stich, K.P. "F.P.G: Over German Trails." *Essays on Canadian Writing* 6 (1977): 148–51.

———. "F.P. Grove's Language of Choice." *Commonwealth Literature* 14 (1979): 9–17.

———. "Grove's New World Bluff." *Canadian Literature* 90 (1981): 111–23.

———. "Extravagant Expression of Travel and Growth: Grove's Quest for America." *Studies in Canadian Literature* 6 (1981): 155–69.

———. "The Memory of Masters in Grove's Self-Portraits." *Canadian Studies/Revue d'études canadiennes* 12 (1982): 153–64.

———. "Narcissism and the Uncanny in Grove's *Over Prairie Trails*." *Mosaic* 19 (1986): 31–41.

———. "Grove's *Stella*." *Canadian Literature* 113/114 (1987): 258–62.

———. "Beckwith's *Mark Twain* and the Dating of Grove's *A Search for America*." *Canadian Literature* 127 (1990): 183–85.

Scobie, Stephen. "The Baroness Elsa." [Poem.] *Canadian Literature* 111 (Winter 1986): 127–29.

"Felix Paul Greve." [Poem.] In *Duino*. Montreal: Signal Editions-Vehicule Press, 1989.

Stobie, Margaret R. *Frederick Philip Grove*. Toronto-Montréal: McClelland & Stewart, 1969.

———. "Frederick Philip Grove and the Canadianism Movement." *Studies in the Novel* 4 (1972): 173–85.

———. *Frederick Philip Grove*. New York: Twayne, 1973.

———. "Grove's Letters from the Mennonite Reserve." *Canadian Literature* 59 (1974): 67–80.

———. "Grove and the Ants." *Dalhousie Review* 58 (1978): 418–33.

———. "Grove in Simcoe." *Canadian Literature* 11 (1986): 130–42.

———. "An Innocent from Abroad: Grove's *A Search for America*." *A Stranger to My Time*. Ed. Paul Hjartarson. Edmonton: NeWest Press, 1986.

Stockdale, John. "What was Frederick Philip Grove?" *Inscape* 11 (1974): 1–11. Rpt. in *The New Hero: Essays in Comparative Quebec/Canadian Literature*. Ed. Ronald Sutherland. Toronto: Macmillan, 1977. "L'Américanité selon Frederick Philip Grove." *Études Littéraires* 8 (1975): 33–41.

Sutherland, Ronald. "Twin Solitudes." *Canadian Literature* 31 (1967): 5–24.

———. *Frederick Philip Grove*. Toronto: McClelland & Stewart, 1969.

Thomas, Clara and John Lennox. "Grove's Maps." *Essays on Canadian Writing* 26 (1983): 75–79.

Thompson, Eric. "Grove's Vision of Prairie Man." *Ariel* 4 (1979): 15–33.

Thompson, J. Lee. "In Search of Order: The Structure of Grove's *Settlers of the Marsh*." *Journal of Canadian Fiction* 3 (1974): 65–73. Rpt. in *Modern Times: A Critical Anthology*. Ed. John Moss. *The Canadian Novel*. Vol. 3. Toronto: NC Press, 1982.

Turner, Margaret E. "Language and Silence in the Literature of Richardson and Grove." In *Future Indicative: Literary Theory and Canadian Literature*. Ed. John Moss. Ottawa: University of Ottawa Press, 1987.

Waddington, Miriam. Rev. of *The Master Mason's House*. *Humanities Association Review* 28 (1977): 297.

Warken, Arlette. "How the Ants Pioneered America: F.P. Grove's *Consider Her Ways* and the Utopian Tradition of H.G. Wells and Jonathan Swift." *Pioneering North America: Mediators of European Literature and Culture*. Ed. Klaus Martens. Würzburg: Königshausen & Neumann, 2000.

Webber, B. "Grove in Politics." *Canadian Literature* 63 (1975): 126–27.

Wiebe, Rudy. "A Novelist's Personal Notes on Frederick Philip Grove." *University of Toronto Quarterly* 47 (1978): 188–99. Rpt. in *A Voice in the Land: Essays by and about Rudy Wiebe*. Ed. W.J. Keith. Edmonton: NeWest Press, 1981.

Wilson, Jenny. "A Comparative Study of Frederick Philip Grove and Theodore Dreiser." M.A. Thesis, University of New Brunswick, 1962.

◆ ENTRIES IN REFERENCE WORKS AND LITERARY HISTORIES

Brockhaus' Konversations-Lexikon. 14th ed. Leipzig-Wien: F.A. Brockhaus, 1892–95.

Ludwig Eisenberg's großes biographisches Lexikon der deutschen Bühne im 19. Jahrhundert. Leipzig: List, 1903.

Lexikon der Deutschen Dichter und Prosaisten vom Beginn des 19. Jahrhunderts bis zur Gegenwart. Ed. Franz Brümmer. 6th ed. Leipzig: Reclam [1913].

Meyers Lexikon. 5th ed. Leipzig: Bibliographisches Institut, 1905.

Pache, Walter. "Frederick Philip Grove (Felix Paul Greve) (1879–1948)." In *Canadian Writers, 1890–1920*. Ed. W.H. New. *Dictionary of Literary Biography*. Vol. 92. Detroit: Gale, 1990.

Martens, Klaus. "Frederick Philip Grove (Felix Paul Greve)." In *Dictionary of Literary Biography. Canadian Science Fiction and Fantasy Writers*. Ed. Douglas Ivison. Forthcoming.

◆ BIOGRAPHIES

Eaton, C.E. "Life and Works of Frederick Philip Grove." M.A. Thesis, University of Acadia, 1940.

Pacey, Desmond. *Frederick Philip Grove*. Toronto: Ryerson Press, 1945. [New ed. 1970.]

Sutherland, Ronald. *Frederick Philip Grove*. Toronto: McClelland & Stewart, 1969.

Spettigue, Douglas O. *Frederick Philip Grove*. Toronto: Copp Clark, 1969.

Stobie, Margaret R. *Frederick Philip Grove*. Toronto: McClelland & Stewart, 1969.

Spettigue, Douglas O. *FPG: The European Years*. Toronto: Oberon, 1973.

Stobie, Margaret R. *Frederick Philip Grove*. New York: Twayne, 1973.

Martens, Klaus. *Felix Paul Greves Karriere: Frederick Philip Grove in Deutschland.* Schriften der Saarländischen Universitäts- und Landesbibliothek. Vol. 3. St. Ingbert: Röhrig Universitätsverlag, 1997.

◆ **BIBLIOGRAPHIES**

Heggie, Grace, and Anne McGaughey, eds. *Index to Canadian Bookman.* Toronto: McLaren Editions, 1993.

Miska, John P. *Frederick Philip Grove: A Bibliography of Primary and Secondary Material.* Ottawa: Microfilm Bibliographies, 1984.

Raths, Deborah. *Register of the Frederick Philip Grove Collection.* Winnipeg: Department of Archives, Manuscripts and Rare Books, University of Manitoba Libraries, 1979.

◆ **THE CULTURAL CONTEXT: LITERATURE AND OTHER MATERIALS**

Anon. *Bericht über das 348. Schuljahr 1876–77.* Beigabe zur Geschichte der St. Johannis-Schule in Hamburg, I: "Die milden Stiftungen des Johanneums." Hamburg, 1878.

Anon. [Dr. P. Reinmüller.] *Jahres-Bericht der Realschule der Evangelisch Reformierten Gemeinde in Hamburg, Seilerstraße (St. Pauli) über das Schuljahr 1894 bis Ostern 1895.* Hamburg: F. Rommerdt, März 1895.

Anon. *Realschule in St. Pauli zu Hamburg: Bericht über das Schuljahr 1897–8.* Program no. 778. Hamburg: Lütcke & Wulff, 1898.

Anon. *65 Jahre Akademischer Ruderclub Rhenus: Clubgeschichte 1890–1955.* Saarbrücken, 1955.

Anon. [Karl Gustav Vollmoeller.] "E.F.G.H., Die Nachgelassenen prosaischen Schriften." *März* 4.12 (17 June 1910): 460–72; 4.13 (1 July 1910): 33–44.

Anon. "Bunbury: Eine Legende von Matta-Fatta." *Die Schaubühne* 3 (17 Jan. 1907): 79–80.

Anon. [Max Bruns.] *Die Entwicklung von J.C.C. Bruns' Verlag, Minden in Westfalen.* Minden: J.C.C. Bruns, [1929–30].

Anon. [Heinrich Stiller.] *Festschrift zur Erinnerung an das achtzigjährige Bestehen der Firma J.C.C. Bruns in Minden, Westf., 1. Januar 1914.* Minden: J.C.C. Bruns, [1914].

Anon. [Dr. Georg Thiel.] "Von Bonn nach Würzburg (3.–15. August 1899)." In *Geschichte des Akademischen Ruderclubs Rhenus zu Bonn: Festschrift zum fünfzehnjährigen Stiftungsfest S.–S. 1905.* Ed. W. Ottendorf, E. Mengelberg and W. Ludwig. Bonn: Carl Georgi, 1906.

Adams, Henry. *The Education of Henry Adams.* Ed. Ernest Samuels. Boston: Houghton Mifflin, 1973.

Alighieri, Dante. *Das neue Leben.* Trans. Karl Federn. Halle: Hendel, 1897.

D'Annunzio, Gabriele. *La Citta Morta.* [1898/1901.] Mailand: Mondadori, 1975.

———. *Francesca da Rimini.* Trans. Karl Gustav Vollmoeller. Berlin: S. Fischer, 1903.

Archäologenbildnisse: Porträts und Kurzbiographien von Klassischen Archäologen deutscher Sprache. Ed. Reinhard Lullies and Wolfgang Schiering. Mainz: Verlag Philip von Zabern, 1988.

"Archäologischer Anzeiger." *Jahrbuch des Kaiserlich Deutschen Archäologischen Instituts*, 15 (1900). Berlin: Georg Reimer, 1901.

August Endell. Der Architekt des Photoateliers Elvira, 1871–1925. Museum Villa Stuck, Munich. Exhibition and catalogue designed by Klaus Sembach and Gottfried von Haeseler. Munich: Stuck Jugendstilverein, 1977.

Baatz, Dietwulf. *Der römische Limes.* 2nd ed. Berlin: Mann Verlag, 1975.

Banning, Rudolf. "Zur Theorie des Segelns." In *Gelehrtenschule des Johanneums.* Program no. 849. Hamburg: Lätcke & Wolf, 1904.

Bäthe, Kristian. *Wer wohnte wo in Schwabing?* Munich: Süddeutscher Verlag, 1965.

Barr, A.E. *The Black Shilling.* Trans. Alfred Peuker. Minden: J.C.C. Bruns, 1907.

Baudelaire, Charles. *Blumen des Bösen.* Minden: J.C.C. Bruns, [1922].

——. *Charles Baudelaire's Werke.* Ed. and trans. Max and Margarethe Bruns. 5 vols. Minden: J.C.C. Bruns, [1901–8].

Bernus, Alexander von. *In Memoriam Alexander von Bernus: Ausgewählte Prosa aus seinem Werk.* Ed. Otto Heuschele. Heidelberg: Lambert Schneider, 1966.

Bierbaum, Otto J. *Prinz Kuckuck. Leben, Taten, Meinungen und Höllenfahrt eines Wollüstlings.* [1906–1907.] Munich: Albert Langen-Georg Müller, [1960].

Blei, Franz. "Nietzsche in Frankreich." *Die Zeit* (18 Jul. 1903): 144–45.

——. "Oscar Wilde." *Rheinisch-Westfälische Zeitung* (8, 12, 15 Jul. 1903): 193–95.

——. *In Memoriam Oscar Wilde.* Leipzig: Insel, 1904.

——. *Der Montblanc sei höher als der Stille Ozean.* Ed. Rolf-Peter Baacke. Hamburg: Europäische Verlagsanstalt, 1994.

——. *Porträts.* Ed. Anne Gabrisch. Berlin: Volk und Welt, 1986.

Bock von Wüllingen, Ferdinand. *Das Geheimnis des Teutonensteins im Hof der Burg Miltenberg.* Amorbach and Miltenberg: Volkhardtsche Druckerei, 1951.

Boehringer, Robert, ed. *Briefwechsel zwischen George und Hofmannsthal.* 2nd expanded ed. Munich-Düsseldorf: Küpper, 1953.

—— and G.P. Landmann, eds. *Stefan George–Friedrich Gundolf. Briefwechsel.* Munich and Düsseldorf: Küpper, 1962.

——. *Mein Bild von Stefan George.* 2nd ed. Munich-Düsseldorf: Küpper, 1967.

Böschenstein, Bernhard. "André Gide und Stefan George." *André Gide und Deutschland / André Gide et l'Allemagne.* Ed. Hans T. Siepe and Raimund Theis. Düsseldorf: Droste, 1992.

Bohnenkamp, Klaus E., and Claude Foucart. "Rudolf Kassners Briefe an André Gide." *Jahrbuch der Deutschen Schillergesellschaft.* Ed. Fritz Martini, Walter Müller-Seidel and Bernhard Zeller. Stuttgart: Kröner, 1986.

Borchardt, Rudolf. *Zehn Gedichte.* Bonn: J. Trapp, 1896.

Borges, Jorge Luis. "About Oscar Wilde." In *Other Inquisitions 1937–1952.* Trans. Ruth L.C. Simms. New York: Washington Square Press, 1966.

Boyle, T. Coraghessan. *The Road to Wellville.* New York: Viking, 1993.

Brandes, Georg, ed. *Die Literatur. Sammlung illustrierter Einzeldarstellungen.* Berlin: Bard, Marquardt & Co., 1904.

Braver, Ines R. "Karl Gustav Vollmoeller: Ein Beitrag zum Verständnis des Dichters." Dissertation, University of New York, 1961.

Browning, Robert. *Pippa geht vorüber*. Trans. W. von Heiseler [Henry von Heiseler]. Leipzig: Insel, 1903.

Bruns, Max. *Aus meinem Blute*. Minden: J.C.C. Bruns, [1898].

——. *Laterna Magica: Ein Anti-Phantasus*. Minden: J.C.C. Bruns, 1901.

——. "Meine Lektüre." I–VI (1901–7). J.C.C. Bruns Archiv, Minden.

——. *Die Gedichte (1893–1908)*. Minden: J.C.C. Bruns, [1909].

——. "Copir-Bücher." J.C.C. Bruns Archiv, Minden.

Buddensieg, Tilmann. "Zur Frühzeit von August Endell: Seine München Briefe an Kurt Breysig." In *Festschrift für Eduard Trier*. Ed. Justus Müller-Hopfstede and Werner Spies. Berlin: Mann Verlag, 1981.

Clarke, George Herbert. "A Canadian Novelist and His Critic." *Queen's Quarterly* 52 (1946): 36268.

Claudel, Paul. *Correspondance avec André Gide*. Ed. Robert Mallet. Paris: Gallimard, 1948.

Closs, August, ed. *Introduction to German Literature. Twentieth Century German Literature*. Vol. 4. London: Cresset Press, 1969.

Curtius, Ludwig. *Deutsche und antike Welt*. Stuttgart: Deutsche Verlags-Anstalt, 1958.

Dauthendey, Max. *Ultra-Violett*. Berlin: Haase, 1893. [New ed. Minden: J.C.C. Bruns, 1899.]

——. *Des großen Krieges Not*. Medan/Sumatra-Munich: A. Langen, 1915.

Delbrueck, Richard. "Die Kuh des Myron." *Mitteilungen des Kaiserlich deutschen Archaeologischen Instituts. Roemische Abteilung* 16 (1901): 42–46.

—— and Karl Gustav Vollmoeller. "Das Quellhaus des Theagenes in Megara." ["Text von Delbrueck, Zeichnungen von Vollmoeller."] *Mitteilungen des Kaiserlich deutschen Archäologischen Instituts. Athenische Abteilung* 25 (1900): 23–33.

Deutsche Reichs-Zeitung. 32 (30 May 1903): 271.

Dickson, Lovat. *H.G. Wells: His Turbulent Life and Times*. London: Macmillan, 1969.

Die Literarische Welt. Ed. Willy Haas. Berlin, 1925–33.

Dolbin, B.F. "Eine Stunde mit Carl Vollmoeller." *Die Literatur* 32.7 (April 1930): 379.

——. "Les Dossiers de Presse de *L'immoraliste* (VI), des *Caves du Vatican* (II) et de la *Symphonie pastorale* (I)." *Bulletin des Amis d'André Gide* 6.40 (October 1978): 64–79.

Eisenberg, Ludwig. *Das geistige Wien: Künstler- und Schriftsteller-Lexikon*. Vol. 1. Wien: Daberkow, 1893.

Ellmann, Richard. *Oscar Wilde*. London: Hamish Hamilton, 1987.

Endell, August. *Ein Werden. Gedichte*. Munich: Knorr & Hirth, [1896].

Endell, Else. Picture postcard to Marcus Behmer from the island of Föhr (26 Dec. 1902). Stadtarchiv München.

Ernst, Jutta. "Zwischen Kunst und Justiz: Die übersetzerische Vermittlung von Weltliteratur und ihre rechtlichen Rahmenbedingungen." In *Literaturvermittler um die Jahrhundertwende: J.C.C. Bruns' Verlag, seine Autoren und Übersetzer*. Ed. Klaus Martens. Schriften der Saarländischen Universitäts- und Landesbibliothek. Vol. 1. St. Ingbert: Röhrig Universitätsverlag, 1996.

Federn, Karl. *Dante*. Leipzig-Berlin-Vienna: E.A. Seemann und Gesellschaft für Graphische Industrie, 1899.

Flaubert, Gustave. *Die Schule der Empfindsamkeit*. Trans. Luise Wolf. Minden: J.C.C. Bruns, [1904].

———. *Madame Bovary*. Intro. Guy de Maupassant. Trans. René Schickele. Minden: J.C.C. Bruns, [1907].

———. *Briefe an seine Nichte Caroline*. Intro. E.W. Fischer. Trans. Sophie von Harbou. Minden: J.C.C. Bruns, [1908].

———. *Salammbo*. Intro. Louis Bertrand. Trans. Friedrich von Oppeln-Bronikowski. Minden: J.C.C. Bruns, [1908].

Forsee, John. "Sparta." *22 Project Files of Writer's Projects, American Guide Series*. Work Projects Administration in Kentucky, Kentucky Department of Libraries and Archives, Frankfort.

Foucart, Claude. "Correspondance André Gide-Dieter Bassermann." *Bulletin des amis d'André Gide* 7.42 (April 1979): 3–39.

Frank, Armin Paul. "Einleitung." *Die literarische Übersetzung: Fallstudien zu ihrer Kulturgeschichte*. Ed. Brigitte Schultze. Göttinger Beiträge zur Internationalen Übersetzungsforschung. Vol. 1. Berlin: Schmidt, 1987.

Frenz, Horst. "Karl Knortz, Interpreter of American Literature and Culture." *German-American Literature*. Ed. Don Henry Tolzmann. Metuchen-London: Scarecrow Press, 1977.

Freud, Sigmund. *Studien über Hysterie*. Leipzig and Vienna: Deuticke, 1895.

Freytag-Loringhoven, Else von. *Baroness Elsa*. Trans. and intro. Paul I. Hjartarson and D.O. Spettigue. Ottawa: Oberon Press, 1992.

———. "Affectionate," "Holy Skirts." In *Poems for the Millennium*. Vol. 1. Ed. Jerome Rothenberg and Pierre Joris. Berkeley, Los Angeles, London: University of California Press, 1995.

Frost, Robert. *The Poetry of Robert Frost*. Ed. E.C. Latham. New York: Holt, Rinehart and Winston, 1969.

Furtwängler, Adolf. *Meisterwerke der griechischen Plastik*. Leipzig: Geisecke & Devrient, 1893.

———. *Beschreibung der Vasensammlungen im Antiquarium*. Königliche Museen zu Berlin. 2 vols. Berlin: Spemann, 1885.

———. "Die bayerische Ausgrabung des Aphaia-Heiligtums im Jahre 1901." In *Aegina. Das Heiligtum der Aphaia*. Ed. Adolf Furtwängler, Ernst R. Fiechter and Hermann Thiersch. Munich: Verlag der Akademie der Wissenchaften, 1906.

Gano, Rebecca. "Early History of Sparta." *Warsaw Independent*, 30 May 1930. [Similar accounts by Gano in the Owenton *News-Herald*, 16 May 1940; 30 Mar. 1950.]

Geibig, Gabriele. *Max Dauthendey: Sein Nachlaß als Spiegel von Leben und Werk.* Würzburg: Schöningh, 1992.

George, Stefan. *Les nourritures terrestres.* ["Le récit de Ménalque." *Ermitage* 1 (1897); "La ronde de la Grenade." *Centaure* 1 (1897).] Paris, 1927.

———. *Baudelaire: Die Blumen des Bösen.* [1901.] *Sämtliche Werke in 18 Bänden.* Vols. 13–14. Stuttgart: Klett-Cotta, 1988.

———. *Shakespeare-Sonnette.* [1909.] *Sämtliche Werke in 18 Bänden.* Vol. 12. Stuttgart: Klett-Cotta, 1988.

———. *Selections from His Works translated into English.* Trans. Daisy Broicher. London: Elkin Matthews, 1910.

———. *Zeitgenössische Dichter. Übertragen von Stefan George.* [1905.] 2 vols. Berlin: Georg Bondi, 1913.

———. *Dante. Die Göttliche Komödie. Übertragungen. Sämtliche Werke in 18 Bänden.* Vols. 9–11. Stuttgart: Klett-Cotta, 1988.

Ghéon, Henri, and André Gide. *Correspondance, 1897–1903.* Ed. Jean Tipy. Paris: Gallimard, 1976.

Gide, André. *Le traité du Narcisse (Théorie de symbole).* Paris: Librairie de l'Art Indépendant, 1891.

———. *Les nourritures terrestres.* Paris: Mercure de France, 1897.

———. *Philoctète.* Paris: Mercure de France, 1899.

———. *Le Prométhée mal enchaîné.*

———. "Le retour de L'enfant prodigue." *Vers et Prose* IX, March- May, 1907.

———. *Le roi Candaule.* Paris: Revue Blanche, 1902.

———. *L'immoraliste.* Paris: Mercure de France, 1902.

———. *Paludes.* Paris: Librairie de l'Art Indépendant, 1895.

———. "Ajax." [Fragment.] 1907.

———. *La Tentative amoureuse.* Paris: Librairie de l'Art Indépendant, 1893.

———. *Saül.* Paris: Mercure de France, 1898.

———. *La porte étroite.* Paris: NRF, 1909.

———. *Les caves du Vatican.* Paris: Éditions de la NRF, 1914.

———. "Philoktet oder der Tractat von den drei Lebensanschauungen." Trans. E.R. Weiss. *Wiener Rundschau* 5:3 (1 Feb. 1901): 50–60.

———. *Philoktet oder der Tractat von den drei Arten der Tugend.* Trans. Rudolf Kassner. Leipzig: Insel, 1904.

———. *Paludes (Die Sümpfe).* Trans. Felix Paul Greve. Minden: J.C.C. Bruns, [1905].

———. *Der Immoralist.* Trans. Felix Paul Greve. Minden: J.C.C. Bruns, [1905].

———. *Der König Candaules.* Trans. Franz Blei. Leipzig: Insel, 1905.

———. *Ein Liebesversuch und andere Novellen.* Trans. Felix Paul Greve. Berlin: Oesterheld, 1907.

———. *Der schlecht gefesselte Prometheus.* Trans. Franz Blei. Munich: Hans von Weber, 1909.

———. *Saül.* Trans. Felix Paul Greve. Berlin: Erich Reiss, 1909.

———. *Die Enge Pforte.* Trans. Felix Paul Greve. Berlin: Erich Reiss, 1909.

———. *Romans. Récits et Soties. Oeucres Lyriques.* Intro. Maurice Nadeau. Paris: Éditions Gallimard-Bibliothèque de la Pleiade, 1958.

——. *Journal I. 1887–1925*. Paris: Gallimard, 1986.

——. *Journal II. 1926–1950*. Paris: Gallimard, 1997.

——. *André Gide-Paul Claudel: Correspondance*.

——. *André Gide-Henri de Régnier. Correspondance 1891–1911*. Ed. David J. Niederauer and Heather Franklyn. Lyon: Presses Universitaires, 1997.

Gissing, George. *Zeilengeld*. Trans. A. Walter. Nördlingen: Greno, 1986.

Goethe, Johann Wolfgang von. "Die Laune des Verliebten." *Werke*. Vol. 4. Ed. Wolfgang Kayser. Hamburg: Wegner, 1968.

Gray, Gypsy M. "Sparta." *History of Gallatin County, KY*. Covington, KY.: Kentucky Historical Societies, 1968.

Gressel, Hans. *Max Bruns als Kritiker seiner Zeit. Stationen einer Wandlung. Land und Leuten dienen. Special Issue*. Ed. Realgymnasium der Stadt Minden. Minden: J.C.C. Bruns, [1976].

Greve, Ludwig, Jochen Meyer et al., eds. *Das 20. Jahrhundert: Von Nietzsche bis zur Gruppe 47*. Marbacher Katalog 36. 2nd ed. Stuttgart: Scheufele, 1993.

Grupp, Peter. *Harry Graf Kessler, 1868–1937. Eine Biographie*. Munich: C.H. Beck, 1995.

Gundolf, Friedrich. *Shakespeare und der deutsche Geist*. Berlin: Bondi, 1911.

Haas, Willy. "Erinnerungen zu André Gides 60. Geburtstag." *Die Literarische Welt* 5.47 (22 Jan. 1929): 3–4.

Hardt, Ernst. *Tantris der Narr*. Leipzig: Insel, 1907.

Hartman, Geoffrey. *The Fate of Reading and Other Essays*. Chicago: University of Chicago Press, 1975.

Heinke, Kurt. "Monographie der algerischen Oase Biskra." Dissertation, Universität Leipzig, 1914.

Heiseler, Henry von. *Zwischen Deutschland und Russland: Briefe 1903–1928*. Ed. Bernt von Heiseler. Heidelberg: Lambert Schneider, 1969.

Heisserer, Dirk. *Wo die Geister wandern: Eine Topographie der Schwabinger Bohème um 1900*. Munich: Diederichs, 1993.

Helbing, Lothar, Claus Victor Bock and Karlhans Kluncker. *Stefan George: Dokumente seiner Wirkung*. Amsterdam: Castrum Peregrini, 1984.

Hemecker, Wilhelm. "Oscar A.H. Schmitz und die 'Blätter für die Kunst.'" *Castrum Peregrini* 45.225 (1996): 62–75.

Herring, Phillip. *Djuna: The Life and Works of Djuna Barnes*. New York: Viking, 1995.

Hesse, Hermann. *Gedenkblätter. Erinnerungen an Zeitgenossen*. Ed. Volker Michels. Frankfurt: Suhrkamp, 1984.

——. *Die Welt im Buch. Leseerfahrungen I. Rezensionen und Aufsätze aus den Jahren 1900–1910*. Ed. Volker Michels. Frankfurt: Suhrkamp, 1988.

Holdheim, W. Wolfgang. *Theory and Practice of the Novel: A Study on André Gide*. Genève: Librairie Droz, 1968.

Holmsen, Bjarne P. [Arno Holz and Johannes Schlaf]. *Die Familie Selicke*. Berlin: S. Fischer, 1890.

Holz, Arno, and Johannes Schlaf, "Die papierne Passion." *Freie Bühne für Modernes Leben*, Vol. 1. (1890): 274–88.

Höroldt, Dietrich, ed. *Geschichte der Stadt Bonn*. Vol. 4. Bonn: Ferd. Dümmlers Verlag, 1989.

Huch, Friedrich. Letters to his mother. Stadtarchiv Braunschweig.

——. *Peter Michel*. Hamburg: Alfred Janßen, 1901.

Huch, Roderich. "Erinnerungen an Kreise und Krisen der Jahrhundertwende in München-Schwabing." *Castrum Peregrini* 110 (1973): 5–49.

Hytier, Jean. *André Gide*. Alger: Charlot, 1938.

Jahn, Kurt. "Die Deutsche Literatur und das Ausland." *Jahresberichte für Neuere Deutsche Literaturgeschichte* 14 (1903): 616–39.

Jaime, Eduard. "Erinnerungen an Karl Vollmoeller." *Neue Literarische Welt* 6 (25 Mar. 1952): 16.

Jahrbuch des Kaiserlich Deutschen Archäologischen Instituts. Vol. 15 (1900). Berlin: Georg Reimer, 1901.

Jammes, Francis and André Gide. *Correspondance, 1893–1938*. Ed. Robert Mallet. Paris: Gallimard, 1948.

Kassner, Rudolf. *Die Mystik, die Künstler und das Leben*. Leipzig, Eugen Diederichs, 1900.

——. "André Gide." *Wiener Rundschau* 3: 1 II. (1901): 60–63.

Kessler, Harry Graf. *Gesichter und Zeiten*. Vol. 1: *Völker und Vaterländer*. [1935.] Berlin: S. Fischer, 1956.

——. *Tagebuch eines Weltmannes*. Ed. Gerhard Schuster and Margit Pehle. Marbacher Katalog 43. Marbach: Deutsche Schillergesellschaft, 1988.

Key, Ellen. *Menschen. Zwei Charakterstudien*. Trans. Francis Maro. Berlin: S. Fischer, 1903.

Klages, Ludwig. *Stefan George*. Berlin: Bondi, 1902.

Klemperer, Victor. "Die Tradition in der gegenwärtigen französischen Literatur." *Die Literarische Welt* 5 (21 June 1929): 1–2.

Kluncker, Karlhans. *Blätter für die Kunst*. Frankfurt: Klostermann, 1974.

——, ed. *Karl und Hanna Wolfskehl: Briefwechsel mit Friedrich Gundolf*. Amsterdam: Castrum Peregrini, 1977.

Kolbe, Jürgen, and Karl Heinz Bittel. *Heller Zauber. Thomas Mann in München 1894–1933*. Berlin: Siedler, 1987.

Landmann, Edith. *Gespräche mit Stefan George*. Düsseldorf-Munich: Küpper, 1963.

Lasker-Schüler, Else. *Gesammelte Werke in drei Bänden*. Ed. Friedhelm Kemp. Munich: Kösel, 1962.

Leppmann, Wolfgang. *Winckelmann: Ein Leben für Apoll*. [1971.] Frankfurt: Fischer Taschenbuch Verlag, 1986.

Lepsius, Sabine. *Ein Berliner Künstlerleben um die Jahrhundertwende*. Munich: Gotthold Müller Verlag, 1972.

Lessing, Gotthold Ephraim. *Philotas: Ein Trauerspiel*. In *Lessings Werke*. Vol. 1. Ed. Kurt Wölfel. Frankfurt: Insel, 1967.

Lessing, Theodor. *Einmal und nie wieder*. [1935.] Gütersloh: Bertelsmann Sachbuch Verlag, 1969.

——. *Der Lotse: Wochenschrift für deutsche Kultur*. Ed. Carl Adolf Mönckeberg and Siegfried Heckscher. Hamburg: Janßen, 1900–02.

Mann, Klaus. *André Gide und die Krise des modernen Denkens* [*André Gide and the Crisis of Modern Thought*]. Reinbek: Rowohlt, 1984.

Mann, Thomas. "Traum von einer schmalen Lorbeerkrone." *Die Gesellschaft* 15.2 (1899): 183.

——. *Buddenbrooks: Der Verfall einer Familie*. Berlin: S. Fischer, 1903.

——. "Gladius Dei." *Gesammelte Werke in dreizehn Bänden*. Vol. 8. Frankfurt: S. Fischer, 1974.

——. "Gedächtnisrede auf Friedrich Huch." In Friedrich Huch, *Gesammelte Werke*. Vol. 1. Stuttgart: Deutsche Verlagsanstalt, 1925.

——. "Lebensabriß." [1930.] *Werke*. Ed. Hans Bürgin, 220–54. Frankfurt: Fischer Bücherei, 1960.

——. *Bekenntnisse des Hochstaplers Felix Krull. Gesammelte Werke in dreizehn Bänden*. Vol. 7. Frankfurt: S. Fischer, 1974.

Mann, Victor. *Wir waren fünf: Bildnis der Familie Mann*. Reinbek: Rowohlt, 1976.

Martens, Klaus. *Die ausgewanderte Evangeline: Longfellows epische Idylle im übersetzerischen Transfer*. Paderborn: Schöningh, 1989.

——. "The Art Nouveau Poe: Notes on the Inception, Transmission and Reception of the First Poe Edition in German Translation." *American Studies/Amerikastudien* 35.1 (1990): 81–93.

——. "Institutional Transmission and Literary Translation: A Sample Case." *TARGET* 3.2 (1991): 225–41.

Martin, Claude. *André Gide*. Rowohlts Monographien, vol. 89 (Ninth edition). Reinbek: Rowohlt, 1995.

Melville, Herman. *Moby-Dick*. Ed. H. Hayford and H. Parker. New York: Norton, 1967.

——. *Redburn*. Ed. H. Hayford, H. Parker and G. Thomas Tanselle. Evanston-Chicago: Northwestern University Press, 1969.

Meredith, George. *Gesammelte Romane*. Trans. J. Sotteck. Berlin: S. Fischer, 1904.

——. *Rhoda Fleming*. Trans. Sophie von Harbou. Minden: J.C.C. Bruns, [1905].

Meyer, Jochen, ed. *Briefe an Ernst Hardt: Eine Auswahl aus den Jahren 1898–1947*. Schiller-Nationalmuseum/Deutsches Literaturarchiv, Marbach, 1975.

Meyer, Richard M. "Ein neuer Dichterkreis." *Preußische Jahrbücher* 28.1 (April-June 1897): 33–54.

Mitteilungen des Kaiserlich Deutschen Archäologischen Instituts. Roemische Abteilung. Vol. 16. Rom: Loescher & Co., 1901.

"Mortgage Records." Gallatin County. Gallatin County Library, Warsaw, KY.

Nelson, Cary. *Repression and Recovery: Modern American Poetry and the Politics of Cultural Memory 1910–145*. Madison: The University of Wisconsin Press, 1989.

Neues vollständiges Verzeichnis unserer Buch- und Kunst-Publikationen bis Ende 1903. Leipzig: Insel, [November] 1903.

New, W.H. *A History of Canadian Literature*. London: Macmillan, 1989.

Nijland-Verwey, Mea, ed. *Wolfskehl und Verwey: Die Dokumente ihrer Freundschaft, 1897–1946*. Heidelberg: Schneider, 1968.

Nordsee-Sanatorium Wyk auf Föhr. Ed. Landesamt für Denkmalpflege Schleswig-Holstein. Text by Peter Schafft. Kiel: Carius-Druck, 1981.

Ott, Ulrich and Friedrich Pfäfflin, eds. *Ricarda Huch 1864–1947*. Marbacher Katalog 47. Marbach: Offizin Scheufele, 1994.

"Passenger Lists: Québec 1965–1921," Microfilm T-4762 (1909, starts with July 25). Ship's Manifest for SS. *Megantic*. "Grove, Fe....P(?). Ticket no. 4825." National Archives of Canada, Ottawa.

Peterfy, Margit. "Themen der Zeit bei J.C.C. Bruns: Via 'Ethik' in das zwanzigste Jahrhundert." In *J.C.C. Bruns' Verlag: Seine Autoren und Übersetzer*. Ed. Klaus Martens. Schriften der Saarländischen Universitäts- und Landesbibliothek. Vol. 1. St. Ingbert: Röhrig Universitätsverlag, 1996.

Pfuhl, Ernst. "Der Raub des Palladions." *Mitteilungen des Kaiserlich deutschen Archaeologischen Instituts. Roemische Abteilung*. Vol. 16 (1901): 33–41.

Pieler, Peter-Hubertus. *Mit uns zieht die neue Zeit: Der Verleger Alfred Janßen und die Reformbewegung*. Herzberg: Bautz, 1994.

Pierce, Lorne. *An Outline of Canadian Literature*. Montreal: Louis Carrier, 1927.

Piper, Reinhard. *Briefwechsel mit Autoren und Künstlern 1903–1953*. Ed. Ulrike Buergel-Goodwin and Wolfram Göbel. Munich-Zürich: Piper, 1979.

Pound, Ezra. *The Cantos of Ezra Pound*. New York: New Directions, 1972.

Przybyszeweski, Stanislaw. *Ferne komm ich her. Erinnerungen an Berlin und Krakau*. Leipzig und Weimar: Gustav Kiepenheuer, 1985.

De Quincey, Thomas. *Der Mord als eine der schönen Künste betrachtet*. Trans. Alfred Peuker. Minden: J.C.C. Bruns, 1913.

Raabe, Paul, H.L. Greve and Ingrid Grüninger, eds. *Expressionismus. Literatur und Kunst 1920–1923*. Ausstellungskatalog. Marbach: Deutsches Literaturarchiv und Schillermuseum, 1960.

Reichert, Klaus. "Vom Jugendstil zur Sachlichkeit: August Endell (1871–1925)." Dissertation, Universität Bochum, 1974.

Reichshandbuch der Deutschen Gesellschaft: Das Handbuch der Persönlichkeiten in Wort und Bild. Vol. 1. Berlin: Deutscher Wirtschaftsverlag, 1930.

Reventlow, Franziska Gräfin zu. *Tagebücher 1895–1910*. Ed. Else Reventlow. Munich-Wien: Langen-Müller, 1973.

——. *Briefe*. Ed. Else Reventlow. Munich-Wien: Langen-Müller, 1975.

——. *Romane*. Ed. Else Reventlow. Munich-Wien: Langen-Müller, 1976.

Rick, Klaus, ed. "Der Strafvollzug in Bonn im Wandel der Zeiten." Unpubl. manuscript, Bonn, 1989.

Rieche, Anita, ed. *150 Jahre Deutsches Archäologisches Institut, Rom*. Ausstellungskatalog, Wissenschaftszentrum Bonn-Bad Godesberg. Essen: Theodor Wiegand Gesellschaft, 1979.

Riley, Emma K. "Sparta, Kentucky." Typed manuscript. By a former postmistress of Sparta. Owen County Library, Owenton, KY.

Rott, Friedrich, ed. *Die Wehrpflicht im Deutschen Reich*. Vol. 1. Kassel: Brunnemann, 1891.

Sarkowski, Heinz. "J.C.C. Bruns in Minden: Hinweis auf einen fast vergessenen Verlag." *Imprimatur* N.F. 6 (1968): 121–31.

Schiller, Friedrich. *Wallenstein. Ein dramatisches Gedicht. 1. Teil: Wallensteins Lager.* In *Schillers Werke in vier Bänden.* Vol. 1. Hamburg-Berlin: Deutsche Hausbücherei, 1967.

Schmitz, Walter, ed. *Die Münchner Moderne.* Stuttgart: Reclam, 1990.

Schröder, Hans Eggert. *Ludwig Klages: Die Geschichte seines Lebens. Erster Teil: Die Jugend.* Bonn: Bouvier, 1966.

Schuchhardt, Walter-Herwig. *Adolf Furtwängler.* Freiburger Universitätsreden. Neue Folge 22. Freiburg: Schulz Verlag, 1956.

Schultess, Friedrich. *Aus drei Jahrzehnten des Hamburgischen Johanneums.* Ed. Carl Schulteß. Hamburg: Otto Meißner, 1927.

Schutte, Jürgen, and Peter Sprengel, eds. *Die Berliner Moderne 1885–1914.* Stuttgart: Reclam, 1987.

Schweitzer, Marcelle. *Gide aux Oasis.* Paris: Editions de la Francité, 1971.

Seekamp, H.-J., R.C. Cockenden and M. Keilson. *Stefan George: Leben und Werk. Eine Zeittafel.* Amsterdam: Castrum Peregrini, 1972.

Shotwell, John B. *Schools of Cincinnati.* Cincinnati: n.p., 1902.

Soergel, Albert. "Karl Gustav Vollmoeller." In *Dichtung und Dichter der Zeit.* Leipzig: Voigtländer, 1911.

———. "Max Bruns." In *Dichtung und Dichter der Zeit.* Leipzig: Voigtländer, 1928.

Stebbins, Theodore, Carol Troyen and Trevor J. Fairbrother, eds. *New World: Masterpieces of American Painting 1760–1910.* Boston: Museum of Fine Arts, 1983.

Stern, Fred B., ed. *Auftakt zur Literatur des 20. Jahrhunderts: Briefe aus dem Nachlaß von Ludwig Jacobowski.* 2 vols. Heidelberg: Lambert Schneider, 1974.

Stevens, Wallace. *The Collected Poems of Wallace Stevens.* New York: Knopf, 1954.

Tebben, Karin, ed. *Deutschsprachige Schriftstellerinnen des Fin de siècle.* Darmstadt: Wissenschaftliche Buchgesellschaft, 1999.

Tgahrt, Reinhard, et al., eds. *Rudolf Borchardt, Alfred Walter Heymel, Rudolf Alexander Schröder.* [Exhibition catalogue.] Deutsches Literaturarchiv im Schiller-Nationalmuseum, Marbach. Munich: Kösel, 1978.

Theis, Raimund. *Franz Blei–André Gide: Briefwechsel 1904–1933.* Beiträge zur Romanistik, Vol. 1. Darmstadt: Wissenschaftliche Buchgesellschaft, 1997.

U., F. "Die Bootsmannschaft am Johanneum." *Das Johanneum* 3.11 (1930): 305–08.

U.S. Census of Agriculture, 1935. Kentucky Statistics by Counties. Washington, D.C.: U.S. Department of Commerce, 1935.

Usener, Walther. "Erste Verse." [Manuscript.] Karlsruhe, 1906. Schiller-Nationalmuseum/Deutsches Literaturarchiv, Marbach.

Vallentin, Antonina. "Berliner Stunden mit H.G. Wells." *Die Literarische Welt* 5.18 (3 Mar. 1929): 1.

Varble, C.N. "History of Sparta." Unpublished typescript, Kentucky Historical Society Collection, Frankfort, KY.

———. "History of Sparta." Unpublished typescript, illustrated with line drawings and photographs (longer and more elaborate version of the manuscript in Frankfort). Privately owned.

Vignazia, Adriana. *Die deutschen D'Annunzio-Übersetzungen*. Frankfurt: Peter Lang, 1995.

Vollmoeller, Karl Gustav. "Über zwei griechische Kammergräber mit Totenbetten." *Mitteilungen des Kaiserlichen deutschen Archäologischen Instituts. Athenische Abteilung* 26 (1901): 333–76.

——. "Griechische Kammergräber mit Totenbetten." Dissertation, Universität Bonn, 1901.

——. *Catherina, Gräfin von Armagnac und ihre beiden Liebhaber*. Berlin: S. Fischer, 1903.

Wilde, Oscar. *Dorian Gray*. Trans. Johannes Gaulke. Leipzig: Max Spohr, 1901.

——. *Salomé*. Trans. Hedwig Lachmann. Leipzig: Insel, 1903.

——. *Dramen*. Trans. Frhr. von Teschenberg. Leipzig: Spohr, 1903.

——. *Der Sozialismus und die Seele des Menschen / Aus dem Zuchthaus zu Reading / Aesthetisches Manifest*. Trans. Hedwig Lachmann and Gustav Landauer. Berlin: Karl Schnabel-Axel Junckers Buchhandlung, 1904.

——. *Das Bildnis des Dorian Gray*. Trans. M[argarethe]. Preiß. Intro. Johannes Gaulke. Leipzig: Reclams Universalbibliothek, [1908].

Wilhelm, Hermann. *Die Münchner Bohème: Von der Jahrhundertwende bis zum Ersten Weltkrieg*. Munich: Buchendorfer Verlag, 1993.

Wolff, Kurt. *Autoren, Bücher, Abenteuer*. Berlin: Wagenbach, 1965.

Wolfskehl, Karl. *Karl Wolfskehl 1869–1969: Leben und Werk in Dokumenten*. Ed. Manfred Schlösser and Erich Zimmermann. Darmstadt: Agora Verlag, 1969.

—— and Hanna Wolfskehl. *Briefwechsel mit Friedrich Gundolf*. Ed. Karlhans Kluncker. Amsterdam: Castrum Peregrini, 1976.

——. *Briefwechsel aus Italien 1933–1938*. Ed. Cornelia Blasberg. Hamburg: Luchterhand, 1993.

Zeller, Bernhard, et al., eds. *Stefan George: Der Dichter und sein Kreis*. Eine Ausstellung des Deutschen Literaturarchivs im Schiller-Nationalmuseum, Marbach. Munich: Kösel, 1968.

Zwymann, Kuno. *Das Georgesche Gedicht*. Berlin: Edelheim, 1902.

INDEX

Flaubert, Gustave 204–14
Food of the Gods, The (Wells) 171, 174
Francesca da Rimini (D'Annunzio) 111
Franklin-Grout 209
Freistatt 217
Frenssen, Gustav 86
Fruits of the Earth (Greve) 4, 58, 178,
    214, 246, 254
Furtwängler, Adolf 60, 69, 77, 80

Gammel, Irene xxviii
Gardone xxix
Gaulke, Johannes 102, 104, 107, 120–2,
    123
General-Anzeiger 52
Georg Müller Publishers 205, 209
George, Stefan 10, 35, 76, 76, 83, 106–7,
    161–2, 271–2
Gesichter und Zeiten (Kessler) 22
Gide, André 61, 73–4, 178, 215, 272
    communication with Greve xiii,
        xxix, 3, 4, 18, 176–83, 184–95
Gmelin, Karl 132, 138
Goudstikker, Sophia 106
Governor General's Award 184
Graef, Botho 10, 35, 37
Graphic Press 253
Grass, Archie 254
Greve, Bertha 1–5, 15, 16, 21, 22
Greve, Carl Eduard 1–2, 3, 15, 16, 154
    and fictional description of 49–50,
        198
Greve, Felix Paul, *see also* Grove,
        Frederick Philip, xxvii, 20, 24, 31,
        32, 40, 41
    and archaeology 59–74
    arrest and imprisonment of 147–60,
        148
    as F.C. Gerden 71, 150, 154, 239
    as playwright 200–4
    as poet and translator 75–125
    as a student in Bonn 17–58
    as translator of Wilde 95–125

avoidance of military service by
    195–6
childhood of 1–16
death of 264, 265
ill health of 46–7, 78, 104–5, 107,
    145, 167, 263–4, 267
in Canada 196, 236–8, 245–65, 273–4
in Manitoba 57, 237–8, 241, 243,
    247–52, 265
in Ontario 252–7
in the United States 237–45
"suicide" of 233, 235
use of pseudonyms 197, 208, 215,
    230, 233, 236, 238, 239
Greve, Henny Frieda Anna Martha 1,
    3–5, 260
Grove, A. Leonard 237, 247, 252, 256,
    262
    and recollections of his father 254–5,
        259–61, 262–4
Grove, Catherine 237, 247, 247, 255,
    256, 263, 264–5
Grove, Frederick Philip, *see* Greve,
        Felix Paul
Grove, Mary (Mrs. A. Leonard Grove)
    264
Grove, Phyllis May 247, 251–2, 256, 260,
    264
Groves, Abe 245, 246–7
Groves, Conrad 245
Gundolf, Friedrich 77, 78, 122, 134

Hamburger Fremdenblatt 231
Harden, Maximilian 142
Hardt, Ernst 10, 35, 36, 36, 37–8, 57, 63,
    70–1
Hartmann, Carl 44
Helena und Damon (Greve) 34, 39, 86,
    99–100, 100, 105, 111, 200
Herr Dames Aufzeichnungen
    (Reventlow) 226
Hesse, Hermann xii, xxx, 215
Heymel, Alfred Walter 98
Hille, Peter 219

Randarabesken zu Oskar Wilde (Wilde)
117, 119, 164, 185
Redlich, Felix 254
Reinhardt, Max 193–4
Reise in Schweden (Greve) 213
Reiseblätter (Flaubert) 199, 207
Reiss, Ernst 214
Reventlow, Franziska zu 80, 81, 83, 85,
87, 91–2, 101–2, 162, 219
Rheinische Friedrich-Wilhelm's
University 17
Rhoda Fleming (Meredith) 168
Riley, Anthony xxviii
Röttger, Karl 205
Rowohlt, Ernst 214
Royal Society of Canada 184
Rubio, Mary 257
Rutherfurd-Clark, Jane Grace 20
Rutherfurd-Clark, Lord 20, 21, 96

Salammbô (Flaubert) 211
Salomé (Wilde) 103, 104, 108, 115, 123,
124
Salz, Arthur 146
Saül (Gide) 193–4, 198
Schafgans, Dr. 175, 176
Schickele, René 211
Schiller, Friedrich 11
Schlaf, Johannes 96
Schliemann, Heinrich 64
Schmidt-Ernsthausen, Renatus 158
Schmitz, Matthias 44
Schmitz, Oscar A.H. 142, 143, 159, 162,
196–7, 217, 226–7, 231–2
Schmitz, Ohaha [maybe remove] 87
Schmitz, Richard 38, 63, 216
Schnabel, Karl 226
Schröder, Fritz 26, 93
Schröder, Rudolph Alexander 98
Schuler, Alfred 76, 81
Schultess, Friedrich 11–16, 13, 66, 76
Schwabinger Beobachter 93
Semester Bericht des ARC Rhenus 19
Sentimentalist (Greve) 199

Settlers of the Marsh (Greve) 58, 74,
144, 183, 246, 249–50, 252
and father figures 257
Sherard, Robert 156
Simplicissimus 82
Simrock, Karl 33
Spettigue, Douglas O. ix, xxvii, xxviii, 1,
15, 18, 178
Sphinx, The (Wilde) 199
Spohr, Max 123
Stiller, Heinrich 123–4, 176
Stobie, Margaret xxviii, 237–8, 240
Styx (Lasker-Schüler) 223–4

Tägliche Rundschau 149
Teppich des Lebens (George) 86, 106
Theis, Raimund xxxi, 190, 194
Thiel, Georg 44, 46
Thiel, Theo 26, 31, 31
Time Machine, The (Wells) 171
Tino von Bagdad (Lasker-Schüler) 220
Tucholsky, Kurt 200
Turn of the Year, The (Greve) 39, 249,
251, 256, 257
Two Generations (Greve) 4, 230, 254,
257

University of Manitoba 184
Usener, Hermann 11, 12, 17, 35, 37
Usener, Walther 37

Vallentin, Richard 201
Vallette, Alfred 188
Valette, Marguerite 226
Vasenwerk (Fürtwangler) 77, 80
Verga, Giovanni 153, 165, 166
Verwey, Albert 76, 106, 229
Vita nuova (Dante) 77
Vollmoeller, Karl Gustav 38, 38, 64–5,
70–1, 73, 111
von Bismarck, Count Otto 25